# iOS and macOS™
# Performance
# Tuning

# iOS and macOS™ Performance Tuning

Cocoa®, Cocoa Touch®, Objective-C®, and Swift™

Marcel Weiher

**✦✦Addison-Wesley**

Boston • Columbus • Indianapolis • New York • San Francisco • Amsterdam • Cape Town
Dubai • London • Madrid • Milan • Munich • Paris • Montreal • Toronto • Delhi • Mexico City
São Paulo • Sydney • Hong Kong • Seoul • Singapore • Taipei • Tokyo

Many of the designations used by manufacturers and sellers to distinguish their products are claimed as trademarks. Where those designations appear in this book, and the publisher was aware of a trademark claim, the designations have been printed with initial capital letters or in all capitals.

The author and publisher have taken care in the preparation of this book, but make no expressed or implied warranty of any kind and assume no responsibility for errors or omissions. No liability is assumed for incidental or consequential damages in connection with or arising out of the use of the information or programs contained herein.

For information about buying this title in bulk quantities, or for special sales opportunities (which may include electronic versions; custom cover designs; and content particular to your business, training goals, marketing focus, or branding interests), please contact our corporate sales department at corpsales@pearsoned.com or (800) 382-3419.

For government sales inquiries, please contact governmentsales@pearsoned.com.

For questions about sales outside the U.S., please contact intlcs@pearson.com.

Visit us on the Web: informit.com/aw

Library of Congress Number: 2016961010

ISBN-13: 978-0-321-84284-8
ISBN-10: 0-321-84284-7

1   17

**Editor-in-Chief**
Greg Wiegand

**Senior Acquisitions Editor**
Trina MacDonald

**Development Editor**
Songlin Qiu

**Managing Editor**
Sandra Schroeder

**Full-Service Production Manager**
Julie B. Nahil

**Project Manager**
Melissa Panagos

**Copy Editor**
Stephanie Geels

**Indexer**
Jack Lewis

**Proofreader**
Melissa Panagos

**Technical Reviewers**
Christian Brunschen
BJ Miller
Christian Neuss
Dominik Wagner

**Editorial Assistant**
Olivia Basegio

**Cover Designer**
Chuti Prasertsith

**Compositor**
Lori Hughes

# Contents at a Glance

# Contents

# About the Author

**Marcel Weiher** is a software engineer and researcher with more than 25 years of experience with Cocoa-related technologies. Marcel's work has always been performance-focused, ranging from solving impossible pre-press problems on the machines of the day via optimizing one of the world's busiest Web properties at the BBC to helping other Apple engineers improve the performance of their code on Apple's Mac OS X performance team.

In addition to helping established companies and start-ups create award-winning software and turn around development teams, Marcel also teaches, blogs, speaks at conferences, contributes to open source, and invents new techniques such as Higher Order Messaging. He also works on programming languages, starting with an Objective-C implementation in 1987 and culminating in the Objective-Smalltalk architecture research language. Marcel currently works as a principal software engineer at Microsoft Berlin and maintains his own software and consulting company, metaobject ltd.

# Introduction

Performance is one of the most important qualities of software programs. You can't have world-beating software without world-beating performance. For a long time, hardware improvements meant that worrying about software performance seemed a waste of time, but with Moore's Law no longer automatically providing significant automatic performance improvements, performance optimization is coming back to the forefront of both computer science and engineering.

In addition, performance for end users seems to have gotten only marginally better, whereas the performance of the underlying hardware has improved by many orders of magnitude. Bill Gates quipped that "the speed of software halves every 18 months," whereas Wirth's law in *A Plea for Lean Software* states, "Software is getting slower more rapidly than hardware becomes faster."[1]

We are so used to this sorry state of affairs that industry veterans were surprised at the original iPad's fluid UI, despite having a CPU with "only" 1 GHz. That's more than 1,000 times faster than my Apple ][, and 40 times faster than my NeXT cube that had a larger screen to deal with. If anything, the surprise should have been that it wasn't faster, especially when considering that it also had a GPU to handle the screen.

This book will try to give insights into the underlying reasons for these developments in the context of Objective-C, Cocoa, and CocoaTouch, and attempt to provide techniques for taking full advantage of the raw power of our amazing computing machines—power that we tend to squander with reckless abandon. It will also try to show when it is actually OK to squander that power, and when it is necessary to pay careful attention. Programmer attention is also a scarce resource, too often squandered attempting to optimize parts of the program that do not matter.

General themes will include latency versus bandwidth, and transactions costs (overhead) versus actual work done, themes that are universal and manifest themselves in different forms at every level of the hardware and software stack.

What you will notice is that due to the speed of our machines, any single operation is, in fact, always more than fast enough, so the crucial equation is $items * cost$. Most optimization is about reducing one or both of the parts of that formula, usually by breaking it up first.

---

1. Niklaus Wirth, *A Plea for Lean Software* (Los Alamitos, CA: IEEE Computer Society Press, 1995), pp. 64–68. http://dx.doi.org/10.1109/2.348001

One frequent method for reducing cost is to realize that *cost* is actually composed of two separate costs, $cost_1$ and $cost_2$, and only one of these needs to be applied to all items: $items \times (cost_1 + cost_2) \rightarrow cost_1 + items \times cost_2$. I would probably call this the fundamental optimization equation; a large part of the optimization techniques fall into this category, and it is also fundamental to the organization of most of the hardware/software stack we deal with every day.

This book has a very regular structure, with four basic areas of performance discussed in turn:

1. CPU performance
2. Memory
3. I/O
4. Graphics and responsiveness

Although an effort has been made to keep the treatment of each subject area independent, there is a logical progression, so at least a passing familiarity with earlier topics helps with later topics.

Within each of these four broad topics, there are again four specific areas of interest:

1. Principles
2. Measurement and tools
3. Pitfalls and techniques
4. Larger real-world examples of applying the techniques

Again, there is a logical structure: You need to have some idea about the principles and know how to measure before you can meaningfully think about actual performance optimization techniques, but again, you should also be able to dip into specific areas of interest if you have a passing familiarity with earlier topics.

This structure yields a total of $4 \times 4 = 16$ chapters, with a special chapter on Swift tucked between memory and I/O for a total of 17. Swift is also used throughout the book where appropriate, but it deserves a chapter of its own due to its unique performance characteristics.

For me, software performance is a passion and a calling that has been a common thread throughout my career. I have learned that performance is something you can't automate, nor can you leave it until the last minute. On the other hand, there are many times when you shouldn't worry about performance in order to have the capacity to concentrate on performance where it is really needed. If that weren't paradoxical enough, having excellent base performance levels is often what makes it possible to get to that state of not having to worry about performance most of the time.

In short, this book is about making software that performs beautifully.

# 1

# CPU: Principles

The interaction between CPU performance and Objective-C has a history going back to the beginnings of Objective-C in the early 1980s and the first public release of Smalltalk. Smalltalk is a dynamic object-oriented language and environment implemented on top of a byte-coded virtual machine with garbage collection and complemented by the first integrated bit-mapped graphical user interface (GUI). It was this environment that Steve Jobs saw during his famous visit to Xerox PARC and decided to popularize with the Lisa and Macintosh computers.

Although it provided amazing capabilities for the time, the Smalltalk environment proved too much for even the emerging workstation-class microprocessors such as the Motorola MC 68000, which was to be at the heart of both the Mac and Lisa, to handle with acceptable performance.

Three approaches emerged to tackle this performance problem—two at the extremes and one a compromise somewhere in the middle.

1. The first approach is represented by the Macintosh Toolbox and original MacOS. The Macintosh completely dropped the expressiveness of Smalltalk's dynamic object-oriented approach and instead retained just the GUI, which was reimplemented in MC 68000 assembly language. This made it possible to popularize the GUI, but left the software engineering and environmental advantages of Smalltalk behind.

   In fact, Steve Jobs said that he was so enthralled with the GUI that he missed the more important pieces of the PARC magic: object-oriented programming and networking.

2. On the other end of the spectrum, the Smalltalk community decided to innovate in implementation technologies to close the performance gap. This led to important innovations such as just-in-time compilation and scavenging garbage collection that dramatically increased performance.

   Moore's Law turned out to be an even bigger contributor, though. Even a naïve Smalltalk-80-style bytecode interpreter on today's hardware is roughly 100 times faster than assembly language on MC 68000 class machines even for basic integer operations directly supported by the CPU hardware, and such integer computation represents pretty much a worst-case for Smalltalk.

3.  The middle-ground approach is the one taken by Objective-C, a hybrid language that integrates a Smalltalk-like dynamic object-runtime on top of the C programming language. Objective-C emerged around the same time as the original Macintosh on machines with comparable computational power. Instead of discarding object techniques completely like the original Mac, or relying purely on technological advances to make them tenable, Objective-C makes both sets of techniques easily available at all times and leaves it to developers to apply those technological options appropriately.

With the right set of decisions, this third approach—Objective-C—makes it possible to achieve both best-of-breed performance and high levels of expressiveness and productivity. However, with great power comes great responsibility: Used less wisely, it is also quite possible to achieve expressiveness worse than C combined with speed slower than Smalltalk. This book will give you the techniques to avoid the latter and achieve the former.

# A Simple Example

But enough theory, let's see some actual code! The task will be simple and purely CPU-bound: summing the integers from 1 to 1,000. We will implement two Objective-C examples demonstrating the range of styles and corresponding performance characteristics available with Objective-C and Cocoa. In addition, we will look at the same example implemented in some other programming languages, which we'll use as reference points for the different Objective-C styles.

Note that this is not a useful method for computing the first $n$ integers. In that case, we would use the closed formula discovered by Gauss: $\frac{n(n+1)}{2}$.

The first thing you might notice when you look at the Objective-C program shown in Example 1.1 is that it looks like pure C. That's OK; Objective-C is a pure superset of C and therefore any C program is also an Objective-C program. Type in the code shown in Example 1.1 and save the file as `sumintc_ex1.m`.

**Example 1.1   Sum integers in Objective-C using primitive types**

```
#include <stdio.h>

int main( int argc , char *argv[] )
{
  int i,sum;
  sum=0;
  for (i=1;i<=1000 ;i++ ) {
    sum+=i;
```

```
  }
  return 0;
}
```

When you compile the code in Example 1.1 using `cc -Os`[1] `-Wall -o sumintc_ex1 sumintc_ex1.m` and then run it with `time ./sumintc_ex1`, you will notice that the runtimes are really fast, on the order of a couple of milliseconds. This is also to be expected, modern CPUs are extremely fast at simple integer arithmetic, and the C program as written translates pretty directly to CPU instructions.

## The Perils of (Micro-)Benchmarking

However, let's run a sanity check to see if we're actually measuring something real. When you compile and run Example 1.2, the program displays approximately the same time as Example 1.1.

**Example 1.2    Sanity check; an empty test program**

```
int main( int argc , char *argv[] )
{
  return 0;
}
```

What's going on here? There are actually several problems.

1. A modern optimizer notices that the result of the computation isn't used and that there are no side effects of the computation itself, and therefore discards the computation.
2. Even if it weren't able to discard the result, the optimizer can and will actually compute the result for this computation statically, so instead of generating code for the loop it just generates code for the result.
3. The number of iterations is small enough, and CPUs fast enough, that total running time is actually dominated by process start-up time; the actual running time of the loop doesn't matter.

In order to get measurable results, we need to make a couple of changes: First, we need to make the task larger so that we are actually measuring it and not process start-up overhead. We can do this by including an outer loop that simply runs the actual loop we want to run a (large) number of times. Second, we use the result, for example, by printing it to `stdout`. Note that both of these requirements combine in a way that seems nonsensical at first: We reset the `sum` variable to 0 every time

---

1. These are the letters capital $O$ and lowercase $s$.

through the inner loop, but then output the value outside the outer loop. This is because we want to print the output just once, but also don't want to change the nature of the task (such as summing to a larger target value). Third, we make the parameters unavailable at compile time, in this case by passing them in on the command line, and so we get the slightly more verbose program shown in Example 1.3.

**Example 1.3    Sum integers avoiding benchmark removal by the optimizer**

```
#include <stdio.h>
#include <stdlib.h>

int main( int argc , char *argv[] )
{
  int i,k,sum;
  int limit=argc > 1 ? atoi(argv[1]) : 1000;
  int step=argc > 2 ? atoi(argv[2]) : 1;
  for (k=0;k<1000000; k++ ) {
    sum=0;
    for (i=1;i<= limit;i+=step ) {
      sum+=i;
    }
  }
  printf("%d\n",sum);
  return 0;
}
```

On my current machine, a Mid 2015 MacBook Pro 15-Inch with a 2.8-GHz Intel Core i7 processor, this yields a much more reasonable execution time of 0.238 s. As we had scaled the result by doing 1 million iterations of the basic task, we know it took 0.238 $\mu$s to execute. The one-time overhead that was completely drowning out the task before is now less than approximately 3% of the total execution time and no longer significant. Increasing the loop counts by a factor of 10 as a cross-check results in execution times that are 10 times longer, so we can now be reasonably confident we are measuring the right thing. Not that this is not a one-time thing; for example, a future optimizer might figure out that the inner loop always computes the same result, and therefore it may only do one iteration of the outer loop.

Another option would have been to compile without optimization using the $-00$[2] flag, but that would have been unrepresentative as most production code will have optimizations on and turning them off makes this code around 6 times slower.

---

2. Capital *O* and number zero.

## More Integer Summing

To check the other end of the Objective-C performance envelope, we maintain the sum as a Foundation object, "NSNumber," as shown in Example 1.4. The loop and loop counter are still plain C, because Objective-C does not have pure object-oriented looping constructs. We also decrease the outermost loop counter by a factor of 100 for reasons that will soon become apparent.

**Example 1.4    Sum integers using objects to represent numbers**

```
#import <Foundation/Foundation.h>

int main( int argc , char *argv[] )
{
  int i,k;
  NSNumber* sum = nil;
  for (k=0; k<10000; k++ ) {
    sum=@(0);
    for (i=1;i<=1000 ;i++ ) {
      sum=@([sum intValue]+i);
    }
  }
  NSLog(@"%@",sum);
  return 0;
}
```

How fast this program runs crucially depends on the runtime selected using compiler flags. First, we need to add `-framework Foundation` in order to compile and link against the Foundation framework that provides the definition of the NSNumber class and the NSLog() function: `cc -Wall -Os -m32 -o example1.4 example1.4.m -framework Foundation`. Selecting the 32-bit runtime using `-m32` creates a program that runs in 2.38 s on my machine. Had we kept the iterations the same it would have taken 238 s, almost 4 minutes, so 1,000 times slower than the previous test program.

The primary reason Objective-C with NSNumber types is so much slower than with primitive types is object allocation—more specifically, heap allocation. When using the 64-bit runtime that is the default now, the runtime for the sample program drops to 0.114 s or 11.4 s normalized to a million iterations. This improvement is due to the use of *tagged pointers* that can represent some objects directly in the object pointer and therefore avoid heap allocation. In both cases, the compiler's optimizer is almost completely out of the picture; runs with and without optimization differ not by a factor of 6 as for the example with primitives, but rather only by at most a few percent less than the run-to-run variation. We will talk more about primitives, objects, and tagged pointers in Chapter 3.

## Swift

Swift was developed as an alternative to and replacement for Objective-C. It is similar to Objective-C in that it is a hybrid language, with the object-oriented parts similar to and built on the same runtime as Objective-C. However, the hybrid nature is much less pronounced because it is a unified design rather than one language grafted onto another.

This is apparent in Example 1.5, which shows direct transliterations of both the primitive integer and the object-based version. The two versions are much closer to each other, with direct initialization of objects from primitive types possible and type-inference taking care of most of the differences.

**Example 1.5    Summation in Swift**

Swift/primitives:

```
var a=0
for j in 0..<10_000_000 {
  a=0
  for i:Int in 0...1000   {
    a=a + i
  }
}
print("a=\(a)")
```

Swift/objects:

```
import Foundation

var a:NSNumber=0
for j in 0..<100000 {
  a = 0
  for i in 0...1000   {
    a=a.integerValue + i
  }
}
print("a = \(a)")
```

In terms of performance, Swift is not quite there yet, with the primitive version approximately 50% slower and the object-based version a surprising three times slower than Objective-C. In my testing, this seems to be typical, with primitive operations usually fairly close to Objective-C performance, and in rare cases equal or even slightly better, but with more complex operations lagging significantly.

While Example 1.5 was purposely coded in a similar style to the Objective-C examples, Example 1.6 shows that a higher-level, more expressive style is also possible. The higher-order function reduce is applied to the range object 0...1000 with the reduction operator + and the starting value 0. It is very similar in expressiveness to very high-level languages such as Ruby or Smalltalk (or functional languages).

**Example 1.6     Summation via reduction in Swift**

```
var a=0;
for j in 0..<1000000 {
  a = (0...1000).reduce(0, combine:+ )
}
print("a = \(a)")
```

With optimizations enabled, the Swift compiler is able to remove these abstractions and produce code that is essentially equivalent to the primitive `for`-loop from Example 1.5. This is extremely impressive and theoretically makes it possible to routinely use such high-level abstractions even in performance-intensive code.

In practice however, there is a snag: With optimization disabled, the code runs pretty much exactly 100 times slower, whereas with the previous examples the difference was at most around a factor of six. Such a discrepancy is more than just significant, it means that performance-wise the non-optimized version is a completely different language, more like an interpreted language such as Ruby or Smalltalk (and even slower than those) than an ahead-of-time compiled language.

You might think that this discrepancy doesn't matter because performance is always measured and programs are always shipped with optimizations enabled. And you'd be right to a certain extent; witness the lengths I went through earlier in this chapter to get useful measurements with optimizations enabled. All those problems would have gone away by simply disabling optimizations.

There is a catch, though. Or more precisely, at least two: First, debug builds default to having optimizations enabled, and those tend to be used almost exclusively during development. With a 100 times performance difference, either your debug build is going to be unusably slow, with an operation that would take half a second in release taking almost a minute in debug, or the debug build is actually usable, in which case the optimization actually isn't needed and is just a waste of time.

The second, potentially even more troubling issue from a performance perspective is that optimizations are opaque, not guaranteed to occur and undiagnosed if they don't occur. That means that a new version of the compiler can silently drop a particular optimization, or non-obvious code changes can mean that a precondition for an optimization is no longer met. These are likely to be isolated incidents, and when the penalty is two to three times, they tend to be bearable. When the penalty could be 100 times or more, that's a performance mine waiting to go off.

In general, performance these days means predictable and controllable performance, and this is neither. We will talk more about these aspects in later chapters.

## Other Languages

Example 1.7 shows integer summation code in a number of other high-level languages. Most of these languages do not feature aggressive optimizers, so the various tricks needed to ensure that computation actually takes place are not necessary. Table 1.1 and the graph in Figure 1.1 show how Objective-C compares to these languages.

**Example 1.7    Summation in various other languages**

PostScript:
```
0 1 1000 { add } bind for
```

PostScript, self-timing and displaying:
```
%!
/Helvetica 25 selectfont 100 100 moveto
/intshow { 20 string cvs show } bind def
usertime

0 10000 { 0 0 1 1000 { add }  for exch pop } bind repeat
exch usertime exch sub intshow ( ms result: ) show intshow

showpage
```

Smalltalk:
```
( 1 to: 1000 ) inject: 0 into: [ :a :b | a+b ].
```

Smalltalk + Higher Order Messaging:
```
( 1 to: 1000 ) reduce + 0.
```

Ruby:
```
 print (1..1000).inject(0) {|sum,x| sum +x }
```

Considering that Objective-C was developed in response to Smalltalk's performance issues, it is interesting to see how Objective-C compares with Smalltalk.

- Squeak is a bytecode interpreter that closely follows the original Smalltalk-80 implementation of the early 1980s.

- Java is an object-oriented, bytecode language whose main implementation, Oracle's HotSpot VM, is a fairly direct descendant of the Strongtalk VM for Smalltalk. Unlike Smalltalk, it also provides primitives in the language.

The result is interesting in that Objective-C brackets the Smalltalk/Java results. When using primitives, Objective-C is slightly faster than Java when also using primitives and 30 times faster than Java when using pure objects and 60 times faster than reasonably modern Smalltalk using pure objects. However, Objective-C using pure objects is slower than Java and comparable to Smalltalk when using tagged objects, and massively slower when using heap-allocated objects.

In fact, Objective-C brackets *all* the languages we have here; it can be either faster or slower than all of them, depending on how it is used. Although our example here

**Table 1.1     Arithmetic features and time to sum 1,000 integers in different languages**

| Language | Objects | Unlimited Precision | Execution Time (µs) |
|---|---|---|---|
| Objective-C (primitives) | No | No | 0.2 |
| Swift (primitives) | No | No | 0.3 |
| Java (primitives) | No | No | 0.4 |
| Strongtalk | Yes | Yes | 5.2 |
| Java (objects) | Yes | No | 6.1 |
| Objective-C (tagged objects) | Yes | No | 11.4 |
| Smalltalk-80 | Yes | Yes | 12.7 |
| Swift (tagged objects) | Yes | No | 31 |
| PostScript | Sort of | Yes | 54.2 |
| Ruby | Yes | Yes | 55.3 |
| Objective-C (objects) | Yes | No | 238.1 |
| MC 68000 Assembler/7.1 MHz | No | No | (estimate) 3,000 |

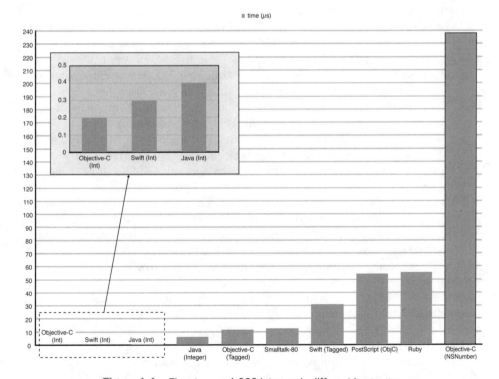

**Figure 1.1**     Time to sum 1,000 integers in different languages

is very trivial, I have found this property to be generally true: Objective-C gives you a wide range from which to choose when trading expressiveness for performance. It is up to you to choose. That is the power of a hybrid language.

# The Power of Hybrids

When Brad Cox created Objective-C, the choice of a hybrid language was very deliberate. In addition to needing more performance than a pure Smalltalk could provide, he envisioned two different purposes: one is implementing components (called "Software-ICs") efficiently, largely in C, and the other is connecting those components together using dynamic message sending.

This hybrid pattern can often be seen where high performance meets dynamic flexibility. One great example is the Unix shell, where filter components such as grep or wc are written in C but hooked up very dynamically using the shell. NumPy is popular for controlling numerical array processing routines written in C or C++ from Python, and at the high end, supercomputing centers used the string-based scripting language Tcl (generally slower than Ruby) to "steer" computations in their clusters.

When performance problems occur in Objective-C, it is almost invariably because this hybrid pattern was disregarded and Objective-C was treated as pure object-oriented language. As Table 1.1 shows, Objective-C is a very bad pure object-oriented language: It is slower than the other pure object-oriented languages, especially with high rates of object creation, while delivering fewer features, being less crash resistant and offering a far less interactive programming environment.

However, Objective-C is an awesome hybrid language, great for connecting coarse grain objects with very fast and flexible dynamic message passing. In addition to allowing the typical hybrid pattern of pre-fab components written in a fast/static language connected by a flexible slower language, Objective-C also allows a more gradual approach that doesn't presuppose where the bottlenecks will be.

You may have wondered at the somewhat odd choice of PostScript in the selection of languages to compare. The reason for this choice is that the particular PostScript interpreter in question is actually written in Objective-C. And not only is it written in Objective-C, it is written in a pure object-oriented fashion, with all PostScript objects (stacks, strings, numbers, matrices) mapped straight to Objective-C objects. Despite apparently contradicting the hybrid pattern and using a more pure object-oriented approach, it outperforms the industry-standard PostScript interpreter shipped with Mac OS X, which is written in straight C.

The contradiction is only superficial. While Objective-C is a hybrid, it is a *single* hybrid language, with both parts reasonably well integrated. That means that although you can take an approach in which you write your core in C or C++ and then layer it in Objective-C wrappers, you can actually take a more productive approach in which you write your core in Objective-C and then optimize. We will take a closer look at how to perform such optimizations in Chapter 3.

# Trends

To say that CPU performance has improved dramatically in the quarter of a century since the original Macintosh with its MC 68000 CPU was introduced is an understatement of colossal proportions. Today's machines are approximately 4,000 times faster, and that's from a base that wasn't too shabby to begin with. This improvement has been achieved by increasing clock-frequencies, adding resources so that most common instructions can execute in a single clock-cycle, and finally duplicating functional units and adding control logic so multiple instructions from a nominally sequential instruction stream can be analyzed and executed in parallel.

None of these advancements have come for free. Pipelining is usually required to allow the many steps in decoding and executing instructions to overlap in order to achieve throughput of one instruction per clock-cycle. In addition, higher clock-frequencies require individual pipeline steps to be physically shorter and less capable and thus the overall pipelines to be even deeper, increasing the cost of pipeline hazards such as stalls or mispredicted branches, making maximum throughput ever harder to achieve and actual performance ever harder to predict.

Whereas CPU and memory speeds were roughly matched in the MC 68000 days, even allowing for some extra DRAM accesses to refresh the screen, today DRAM access times are around 100 times too slow to directly supply the CPU with data. This makes it necessary to place large and complex caches between the CPU and main memory. Of course, caches make access times slower in the worst case, so again we have to hope that the average case works in our favor, and predictability is also adversely affected again. Another aspect here is that the relative performance of components has changed over the years. Where it used to make sense to have precompute tables of expensive computations, nowadays it is very often cheaper to just compute rather than wait for main memory.

Finally, exploiting instruction-level parallelism (ILP) has meant putting a lot more functional units onto the die, as well as additional control logic to detect and extract potentially parallel instructions and to make sure their effects are made visible to the running program as if they had executed sequentially.

As all of these mechanisms have now reached the point of diminishing returns, the free ride that software developers have enjoyed over the last couple of decades has come to a screeching halt. We can no longer rely on the next generation of CPUs to cover both users' increased expectations and our performance sins of the past—performance sins that have eaten up much if not all of the gains made in hardware.

In fact, many luminaries have quipped that software tends to get slower at a slightly faster rate than hardware gets faster, and that was when hardware *was* still getting faster. A test pitting a Mac Plus against an Athlon powered PC in Word and Excel application benchmarks showed the (Motorola MC 68000–powered) Mac Plus beating the modern machine's performance in 63% of the most common tasks and over 50% of the tasks selected.[3]

So we not only cannot regress current performance by adding new features, we probably also have to actually improve performance to meet user demands for handling ever larger data sets. Although additional hardware-based performance is available in the form of additional cores and GPUs, utilizing those additional hardware resources is often harder than just not wasting CPU cycles quite as egregiously as before.

Last but not least, a whole new generation of mobile devices such as the iPhone confronts us with CPUs that have vastly lower performance available, not least because of power limitations.

## Cost of Operations

At its heart, optimization is the art of balancing cost with outcomes, ideally achieving the best outcome at minimal cost. Balancing costs is hard without knowing what those costs are, so it is important to really familiarize yourself with the costs of common operations that are important for your application areas (and of course measure, measure, measure, which we will cover in Chapter 2).

Tables 1.2 through 1.6 show the cost of common CPU-oriented operations on different pieces of hardware. These costs are shown both in absolute terms and relative to each other, which is why the tables are 2D, with specific operations listed both in the rows and columns. If you want to find out how much one operation costs in terms of another, just check the intersection of the column of one operation with the row of the other.

All basic operations are individually incredibly fast on modern CPUs, so the times in Table 1.2 are usefully expressed in nanoseconds (billionths of a second). The absolute times of these operations are so far removed from the time scales that a human being can intuitively grasp so as to be almost meaningless; this was illustrated by the student from Bentley's *Programming Pearls* who gave the running time of an algorithm as 1.83, but wasn't really sure whether it was milliseconds or microseconds.

Table 1.2 instead focuses on *relative cost*, so you can see that a message send is about as costly as an integer division, and one object allocation costs the same as 45 message sends. So if we are wrapping an integer division in a message send, our overhead is 100%, which is somewhat questionable but may be acceptable depending on our circumstances. Wrapping an integer addition in a way that requires an object allocation, on the other hand, would cause our relative overhead to be a factor of 1,000, so our program is 1,000 times slower than it needs to be in that area.

---

3. http://hallicino.hubpages.com/hub/_86_Mac_Plus_Vs_07_AMD_DualCore_You_Wont_Believe_Who_Wins

Table 1.2     Relative cost of common operations on MacBook Pro Retina, late 2013

| Operation | add | multiply | 1 ns | message | divide | autorelease | alloc | 1/10th s |
|---|---|---|---|---|---|---|---|---|
| add | 1 | 2.2 | 3.4 | 22 | 23 | 644 | 1,012 | 3.374e+08 |
| multiply | | 1 | 1.5 | 9.8 | 10 | 291 | 457 | 1.523e+08 |
| 1 ns | 0.3 | 0.66 | 1 | 6.5 | 6.7 | 191 | 300 | 1e+08 |
| message | | | | 1 | 1 | 30 | 46 | 1.548e+07 |
| divide | | | | | 1 | 28 | 45 | 1.489e+07 |
| autorelease | | | | | | 1 | 1.6 | 5.24e+05 |
| alloc | | | | | | | 1 | 3.333e+05 |
| 1/10th s | | | | | | | | 1 |

Table 1.3     Relative cost of common operations on iPhone 5S

| Operation | 1 ns | multiply | message | divide | autorelease | alloc | 1/10th s |
|---|---|---|---|---|---|---|---|
| 1 ns | 1 | 3.9 | 4.6 | 6.2 | 209.7 | 274 | 2147484 |
| multiply | | 1 | 1.2 | 1.6 | 53 | 70 | 545600.5 |
| message | | | 1 | 1.3 | 45 | 59 | 464320.8 |
| divide | | | | 1 | 34 | 44 | 346927.9 |
| autorelease | | | | | 1 | 1.3 | 10241.72 |
| alloc | | | | | | 1 | 7837.331 |
| 1/10th s | | | | | | | 1 |

Table 1.4     Relative cost of common operations on Simulator MacBook Pro 15-inch

| Operation | 1/10th s | 1 ns | multiply | message | divide | autorelease | alloc |
|---|---|---|---|---|---|---|---|
| 1/10th s | 1 | -4.7e-07 | -5.6e-07 | -1.3e-06 | -4.1e-06 | -4e-05 | -0.00017 |
| 1 ns | -2.1e+06 | 1 | 1.2 | 2.8 | 8.8 | 85 | 370.8 |
| multiply | | | 1 | 2.3 | 7.3 | 70 | 307.2 |
| message | | | | 1 | 3.1 | 30 | 132.9 |
| divide | | | | | 1 | 9.7 | 42 |
| autorelease | | | | | | 1 | 4.4 |
| alloc | | | | | | | 1 |

**Table 1.5**   **Relative cost of common operations on iPhone SE**

| Operation | 1 ns | multiply | message | divide | autorelease | alloc | 1/10th s |
|---|---|---|---|---|---|---|---|
| 1 ns | 1 | 2.2 | 3.3 | 4.5 | 92 | 121.9 | 2147484 |
| multiply | | 1 | 1.5 | 2 | 42 | 56 | 977906.9 |
| message | | | 1 | 1.3 | 28 | 36 | 642574.4 |
| divide | | | | 1 | 21 | 27 | 481606.6 |
| autorelease | | | | | 1 | 1.3 | 23263.07 |
| alloc | | | | | | 1 | 17616.91 |
| 1/10th s | | | | | | | 1 |

**Table 1.6**   **Relative cost of common operations on iPhone 3G**

| Operation | 1 ns | add | multiply | divide | message | autorelease | alloc | 1/10th s |
|---|---|---|---|---|---|---|---|---|
| 1 ns | 1 | 9.7 | 23 | 92 | 140 | 6,700 | 9,400 | 1e+08 |
| add | | 1 | 2.4 | 9.5 | 14 | 691 | 969 | 1.031e+07 |
| multiply | | | 1 | 4 | 6.1 | 291 | 409 | 4.348e+06 |
| divide | | | | 1 | 1.5 | 73 | 102 | 1.087e+06 |
| message | | | | | 1 | 48 | 67 | 7.143e+05 |
| autorelease | | | | | | 1 | 1.4 | 1.493e+04 |
| alloc | | | | | | | 1 | 1.064e+04 |
| 1/10th s | | | | | | | | 1 |

However, even high relative overhead will not matter if the operations in question are not executed frequently, so the final column of Table 1.2 shows how many operations of a particular kind can be executed in 1/10th of a second, which is roughly the response time that most humans will perceive as instantaneous. So if we want to maintain instantaneous response for our app, we could do up to half a billion integer additions, but we had better not try to allocate more than around 400,000 objects.

Table 1.3 shows that phones still lag desktop and laptop CPUs by a significant margin, even though the gains relative to an iPhone 3G shown in Table 1.6 are enormous. Not only are all operations anywhere slower, but some of the relationships between operations also change.

# Computational Complexity

A discussion of the principles of CPU performance would not be complete without some reference to computational complexity, the theory dealing with the resource consumption of algorithms and the dreaded Big O. The bad news is that problems due to an algorithm in an unfortunate complexity class are usually really, really bad. The good news is that because they are so bad, these problems tend to be easy to spot and reasonably straightforward to fix.

For example, the code in Example 1.8 should at least raise an eyebrow: We are trying to figure out which rows of a table view are selected, as determined by an array of selected `WLTask` objects that is passed into the method. The outer `for` loop is executed once for each row in the table view, so the overall loop is $O(n)$ in the number of rows. However, the check is performed using the `indexOfObject:` method, which is $O(m)$ in the size of the array. Multiplying yields $O(m \times n)$, which is OK when only a single object is selected and therefore $m$ is 1. However, what if the user selects all of the objects? In this case, $n = m$ and therefore $O(m \times n)$ becomes $O(n^2)$. Oops!

**Example 1.8  Slightly hidden quadratic algorithm via indexOfObject:**

```
- (NSMutableIndexSet *)rowsOfSelectedTasks:(NSArray *)selectedTasks
{
    NSMutableIndexSet *selectedRows = [NSMutableIndexSet indexSet];
    for (int row = 0; row < (int)self.tableView.numberOfRows; row++)
    {
        WLTask *task = [self taskAtRow:row];
        if (task != nil)
        {
            NSUInteger index = [selectedTasks indexOfObject:task];
            if (index != NSNotFound)
            {
                [selectedRows addIndex:row];
            }
        }
    }
    return selectedRows;
}
```

We solved the problem by turning the `NSArray` that is passed as an argument into an `NSSet`, which has amortized $O(1)$ for checking presence. Example 1.9 has the same problem but is more difficult to solve because the two sources of $O(n)$ complexity that combine into $O(n^2)$ are split over two methods. This makes the source of the quadratic complexity harder to spot, and also makes it more difficult to solve because there is no obvious place to construct a temporary `NSSet`.

**Example 1.9  Hidden quadratic algorithm via occurs-check**

```
-(void)addObjectIfAbsent:(id)newObject
{
    if ( NSNotFound !=  [array indexOfObject:newObject]  )  {
        [array addObject:newObject];
```

```
    }
}

-(void)addObjects:(NSArray *)newObjects
{
  for ( id obj in newObjects ) {
    [self addObjectIfAbsent:obj];
  }
}
```

By adding the presence check, which runs in linear time for an array, adding $n$ objects using this method now will take time on the order of $n^2$. If you wish to have a presence check, it would be better to add an additional `NSMutableSet`, which will do the presence check in effectively constant time, restoring the overall operation to linear time. This pattern of nesting a linear operation within a linear operation resulting in a total quadratic operation is so common that is has been given the name *accidentally quadratic*. Watch out for it in your code.

However, we will be dealing with constant factors instead of different complexity classes most of the time.

## Summary

Computers are fast. This trivial observation has surprising consequences. Most of our code is less performance critical than it has ever been, because computers are so fast that it doesn't matter if you control your supercomputers with Tcl or your iOS animations with Ruby or JavaScript. However, the parts of the code that are performance critical are more performance critical than ever, and this is because we do more with our computers and we no longer tolerate bad performance.

At the same time, the seemingly eternal promise of the *Sufficiently Smart Compiler* that just takes our high-level code and magically makes it fast has not materialized, and hardware is no longer making our existing code faster by itself. So we need to optimize, and although automated help is appreciated, we need to make intelligent decisions and have the instruments to gather the information needed for those decisions and the tools to then turn those decisions into code.

Using the right toolbox and mindset, we can achieve great performance within the constraints of our environment, while at the same time keeping our code clean, expressive, and fun.

# 2

# CPU: Measurement and Tools

Measurement plays an absolutely crucial part in performance optimization. We cannot control what we cannot measure, and controlling performance parameters—hopefully by improving them—is the goal of the exercise. Without measuring to control our results, we cannot be sure that what we are doing actually improves the situation, rather than making it worse.

Another important aspect is analysis; after all, it helps tremendously to have a good idea what may be the problem before we try to fix it. However, unlike verification, measurement for analysis has just a helper function, being one of the sources for forming our hypothesis about the nature of the problem. When a problem is obvious, it can be expedient to skip measurement for analysis and act directly on the current hypothesis. Of course, this increases the risk that you get your hypothesis wrong, and verification will tell you that you missed and need to try again. So this is very much a personal choice based on your experience, hit rate, and tolerance for extra work because you guessed wrong.

Apart from the pure discovery step, performance measurement should be looked at like scientific experiments designed to answer specific questions in relation to an existing hypothesis, meaning the tools should always be used to answer a specific question that you have. Just gathering lots of data and chasing numbers without a specific performance hypothesis about the system and a specific question you want answered by your measurements is rarely effective, unless you are happy with spending a couple of days optimizing your system's idle loop.[1]

Fortunately, Mac OS X has plenty of tools to answer a variety of questions you might have about CPU performance. The task is made even easier by the fact that CPU time is a quantity that is tracked for every process by the scheduler as part of normal operations, and tends to be very deterministic for a given program. So in many simple cases, that time tracked by the system can simply be queried and will be accurate. If more fine-grain information is required, sampling tools can give

---

1. J.L. Bentley, *Programming Pearls* (Boston: Addison-Wesley, 2000).

resolution down to the function and even statement level, though with greater potential for error.

# Command-Line Tools

Mac OS X includes a good number of command-line performance tools that can provide good answers to simple performance questions. It is usually a good idea to try to use the simplest tool available that is capable of answering your question.

So you might want to try these tools first when you have a performance question, and bring out the big guns, with their associated overhead, if and when you need more detailed analyses.

## top

For example, you might want to consider having one `top` process running in a Terminal window at all times. The `top` program is mostly a discovery tool and provides a continuously updated display of a large number of system performance parameters. Monitoring these parameters will give you a good idea of what the system "looks" like when it is functioning normally and will alert you to abnormal conditions such as a process suddenly consuming a lot of resources, including the CPU.

Let's look at some sample `top` output:

```
● ○ ○                    Terminal — top — 85×25
Processes: 71 total, 3 running, 68 sleeping, 277 threads         16:58:47
Load Avg: 0.37, 0.26, 0.19  CPU usage: 48.39% user, 5.44% sys, 46.16% idle
SharedLibs: 6212K resident, 6920K data, 0B linkedit.
MemRegions: 10302 total, 1150M resident, 19M private, 324M shared.
PhysMem: 569M wired, 1446M active, 469M inactive, 2484M used, 1611M free.
VM: 143G vsize, 1037M framework vsize, 84202(1) pageins, 0(0) pageouts.
Networks: packets: 1495/351K in, 2055/411K out.
Disks: 80378/1948M read, 19413/419M written.

PID   COMMAND     %CPU TIME     #TH  #WQ  #POR #MRE RPRVT  RSHRD  RSIZE  VPRVT
475-  sumintsm    99.5 00:12.25 1/1  0    16   632+ 734M+  240K   735M+  748M+
0-    kernel_task 2.2  01:25.84 62/2 0    2    736  13M    0B     218M+  62M
478   quicklookd  1.0  00:00.08 7    4    79-  82+  2224K- 12M+   6332K+ 43M-
457   top         1.0  00:01.78 1/1  0    30   33   1136K+ 264K   1712K+ 17M
119   Finder      0.7  00:08.73 12   5    203- 348+ 15M+   66M+   37M+   51M+
60    WindowServer 0.3 00:57.02 5    2    267+ 999  10M+   111M-  114M+  54M+
238-  Microsoft Wo 0.3 00:29.50 6    1    136  580  35M    49M    89M    105M
450   Terminal    0.3  00:13.11 5    1    115  940  27M    36M    49M    43M
118   SystemUIServ 0.2 00:01.64 3    1    253  277  9456K+ 26M    17M+   35M+
52    coreservices 0.2 00:02.83 5    2    318+ 195  2688K+ 18M    19M+   16M
204   Quartz Debug 0.1 00:16.34 6    1    111  107  4188K  25M    9452K  32M
15    configd     0.1  00:02.28 6    2    246  92   1424K  9164K  3604K  15M
34    mds         0.0  00:21.14 5    4    99   816  119M+  18M    75M+   274M
177   mdworker    0.0  00:08.83 5    2    96   250  12M    12M    62M+   65M
39    fseventsd   0.0  00:00.32 12   2    93+  65+  1076K+ 244K   1600K+ 25M+
```

In this case, we see that the `sumintsm` is using a lot of CPU capacity, essentially all of one CPU, and that it's been doing that for quite some time, accumulating a total of over 9 s of CPU time. The CPU usage line in the header shows us that we have a two-processor system, because the process taking almost 100% of one CPU is still only taking slightly less than 50% of the total CPU capacity available in the system. This sort of display suggests that we have something worth investigating more closely.

I tend to run `top` with the `-u` flag that sorts by current %CPU when running in a general "tell me what the system is doing" mode so that the most active processes are always near the top, but without that flag when I am trying to focus on a specific process, so it stays in the same place in the output. Check out the man page for many other sophisticated options to control display, analysis, and sampling rate.

## time

We already used the `time` command earlier to give us measurements of the different summation programs. It is one of the simplest performance measurement tools available, as it just executes its argument and reports the CPU time and the wall clock time taken by execution of the whole program. CPU time is broken down into time spent in user-space and kernel space (sys).

As it provides only a few numbers and requires no setup, it is perfect for quickly testing out algorithms that can be extracted into a command-line tool. Analysis of larger programs is not supported, again, unless parts can be extracted into a tool. Let's look more closely at the `time` output running our test program:

```
$ time ./sumintsc

    500500

    real        0m0.764s
    user        0m0.735s
    sys 0m0.006s
```

The fact that `real` time is almost identical to `user` time means that the program is almost certainly CPU bound, so focusing on CPU performance is the correct approach for improving its overall performance. On an unloaded system, a large difference between real and user + sys will mean that the program is not CPU bound, but waiting either for I/O or for other programs. If not enough CPUs are available for the system load, it could also mean that the kernel preempted the program. As this is indistinguishable from the other situations, it is important to have sufficient idle CPU resources in the system to run the test program. Fortunately, with modern multicore computers, this is becoming less of a problem.

One thing to watch out for is that time exists both as a separate program in `/usr/bin/time` and as a built-in shell command. You will usually get the built-in command, but the man page explaining some extra options applies to the command in `/usr/bin`.

## `sample`

While `time` and `top` give you a good first outside view of what a process is doing, `sample` lets you take a quick peek inside. Say that you see some anomaly in the `top` window you have running. You can quickly dash off a `sample <processName>` in another Terminal window and it will write a sampling-based call tree both to the standard output and to a file in `/tmp` that you can peruse at your leisure. Let's look at the sample output for our Objective-C integer summation program:

```
Analysis of sampling sumints_objc (pid 16000) every 1 millisecond
Process:        sumints_objc [16000]
Path:           /tmp/sumints_objc
Load Address:   0xc7000
Identifier:     sumints_objc
Version:        0
Code Type:      X86
Parent Process: bash [15800]

Date/Time:      2016-05-01 14:31:22.503 +0200
Launch Time:    2016-05-01 14:31:20.545 +0200
OS Version:     Mac OS X 10.11.4 (15E65)
Report Version: 7
Analysis Tool:  /usr/bin/sample
----

Call graph:
    2704 Thread_1945987   DispatchQueue_1: com.apple.main-thread  (serial)
      2704 start  (in libdyld.dylib) + 1  [0x96d726ad]
        2267 main  (in sumints_objc) + 197  [0xc7ef5]
        + 1922 +[NSNumber numberWithInt:]  (in Foundation) + 68
        + ! 1818 -[NSPlaceholderNumber initWithInt:]  (in Foundation) + 49
        + ! : 1526 CFNumberCreate  (in CoreFoundation) + 636
        + ! : | 934 _CFRuntimeCreateInstance  (in CoreFoundation) + 285
        + ! : | + 860 CFAllocatorAllocate  (in CoreFoundation) + 134
        + ! : | + ! 835 __CFAllocatorSystemAllocate  (in CoreFoundation) + 24
        + ! : | + ! : 702 malloc_zone_malloc  (in libsystem_malloc.dylib) + 75
        + ! : | + ! : | 680 szone_malloc  (in libsystem_malloc.dylib) + 24
        + ! : | + ! : | + 235 szone_malloc_should_clear  (in libsystem_malloc.dylib)
        + ! : | + ! : | + 195 szone_malloc_should_clear  (in libsystem_malloc.dylib)
        + ! : | + ! : | + ! 195 tiny_malloc_from_free_list  (in libsystem_malloc.dyl
  ...
  Total number in stack (recursive counted multiple, when >=5):

Sort by top of stack, same collapsed (when >= 5):
        objc_msgSend  (in libobjc.A.dylib)         288
        CFNumberCreate  (in CoreFoundation)         261
        szone_malloc_should_clear  (in libsystem_malloc.dylib)         237
        _CFRuntimeCreateInstance  (in CoreFoundation)         209
        CFNumberGetValue  (in CoreFoundation)         207
        tiny_malloc_from_free_list  (in libsystem_malloc.dylib)         195
        _platform_bzero$VARIANT$sse42  (in libsystem_platform.dylib)         179
        object_setClass  (in libobjc.A.dylib)         168
        _os_lock_spin_lock  (in libsystem_platform.dylib)         139
  ...
Binary Images:
    0xc7000 -    0xc7fff +sumints_objc (0) <398FF7DD-6AD1-3014-8597-4AD7BB60971E> /tm
0x8fe7a000 - 0x8feae67f  dyld (0.0 - ???) <872065EE-ED21-3B30-96A5-2CC56D735FB7> /us
0x904ce000 - 0x904d9ff7  libChineseTokenizer.dylib (16) <AE3E240D-C4AC-39D0-882F-4F8
  ...
```

Sample output is broken up into four sections:

1. A header giving various bits of metadata about the process being sampled. I usually ignore and/or filter it.
2. The call graph, which is the meat of the information gathered.
3. A sorted list of the most expensive/most used leaf functions.
4. A trailer showing an overview of the code/libraries included in the running process, which I also usually ignore.

Sample output contains a lot of information, not all of which is necessarily useful at any particular time. In particular, the wealth of output can obscure the actually relevant information. The **Call graph** section, for example, is used to convey the call hierarchy, and children of a particular node are sorted so that the heaviest subtree is shown first. We can easily see that allocating NSNumber objects using _CFRuntimeCreateInstances takes approximately one third of the total time spent. However, finding the other two thirds of the time is a bit trickier because instead of other functions at that level we get to see the implementation details of _CFRuntimeCreateInstances that are potentially interesting tidbits, but not really actionable pieces of information.

The fact that sample output is textual opens the possibility to a wide variety of ad-hoc postprocessing using Unix text tools from the command line. A simple example using grep and head to remove uninteresting detail is shown below. It cuts off the call graph at a specified depth and so allows us to see *all* the direct descendants responsible for the runtime of our main function. It achieves this by removing all lines that start with at least a specific number (in this case 14) of non-numeric characters. As specific entries are indented and start with the number of samples encountered, this effectively filters out all entries that are more deeply nested.

```
$ egrep -v  "^[^0-9]{14}" samples.txt | head -20
Analysis of sampling sumintsm (pid 4710) every 1 millisecond
Call graph:
    2704 Thread_1945987    DispatchQueue_1: com.apple.main-thread  (serial)
      2704 start  (in libdyld.dylib) + 1  [0x96d726ad]
        2267 main  (in sumints_objc) + 197  [0xc7ef5]
        + 1922 +[NSNumber numberWithInt:]  (in Foundation) + 68  [0x9d6c5d44]
        + 125 objc_msgSend  (in libobjc.A.dylib) + 80,20,...  [0x954d2ce0,0x954d2ca4
        + 111 +[NSNumber numberWithInt:]  (in Foundation) + 86  [0x9d6c5d56]
        + 54 +[NSNumber numberWithInt:]  (in Foundation) + 92,78,...  [0x9d6c5d5c,
        + 53 +[NSNumber numberWithInt:]  (in Foundation) + 46  [0x9d6c5d2e]
        + 1 -[NSObject autorelease]  (in libobjc.A.dylib) + 0  [0x954d522a]
        + 1 DYLD-STUB$$objc_msgSend  (in Foundation)
        227 main  (in sumints_objc) + 166  [0xc7ed6]
        + 207 -[__NSCFNumber intValue]  (in CoreFoundation)
        + 20 -[__NSCFNumber intValue]  (in CoreFoundation)
        162 objc_msgSend  (in libobjc.A.dylib) + 80,20,...  [0x954d2ce0,0x954d2ca4,
        40 main  (in sumints_objc) + 184,151,...  [0xc7ee8,0xc7ec7,...]
        5 DYLD-STUB$$objc_msgSend  (in sumints_objc) + 0  [0xc7f56]
```

If the filtering done by the command line turns out to be generally useful, it's easy to capture that know-how in a little script, like the following:

```
#!/bin/sh
file=$1
```

```
numindent=$(($2*2+4))
echo $numindent
egrep -v  "^[^0-9]{$numindent}" $file | sed 's/) +.*$/)/g' |  head -20
```

This also cleans up the output a little more:

```
$ filtersample samples.txt 6
Call graph:
    2704 Thread_1945987   DispatchQueue_1: com.apple.main-thread (serial)
      2704 start  (in libdyld.dylib)
        2267 main  (in sumints_objc)
        + 1922 +[NSNumber numberWithInt:]  (in Foundation)
        + 125 objc_msgSend  (in libobjc.A.dylib)
        + 111 +[NSNumber numberWithInt:]  (in Foundation)
        + 54 +[NSNumber numberWithInt:]  (in Foundation)
        + 53 +[NSNumber numberWithInt:]  (in Foundation)
        + 1 -[NSObject autorelease]  (in libobjc.A.dylib)
        + 1 DYLD-STUB$$objc_msgSend  (in Foundation)
        227 main  (in sumints_objc)
        + 207 -[__NSCFNumber intValue]  (in CoreFoundation)
        + 20 -[__NSCFNumber intValue]  (in CoreFoundation)
        162 objc_msgSend  (in libobjc.A.dylib)
        40 main  (in sumints_objc)
        5 DYLD-STUB$$objc_msgSend (in sumints_objc)
```

This type of analysis, showing a certain level of detail across several different methods or functions, is very valuable but at the same time difficult to achieve with GUI tools such as Instruments. Command-line tools make it possible to capture specific recurring analyses as reusable scripts.

# Xcode Gauges

Xcode includes lightweight profiling that is "always on" for programs launched by Xcode. An overview is shown in the *Debug Navigator*, to the left of the main pane, with labeled bar graphs for **CPU**, **Memory**, **Energy**, **Disk**, and **Network** Usage. Clicking on any of the small graphs in the Debug Navigator brings up a more detailed view for that particular aspect. Figure 2.1 shows the Debug Navigator in the left pane and the detailed CPU view in the main editor area.

# Instruments

If sample and time don't give you the answers you need and the Xcode gauges don't yield enough resolution, you probably want to turn to Instruments, a very versatile and powerful but also sometimes somewhat intimidating tool. Instruments has a wide variety of data-gathering options integrated with a sophisticated GUI for analyzing that data and finding the guilty parties. It is a very large tool, with excellent Apple-provided documentation that is also under constant development. For detailed

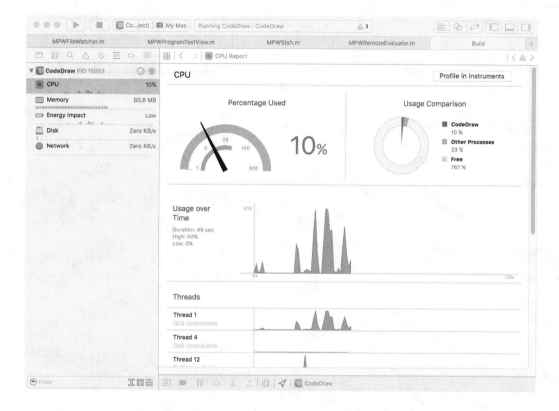

**Figure 2.1**    Xcode built in CPU profiling

use instructions, you should probably refer to that documentation; I will provide some basics and usage scenarios that I have found useful.

As a sampling tool, Instrument's output should generally be seen as indicative, not definitive, because it is prone to aliasing effects like any other form of sampling. This isn't a problem if you use data gathering for hypothesis building as described at the start of this chapter. While increasing the sampling frequency might seem an like an obvious remedy to this problem, higher sampling frequencies actually tend to decrease accuracy due to sampling overhead and jitter as well as increasing the resource requirements and the chance of interfering with the process under observation.

## Setup and Data Gathering

I usually start Instruments from Xcode, either by choosing the *Profile* option from the *Product* menu or clicking a button on one of Xcode's gauges. That way, Instruments is already set up to look at your program. By default it will then present the selection screen in Figure 2.2. I typically choose the *Time Profiler* instrument that is helpfully

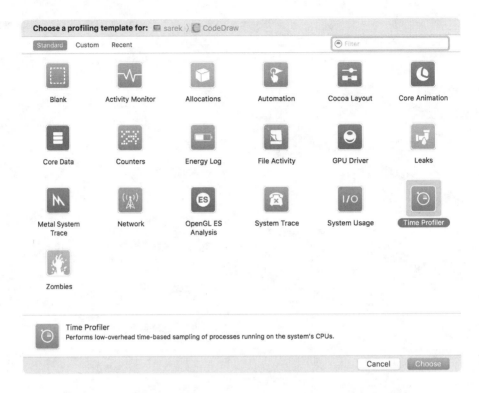

**Figure 2.2**    Instrument selection screen

already preselected. In fact, when launching from Xcode you can even skip the selection step by defining a default instrument in XCode's scheme editor for the scheme you are profiling.

After having selected the Time Profiler instrument, Instruments will show a trace document. The trace document window, from top to bottom, contains a toolbar, the timeline pane that shows a timeline for every instrument in the trace document (there can be multiple), the large detail pane that shows details (usually trace data) for the instrument currently selected in the timeline pane, and finally the inspector pane to the right of the detail pane showing more detail and configuration options of the instrument in question.

Figure 2.3 shows a trace document configured with the single Time Profiler instrument we selected previously. You can now configure your profiling target, instrument, and profiling options. Alternately, you can just accept the defaults, which are fine for a wide variety of profiling tasks, and click the big red record button at the left of the toolbar to start your profiling session.

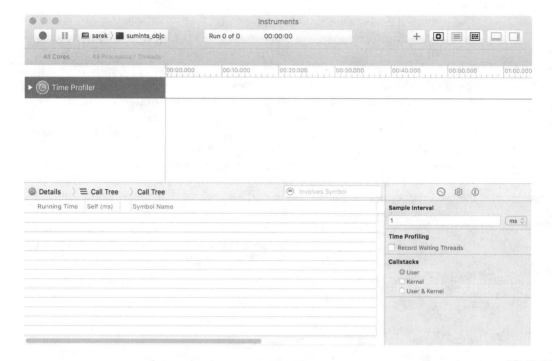

**Figure 2.3**   CPU Instrument before profiling

## Profiling Options

As I mentioned, the default profiling options are adequate for a wide variety of profiling tasks. On the other hand, customizing your profiling session can transform Instruments into a highly tuned profiling machine, and my guess is that once you've used them you will quickly find them indispensable.

First, there are a number of variations for starting a profiling session in addition to hitting *Profile* in Xcode. Using the device selector in the top left of the toolbar (to the right of the record and pause buttons), you can profile programs that are already running or launch arbitrary GUI or command-line programs on any attached device enabled for debugging. You can even switch an iOS device to untethered profiling if you need freedom of movement, for example, to profile code using the accelerometers.

The Instruments Dock menu also has additional entries that allow you to start profiling sessions without interacting with the Instruments UI. This can be important if you want to capture information from an application running on the same computer as Instruments itself without deactivating that application, which is what would happen if you interact with the Instruments UI. An even more hands-off approach is starting a profiling session using the `instruments` command-line tool.

The command `instruments -t "Time Profile" -l 2000 -D sumintsm-cpu.trace sumintsm` starts the `sumintsm` command-line program, profiles it for 2 s (2,000 ms) using the *Time Profiler* instrument, and then writes the resulting data to the trace document `sumintsm-cpu.trace`, appending run data if the file already exists. The command-line program has a much smaller footprint than the GUI application and doesn't load any of the UI frameworks or resources.

I personally found this capability essential when I was tasked with measuring and improving *cold launch* performance of various apps in the iWork suite. A cold launch refers to a launch of the app right after boot and log-in, in which case the UI frameworks are not yet memory resident. It is an important metric because it is very visible to users. However, launching the Instruments GUI app loads the majority of the GUI frameworks, meaning that with the app present any information gathered is no longer representative of a cold launch.

Two other extremely useful options can be set in the *Record Options* sheet shown in Figure 2.4 and available from the *File* menu: a *time limit* and *window limit*. Both limit profiling to a specified number of seconds, the difference is that the *time limit* does it from the start of the recording, the *window limit* from the end.

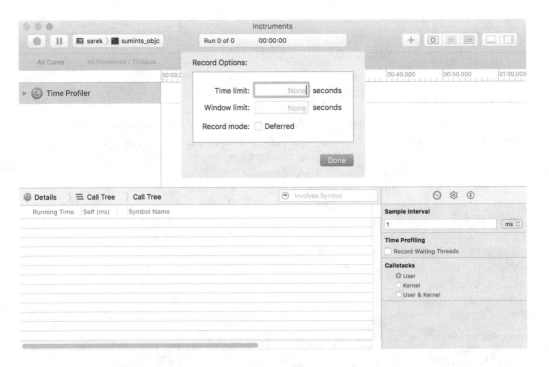

**Figure 2.4**  CPU Instrument with recording options

The *time limit* is useful for creating consistent, repeatable, and thus comparable profiles, for example by profiling an application for 2 s from launch and comparing what happens in those 2 s with different optimizations. It can also be convenient to simply not have to hit the stop button.

The *window limit* has two main use-cases that I am aware of: first, it allows you to capture a profile of a specific activity that might require long setup in an application without also capturing the long setup in the profile. A related but possibly more significant case is if the setup is indeterminate: let's say you have an event that you want to profile, but that you can't reproduce deterministically. With *window limit* set to 10 s you can just let Instruments run continuously, and when you see the behavior you are targeting, hit the stop button. Your trace will now contain the 10 s before you hit stop, hopefully including the event you are interested in.

Although there will be some impact from having Instruments running, the fact that we have multiple CPUs means that your target app can often run mostly unimpeded by the profiling. Use of the *window limit* means that memory doesn't fill up, which will otherwise happen very quickly.

Setting a *window limit* will automatically activate the *Defer* flag, which means that you can't interact with Instruments until after profiling is done, in order to minimize interference with the program being profiled. You can also set this flag manually without the *window limit* option.

I prefer always having at least a time limit set, in order to prevent runaway profiling sessions.

Finally, you can also configure the Instrument(s) being used. In the case of the *Time Profiler* instrument, the choices roughly correspond to the `real`, `user`, and `sys` components reported by the command-line `time` command: by default, *Time Profiler* reports `user` time, meaning time spent running the CPU on behalf of the user program. Selecting *Record Waiting Threads* corresponds to the `real` component, meaning wall-clock time, so tracking time waiting for I/O is also included. This can be useful at times, but will usually require some sophisticated data mining for interactive programs in order to remove the time spent waiting for the user. Finally, you can also look at time and call stacks spent in the kernel, corresponding to the `sys` component. I've used this maybe once or twice in my career. Other instruments will offer different configuration options.

## Basic Analysis

Unlike earlier performance tools, Instruments allows you to start analyzing while the profile is still being gathered. This can be convenient, but beware that such interactions can negatively affect the program being profiled if it's running on the same machine, and therefore there can also be a negative impact on the quality of the data you are gathering. Figure 2.5 shows a CPU trace during profiling: The record button has been replaced by a stop button, the timeline is starting to fill (with a fairly uninteresting rectangular graph because the `sumintsm` program is purely CPU bound), and the details pane is starting to show functions.

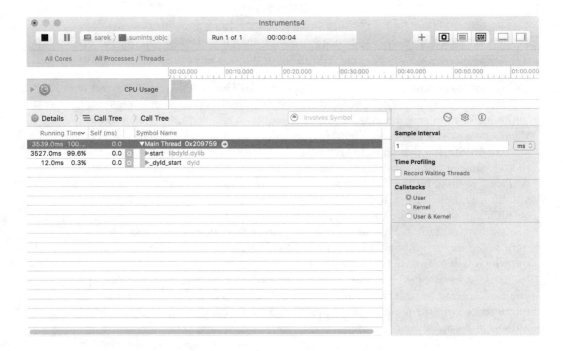

**Figure 2.5**   CPU Instrument during profiling

Each line in the Details view shows a single function or method. (Objective-C methods are implemented as C functions, so I will just call them functions.) For each function, it shows the total running time of that function and all its children (functions it calls) in milliseconds, as well as the percentage of the entire trace's running time that total time represents and the time spent in the function itself, without the calls to children. The little icon represents the source of the function, for example, a head silhouette for user-supplied functions, a mug for Cocoa, and a little gear for system functions. Finally, you have the name of the function in an outline view, along with the name of the library.

I tend to wait with my analysis until the run is finished, but whether you start analyzing the data during the run or afterward, you will probably start to drill down using the exposure triangles in front of the function names. My first move is usually to alt-click on the topmost exposure triangle; this will expand the entire profile underneath, and since entries are initially sorted by time spent, this will automatically reveal the most expensive branch in the call graph, shown in Figure 2.6. From there I can start exploring.

I was surprised to learn that many developers are not aware of the alt-click trick, despite the fact that it appears to be a system-wide feature of outline views. It certainly also works in Finder's list view.

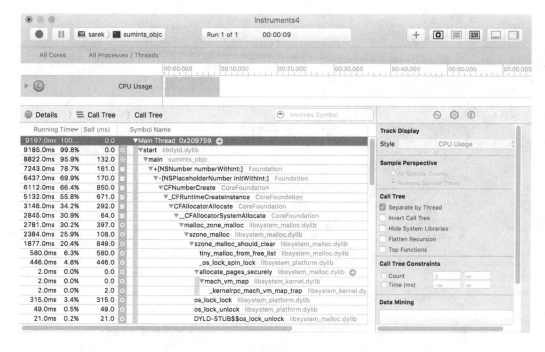

**Figure 2.6**   CPU Instrument after profiling is completed and trace expanded

Drilling down can be approached from either side: start top-down with the total program, and see where the time is going (Figure 2.6), or start at the highest cost leaf functions and see where the requests for their services are coming from (Figure 2.7).

## Source Code

Double clicking on a line of the CPU profile will reveal the source code of the function or method in question, annotated with the profile information on a line-by-line basis. As Figure 2.8 shows, the result is also colored to direct you instantly to the hotspots.

If source code is not available—for example, if you didn't compile with debug symbols or if you are looking at a system library—Instruments will show you annotated assembly code instead of source code, as seen in Figure 2.9.

If you want, you can also see the assembly code side by side with the source, as shown in Figure 2.10.

Getting precise line-by-line hotspot information is much more precise than the whole-function granularity of the normal call graph, and it can be absolutely invaluable, as it points you directly to the specific code that is slow. Sometimes it seems a bit too easy.

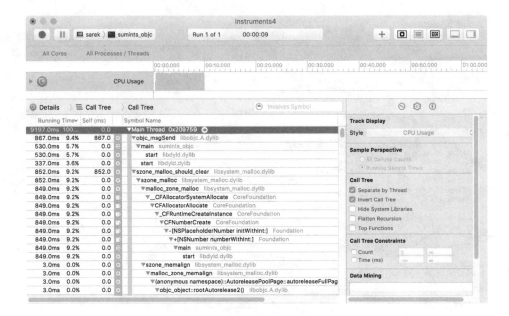

**Figure 2.7**    CPU Instrument in "heavy" view

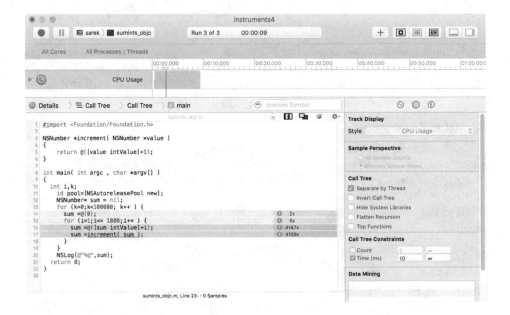

**Figure 2.8**    CPU Instrument showing source code

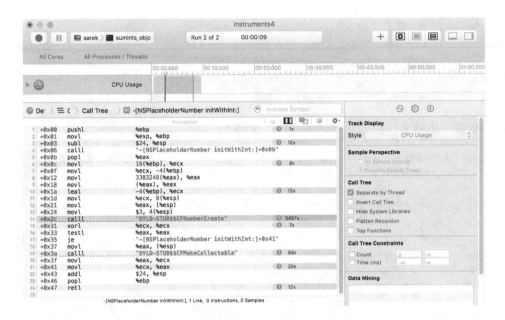

**Figure 2.9**    CPU Instrument showing assembly code

**Figure 2.10**    CPU Instrument showing source and assembly code

## Data Mining I: Focus

The simplest form of data mining happens when you either click the right arrow next to a line of the profile, or select *Focus on subtree* from the data-mining context menu in Figure 2.11: The call graph displayed in the Details view now starts with the node that was selected, with all percentages now relative to this node (which is at 100% by definition). I use this mostly to get rid of symbols only involved in program start; other than that, I generally prefer to see context.

Figure 2.12 shows the call graph of a slightly modified `sumints` program that does the sums twice—once in the `main` function and once in a helper function.

The main users of the CPU are two calls to [NSNumber numberWithInt: one in `main` and one in the helper. If we want to look more closely at the cost of [NSNumber numberWithInt:, we might choose to focus, resulting in the focused graph shown in Figure 2.13.

However, closer inspection reveals that this is not exactly what we want, because it focuses only on a single instance of the [NSNumber numberWithInt: call, the first one in this case (you can check that the total milliseconds shown is roughly the same as the number previously shown for the first call).

However, what we want to see is the total cost of [NSNumber numberWithInt:, no matter where it is called. Seeing the cost of a specific function no matter where it is called is a frequent requirement, and for leaf functions it is easily accomplished by switching to the inverted call graph. For functions in the middle, there is no obvious way to accomplish this, which is why there is a specific data-mining feature called *Focus on calls made by . . .* in the data-mining context menu (Figure 2.11).

This is one of those features that you really have to know is there and why it's there in order to make use of it. The result can be seen in Figure 2.14. Once you've used this multiple-focus feature, you won't know how you ever managed without it. To the best of my knowledge, it is the only way to get at this information, except for doing further massaging of `sample` output.

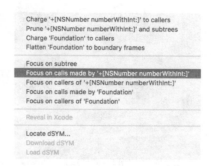

**Figure 2.11**   Instruments data-mining context menu

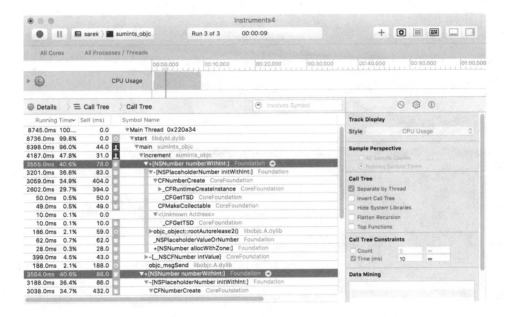

**Figure 2.12**    CPU Instrument non-focused

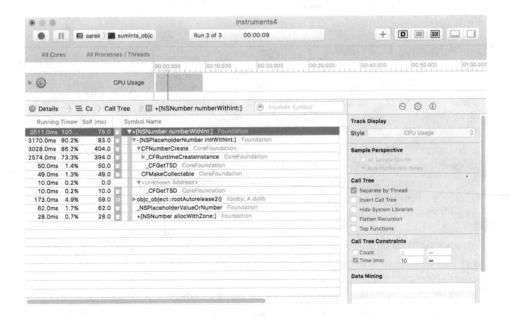

**Figure 2.13**    CPU Instrument focused on a single instance of a method

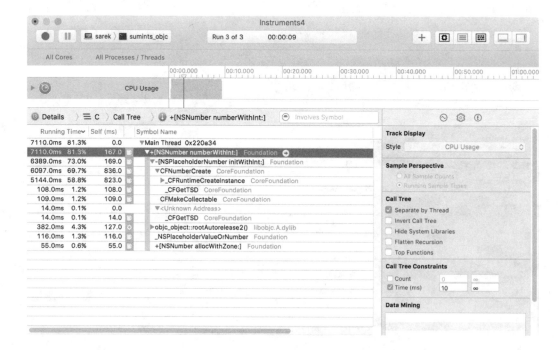

**Figure 2.14**    CPU Instrument focused on all occurrences of a function

## Data Mining II: Pruning

In analyzing trace data, you will often find that the data that is of interest to you is drowned out by all the data that is not, and that effectively becomes noise. While this is one reason to choose both your questions and your tools wisely, and focusing can also help, the data-mining functions in Instruments can also directly remove such noise.

In many situations, the "heavy" view will show a number of hotspots, and the hotspots in question will be fairly generic system functions that you have no control over. Favorites include objc_msgSend(), malloc(), and free(). These functions most likely aren't the actual problem, and you probably won't be optimizing them. They are part of the system.

Instead, the problem will be that these functions are getting called too often, something that a sampling tool like Instruments cannot distinguish from the function itself being slow, because it doesn't count function entries and exits. Rather, it only sees that the program counter was inside the function when the process got sampled.

While you can walk up the inverted call graph to find the actual culprits, this can quickly become repetitive and tedious. Instead, you can simply prune these functions so they do not appear in the call graph at all. There are two general methods for this, one of which is actual "pruning," meaning that these functions and the time spent in

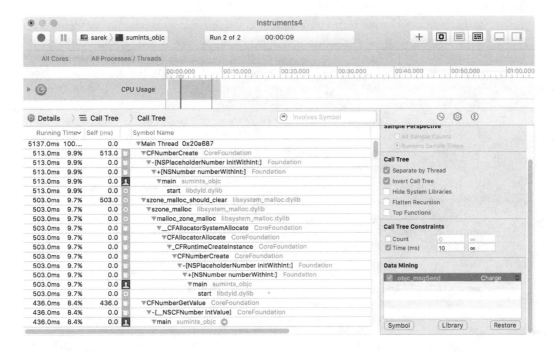

**Figure 2.15**    CPU Instrument data mining active: objc_msgSend() charged to caller

them is removed completely. This is rarely what you want because it distorts the actual running time.

More useful in most cases is the option to *Charge xxx to callers* available from the data-mining context menu, which removes the function from the display without removing the time, which is simply and correctly attributed to the function's callers. The result of charging objc_msgSend() to callers can be seen in Figure 2.15.

One thing to keep in mind while looking at the call graphs is that although call return does imply some partial temporal order, that order is very limited at best. If you want to see what actually happens over time, use the time-track pane to select different instances of time.

# Internal Measurement

Instead of just poking at your program with external instruments, you can also add instrumentation to the code itself. This will avoid or greatly reduce sampling artifacts, increase precision, and also make data gathering potentially very simple: just run the program. Internal measurement also allows you to focus on precisely the aspects you want to measure, instead of having to extract that information from potentially large amounts of superfluous data. On the other hand, inserting the measurement code may affect the routine being measured, and for that reason is often infeasible for measuring routines that execute very quickly. It also means adding extra code with potential bugs to the project, whereas external tools keep the original code clean.

If your applications log significant events using NSLog(), you are already doing some internal measurement because the logs produced by NSLog() have a millisecond-precision timestamp pre-pended. So if you have a log of application activity, you already know how long it took to get from one of these significant events to another, in real time (not CPU time). Due to the coarse nature, lack of precision, and high overhead of this method, in addition to the clutter it might produce in the logs, it should really not be used for any significant performance monitoring. However, it can be extremely useful when all you have is a customer logfile.

More sophisticated measurement involves using the getrusage() system call to get actual CPU usage information from the operating system, containing the same information used by the time and top commands, but without the overhead of starting up a separate process. Example 2.1 is a version of the integer summation program from Chapter 1 amended with self-timing capabilities via getrusage().

**Example 2.1    Adding self-timing to the integer summer**

```
#import <Foundation/Foundation.h>

long long usermicros()
{
  struct rusage usage;
  getrusage( RUSAGE_SELF, &usage );
  return usage.ru_utime.tv_sec * 1000000 + usage.ru_utime.tv_usec;
}

int main( int argc , char *argv[] )
{
  int i,k;
  long start=usermicros();
  NSNumber* sum=nil;
  for (k=0; k<100000; k++ ) {
    sum=@(0);
    for (i=; i<=1000; i++ ) {
      sum=@([sum intValue]+i);
    }
  }
  NSLog(@"%@ user: %lld microseconds",sum,usermicros()-start);
  return 0;
}
```

This allows much smaller time intervals to be measured accurately and a lot of measurements to be performed simultaneously. In fact, the performance tables shown in Chapter 1 and used throughout the book were generated using this method.

## Testing

Once you have automated internal performance measurement in place, you can also use it in unit tests in order to make performance requirements testable and to make deviation from those requirements detectable automatically.

Unit tests are also crucial in ensuring that your code keeps working as you optimize. Having the safety of the unit tests gives you the freedom to experiment with faster implementations.

Fast unit tests are also important because that allows unit tests to be run continuously with every build. (My full unit test suite of currently slightly over 1,000 tests runs in 1 to 2 s, which is a bit on the slow side but still acceptable.)

Xcode now includes performance tests as part of the XCTest framework. So far, I have not found these performance tests very useful. First, they use Xcode user interface magic that's not transparent to store the test results. I prefer my tests to be self-contained and fully specified in code and not rely on outside context, especially machine- or user-specific context. Second, these performance tests can only be used to guard against performance regressions, not drive performance improvements in a test-first style.

Of course, there is a reason for asking existing performance levels in a performance test, and then storing that on a per-host basis: Absolute performance levels are machine dependent, and a test that succeeds on a high-spec Mac Pro might fail on a MacBook Air. The answer to this conundrum is to run relative performance tests as shown in Example 2.2. Instead of codifying a specific time in which the test must be completed, we specify a ratio between a slow method and the faster method.

**Example 2.2    Unit test codifies performance improvement**

```
-(void)testPerformanceOfNewFastShouldBeTwiceOfOldSlow
{
  long long timeslow=-usermicros();
  ... old slow implementation ...
  timeslow += usermicros();
  long long timefast = -usermicros();
  ... new fast implementation ...
  timefast += usermicros();
  double improvement = (double)timeslow / (double)timefast;
  XCTAssertGreaterThan( improvement, 2.0 , @"should be faster");
}
```

This way, we can also codify performance improvements that we would like to see into our tests and then use those failing test cases to drive the performance tests until the performance test succeeds, just like we do with features in test-driven development.

# Dtrace

`dtrace` can be regarded as a combination of external and internal measurement devices on steroids, with kernel support and full scriptable tracing facilities. In short, it can do almost anything, but that power comes at the price of even simple tasks requiring significant know-how and effort. In my personal experience, the vast majority of performance-measurement tasks are fairly straightforward and already covered by existing tools.

# Optimization Beyond the Call of Duty

Soon after starting to work at one particular company, I was asked to help a colleague who had been tasked with an optimization problem; there was some problem with mail indexing being slow. My brief was that he had been working at this problem for about a month without any visible progress, and concern was spreading throughout several groups.

My inquiry about the status of the investigation revealed that the developer in question had been doing impressive work on string searching algorithms, with comparative statistical analyses of several advanced variants of Boyer-Moore-type string algorithms to find out which one would squeeze out the last percent of performance for the types of data sets in question.

All good stuff, but 10 minutes of sampling and code review revealed that the original program was using code that essentially looked like Example 2.3, except that the function pointer was passed into the function in question.

**Example 2.3    Inefficient string search**

```
comparisonFunc=isCaseSensitive ? strncmp : strncasecmp
int len=strlen(target)
int max=strlen(source)-len;
for ( i=0; i< max; i++) {
   if ( ! comparisonFunc( source+i, target, len ) ) {
      // success
   }
}
```

This is perfectly workable code, but it is slower than necessary for one and possibly two reasons: First, we are calling the full string comparison function for every single character of the potentially large input string, and second we are calling that function through a function pointer.

The first problem is the crucial one. Although we will need to call the comparison function to determine whether there is a full string match at a particular location in the source, the vast majority of locations will not match, so the bulk of the work is rejecting candidate locations, not matching them. With that insight, it becomes clear that we can reject most candidate locations much more cheaply by simply looking at their first character, without incurring the overhead of a function call.

The second problem is only significant in that without the function pointer the compiler could have done that job for us: string comparison functions belong to a class of "special" functions that compilers are aware of and may generate specialized, inlined code rather than a function call to a library function. However, the compilers can't see "through" the function pointer and thus can't inline the code for us.

With that brief insight, the fix was simple: Pull out the first character of the string comparison as shown in Example 2.4.

**Example 2.4   Slightly more efficient string search**

```
comparisonFunc = isCaseSensitive ? strncmp : strncasecmp
int len=strlen(target)
int max=strlen(source)-len;
for ( i=0;i< max;i++) {
   if ( tolower( source[i] ) == tolower( target[0] )  &&
        ! comparisonFunc( source+i , target, len ) ) {
      // success
   }
}
```

Since `strncasecmp()` is defined as converting both its input strings to lowercase, this is equivalent to calling the string functions. Another option would have been to not use a function pointer in order to let the compiler use its inlining prowess, but that would have meant duplicating the code—not a good option when considering the alternatives.

The code in Example 2.4 is far from optimal. First, we do not adjust the string pointer and length in the call to `comparisonFunc()` to reflect the fact that we've already checked the first character. In fact, we can't do that, because the first character check is actually a bit too lenient: It always uses the `tolower()` function even in the non-case-insensitive case, getting some false matches. These false matches for the first character don't matter for correctness because they will be filtered out by the call to `comparisonFunc()`.

All these performance deficiencies and the fact that the code is also much less efficient than the advanced string algorithms being examined didn't matter one bit: The one line change not only improved performance by an order of magnitude, that improvement was also sufficient to make the indexing process disk-bound, meaning further algorithmic improvement didn't affect performance. Elapsed time: less than an hour.

# Summary

This chapter introduced performance measurement from command-line tools via the Instruments profiler to internal measurement and performance tests. While mastering these tools is important and can give you a great head start in improving your code's performance, it is important to always remember not to be blinded by the tools. The measurements they help you gather are just means to support or refute hypotheses you have formed about the performance, not ends in themselves. If you keep that in mind, and optimize what needs optimization, you will already have a leg up on most of your competition.

# 3

# CPU: Pitfalls and Techniques

Having had a look at the parameters driving performance and techniques for identifying slow code, let's now turn to actual techniques for making code run fast. We will look at efficient object representations and ways for those objects to communicate and access data. We will also examine streamlining computation. In all this, the objective will typically be to effectively combine the "Objective" and the "C" parts of Objective-C to achieve the desired balance between performance and encapsulation.

In general, the basic idea is for objects to have C on the inside and messages on the outside, and for the objects themselves to be fairly coarse-grained, mostly static entities. When following these principles, it is possible to start with a fully object-oriented implementation without worries, but with the knowledge that it will be possible to later optimize away any inefficiencies. It has been my experience that it is quite possible to achieve the performance of plain C, and sometimes even beyond.

However, there are pitfalls that not only make an Objective-C program slow (slower than so-called scripting languages), but even worse can be major obstacles to later optimization efforts. These pitfalls usually lie in library constructs that are easy to use but have hidden performance costs, costs that are not localized within a single object where they could be eliminated, but present in interfaces and therefore spread throughout the system and much harder to expunge.

The following will show different options for data representation, communication, and computation, along with their respective trade-offs in terms of coupling, cohesion, and performance.

## Representation

One of the primary tasks of a program, especially an object-oriented program, is to represent data. Due to the hybrid nature of the language, an Objective-C programmer has many options available for this task.

Without any claims of completeness, structured data can be represented using a C `struct`, Objective-C object, or various forms of key-value stores, most prominently

Foundation's `NSDictionary` and CoreFoundation's `CFDictionary`, which are both getting more and more use. Simple scalars can be represented as C `float`, `double`, or `int` and their multitude of variations, Foundation `NSInteger` and CoreGraphics `CGFloat` typedefs, and finally Foundation `NSNumber` and CoreFoundation `CFNumber` objects. Note that the naming conventions are a bit confusing here: The names `NSInteger` and `NSNumber` strongly suggest that these two types are related—for example, with `NSInteger` being a specific subclass of `NSNumber`—but in fact they are completely unrelated. `NSInteger` is a typedef that resolves to a 32-bit `int` on 32-bit architectures and to a 64-bit `long` on 64-bit architectures, whereas `int` is 32 bits in both cases. Similar with `CGFloat`, which turns into a 32-bit `float` on 32-bit architectures and a 64-bit `double` on 64-bit architectures. Example 3.1 shows a few of the possible number representations.

**Example 3.1   Numbers as primitives and objects**

```
#import <Foundation/Foundation.h>

int main()
{
  int a=1;
  float b=2.0;
  NSNumber *c=[NSNumber numberWithInt:3];
  CFNumberRef d=CFNumberCreate(kCFAllocatorDefault,
                  kCFNumberFloatType, (const void*)&b );
  NSNumber *e=@(5);
  NSLog(@"a=%d b=%g c=%@ d=%@ e=%@",a,b,c,d,e);
  return 0;
}
```

In order to come to a good solution, the programmer must weigh trade-offs between decoupling and encapsulation on one hand and performance on the other hand, ideally getting as much decoupling and encapsulation without compromising performance, or conversely maximizing performance while minimizing coupling.

## Primitive Types

Possibly the easiest call to make is in the representation of simple scalar types like characters/bytes, integers, and floating point numbers: use the built-in C primitive types whenever possible, and avoid object wrappers whenever possible.

With the language supporting them natively, scalars are convenient to use and perform anywhere from 10 to more than 100 times better than their corresponding Foundation object `NSNumber` or its CoreFoundation equivalent `CFNumber`. Table 3.1 gives the details: the first three columns are times for different arithmetic operations on scalar types. The differences in timings for 32- and 64-bit addition and

**Table 3.1    Primitive operations in 32- and 64-bit architectures**

| Operation | add | multiply | divide | -intVal | NS(int) | CF(float) | NS(float) |
|---|---|---|---|---|---|---|---|
| 64-bit (ns) | 0.67 | 0.79 | 14 | 15 | 44 | 169 | 190 |
| 32-bit (ns) | 0.72 | 0.76 | 7.8 | 22 | 232 | 182 | 211 |

multiplication are probably measuring artifacts, though they were stable when preparing these measurements and it is important to report actual results as measured, not what we *think* the results should be.

Division is slower than the other arithmetic operations because dividers in CPUs usually only handle a few bits at a time, rather than a full word, which also explains why 64-bit division is significantly slower than 32-bit division.

Compared to entities that can usually be stored in registers and manipulated in a single clock cycle (or less on superscalar designs), any object representation has excessive overhead, and Objective-C's fairly heavyweight objects are doubly so. Foundation and CoreFoundation make this overhead even worse by providing only immutable number objects, meaning any manipulation must create new objects. Finally, scalars like numbers and characters tend to be at the leaves of any object graph and therefore are the most numerous entities in a program, with every object containing at least one but more likely many instances of them.

On the flip side, there is little variation or private data that would benefit from the encapsulation and polymorphism that are made possible by an object representation, and number objects are in many ways even less capable than primitive types, for example, by not providing any arithmetic capabilities. This could change in the future if Foundation or another framework provided a number and magnitudes hierarchy similar to that of Smalltalk or LISP, where small integers automatically morph into infinite precision integers, fractions, floating point, or even complex numbers as needed. Alas, Foundation provides none of these capabilities, though the introduction of tagged integers in the 64-bit runtime on OS X 10.7 along with the addition of number literals in 10.8 could be a sign of improvements in the future.

Of course, there are times when an object is required by some other interface, for example, when adding content to an NSArray or NSDictionary. In this case, you must either use NSNumber or an equivalent or provide alternatives to those interfaces—an option we will explore more later in the chapter.

One wrinkle of Table 3.1 is that although most times are similar between 32 and 64 bits, two numbers are different. The division result is about twice as slow on 64 bit, whereas the creation of integer NSNumber objects is six times faster. The division result is easily explained by the fact that the integer division hardware on the particular CPU used processes a fixed number of bits per cycle, and 64-bit operands simply have twice as many bits. The multiply and add circuits, on the other hand, operate on full 64-bit words at once.

**Table 3.2    Tagged and regular pointers**

| Bits | 8–32/64 | 4–7 | 3 | 2 | 1 | 0 |
|---|---|---|---|---|---|---|
| Regular pointer | upper address bits | | | | 0 | |
| Tagged pointer | value | subtype | | tag id | | 1 |

The difference in allocation speeds for integer objects on the other hand has nothing to do with the CPU differences and everything with the fact that Apple introduced tagged integers in OS X, but only in the modern runtime, and only for the 64-bit version of that runtime. Tagged integers are a technique taken from old LISP and Smalltalk systems where the value of an integer object is encoded not in an allocated structure pointed to by the object, as usual, but rather in the object pointer itself. This saves the pointer indirection when accessing and especially the memory allocation when creating or destroying the data (integers in this case). This representation takes advantage of the fact that object pointers are at least word aligned, so the lower 2 or 3 bits of a valid object pointer are always 0 on 32-bit and 64-bit systems, respectively. Table 3.2 shows how the tagged pointer representation puts a "1" in the low bit to distinguish tagged pointers from regular pointers, another 7 bits for typing the value, and the remaining 24 or 56 bits to store a value.

In fact, it is puzzling that the performance for integer NSNumber creation isn't much better than it is, since all it takes is the bit-shift and arithmetic OR shown in the makeInt() function of Example 3.2, possibly with some tests depending on the source and target number type—operations that should be in the 1 to 2 ns total range.

**Example 3.2    Summing manually created tagged NSNumber objects**

```
#import <Foundation/Foundation.h>

#define kCFTaggedObjectID_Integer ((3 << 1) + 1)
#define kCFNumberSInt32Type 3
#define kCFTaggedIntTypeOffset 6
#define kCFTaggedOffset 2
#define kCFTaggedIntValueOffset (kCFTaggedIntTypeOffset+kCFTaggedOffset)
#define MASK (kCFNumberSInt32Type<<kCFTaggedIntTypeOffset)
#define kCFTaggedIntMask (kCFTaggedObjectID_Integer | MASK)

static inline int getInt( NSNumber *o ) {
  long long n=(long long)o;
  if ( n & 1 ) {
    return  n >> kCFTaggedIntValueOffset;
  } else {
    return [o intValue];
  }
}

static inline NSNumber *makeInt( long long o ) {
```

```
  return (NSNumber*)((o << kCFTaggedIntValueOffset) | kCFTaggedIntMask);
}

int main( int argc , char *argv[] )
{
  NSNumber* sum = nil;
  for (int k=0;k<1000000; k++ ) {
    sum =makeInt(0);
    for (int i=1;i<=1000;i++) {
      sum =makeInt(getInt(sum)+i);
    }
  }
  NSLog(@"%@/%@ -> '%@'",sum,[sum class],[sum stringValue]);
  return 0;
}
```

The reason of course is that Apple has so far hidden this change behind the existing messaging and function call application programming interfaces (APIs) going through CoreFoundation. We are also advised that the representation, including the actual tags, is private and subject to change. What we are leaving on the table is significant: The code in Example 3.2 runs in 1.4 s, compared to 11.4 s for the Foundation/CoreFoundation-based code from Chapter 1.

Hopefully this will change in the future, and the compiler will become aware of these optimizations and be able to generate tagged pointers for integer objects and some of the other tagged types that have been added in the meantime. But as of OS X 10.11 and Xcode 7.3, it hasn't happened.

## Strings

A data type that almost qualifies as a primitive in use is the string, even though it is actually variable in length and doesn't fit in a processor register. In fact, Objective-C strings were the first and for a long time the only object that had compiler support for directly specifying literal objects.

There are actually several distinct major uses for strings:

1. Human readable text
2. Bulk storage of serialized data as raw bytes or characters
3. Tokens or keys for use in programming

While these cases were traditionally all handled uniformly in C using `char*` pointers, with some `NUL` terminated and others with a length parameter handled out of band, conflating the separate cases is no longer possible now that text goes beyond 7-bit ASCII.

Cocoa has the `NSString` class for dealing with human readable text. It handles the subtleties of the Unicode standard, delegating most of the details to `iconv` library. This sophistication comes at a cost: roughly one order of magnitude slower performance than raw C strings. Table 3.3 shows the cost of comparing 10- and 32-byte `C-Strings` with 10- and 32-character `NSString` objects.

Table 3.3   **NSString and C-String operations**

| Operation | 1 ns | !strcmp(10) | strcmp(32) | !nscmp(10) | ns append | nscmp(32) |
|---|---|---|---|---|---|---|
| 1 ns | 1 | 3.3 | 10 | 76 | 77 | 82 |
| !strcmp(10) | | 1 | 3 | 23 | 23 | 25 |
| strcmp(32) | | | 1 | 7.5 | 7.6 | 8.2 |
| !nscmp(10) | | | | 1 | 1 | 1.1 |
| ns append | | | | | 1 | 1.1 |
| nscmp(32) | | | | | | 1 |

Although NSStrings are expensive, this is an expense well spent when the subject matter really is human-readable text. Implementing correct Unicode handling is complex, error prone, and inherently expensive. In addition, the option of having multiple representations with a common interface is valuable, allowing string representations optimized for different usage scenarios to be used interchangeably. For example, literal NSStrings are represented by the NSConstantString class that stores 8-bit characters, whereas the standard NSCFString class (backed by CFString CoreFoundation objects) stores 16-bit unichars internally. Subclasses could also interchangeably provide more sophisticated implementations such as ropes, which store the string as a binary tree of smaller strings and can efficiently insert/delete text into large strings.

Starting with OS X 10.10, string objects on the 64-bit runtime also got the tagged pointer treatment that we previously saw for integers. This may seem odd, as strings are variable-length data structures, arrays of characters. However, 64 is quite a lot of bits, enough to store seven 8-bit characters and some additional identifying information such as the length. In fact, when I myself proposed tagged pointer strings back in 2007, I also had variants with eight 7-bit ASCII strings, or an even tighter packing that ignores most of the control and special characters to use only 6 bits and thus have room for 9 characters. I don't know if any of those variants are implemented.

Example 3.3 illustrates the different NSString implementation types: a literal is an instance of __NSCFConstantString, a CF variant of NSConstantString. Creating a mutable copy creates a new string object, whereas creating a copy of that mutable copy creates a tagged pointer string because the string is only 5 characters long. All of this is implementation dependent, but the differences are relevant when looking at NSDictionary lookup performance.

Example 3.3   **Show differences between normal, constant, and tagged strings**

```
#import <Foundation/Foundation.h>

void printString( NSString *a ) {
```

```
  NSLog(@"string=%@ %p class: %@",a,a,[a class]);
}

int main()
{
  NSString *cs=@"Const";

  printString(cs);
  printString([cs mutableCopy]);
  printString([[cs mutableCopy] copy]);
}
cc -Wall -o taggedstring taggedstring.m -framework Foundation
./taggedstring
string=Const 0x108fe2040 class: __NSCFConstantString
string=Const 0x7fb359c0d630 class: __NSCFString
string=Const 0x74736e6f4355 class: NSTaggedPointerString
```

While great for human readable text, NSString objects are somewhat heavyweight to be used for serialized data, which is handled more safely and efficiently by the NSData class. Unlike NSString, which requires an encoding to be known for text data and can therefore not be safely used on arbitrary incoming data (it will raise an exception if the data does not conform to the encoding), NSData can be used with arbitrary, potentially binary data read from the network or a disk. For performance, it is possible to get a pointer to the NSData's contents via the -byte or -mutableBytes methods for processing using straight memory access, whereas NSString (rightfully) protects its internal data representation, with processing only possible by sending high-level messages or by copying the data out of the NSString as 16-bit unichar character data or encoded 8-bit bytes.

When parsing or generating serialized data formats, even textual ones, it is significantly more efficient to treat the serialized representation such as the JSON in Example 3.4 as raw bytes in an NSData, parse any structure delimiters, numbers, and other non-textual entities using C character processing, and create NSString objects exclusively for actual textual content, rather than reading the serialized representation into an NSString and using NSScanner or other high-level string processing routines.

**Example 3.4    Textual content of JSON file is shown in bold**

```
[ { "name": "AAPL",   "price": 650.1,     "change": 20.41  },
  { "name": "MSFT",   "price": 62.79,     "change": -0.9   },
  { "name": "GOOG",   "price": 340.79,    "change": -5.2   }, ]
```

Even the strings that appear in such a file tend to be structural rather than actual content, such as the dictionary keys in Example 3.4. These types of structural strings are also represented as NSString objects in Cocoa, just like human-readable text.

While convenient due to the literal NSString syntax (@"This is a constant string"), this conflating of human-readable text and functional strings can at times be unfortunate in terms of performance. Fortunately, many types of keys that are more optimized exist—for example, basic C strings, message names, and instance variable names.

# Objects

Since you're programming in Objective-C, it is likely that objects are going to be your major data-structuring mechanism.

Use C inside the objects. The messaging interface hides the representation, and users are none the wiser. Try to avoid using fine-grain, semantic-free objects to implement the coarse-grain, semantics-bearing objects.

## Accessors

Accessors are methods that just read or write an object's internal data, corresponding roughly to memory read and write instructions. According to good object-oriented style, attributes of an object should not be accessed directly, certainly not from outside the object, but preferably also from within. Objective-C 2.0 properties handle the burden of creating accessors.

However, accessors should also at least be minimized and ideally should be eliminated altogether, because they turn objects from intelligent agents that respond to high-level requests for service to simple data-bearing structures with a higher cost of access. Apart from a cleaner design, passing high-level requests into an object also makes sense from a performance point of view because this means the transaction costs of a message send is paid only once, at which point the method in question has access to all parameters of the message and the object's instance variables, instead of using multiple message sends to gather one piece of data from the object at a time.

Of course, in reality, accessors or property definitions are a common feature of Objective-C programs, partly because program architecture deviates from object-oriented ideals and partly because accessors for object references in Objective-C are also needed to help with reference counting, as shown in Example 3.5.

**Example 3.5    Object accessors need to maintain reference counts**

```
-(void)setInteger:(int)newInteger {
    _integer=newInteger;
}
-(void)setObject:(id)newObject {
    [newObject retain];
    [_object release];
    _object=newObject;
}
```

As with other repetitive boilerplate, it makes sense to automate accessor generation, for example, by using Xcode macros, preprocessor macros that generate the accessor code. Alternately, the language can take over: Since Objective-C 2.0 properties can automatically synthesize accessors and with Automatic Reference Counting (ARC), the actual reference counting code was moved from the accessors to the code-generation of all variable access.

A caveat with using properties for generating accessors is that the generated code is not under user control, with the default `atomic` read accessors up to five times slower than a straightforward implementation, because they `retain` and `autorelease` the result, place a lock around the read in case of multithreaded access, and finally need to wrap all of that in an exception handler in order to release the lock in case of an exception. An alternative is the accessor macros shown in Example 3.6. These macros generate the correct accessor code just like properties. However, this generation is under user control, meaning not only that you get to decide what code gets run, but also that you can (a) change your mind and (b) extend the idea further without having to modify the compiler, as I will show later.

**Example 3.6    Accessor macros**

```
#if !__has_feature(objc_arc)
#define ASSIGN_ID(var,value) \
   { \
     id tempValue=(value);\
       if ( tempValue!=var) {  \
         if ( tempValue!=(id)self ) \
           [tempValue retain]; \
         if ( var && var!=(id)self) \
           [var release]; \
         var = tempValue; \
       } \
   }
#else
#define ASSIGN_ID(var,value)     var=value
#endif

#ifndef AUTORELEASE
#if !__has_feature(objc_arc)
#define AUTORELEASE(x)  ([(x) autorelease])
#else
#define AUTORELEASE(x)   (x)
#endif
#endif

#define setAccessor( type, var,setVar ) \
-(void)setVar:(type)newVar { \
    ASSIGN_ID(var,newVar);\
} \
```

```
#define readAccessorName( type, var , name )\
-(type)name { return var; }

#define readAccessor( type, var ) readAccessorName( type, var, var )

#define objectAccessor( objectType, var, setVar ) \
    readAccessor( objectType*, var )\
    setAccessor( objectType*, var,setVar )
```

In OS X 10.11, the slowdown has apparently been reduced to around 35%, with or without ARC enabled.

Due to the pervasiveness of accessors, this overhead is serious enough that teams at Apple sped up whole programs by more than 10% just by switching properties from `atomic` to `nonatomic`. An improvement of 10% may not seem much when we are frequently talking about improvements of 10 to 100 times, but it is actually huge when we are talking about the whole program, where significant engineering effort is often expended for single-digit percentage improvements. And here we get double digits with a single change that had no other effect. So why does `atomic` exist? And why is it the default?

The idea was to protect against code such as that shown in Example 3.7. This code has a stale reference to an object instance variable that was actually released when the pointer went stale, similar to some early Unix `malloc()` implementations having a `free()` function that delayed freeing its memory until the next call to `malloc()`, in essence avoiding a potential crash in buggy code such as that in Example 3.7.

**Example 3.7    Stale pointer reference**

```
...
  id myWindowTitle=[window title];
  [window setTitle:@"New Window title"];   // windowTitle goes stale
  [self reportTitle:myWindowTitle];        // crashes pre-ARC
....
```

The crash will occur if `title` is held onto by the window, and only by the window, because in that case `setTitle:` will release the title and the reference to this object in `myWindowTitle` will not only be stale, that is, no longer pointing to the window's title—but also invalid. Having auto-releasing accessors such as the ones provided by the `atomic` keyword will prevent a crash in this case, but at the cost of hiding the fact that the reference has, in fact, gone stale. I can see two potential reasons for writing this code. The first is that of a simple but slightly premature optimization if the title is used several times and we don't want to go fetch it from the window every time. In this case the code is simply wrong, because you'd actually want to get the new value from the window after it was set, and `atomic` in this case just masks the incorrect code. A crash would alert the programmer to the fact that the logic is amiss. The second case is that in which the programmer actually intended to stash away the old value. In this case, the code is also plain buggy, because the programmer is well aware that the new value will make the old value invalid—that's why they are stashing it! The corrected code in Example 3.8 not only doesn't need `atomic`, it also makes the intention of the code clear.

**Example 3.8     Non-stale pointer reference**

```
...
  id oldWindowTitle=[[window title] retain] autorelease];
  [window setTitle:@"New Window title"];
  [oldWindowTitle doSomething];    // clear that we want old title
....
```

Note that ARC also prevents the crash, and therefore also hides the staleness of the pointer, just like `atomic` did—by aggressively retaining objects even when they are stored into local variables. The advantage is that you don't have to think as much about the lifetime of your objects. The disadvantage is that you don't have to think as much about the lifetime of your objects, and you get significantly more reference-counting traffic, which impacts performance.

So while it is unclear whether `atomic` would be beneficial at all even if there were no performance penalty, the significant slowdown in a very common operation makes it highly questionable at best. The fact that the collection classes do not support this pattern (for performance reasons) and iOS's UIKit explicitly sets `nonatomic` for over 99% of its property declarations shows that Apple itself is not of one mind in this case.

Even slower than `atomic` accessors is access via key-value coding (KVC): A call such as `[aTester valueForKey:@"attribute"]` is not only more verbose than the equivalent direct message send `[aTester attribute]`, and not only more error prone because the compiler cannot check the validity of the string passed to `valueForKey:`, it is also 20 times slower. If runtime parameterization of the value to get is required, using `[aTester performSelector:@selector (attribute)];` is only twice as slow as a straight message send and 10 times faster than `valueForKey:`.

You might expect from these basic performance parameters that technologies built on top of KVC such as key-value observing (KVO) and Cocoa Bindings can't be too speedy, and you'd be right: Adding a single KVO observer adds a factor of 100 to the time of a basic set accessor (600 ns vs. 6 ns) and a single binding a factor of 150 (900 ns).

KVO and bindings also do not protect against cascading update notifications, which can lead to at least quadratic performance if there are transitive dependencies (b depending on a and c depending on both a and b will result in c being evaluated twice), and can lead to infinite recursion and crashes if there are dependency loops. So for larger data sets or complex dependencies, it is probably a good idea to investigate using a proper constraint solver in the tradition of the 1978 Xerox PARC *ThingLab* or later developments such as *DeltaBlue, Amulet,* or *Cassowary*. In fact, it appears that *Cassowary* was adopted by Apple for Mountain Lion's auto-layout mechanism.

## Public Access

When sending messages to access instance variables is too slow, those instance variables can be made @public. In this case, access time is essentially the same as for a C struct, (non-fragile instance variables mean that the offset is looked up in the class instead of being hard-coded at compile-time, slightly affecting the result) but then again so is safety and encapsulation: none of either. The case can therefore be made that if @public access is required, one should use a struct instead. In fact, there are some additional benefits to a struct, mainly that it can be allocated on the stack in an auto variable, passed by value to a function, or directly embedded into another object or struct or array, whereas an Objective-C object must be expensively allocated on the heap and can only be accessed indirectly via pointer.

However, there are also some benefits to keeping such an open object a true Objective-C object—namely, it can have additional functionality attached to it, access can be granted or denied on a per-field basis, and it may be used compatibly with other objects that are not aware of its publicly accessible instance variables. As an example, the PostScript interpreter mentioned in Chapter 1 uses a string object that has all its instance variables public, shown in Example 3.9, but at the same time can be used largely interchangeably with Cocoa NSString objects.

**Example 3.9    Full public string object definition**

```
@interface MPWPSString : MPWPSCompoundObject
{
    @public
    unsigned char *bytes;
    unsigned    length,capacity;
}
```

Of course, breaking encapsulation this way makes evolution of the software harder and should be considered as a last resort when all other techniques have been tried, performance is still not adequate, and careful measurement has determined that the access in question is the bottleneck.

## Object Creation and Caching

As we have seen so far, object creation is expensive in Objective-C, so it is best to use objects as fairly static and coarse-grained entities that exchange information via messages, preferably with mostly scalar/primitive arguments. If complex arguments cannot be avoided and high rates of creation/exchange need to be maintained, both Objective-C and Swift can resort to `structs` instead of objects, which like primitives can be stack allocated, allocated in groups with a single `malloc()`, and passed by value as well as by reference. However, this often means either switching between objects and structs when modeling the problem domain, or even foregoing object modeling altogether.

Another option to lessen or even eliminate the performance impact of object creation when high rates of (temporary) object creation cannot be avoided, is object caching: reusing objects that have already been allocated. The advantage of object caching over using structs is that performance considerations do not interfere with the modeling of the problem domain and all the code involved. Instead, a pure performance fix can be applied if and when performance turns out to be a problem.

Table 1.2 shows that reusing just one object instead of allocating a new one, we have not only saved some memory, but also CPU time equivalent to approximately 50 message sends, allowing us to use objects where otherwise we might have had to revert to C for performance reasons. Object reuse was common in object-oriented languages until generation-scavenging copying garbage collectors with "bump pointer" allocation came online that made temporary objects extremely cheap. Alas, C's memory model with explicit pointers makes such collectors that need to move objects nigh impossible, so object reuse it is!

In order to reuse an object, we have to keep a reference to it in addition to the reference we hand out, for example, in an instance variable or a local collection. We can either do this when we would have otherwise deallocated the object, or we can keep a permanent reference. Then, when it comes time to create another object of the desired class, we check whether we already have a copy of it and use that already allocated copy instead.

## Mutability and Caching

When is it safe to reuse an object? Immutable value objects, for example, can be reused as often as desired, because different copies of the same value object are supposed to be indistinguishable. Foundation uses this strategy in a number of places for some global uniquing. Small number objects are kept in a cache once allocated, and constant string objects are merged by the compiler and linker and shared.

In order to cache objects behind the client's back, these objects must be immutable, because sharing between unwitting clients becomes impossible if changes made by one client become visible to another. However, immutability forces creating a new object on every change, and creating a new (uncached) number object every time a new value is needed is around 30 to 40 times more expensive than just setting a new value, even if done safely via an accessor. So how can we reuse mutable objects?

One way, chosen by the UIKit for table cells, is to have a documented API contract that guarantees reusability. Another is to take advantage of the Foundation reference counting mechanism, which we use to track if the only reference left to the object is the one from the cache, in which case the object can be reused. Instead of

**Table 3.4   Reference counts for object caching**

|               | in-use   | unused   | unused action |
|---------------|----------|----------|---------------|
| retain/release | $RC > 0$ | $RC = 0$ | deallocate    |
| object caching | $RC > 1$ | $RC = 1$ | reuse         |

using the $1{\rightarrow}0$ transition to see whether the object needs to be deallocated, we use the $RC = 1$ state to see whether the object can be reused, because the cache is keeping a single reference. Table 3.4 summarizes this information.

Example 3.10 shows how this reference-count-aware[1] cache can be implemented, though the actual implementation that's part of a generic object-cache class is much more heavily optimized. The instance variables referenced here are defined in Example 3.18 and discussed in detail in the "IMP Caching" section in this chapter.

**Example 3.10    Circular object cache implementation**

```
-getObject
{
    id obj;
    objIndex++;
    if ( objIndex >= cacheSize ) {
        objIndex=0;
    }
    obj=objs[objIndex];
    if ( obj == nil || [obj retainCount] > 1 ) {
        if ( obj != nil ) {
            [obj release];         //--- removeFromCache
        }
        obj=[[objClass alloc] init];
        objs[objIndex]=obj;
    } else {
        obj=[obj reinit];
    }
    return obj;
}
```

The MPWObjectCache keeps a circular buffer of objects in its cache that's a C array of ids. When getObject[2] method is called to create or fetch an object, it

---

1. Though Apple generally recommends against calling retainCount, this use is not of the problematic kind.
2. id is the default return type and elided.

looks at the current location and determines whether it can reuse the object or needs to allocate a new one and then bump the location. It assumes objects know how to reinitialize themselves from an already initialized but no longer valid state. The circular buffer structure gives objects that were vended by the cache some time before we try to reuse them, similar to the young space in a generation-scavenging collector. At around 9.5 ns per pop, allocating from the (optimized) object cache is around 15 times faster than straight object allocation, so this is a very worthwhile optimization.

Wraparound of the index is handled via an if-check rather than a modulo operation, because a modulo is a division, and as we saw earlier in this chapter, division is one of the few arithmetic operations that is still fairly slow even on modern CPUs. A different way of implementing a modulo would be by and-ing the low bits of the index, but that would restrict the cache size to powers of 2. Finally, there are many variations of probing and retirement policies that will have different performance characteristics, for example, attempting at least $n$ consecutive slots or using random probing. So far, this very simple algorithm has proved to be the best balance for a wide variety of use-cases.

Another potential way of using reference counts is to stick to the $1 \rightarrow 0$ transition the way traditional reference counting does and then override `dealloc` to enqueue the object in a global cache instead of deallocating regularly. However, that sort of approach, unlike the object cache presented here, couples the target class tightly to the caching behavior and requires use of a global cache. I therefore recommend against that type of global cache, despite the fact that it is quite popular. Not requiring locking, scoping the cache to the lifetime of another object and the specific circumstance of that object's use patterns are a large part of what makes object caching via a cache object powerful and fast.

## Lazy Evaluation

Another use of caching is lazy evaluation of properties. When a message requests a property of an object that is expensive to compute and may not even be always needed, the object can delay that computation until the property is actually requested instead of computing the property during object initialization. Alternately, the result of an expensive computation can be cached if it is likely that the computation will be used in the future and if it is known that the parameters of the computation haven't changed.

Lazy accessors have become common enough in my code that they warrant a specialized accessor macro, shown in Example 3.11.

**Example 3.11   Lazy accessor macro**

```
#define lazyAccessor( type, var ,setVar, computeVar )   \
        readAccessorName( type,var, _##var ) \
        setAccessor( type, var, setVar ) \
-(type)var { \
        if ( ![self _##var] )  { \
```

```
                [self setVar:[self computeVar]]; \
        } \
        return [self _##var]; \
} \
```

The accessor builds on the macros from Example 3.6 but also has a parameter `computeVar` that defines the message to be sent to compute the result. When the getter is called, it checks whether it has a result. If it has a result, it just returns it; if not, it calls the `computeVar` method and then stores the result before returning it. Another less frequent accessor macro is the relay accessor that simply forwards the request to an instance variable.

## Caching Caveats

> There are only two hard things in Computer Science: cache invalidation and naming things.
>
> ———————————————————
>
> **Phil Karlton**

With all this caching going on, it is important to remember that caching isn't without pitfalls of its own. In fact, a friend who became professor for computer science likes to ask the following question in his exams: "What is a cache and how does it slow down a computer?"

In the worst case of a *thrashing* cache with a hit rate of 0%, the cache simply adds the cost of maintaining the cache to the cost of doing the non-cached computation, and an easy way of reaching a 0% hit rate with the very simple cache policy used so far is invalidating a cache item just before it is needed again, for example, by having a linear or circular access pattern and a cache size that is smaller than the working set size, even by just a single item.

Additionally, caches use up memory by extending the lifetime of objects, and therefore increase the working set size, making it more likely to either push working-set items to a slower memory class (L1 cache to L2 cache, L2 cache to main memory, main memory to disk...) or even run out of memory completely on iOS devices, resulting in the process being killed. Global, transparent caches like CoreFoundation's `CFNumber` cache fare worst in this regard, because they have effectively no application-specific information helping them determine an appropriate size, leading to caches with arbitrary fixed sizes, like 12.

In addition, they can have puzzling bugs and side effects that, because of their transparent nature, are hard for clients to work around. Example 3.12 demonstrates how different constant strings and number objects allocated by completely different means but with the same numeric value turn out to be the same actual object, as shown by logging the object pointer with the "%p" conversion directive.

**Example 3.12    Globally uniqued Foundation string and number objects in 32 bit**

```
#import <Foundation/Foundation.h>

NSString *b=@"hello world";
int main( int argc, char *argv[] ) {
    NSString *a=@"hello world";
    printf("NSStrings a=%p=b=%p\n",a,b);
    for ( int i=1; i<15; i++) {
        NSNumber *c=[NSNumber numberWithLongLong:i];
        CFNumberRef d=CFNumberCreate(NULL,  kCFNumberIntType,&i);
        printf("%d NSNumber: %p type: %s \
                CFNumberCreate: %p type: %s\n",
                i,c,[c objCType],d,[(id)d objCType]);
    }
    return 0;
}
cc -Wall -m32 -o uniqueobjs uniqueobjs.m -framework Foundation
./uniqueobjs
NSStrings a=0x6b014=b=0x6b014
11 NSNumber: 0x78e7ac30 type: i CFNumberCreate 0x78e7ac30 type: i
12 NSNumber: 0x78e7ac40 type: i CFNumberCreate 0x78e7ac40 type: i
13 NSNumber: 0x78e7ac60 type: q CFNumberCreate 0x78e7ab90 type: i
14 NSNumber: 0x78e7aba0 type: q CFNumberCreate 0x78e7abb0 type: i
```

At the time this test was run, the cutoff for the cache was 12, requests up to that value get a globally unique, cached object, whereas values larger than that result in an allocation. Also note that the objCType of all cached values is "i," a 32-bit integer, despite the fact that we specifically asked for a long long, type code "q". Once outside the cacheable area, the requested type is honored.

The reason for this odd behavior is that the cache used to always cache the first object created for a specific value, regardless of the type requested. So if the first request for the integer 5 was for a long long, then all subsequent requests for a "5" would return that long long NSNumber. However, this could and did break code that was not expecting a "q" (long long) type code in its NSNumber objects, for example, object serializers that used the type code and did not handle the "q" code! This bug was fixed by ignoring the requested type-code for the cached numbers and using "i" instead, which is in fact just as incorrect as the other case, but in practice appears to cause fewer problems. On the 64-bit runtimes, the cache is disabled because all these small integers are implemented as tagged pointers.

Another pitfall is the use of NSDictionary or NSSet instances to cache de-duplicate string objects. While they may reduce peak memory usage in some cases, they can also increase memory usage by unnecessarily and arbitrarily extending the lifetime of the stored strings. Furthermore, the fact that NSString objects have to be created before they can be tested for membership means that the CPU cost has already been paid before the cache is tested, so the cache actually *increases* CPU use. The way to improve this situation is to create a cache that can be queried using C-strings, either with a custom cache or with a custom set of callbacks for CFDictionary.

## Pitfall: Generic (Intermediate) Representations

One of the fun features of the NeXTStep system that is the ancestor of OS X and iOS was its programmable graphics and window system based on DisplayPostscript. Just as the transition to OPENSTEP brought us Foundation with the basic object model of NSString, NSNumber, NSDictionary, and NSArray, I happened to be working on a kind of "PostScript virtual machine" that redefined PostScript operators to return graphical objects in a structured format rather than paint them on the screen, similar to the "distillery" code that to the best of my knowledge still powers Adobe's Acrobat Distiller PostScript to PDF converter to this day.

As I looked at my fresh install of OPENSTEP, I noticed that the binary object sequence (BOS) format created by the interpreter's printobject command included numbers, dictionary, arrays, and strings, mapping perfectly onto the data types provided by the brand new Foundation framework! So all I had to do was create a generic mapper to convert BOS format to Foundation, access the information encoded in those Foundation objects, and use that information to populate my domain objects, which included paths, images, text, and various graphics state parameters such as colors, transformation matrices, font names, and sizes.

While this approach allowed me to construct a prototype graphical object reader reasonably quickly, the performance was "majestic." In a complete surprise, the limiting factor was neither the PostScript procedures that had to emulate the drawing commands and produce output, nor the serialization operator in the PostScript interpreter or the deserialization code, or even the somewhat pokey byte-oriented communications channel. No, the major limiting factor was the creation of Foundation objects, a factor I never would have thought of. After the shock of my disbelief wore off, I replaced the parts that had converted the BOS to Foundation objects with a simple cover object that kept the original data "as-is" but was able to access parts using a generic messaging interface. The parser then accessed this messaging interface instead of converted objects, and performance improved threefold.

This was the first time I learned the lesson that generic intermediate object representations, also known as data transfer objects, are just a Bad Idea™, at least if you care about performance and are using Objective-C. While the general principle holds true in other languages, Objective-C drives that message home with a particular vengeance because of the 1:5:200 performance ratio between basic machine operations, messaging, and object allocation.

Of course, I had to relearn that lesson a couple of times before it finally managed to stick, but the reason why it is true is actually pretty simple: a generic representation will usually have significantly more objects than a final object representation because it needs to use dictionaries (object header + key and value storage) instead of plain old Objective-C objects (somehow the "POOO" acronym as analogous to Java's Plain Old Java Objects [POJO] never caught on), object keys where objects can use instance variable offsets, and object values where objects can use simple scalar primitive types. So not only will you be creating objects that are significantly more expensive individually, but you will also need to create many more of these objects. Multiplying out these two factors makes generic intermediate object representations pretty deadly for performance in Objective-C and Swift.

Alas, Apple also makes this anti-pattern extremely convenient, so it has become pretty much the default for accessing any sort of serialized representation. A typical example is JSON parsing, with the only method directly supported by the frameworks being converting the JSON to and from in-memory property lists, that is, Foundation collections, `NSNumber`, and `NSString` objects. Even the plethora of Swift JSON "parsing" examples that have sprung up on the Internet essentially all first call `NSJSONSerialization` to do the actual parsing and generation.

## Arrays and Bulk Processing

When dealing with a collection of entities accessed by integer indexes, Foundation `NSArray` improves on plain C arrays (`array[index]`) with a number of convenient services: automatic handling of memory management (`retain / release`), automatic growth, sorting, searching, subarray generation, and a memory model that allows efficient addition and removal of objects at both ends of the array.

What's missing is a set of arrays of primitives types such as `float`, `double`, or `int` with similar sets of services, as it should be clear by now that wrapping the scalar values in `NSNumber` objects and sticking those in an `NSArray` will not perform particularly well. Such a wrapper is easy to write, and a number of them exist; for example, the author's `MPWRealArray`, the arrays in `FScript`, or `SMUGRealVector`.

As Figure 3.1 shows, the performance benefits of having a homogenous collection of scalars are overwhelming: Summing the values in an array filled with 10,000 numbers is 5 times faster than summing `NSNumbers` in an `NSArray` even if the individual numbers are accessed via a messages send, and 17 times faster when the array is asked to perform the operation in bulk.

The differences are even more pronounced for creating such an array and filling it with the values from 1 to 10,000: The homogenous array is 20 times faster than creating the same values as an `NSArray` of `NSNumbers`, even when every real value is added inefficiently using a separate message send. Moving to bulk operations, where the loop is executed inside the real array, takes the difference to a factor of 270.

Better yet, representing the numbers as a contiguous C array of floats allows us to use the vector processing tools built into OS X such as vDSP library. Using vDSP functions, summing using the `MPWRealArray` code in Example 3.13 becomes yet another 10 times faster than even the bulk processing scalar code, bringing the performance relative to the `NSArray` + `NSNumber` combination to 1.3 μs.

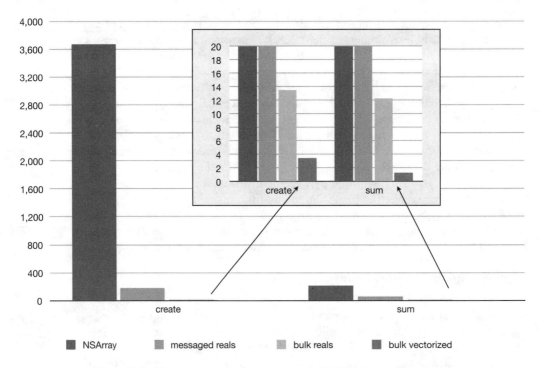

**Figure 3.1**    Time to create and sum a numeric 10,000-element array (microseconds)

**Example 3.13    Summing using vDSP**

```
@interface MPWRealArray : NSObject
{
    int capacity;
    NSUInteger count;
    float *floatStart;
}

-(float)vec_reduce_plus
{
    float theSum=0;
    vDSP_sve ( floatStart, 1, &theSum, count );
    return theSum;
}
```

This takes the time for a single addition to only 0.13 ns, showing off the true power of our computing buzz saws. Creation is also another 4 times faster when adding vector functions bulk real processing; at 3.5 $\mu$s for the entire array, this is now 1,000 times faster than creating an equivalent NSArray of NSNumbers.

To bring this into perspective, a factor of 1,000 is close to the difference between the clock speed of a Mac Pro and that of the author's Apple ][+ with its 1-MHz 6502 processor!

Of course, you don't have to use an array object. If performance is critical, you can also always use a plain C array, which can store any type of primitive, struct, or object. However, this method is without the conveniences of growability, taking care of reference counting, safe access, or convenience methods.

Swift crosses the `NSArray` of Foundation with plain C arrays to get the Swift array type: It provides most or all of the conveniences of an array object like `NSArray` or `MPWRealArray`, while at the same time using generics to be applicable to all types like a plain C array. The big advantage is that the temptation to use an array of `NSNumber` objects or similar when you just wanted to store some integers or reals has lessened dramatically. You just write `[Int]` when you want an array of integers, or with type inference provide a literal array of integers. Access times are reasonable and you still get growability and bounds checking.

The downside is that while it is harder to get unreasonably bad performance, it is also currently hard to get the best possible performance. In my tests, the Swift summation code was around 4 to 5 times slower than the equivalent Objective-C code, though that is probably going to change as the optimizer is improved. Speaking of the optimizer, unoptimized Swift array code was a shocking 1,000 times slower than reasonably optimized Objective-C code, on par with the object-based code provided here as a counterexample despite using primitives.

It is not exactly clear how Swift manages to be this slow without the optimizer, the typical factor for C code being in the 3 to 4 range, and Objective-C often not affected much at all. What *is* clear is that with this type of performance difference, unoptimized debug builds are probably out of the question for any code that is even remotely performance sensitive: when a task taking 100 ms optimized would take almost 2 minutes in a debug build, you can't really debug.

## Dictionaries

The use of strings as keys mentioned in the "Strings" section of this chapter is usually in conjunction with some sort of key-value store, and in Cocoa this is usually an `NSDictionary`. An `NSDictionary` is a hash table mapping from object keys to object values, so features average case constant $O(k)$ read access time.[3]

However, the generic nature of the keys means that, as Table 3.5 and Table 3.6 show, $k$ is a relatively large number in this case, 23 to 100 ns or 10 to 50 times slower than a message-send. Furthermore, `NSDictionary` requires primitive types to be wrapped in objects, with the performance consequences that were discussed in the "Primitive Types" section in this chapter.

---

3. The average constant access time isn't guaranteed by the documentation, but it has always been true, and the CFLite source code available at `http://opensource.apple.com` confirms it.

**Table 3.5    Cost of dictionary lookups by type of stored and lookup key, large key**

| | Time to lookup by lookup key type (ns) | | | |
|---|---|---|---|---|
| Stored keys | Constant string | Regular string | Mutable string | CoreFoundation |
| Constant string | 35 | 78 | 78 | 83 |
| Regular string | 78 | 80 | 80 | 85 |

Table 3.5 shows the more general cost of dictionary access, which is around 80 ns per read if you don't have hash collisions (when two or more keys map onto to the same slot in the hash table). A single collision adds another 20 ns or so. The only time that deviates from the roughly 80 ns standard is when you have constant strings both as the keys of the dictionary and the key to look up. In this case, the lookup can be more than twice as fast, probably due to the fact that constant strings can be compared for equality using pointer equality due to being uniqued.

For small keys up to 7 characters, the tagged pointer optimization introduced in OS X 10.10 also helps. As with constant strings, pointer comparison is sufficient here because the value is stored in the pointer, but only if both strings are of the same type, either both tagged pointers or both constant strings. Table 3.6 shows this effect: When the key classes match, both constant strings and tagged pointer strings take around 22 ns for a single lookup, but there is no benefit if the classes do not match.

So in order to get optimized dictionary performance, you need to make sure that the class of the key used to store the value into the dictionary and the class of the key used to retrieve the value match. If a string literal (@"key") was used to store the value, it is best if a string literal is used to retrieve it.

If you cannot use a string literal on retrieval, your keys are short enough to fit in a tagged pointer string. And if you retrieve values more often than you store them, it may be helpful to convert the keys you use to store the values to tagged pointer strings as was shown in Example 3.3: first do a mutable copy of the original key and then a copy of the mutable copy. This will make your retrievals 2 to 4 times faster, depending on the circumstances. (The detour via a mutable copy is necessary because

**Table 3.6    Cost of dictionary lookups by type of stored and lookup key, small key**

| | Time to lookup by lookup key type (ns) | | | |
|---|---|---|---|---|
| Stored keys | Constant string | Tagged string | Mutable string | CoreFoundation |
| Constant string | 23 | 64 | 52 | 74 |
| Tagged string | 51 | 21 | 44 | 47 |

all immutable strings, including constant strings, will just return `self` when asked to `copy` themselves.)

Even with these optimizations for small and constant strings, it is therefore best to look for alternatives to `NSDictionary` when there is a chance that performance may be relevant, unless what is needed exactly matches the capabilities of `NSDictionary`. The vast majority of dictionary uses are much more specialized, for example, using only fixed strings as keys, and often having only a bounded and small set of relevant or possible keys. The XML parser in Chapter 4 uses two types of specialized dictionaries: `MPWXMLAttributes` for storing XML attributes that supports XML semantics such as ordering and multiple values for a key and is tuned for those use-cases, and the `MPWSmallStringTable` that maps directly from a predefined set of C strings to objects.

`MPWSmallStringTable` does not use a hash-table but operates directly on the byte-by-byte character representation, trying to eliminate nonmatching strings as quickly as possible. While it is also approximately 4 times faster than `NSDictionary` for the small constant string cases that `NSDictionary` is specially optimized for, its main use is in dealing with externally generated string values, and for this use-case it is anywhere from 5 to 15 times faster than `NSDictionary`.

Swift dictionaries, which are and use value types, and which benefit from generics, are obviously faster than heavyweight `NSDictionary` objects that use slow objects, right? Alas, that is currently not the case: In all my tests, Swift `Dictionary` access was significantly slower than even `NSDictionary`. For example, a `[String:Int]` map, which maps two value types and is therefore unencumbered by any legacy Objective-C objects and "slow" dynamic dispatch, took anywhere from 140 ns to 280 ns per lookup, depending mostly on whether the key was a string literal or was provided externally, respectively. This slowdown of 3 to 7 times, compared to `NSDictionary` (and 17 to 25 times compared to `MPWSmallStringTable`) was largely independent of compiler flags, though as typical of Swift, compiling without any optimization causes a significant slowdown.

The easiest alternative to `NSDictionary` is to just define objects and use plain messaging to access their contents, especially when the dictionary in question has a reasonably small and mostly fixed set of keys. Not only is the first line of Example 3.14 anywhere from 10 to 100 times faster, it is also a cleaner design because message names are scoped by their class, whereas dictionary keys pollute the global namespace and must therefore use unwieldy long names.

**Example 3.14    One of these is 100 times faster**

```
[myParagraph setLeading: 10.0];
[myParagraph setAttribute:[NSNumber numberWithFloat:10.0]
                forKey:kMPWParaStyleLeading];
```

Why might one prefer to use a dictionary instead of an object? With the nonfragile instance variables of the Objective-C 2.0 64-bit runtime and associated storage, future-proofing against additional required instance variable is no longer an issue. Potentially sparsely populated objects can be handled by partitioning into one or more subobjects to which the corresponding message are delegated and that are allocated as needed.

As long as clients are provided with a messaging interface, the implementation can be varied and optimized to fit. While it is tempting to provide a key-value based interface instead, the flexibility it appears to offer is an illusion. Once an NSDictionary-like key-value interface is provided to clients, the performance characteristics are pretty much locked in, because mapping from NSString external keys to messages or instance variable offsets internally is just about as costly in terms of CPU usage as an NSDictionary proper. So instead, if an NSDictionary-based internal representation is desired, it can and probably should be wrapped in an object that maps its accessor messages to the dictionary.

The Macro in Example 3.15 allows you to add a messaging interface to a key in a dictionary either statically by writing dictAccessor( var, setVar , [self _myDict] ) in your implementation, where var is the key and [self _myDict] is an expression that returns the dict to be used, or dynamically at runtime, using the imp_implementationWithBlock() function to turn a block into a method implementation.

# Messaging

> I'm sorry that I long ago coined the term "objects" for this topic because it gets many people to focus on the lesser idea. The big idea is "messaging."
>
> Alan Kay

Whereas objects in Objective-C are little more than slightly specialized C structures, the efficient and highly flexible message dispatch system is at the heart of Objective-C. It combines true object encapsulation and the dynamicism of languages such as Ruby or Smalltalk. Not only are Objective-C messages powerful, they are also relatively cheap, only around twice the cost of a C function call and within an order of magnitude of basic machine operations. Even an unoptimized message send is around 10 times faster than keyed access via NSString, and 50 times faster than object-creation, despite the fact that in the current Objective-C runtime, an Objective-C selector, is really just a C string.

The reason that messaging via string selectors is so quick is that the compiler, linker, and runtime conspire to guarantee that every C string representing an Objective-C selector has a unique address, and therefore the Objective-C messenger function objc_msgSend() does not have to concern itself with the string that the selectors point at, but just uses the pointer itself as an uninterpreted unique integer

**Example 3.15    Generate and test dictionary-backed accessor method (statically or dynamically)**

```
#import <Foundation/Foundation.h>
#import <objc/runtime.h>
#define dictAccessor( objectType, var, setVar, someDict ) \
    -(objectType*)var { return someDict[@""#var]; } \
    -(void)setVar:(objectType*)newValue { \
        someDict[@""#var]=newValue;\
    }\
@interface MyObject : NSObject
@property (retain) NSMutableDictionary *dict;
@end
@interface MyObject(notimplemented)
@property (retain) NSString *a;
@property (retain) NSString *b;
@end
@implementation MyObject
-(instancetype)init {
  self=[super init];
  self.dict=[NSMutableDictionary new];
  return self;
}
-(void)addDictAccessorForKey:(NSString*)key
{
  SEL selector=NSSelectorFromString( key );
  id (^block)()=^{
    return self.dict[key];
  };
  imp=imp_implementationWithBlock( block );
   class_addMethod([self class], selector, imp , "@:");
}
dictAccessor( NSString, b, setB , self.dict )
@end
int main()
{
        MyObject *m=[MyObject new];

        [m addDictAccessorForKey:@"a"];
        m.dict[@"a"]=@"Hello";
        m.b=@"World!";
        NSLog(@"m.a: %@ m.b: %@",m.a,m.b);
        return(0);
}
```

value. In fact, as Brad Cox writes in *Object-Oriented Programming: An Evolutionary Approach*, this selector-uniquing process was the main driver for converting Objective-C from a set of C macros to an actual preprocessor, which then made it possible to create a distinct syntax.

On Mac OS X 10.11 with Xcode 7.3.1, the code in Example 3.16 prints `selector: 'hasPrefix:'`, but the compiler already warns that `cast of type 'SEL' to 'char *' is deprecated; use sel_getName instead`. In the GNU runtime, selectors are structure that reference both the message name and its type encoding.

**Example 3.16    Printing a selector as a C string using Apple's runtime**

```
#import <Foundation/Foundation.h>

int main()
{
  SEL a=@selector(hasPrefix:);
  printf("selector: %s\n",(char*)a);
  return 0;
}
```

## IMP Caching

Although developers new to Objective-C tend to worry most about message sending, for example, compared to C++ virtual function invocation, the Objective-C messenger function objc_msgSend() (or objc_msg_lookup() in GNU-objc) has been highly optimized and is usually not a bottleneck.

In the rare cases that it does become a factor, it is possible to retrieve the function pointer from the runtime and call that instead. The technique is known as IMP caching because the type definition of an Objective-C method pointer is called an IMP (implementation method pointer, or just IMPlementation). IMP caching can be useful in a tight loop with a fixed receiver when the method itself is trivial and therefore message dispatch is a major contributor. Example 3.17 shows a greater than 2.5-times improvement in runtime from 2.8 ns to 1.08 ns after subtracting loop overhead.

**Example 3.17    Replacing a plain message send with an IMP-cached message send**

```
#import <MPWFoundation/MPWFoundation.h>
@interface MyInteger : NSObject
@property (assign) int intValue;
@end

@implementation MyInteger
@end
```

```
int main()
{
  MyInteger *myObject=[MyInteger new];
  int a=0;
  myObject.intValue=42;
  for ( int i=0; i<1000; i++) {
    a+=[myObject intValue];
  }

  IMP intValueFun=[myObject methodForSelector:@selector(intValue)];
  for ( int i=0; i<1000; i++) {
    a+=(int)intValueFun( myObject, @selector(intValue) );
  }
}
```

Due to the dynamic nature of Objective-C, there is no automatic way of determining at compile time whether this optimization is safe, which is one reason the Objective-C compiler doesn't do it for you. Fortunately, it is usually very easy for a developer to make that determination. While there are numerous ways for the IMP to change during execution (for example, loading a bundle that includes a category, and using runtime functions to add, remove, or change method implementations or even change the class of the object in question), all of these are rare events that happen fairly predictably.

It is the developer's job to ensure that either none of these events happen, or alternately, that they do not have an impact on the computation.

A special case that needs to be considered when doing IMP caching is the nil receiver. The Objective-C messenger quietly ignores messages to nil, simply returning zero instead of dispatching the message. This short-circuiting protects receivers from having to worry about a nil self pointer, and sender from having to special case nil-receivers. IMP caching breaks this protection on several counts: If the receiver is nil when requesting the IMP, a NULL function pointer will be returned, and invoking such a NULL function pointer will crash the program. On the other hand, if a correct function pointer was obtained from an earlier, non-nil object pointer, calling that function pointer will call a method with a nil self pointer. Any instance variable access from within that method will also crash the program.

So you will need to ensure both that you are not getting a NULL IMP and that you don't call an IMP with a nil receiver.

IMP caching can be particularly useful when sending messages to "known" objects such as delegates or even self. Example 3.18 shows part of the actual header of the object cache discussed in the "Mutability and Caching" section of this chapter. In addition to the cache itself ( objs, cacheSize ) and the current pointer into the cache objIndex, it also maintains IMP pointers for all the message sent in the -getObject method from Example 3.10, allowing the actual -getObject to run without once invoking the messenger. In addition, it makes the IMP for the -getObject method itself available in a @public instance variable, along with a GETOBJECT() C-preprocessor macro to invoke it. The GETOBJECT macro is actually slightly less code to write than a normal alloc-init-autorelease, is 8% faster even with a cache miss, is 15 times faster with a cache hit, and last but not least decouples the user of the cache from the specific class used.

**Example 3.18    Definition and use of an object cache for integer objects**

```
@interface MPWObjectCache : MPWObject
{
    id          *objs;
    int         cacheSize,objIndex;
    Class       objClass;
    SEL         allocSel,initSel,reInitSelector;
    IMP         allocImp,initImp,reInitImp,releaseImp;
    IMP         retainImp,autoreleaseImp;
    IMP         retainCountImp,removeFromCacheImp;
    @public
    IMP         getObject;
}

+(instancetype)cacheWithCapacity:(int)newCap class:(Class)newClass;
-(instancetype)initWithCapacity:(int)newCap class:(Class)newClass;
-getObject;
#define GETOBJECT( cache ) \
    ((cache)->getObject( (cache), @selector(getObject)))
...
@end
integerCache=[[MPWObjectCache alloc] initWithCapacity:20
         class:[MPWInteger class]];
MPWInteger *integer=GETOBJECT( integerCache );
[integer setIntValue:2];
```

If IMP caching is insufficient and you have the source code of the method you need to call available, you can always turn it into a C function, an inline function, or even a preprocessor Macro.

Considering how little of a problem dynamic dispatch is in practice, and how easy it is to remove the problem in the rare cases it does come up, it is a little surprising how much emphasis the Swift team has placed on de-emphasizing and removing dynamic dispatch from Swift for performance reasons.

## Forwarding

While close to C function call speeds on one end, Objective-C messages are flexible enough to take the place of reified messaging and control structures on the other end. For example, Cocoa does not have to use the *Command* pattern because messages carry enough runtime information to be reified, stored, and introspected about so something like the NSUndoManager can be built using the fast built-in messaging system.

For your own projects, I would always recommend mapping any requirements for dynamic runtime behavior onto the messaging infrastructure if at all possible, and with a full reflective capabilities what is possible is very broad. The code in Example 3.19 will execute the message to the object in question as a Unix shell command, so [object ls] will execute the ls command, and [object date] the date command. A more elaborate example would translate message arguments to script arguments.

**Example 3.19   Mapping sent messages to shell commands**

```
#import <Foundation/Foundation.h>
@interface Shell:NSObject
@end
@interface Shell(notimplemented)
-(void)ls;
@end
@implementation Shell

-(void)forwardInvocation:(NSInvocation*)invocation {
  system( [NSStringFromSelector( [invocation selector])
          fileSystemRepresentation] );
}
-(void)dummy {}
-methodSignatureForSelector:(SEL)sel
{
   NSMethodSignature *sig=[super methodSignatureForSelector:sel];
   if (!sig) {
      sig=[super methodSignatureForSelector:@selector(dummy)];
   }
   return sig;
}
@end

int main()
{
    Shell *sh=[Shell new];
    [sh ls];
    return 0;
}
```

Example 3.20 reads the file that is named by the sent message instead of executing it, and perhaps somewhat more realistically, Example 3.21 looks up the selector in a local dictionary.

**Example 3.20    Mapping sent messages to file contents**

```
#import <Foundation/Foundation.h>
@interface Filer:NSObject
@end
@interface Filer(notimplemented)
-(NSString*)hello;
@end
@implementation Filer

-(void)forwardInvocation:(NSInvocation*)invocation {
  NSString *filename=NSStringFromSelector( [invocation selector]);
  NSString *contents=[[NSString alloc]
                              initWithContentsOfFile:filename
                              encoding:NSISOLatin1StringEncoding
                              error:nil];
  [invocation setReturnValue:&contents];
}
-(NSString*)dummy { return @""; }
-methodSignatureForSelector:(SEL)sel
{
    NSMethodSignature *sig=[super methodSignatureForSelector:sel];
    if (!sig) {
       sig=[super methodSignatureForSelector:@selector(dummy)];
    }
    return sig;
}
@end

int main()
{
    Filer *filer=[Filer new];
    NSLog(@"filer: %@",[filer hello]);
    return 0;
}
```

**Example 3.21    Mapping sent messages to dictionary keys**

```
-(void)forwardInvocation:(NSIvocation*)invocation {
    id result=[[self dictionary] objectForKey:
             NSStringFromSelectr([invocation selector])];
    [invocation setReturnValue:&result];
}
```

## Uniformity and Optimization

Although there is no actual performance benefit for the *implementations* of Examples 3.19 to 3.21, the benefit comes from using the fastest plausible *interface*, an interface that can be kept the same all the way from reading files (3.20) via using runtime introspection to look up keys (3.21), generating accessors to a keyed store at runtime or compile time (3.15) or switching to an accessor for an actual instance variable, and finally IMP caching that message send. You don't have to start out fast, but you have to use interfaces that allow you to become fast should the need arise.

The more I have followed Alan's advice to focus on the messages, the better my programs have become, and the easier it has been to make them go fast.

# Methods

Objective-C methods generally fall into two rough categories: lean and mean C data manipulation on one hand and high-level coordination using message sends on the other.

For the data-manipulation methods, all the usual tricks in the C repertoire apply: moving expensive operations out of loops (if there is no loop, how is the method taking time?), strength reduction, use of optimized primitives such as the built-in memory byte copy functions or libraries such as vDSP, and finding semantically equivalent but cheaper replacements. Fortunately, the compiler will help with most of this if optimization is turned on. In fact, instead computing the end-results of the loops, LLVM/clang managed to optimize away most of the simple loops from our benchmark programs unless we specifically stopped it.

In order to keep data manipulation methods lean and mean, it is important to design the messaging interface appropriately, for example, passing all the data required into the method in question, rather than having the method pull the data in from other sources.

High-level coordination methods should generally not be executed very often and therefore do not require much if any optimization. In fact, I've had excellent performance results even implementing such methods in interpreted scripting languages. A method triggering an animation lasting half a second, for example, will take less than 0.2% of available running time even if it takes a full millisecond to execute, which simply won't be worth worrying about.

## Pitfall: CoreFoundation

One of the recurring themes in this chapter has been leveraging C for speed and making careful tradeoffs between the "C" and the "Objective" parts of the language in order to get a balance between ease of use, performance, and decoupling and dynamicism that works for the project at hand.

However, it is possible to get this terribly wrong, as in the case of CoreFoundation. CoreFoundation actually throws out the fast and powerful bits of Objective-C (messaging, polymorphism, namespace handling) and manages to provide a cumbersome monomorphic interface to the slow bits (heap allocated objects). It then encourages the use of dictionaries, which are an order of magnitude slower still. The way CoreFoundation provides largely monomorphic interfaces to CoreFoundation objects that actually have varying internal implementations means that each of those functions, with few exceptions, has to check dynamically what representation is active and then run the appropriate code for that representation. You can see this in the OpenSource version of CoreFoundation available at http://opensource.apple.com/source/CF.

An Objective-C implementation leaves that task to the message dispatcher, meaning that both method implementations can be clean because they will only be called with their specific representation, also making it easier to provide a greater number of optimized representations.

While I've often heard words to the effect that "our code is fast because it just uses C and CoreFoundation and is therefore faster than it would be if it were to use Objective-C," this appears to be a myth. I've never actually found this claim to be true in actual testing. In fact, in my testing, pure Objective-C equivalents to CoreFoundation objects are invariably faster than their CoreFoundation counterparts, and often markedly so. Sending the `-intValue` message shown in Example 3.17 is already 30% faster than calling the CoreFoundation `CFGetIntValue()` function, despite the message-passing overhead. Dropping down to C using IMP caching makes it over 3 times faster than the CoreFoundation equivalent.

The same observations were made and documented when CoreFoundation was first introduced, with users noticing significant slowdowns compared to the non-CoreFoundation OPENSTEP Foundation (apps twice as slow on machines that were supposed to be faster[4]). This obviously does not apply to the NSCF★ classes that Apple's Foundation currently uses; these cannot currently be faster than their CoreFoundation counterparts because they call down to CoreFoundation.

## Multicore

As we saw in Chapter 1, Moore's Law is still providing more transistors but no longer significant increases in clock frequency or performance per clock cycle. This shift in capabilities means that our single-threaded programs are no longer getting faster just by running them on newer hardware. Instead, we now have to turn to multithreading in order to take advantage of the added capabilities, which come in the form of additional cores. Getting multithreading right is a hard problem, not just due to the potential for race conditions and deadlocks, but also because the addition of thread management and synchronization actually adds significant overhead that can be difficult to break even on, despite the additional CPU resources that are unlocked with multithreading.

---

4. http://www.cocoabuilder.com/archive/cocoa/20773-does-ppc-suck-or-has-apple-crippled-cocoa.html#20773

Due to the pretty amazing single-core performance of today's CPUs, it turns out that the vast majority of CPU performance problems are not, in fact, due to limits of the CPU, but rather due to suboptimal program organization.[5] I hope the factors 3 to 4, 10 to 20, and 100 to 1,000 of often easily attainable performance improvements I have presented so far will convince you to at least give the code-tuning option serious consideration before jumping into multithreading, which at best can achieve a speedup to the number of cores in the system—and this is only for perfectly parallelizable, so-called "embarrassingly parallel" problems.

$$S(N) = \frac{1}{(1 - P) + \frac{P}{N}} \tag{3.1}$$

Amdahl's Law (Equation 3.1), relating the potential speedup ($S$) due to parallelization with $N$ cores ($S(N)$) to the fraction of the program that can be parallelized ($P$) shows that the benefit of newer cores peters off very quickly when there are even small parts of the program that cannot be parallelized. So even with a very good 90% parallelizable program, going from 2 to 4 cores gives a 70% speedup, but going from 8 to 12 cores only another 21%. And the maximum speedup even with an infinite number of cores is factor 10. For a program that is 50% parallelizable, the speedup with 2 cores is 33%, 4 cores 60% and 12 cores 80%, so approaching the limit of 2.

While I can't possibly do this topic justice here, it being worthy of at least a whole book by itself, I can give some pointers on the specifics of the various multithreading mechanisms that have become available over the years, from `pthreads` via `NSThread` and `NSOperationQueue` all the way to the most recent addition, Grand Central Dispatch (GCD).

## Threads

Threading on OS X is essentially built on a kernel-thread implementation of POSIX threads (`pthreads`). These kernel threads are relatively expensive entities to manage, somewhat similar to Objective-C objects, only much more so. Running a function `my_computation( arg )` on a new POSIX thread using `pthread_create`, as in Example 3.22, takes around 7 $\mu$s to of threading overhead on my machine in addition to the cost of running `my_computation()` by itself, so your computation needs to take at least those 7 $\mu$s to break even, and at least 70 $\mu$s to have a chance of getting to the 90% parallelization (assuming we have a perfect distribution of tasks for all cores).

Creating a new thread using Cocoa's `NSThread` class method `+detachNewThreadSelector:...` adds more than an order of magnitude of overhead to the tune of 120 $\mu$s to the task at hand, as does the `NSObject` convenience method `-performSelectorInBackground:...` (also Example 3.22).

---

5. James R. Larus. "Spending Moore's dividend," *Communications of the ACM* No. 5 (2009).

Taking into account Amdahl's Law, your task should probably take at least around 1 ms before you consider parallelizing, and you should probably consider other optimization options first.

**Example 3.22    Creating new threads using pthreads, Cocoa NSThread, or convenience messages**

```
pthread_create( &pthread, attrs, my_computation, arg );
[NSThread detachNewThreadSelector:@selector(myComputation:)
        toTarget:self
        withObject:arg];
[self performSelectorInBackground:@selector(myComputation:)
      withObject:arg];
```

So, similar to the balancing of OOP vs. C, getting good thread performance means finding independent tasks that are sufficiently coarse-grained to be worth off-loading into a thread, but at the same time either sufficiently fine-grained or uniformly sized that there are sufficient tasks to keep all cores busy.

In addition to the overhead of thread creation, there is also the overhead of synchronizing access to shared mutable state, or of ensuring that state is not shared—at least, if you get it right. If you get it wrong, you will have crashes, silently inconsistent and corrupted data, or deadlocks. One of the cheapest ways to ensure thread-safe access is actually `pthread` thread-local variables, accessing to such a variable via `pthread_getspecific()` is slightly cheaper than a message send. But this is obviously only an option if you actually want to have multiple separate values, instead of sharing a single value between threads.

In case data needs to be shared, access to that data generally needs to be protected with `pthread_mutex_lock()` (43 ns) or more conveniently and safely with an Objective-C `@synchronized` section, which also protects against dangling locks and thus deadlocks by handling exceptions thrown inside the `@synchronized` section. Atomic functions can be used to relatively cheaply (at 8 ns, around 10 times slower than a simple addition in the uncontended case) increment simple integer variables or build more complex lock-free or wait-free structures.

## Work Queues

Just like the problem of thread creation overhead is similar to the problem of object-allocation overhead, so work queues are similar to object caches as a solution to the problem: They reuse the expensive threads to work on multiple work items, which are inserted into and later fetched from work queues.

Whereas Cocoa's `NSOperations` actually take slightly longer to create and execute than a `pthread` (8 $\mu$s vs. 7 $\mu$s), dispatching a work item using GCD introduced in Snow Leopard really is 10 times faster than a `pthread`, at 700 ns per item for a simple static block, and around 1.8 $\mu$s for a slightly more complex block with arguments like the one in Example 3.23.

**Example 3.23    Enqueuing GCD work using straight blocks**

```
dispatch_async(
    dispatch_get_global_queue(DISPATCH_QUEUE_PRIORITY_DEFAULT, 0),
    ^{ [self myComputation:arg]; } );
```

I personally prefer convenience messages such as the -async Higher Order Message (HOM),[6] which simplifies this code to the one shown in Example 3.24 at a cost of an extra microsecond.

**Example 3.24    Enqueuing GCD work using HOM convenience messages**

```
[[self async] myComputation:arg];
```

In the end, I've rarely had to use multithreading for speeding up a CPU-bound task in anger, and chances are good that I would have made my code slower rather than faster. The advice to never optimize without measuring as you go along goes double for multithreading. On the flip side, I frequently use concurrency for overlapping and hiding I/O latencies (Chapter 12) or keeping the main thread responsive when there is a long running task, be it I/O or CPU bound (Chapter 16). I've also used libraries that use threading internally, for example, the vDSP routines mentioned earlier or various image-processing libraries.

# Mature Optimization

> We should forget about small efficiencies, say about 97% of the time; premature optimization is the root of all evil.
>
> D.E. Knuth

Optimizing Objective-C programs is, in the end, not necessarily hard. In fact, this very amenability to optimization in general and late-in-the-game optimization in particular is a large part of what makes this language popular with expert programmers: you really can leave the "small efficiencies," a few of which we've shown, for later.

Although Knuth's quote above is well-known, what is *less* well-known is that it is just an introduction to extolling the importance and virtues of optimization. It continues as follows:

> Yet we should not pass up our opportunities in that critical 3%. A good programmer will not be lulled into complacency by such reasoning, he will be wise to look carefully at the critical code; but only after that code has been identified.

---

6. Implementation can be found at https://github.com/mpw/HOM.

And the section before the one in question couldn't be more different:

> The conventional wisdom shared by many of today's software engineers calls for
> ignoring efficiency in the small; but I believe this is simply an overreaction to the
> abuses they see being practiced by penny-wise-and-pound-foolish programmers,
> who can't debug or maintain their "optimized" programs. In established
> engineering disciplines a 12% improvement, easily obtained, is never considered
> marginal; and I believe the same viewpoint should prevail in software engineering.
> Of course I wouldn't bother making such optimizations on a one-shot job, but
> when it's a question of preparing quality programs, I don't want to restrict myself
> to tools that deny me such efficiencies.
>                 "Structured Programming with Go To Statements," Knuth, 1974.

The quote is embedded in the paper "Structured Programming with Go To
Statements" from 1974, which is largely about achieving better performance via the
use of go to statements. It is in fact, in large part, an advocacy piece *for* program
optimization, not against it, containing such gems as the idea that engineers in other
disciplines would be excluded from practicing their profession if they gave up
performance as readily as programmers.

What makes Objective-C so powerful is that once you have the information as to
what needs optimization, you can really pounce, smash-bits, and exploit all the
hardware has to give. Both until that point and for the parts that don't need it, you
can enjoy the remarkable productivity of a highly dynamic object-oriented language.

Swift takes a different approach: make everything much more static up-front and
then let the compiler figure it out. While superficially sound, this approach inverts
Knuth's dictum by making microperformance a deciding factor in not just application
modeling, but language design. In addition to the approach being questionable in
principle, it currently just doesn't work: Swift is not just slower than optimized
Objective-C, it is often significantly slower than non-optimized Objective-C,
without any further recourse than waiting for the compiler to get better or rewriting
your code in C. So that questionable premature optimization doesn't even pay off.

That said, a little bit of structural forethought and planning is extremely helpful in
order to enjoy the benefits of late optimization: You should have an idea of the order
of magnitude of data you will be dealing with (one, a thousand, a million?), what
operations you need to support, and whether the machine you are targeting can
handle this amount of data, at least in principle.

As you are designing the system, keep in mind the asymmetric 1:5:50:200
relationship for primitive operations : messaging : key-value access : object creation
that we have illuminated throughout this chapter. With that in mind, see if your most
numerous pieces of data can be mapped to primitives, and try to keep your interfaces
as message-centric as possible. The messaging system has a nice sweet spot in the
relationship between cost and expressiveness.

The arguments of those messages should be as simple (primitive types preferred)
and expressive as possible. Large-volume data should be contained in bulk objects and

hidden behind bulk interfaces. Key-value stores, if needed, should be hidden behind messaging interfaces and temporary objects should be avoided, especially as a requirement for an interface. If temporary objects can't be avoided, try to keep your APIs defined in such a way that you will be able to "cheat" with object caches or other techniques for reusing those objects when the time comes.

Fortunately, these measures tend to simplify code, rather than make it more complicated. Simpler, smaller, well-factored code is not only often faster than complicated code, because code that isn't there doesn't take any time to run, it also makes a much better basis for future optimization efforts because modifying a few spots will have a much greater impact.

# 4

# CPU Example: XML Parsing

My forays into XML parsing started long before Cocoa had acquired XML parsers, at a company (www.infopark.com) building a Web Content Management System (CMS) in Objective-C on Solaris and a bunch of other Unix platforms. Apple had just been acquired by NeXT (or was it the other way around?), so even Cocoa was actually called OPENSTEP and barely starting to morph into Yellow Box on Rhapsody.

You will therefore not see any "newfangled" technologies such as Swift, ARC, or even Objective-C 2.0 properties. However, historical accuracy is only one small reason; after all, it would have been easy to update the code. The more important reason is that these technologies are not adequate at these performance levels. When the placement of a single `-retain` can make a significant difference in overall performance, you can't have the compiler insert them semi-randomly and hope the optimizer will get rid of all of them.

One of the cooler features of the CMS was that it had a website importer that could suck in your existing website and bring it into full multiuser online editing and version control all with the click of a button, similar to the way NeXT's Enterprise Object Framework and WebObjects could automatically connect to a legacy database (mainframe with the 3270 adapter), extract the schema, and automatically create a simple online CRUD app within seconds—where teams of programmers had often struggled for months.

Alas, the magic of the auto import was hampered by the fact that it took nonmagical amounts of time, so I started to look at how to make it a bit more magical on the performance front.

One of the main culprits turned out to be our custom HTML "tag-soup" parser, which simply broke up the input into the categories *tag* and *not tag*, and then processed that tag soup to extract metadata such as the title, converted URLs in image, and anchor tags into database references if they resolved to other imported content or external reference objects if they did not.

The basic parser had been constructed using the parser construction toolkits *flex* and *bison*, which seemed like the obvious tools for the job. It clocked in at a disappointing 200 KB/s on a then state-of-the art SPARC Ultra that had replaced our pokey but reliable SPARCStation 5 as main (shared) development box.

Considering the clock speed of the machine of upwards of 100 MHz, the memory access speed below 100 ns, it seemed we should be able to do at least an order of magnitude better.

# An HTML Scanner

Instead of analyzing the complex, table-driven code created by the parser-generator, it seemed simpler to use an experimental additive approach: build the simplest possible solution to the most relevant and hopefully performance-dominant subproblem of the original problem and then enrich while keeping performance impacts of the enrichments as minimal as possible.

The very least that an HTML parser has to do is look at every character in the source file and figure out whether it belongs to a tag or to text that is outside a tag, splitting the HTML source bold text into the open tag , the text bold text and the close tag . A simple way to do this is with a state machine like the one in Example 4.1. It has two states, inTag and inText. When in the inText state, a left angle bracket switches to the inTag state, and when in the inTag state, a right angle bracket switches back to the inText state. Every state transition is used to report the region that was just completed using the provided callback function.

**Example 4.1   Simplest XML Scanner**

```
typedef enum {
        inText = 0,
        inTag,
        inSgmlTag} ScanState;

typedef int (*CallbackFun)(ScanState,const char*,size_t);
int scanHtml(const char *data,int len,CallbackFun note)
{
  const char *end = data+len;
  const char *start = data;
  const char *cur = start;
  ScanState state = inText;
  int count=0;

  while ( cur < end ) {
    switch (state) {
      case inText:
        if ( *cur == '<' ) {
            count += note( state, start, cur-start );
            state = inTag;
```

```
            start = cur;
        }
      break;
    case inTag:
      if ( *cur == '>' ) {
            count += note( state, start, cur-start );
            state = inText;
            start = cur;
      }
      break;
    }
  cur++;
  }
  return count;
}
```

Since characters are the most common entities in the problem-space, the assumption is also that the code that actually has to examine every character is a good proxy for the overall cost of an XML/HTML parser, even if the operations on the characters are less costly than those on higher-level entities such as tags or elements. This assumption would later prove wrong.

The code in Example 4.2 uses the callback function to count tags. It clocked in at around 7 MB/s on the same hardware that managed just 200 KB/s with the previous parser, an improvement of 35 times. On modern hardware, it performs at around 600 MB/s or about 1.6 ns per byte.

**Example 4.2   Counting tags**

```
int  countTags(ScanState state, const char *ptr, size_t len )
{
  return state == inTag ? 1:0;
}

int main( int argc, char * argv[] ) {
  [NSAutoreleasePool new];
  int i;
  int numTags=0;
  NSString *filename=[NSString stringWithUTF8String:argv[1]];
  NSData *xml=[NSData dataWithContentsOfMappedFile:filename];
  numTags += scanHtml( [xml bytes], [xml length], countTags );
  printf("numTags: %d\n",numTags);
  return 0;
}
```

Note that the code doesn't actually do any processing of the data itself, it just provides the `noteParsed` function with pointers to sections of the original data, *annotated* as `text` or `tag`. The difference between this type of *non-extractive* processing—which just annotates a piece of data—and more normal *extractive* processing—which actually processes the data—is shown in Figure 4.1 using the XML text `<greeting>hello world!</greeting>` as an example.

In extractive processing (shown in the top of Figure 4.1), we allocate a new string object for every significant XML structure we encounter in the original data—in this case an open tag, some content, and a close tag. We then proceed to copy the parsed content from the original data into the new structures, and then proceed with further specific processing.

In non-extractive processing, we don't really do anything once we encounter an element of interest, we just notify our client what the element is and where it can be found in the original bytes.

This is already sufficient for many kinds of processing, for example, extracting just the text content or counting tags, but it doesn't yet deal with decoding the tags, attributes, or other structured elements of the file. It can also reproduce the original file verbatim and do partial processing on a few interesting bits.

One bit of inefficiency in the code in Example 4.1 is that it follows the prototypical state-machine code very closely, going through the `switch` statement for every character and then testing the current character for the condition. This repeated checking of the state is redundant because once we are in a state, we know that we will stay in that state until we encounter the character that causes the state to switch. Turning the `if` conditionals for the exit condition into `while` loops for the continuation condition fixes this and speeds up the scanner variant in Example 4.3 to slightly over 1 GB/s.

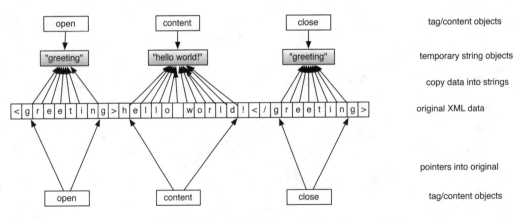

**Figure 4.1**    Extractive vs. non-extractive processing

**Example 4.3     Unrolled state machine**

```
...
    case inText:
      while ( cur < end && *cur != '<' ) {
        cur++;
      }
      count+=note( state, start, cur-start );
      state=inTag;
      start=cur;
      break;
...
```

This ability to "correctly do nothing very quickly" is helpful not just as performance baseline, but also as the actual basis for further processing. Of course, the code as shown isn't actually correct yet, because XML attributes are allowed to contain the unquoted right angle bracket (yes, it's weird, but that's what the spec said), so the real parser has to correctly interpret attributes in order to tell tags apart. Along with some other details, such as identifying entities (e.g., &amp;), XML comments, processing instructions, ignorable whitespace, CDATA sections, and the actual parts and variants of tags, this adds enough complexity to bring the basic processing rate down to between 330 and 460 MB/s, depending on the contents of the file.

# Mapping Callbacks to Messages

Passing a callback to the scanner as a function pointer is already pretty close to providing a message interface; however, it makes the interface very complex, as shown in Example 4.4, which is the actual XML scanner interface used today. Example 4.5 shows the Objective-C translation of that callback-based interface, and Example 4.6 shows how the messages in the Objective-C protocol are mapped onto the callbacks needed by the scanner. That way, when the scanner calls its callbacks, it directly executes the methods in the delegates implementation of the MPWXmlScannerDelegate protocol.

**Example 4.4     Complete scanner interface**

```
typedef BOOL (*ProcessFunc) (void*, void* ,const xmlchar*,int,int);
typedef BOOL (*AttrFunc) (void*,void*,const xmlchar*,int,
                                      const xmlchar*,int);
static int scanXml(const xmlchar *data,
                   unsigned int charCount,
                   ProcessFunc openTagCallback,
                   ProcessFunc closeTagCallback,
                   ProcessFunc declarationCallback,
                   ProcessFunc processingInstructionCallback,
```

```
                          ProcessFunc entityReferenceCallback,
                          ProcessFunc textCallback,
                          ProcessFunc spaceCallback,
                          ProcessFunc cdataCallback,
                          AttrFunc attributeValueCallBack,
                          void *clientData)
```

**Example 4.5    The XML Scanner delegate Objective-C Protocol**

```
@protocol MPWXmlScannerDelegate
@optional
-(BOOL)beginElement:(const char*)fq length:(int)len nameLen:(int)l;
-(BOOL)endElement:(const char*)fq length:(int)len;
-(BOOL)makeText:(const char*)start length:(int)len
        firstEntityOffset:(int)eo;
-(BOOL)makeSpace:(const char*)start length:(int)len;
-(BOOL)makeCData:(const char*)start length:(int)len;
-(BOOL)makeSgml:(const char*)start length:(int)len nameLen:(int)l;
-(BOOL)makePI:(const xmlchar*)start length:(int)len nameLen:(int)l;
-(BOOL)attributeName:(const xmlchar*)n length:(int)l
          value:(const char*)v length:(int)vl;
-(BOOL)makeEntityRef:(const xmlchar*)start length:(int)len;

@end
```

**Example 4.6    Map delegate messages to scanner callback functions**

```
#define IMPSEL(theSel) [delegate methodForSelector:@selector(theSel)]

-(void)_initDelegation
{
  if ( nil != delegate ) {
    text = IMPSEL(makeText:length:firstEntityOffset:);
    space = IMPSEL(makeSpace:length:);
    cdataTagCallback = IMPSEL(makeCData:length:);
    sgml = IMPSEL(makeSgml:length:nameLen:);
    pi = IMPSEL(makePI:length:nameLen:);
    openTag = IMPSEL(beginElement:length:nameLen:namespaceLen:);
    closeTag = IMPSEL(endElement:length:namespaceLen:);
    attVal =
        IMPSEL(attributeName:length:value:length:namespaceLen:highBit:);
    entityRef = IMPSEL(makeEntityRef:length:);
  }
}

-(BOOL)scan8bit:(NSData*)aData
```

```
{
    BOOL success = NO;
    [self setData:aData];
    success = (scanXml( [data bytes], [data length] / sizeof(xmlchar),
            openTag, closeTag, sgml,pi, entityRef,
            text,space,cdataTagCallback,attVal,
            delegate ) == SCAN_OK);
    [self setData:nil];
    return success;
}
```

The mapping is made easier by the fact that both the ProcessFunc and the AttributeFunc were chosen to conform to the Objective-C method calling convention, which means that their first argument is the delegate object and the second parameter is extraneous, being the slot reserved in Objective-C messages for the selector that's passed in the hidden _cmd argument.

The upshot of this chicanery is that on one hand the users of this scanner class can implement plain old Objective-C classes and methods, but on the other, the implementation will interface these methods to the high-performance C scanner at zero extra cost during the parse.

The length parameters are currently all of int type, so they are "limited" to 32 bits, and due to the sign bit actually to 31 bits, or around 2 GB. While this does impose a limit on the total size of the XML file, it might make sense to upgrade these to size_t if XML files with very large individual elements are required.

# Objects

The approach described above sped up the tag-soup parser of the CMS import process sufficiently that it was now quite speedy, and more importantly, limited by factors other than the parser, such as database performance or I/O bandwidth. A number of years later, I became interested in mixing high-quality documents with structured data such as invoices in lieu of having databases generate invoices, for example. XML with namespaces looked like it might do the job, but I had to see whether it would have the performance to use the documents instead of a centralized database for queries and such.

By the time XML parsing became a practical need again, rather than just a theoretical consideration, two standard APIs for XML parsing had become widely accepted, and so there was hope of just reusing an existing solution rather than having to roll my own. First was the W3C's *Document Object Model* (DOM), which specified a tree of *Node* objects representing the information content of an XML file, the *XML Infoset*. Once a document has been parsed, the tree of DOM Nodes can be asked about its properties such as the name of an element or attribute, or navigated by listing attributes or child elements. The entire DOM tree must be resident in memory.

Having to have the entire document in memory at once presented a problem for processing very large documents that the *Simple API for XML* (SAX) was designed to solve. Instead of a complete document that can be examined, a SAX parser sends the client messages for individual events in the XML file (such as "open tag encountered," "character data encountered") as they occur in the file, and then forges ahead without retaining much further state.

Mac OS X started providing the SAX interface with the `NSXMLParser` class in Mac OS X 10.3 and the DOM interface in 10.4 using `NSXMLDocument`. iOS only has `NSXMLParser` and so does not provide an Objective-C level DOM interface, probably due to memory considerations.[1]

For my particular application, streaming seemed the way to go since the documents could potentially get large and I would typically be interested in some small subset of the entire document.

The first attempts with NSXMLParser, which wraps libxml2, were disappointing, and given the earlier experience with XML parsing, it seemed I should be able to do better. Alas, my own trivial attempts at creating an `NSXMLParser`-compatible SAX API by wrapping objects around the output of my C scanner were more than disappointing, slower even than the built-in parsers. Further investigation revealed that a third parser, the opengroupware project's SOPE XML parser, which also wraps libxml2 in Objective-C, achieved performance almost identical to NSXMLParser at around 7 MB/s. Obviously there was something going on.

The something was object allocation, with a little bit of API mismatch thrown in for good measure. You might recall from Chapter 3 that object allocation costs around 200 ns on current hardware, whereas we saw earlier in this chapter that character data can be processed at approximately 3 to 4 ns/character. The disparity is large enough that it overcomes the "bulk dominates" rule of thumb for many inputs, as demonstrated by following example:

```
<a href="http://www.apple.com">apple</a>
```

Even with a reasonably efficient SAX object encoding, this 39-character XML fragment creates a minimum of 6 objects:

1. The string name of the opening tag a
2. A dictionary for the attributes
3. The string key `href`
4. The string value `http://www.apple.com`
5. The content `apple`
6. A string for the close tag a

With a rate of one object per 6.5 characters (39/6), 85% to 90% of the time is spent just creating the objects representing the XML content, with only 10% to 15%

---

1. This is one area where the simulator and the device differ: the simulator actually has `NSXMLDocument`.

dedicated to scanning. As a quick back-of-the-envelope performance estimate, this implies an upper performance bound of about 25 MB/s for an object-oriented XML API, and that's only for the unrealistic assumption that scanning and object creation are the only activities. It also implies that the effort optimizing the scanner was a complete waste of time unless we can speed up or finesse the object-allocation issue.

Furthermore, libxml2 provides a "final" interface for interacting with XML data, rather than just a simple scanner, so it already does a significant amount of processing. For example, its SAX interface delivers NUL terminated strings, meaning it has to `malloc()` buffers and copy the strings from the actual XML content into those buffers. This processing is necessary or at least desirable for a final consumer of the API, but it doesn't come for free, with libxml2 clocking in around 100 MB/s. For someone only wrapping the results in yet another API, much of this processing has to be duplicated; for example, the character data is copied from the buffer `malloc()ed` by libxml2 into a buffer allocated by Foundation. This *API mismatch* problem occurs frequently and is something to watch out for when wrapping C APIs or when creating such APIs.

# Objects, Cheaply

Before moving on, we obviously need to check whether our back-of-the-envelope calculations about the relative cost of object creation in XML parsing are true. Using the *Invert Call Tree* setting of the *Time Profile* instrument should point us to the obvious bottlenecks of a program, and our reasoning leads us to believe that we should have such a bottleneck in object allocation.

Figure 4.2 seems to indicate that this is the case, but it is a little too cluttered to actually be sure what is going on. One of the many handy data-mining features in Instruments is the ability to remove a function from the call tree and charge its cost to the callers of said function. Using this charging feature to remove many of the helper functions used in allocation yields the much clearer picture seen in Figure 4.3. The `malloc` library functions `free()` and `calloc()` alone account for over 31% of the total runtime, and the vast majority of the function in that top 31% is related to storage allocation.

Fortunately, we have object caching to help us with this case, and it seems ideally suited for SAX-style parsing: The objects are created temporarily and then immediately discarded by the parser, and a lot of very similar objects are being created.

However, we can't use ordinary `NSString` objects for this task because they aren't really amenable to being reinitialized, and also want to copy the character content into their private buffer, which would defeat the purpose of avoiding object allocations by requiring buffer allocations. The `MPWSubData` class shown in Example 4.7 encapsulates the concept of *range of bytes in buffer that can be a string* in a simple Objective-C class.

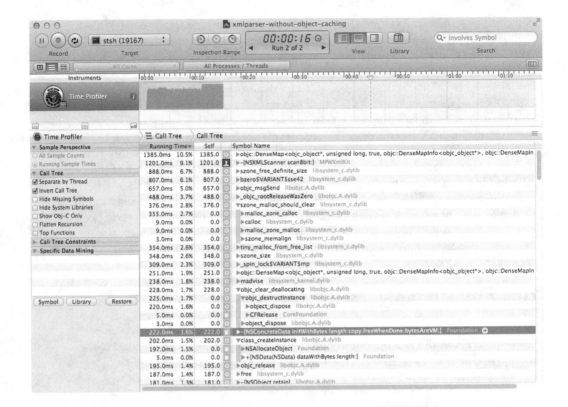

**Figure 4.2**    Performance of non-optimized XML SAX parser

**Example 4.7    MPWSubData class definition**

```
@interface MPWSubData : NSString <NSCoding>
{
  NSData*      referencedData;
  const void *myBytes;
  unsigned int myLength;
}
```

One subtlety of MPWSubData is that it works a lot like a NSData, but is actually a NSString subclass, so it is NSString compatible. This only works with string encodings that have a 1:1 mapping between bytes and characters, such as ASCII or ISOLatin1. As almost all XML content these days is UTF-8-encoded, which does not fit this requirement, this seems like a nonstarter at best. However, it turns out that, by design, ASCII is a subset of UTF-8, so the parser detects when fragments are

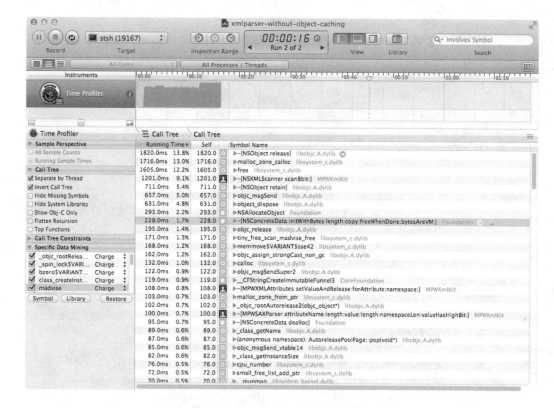

**Figure 4.3**  Performance of non-optimized XML SAX parser, pruned results

pure ASCII and uses MPWSubData for those fragments, resorting to creating a plain NSString when the data cannot be represented as ASCII.

Fortunately, most content happens to be representable in the ASCII subset of UTF-8, for example, almost all the actual XML machinery such as tags and attributes and so forth. This XML-specific data is also the data that is temporary, so exactly the data where not-creating permanent objects pays off, so the whole scheme turns out to work rather well.

An MPWSubData object is initialized with the buffer that it is referencing (an NSData and the location and length of its referenced section within the data (see Example 4.8). It retains the referenced NSData so the underlying buffer doesn't get deallocated out from underneath it. Since it will typically be used multiple times with the same buffer, it optimizes for the case that the buffer has already been set up correctly in order to avoid the unnecessary reference counting operations, which would otherwise significantly impact total performance.

**Example 4.8    Reinitializing an MPWSubData**

```
-reInitWithData:(NSData*)data bytes:(const char*)bytes
                                length:(unsigned)len
{
  if ( data != nil ) {
    if ( referencedData != data ) {
      [referencedData release];
      referencedData=[data retain];
    }
  } else {
    [NSException raise:@"subdata (re-)initialized with nil data"
        format:@"subdata (re-)initialized with nil data"];
  }
  myBytes=bytes;
  myLength=len;
  return self;
}
```

# Evaluation

With the object cache in place and delivering MPWSubData objects, most of the object creation that would have taken place in the SAX parser is replaced with reinitializing a couple of pointers and manipulating the circular buffer. On my 291-MB sample file, this takes the processing rate from 27 MB/s to 163 MB/s, an improvement of 5 times. The profile shown in Figure 4.4 also shows that object allocation is now much more subordinate and most of the time is spent actually scanning the XML file, though even our optimized -getObject method still manages to make a showing!

It is important to note that in a sense, object allocation has only been delayed, not eliminated. If the client retains every object it receives via this interface, the caches will have little effect and the parser will need to create new objects every time instead of reusing previously allocated objects. However, delaying turns into eliminating in almost all practical scenarios, as the vast majority of the "strings" created during parsing of a textual file format do not end up as strings in the final output, even when the final output is completely retained in memory. We showed this in the "Strings" section of Chapter 3 when discussing strings: most of the original data is structural, being replaced by object structure; some is numeric content, usually replaced by primitive number; and only a tiny rest is actual textual content.

On OS X 10.8 through 10.11, Apple's NSXMLParser manages 44 MB/s on the same file, which is both faster than our unoptimized version and also significantly faster than the NSXMLParser implementations in previous OS versions, even when controlling for improvements in hardware. However, it seems that in achieving this

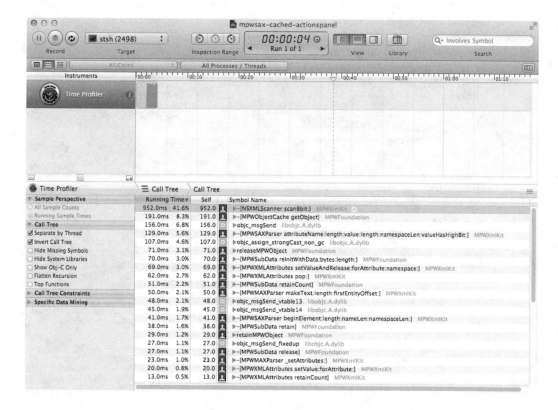

**Figure 4.4**    Performance of an optimized XML SAX parser

performance improvement it has run afoul one of the pitfalls of caching: caching (way) too much. The first indicator is the top output in Figure 4.5, showing 997 MB of RPRVT memory use (dirty memory used by the process itself and not shared). Running the heap tool in the output below shows that this initial assessment was essentially correct, but too low: there are 320 MB of NSString objects, 270 MB of NSDictionary, and 1.1 GB of "non-object" memory allocated on the heap, for a grand total of over 1.6 GB, or an expansion factor of around 5 compared to the XML file size (which is memory mapped and therefore does not show up in heap).

| COUNT | BYTES | AVG | CLASS_NAME | TYPE | BINARY |
|-------|-------|-----|------------|------|--------|
| ===== | ===== | === | ========== | ==== | ====== |
| 5065886 | 327737200 | 64.7 | __NSCFString | ObjC | CoreFoundation |
| 1069417 | 271887024 | 254.2 | __NSDictionaryM | ObjC | CoreFoundation |
| 2921 | 1155338256 | 395528.3 | non-object | | |
| 8 | 5760 | 720.0 | CFBasicHash | CFType | CoreFoundation |

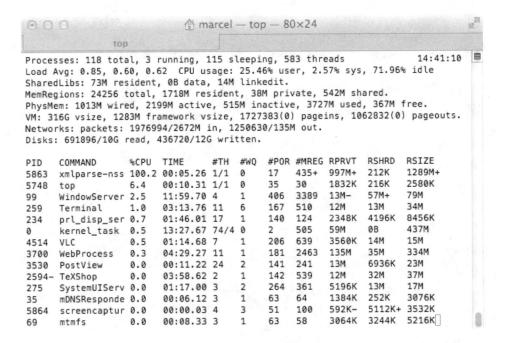

```
    ○ ○ ○                    🏠 marcel — top — 80×24                        ↙

              top

Processes: 118 total, 3 running, 115 sleeping, 583 threads        14:41:10   ▤
Load Avg: 0.85, 0.60, 0.62  CPU usage: 25.46% user, 2.57% sys, 71.96% idle
SharedLibs: 73M resident, 0B data, 14M linkedit.
MemRegions: 24256 total, 1718M resident, 38M private, 542M shared.
PhysMem: 1013M wired, 2199M active, 515M inactive, 3727M used, 367M free.
VM: 316G vsize, 1283M framework vsize, 1727383(0) pageins, 1062832(0) pageouts.
Networks: packets: 1976994/2672M in, 1250630/135M out.
Disks: 691896/10G read, 436720/12G written.

PID   COMMAND      %CPU   TIME      #TH  #WQ  #POR #MREG RPRVT  RSHRD  RSIZE
5863  xmlparse-nss 100.2  00:05.26  1/1  0    17   435+  997M+  212K   1289M+
5748  top          6.4    00:10.31  1/1  0    35   30    1832K  216K   2580K
99    WindowServer 2.5    11:59.70  4    1    406  3389  13M-   57M+   79M
259   Terminal     1.0    03:13.76  11   6    167  510   12M    13M    34M
234   prl_disp_ser 0.7    01:46.01  17   1    140  124   2348K  4196K  8456K
0     kernel_task  0.5    13:27.67  74/4 0    2    505   59M    0B     437M
4514  VLC          0.5    01:14.68  7    1    206  639   3560K  14M    15M
3700  WebProcess   0.3    04:29.27  11   1    181  2463  135M   35M    334M
3530  PostView     0.0    00:11.22  24   2    141  241   13M    6936K  23M
2594- TeXShop      0.0    03:58.62  2    1    142  539   12M    32M    37M
275   SystemUIServ 0.0    01:17.00  3    2    264  361   5196K  13M    17M
35    mDNSResponde 0.0    00:06.12  3    1    63   64    1384K  252K   3076K
5864  screencaptur 0.0    00:00.03  4    3    51   100   592K-  5112K+ 3532K
69    mtmfs        0.0    00:08.33  3    1    63   58    3064K  3244K  5216K▯
```

**Figure 4.5**   `top` output for NSXMLParser parsing a 291-MB XML file

Using 5 times the memory of the input file is less than ideal even for a DOM parser that is supposed to retain the complete file in memory, though it may be unavoidable. However, having *any* memory increase that is proportional to the size of the input file is really unacceptable for a *streaming* SAX parser, which should have a constant memory footprint regardless of the size of the input file. Not only having such a proportional increase in the first place, but having it be 5 times the size of the input is comically bad.

Our parser is around 4 times faster than NSXMLParser, and also remains a true streaming processor. Memory use as recorded by `top` in Figure 4.6 remains constant at around 900 KB, which is close to the overhead of an Objective-C process. This memory remains constant regardless of the size of the input file: the `top` output shows 15 s of CPU use because we had to run the parser 10 times on the input in order to have time to take the screenshot, meaning that by this time the parser had processed around 2 GB of XML data, but memory is still at 900K. The heap output that follows shows that essentially no objects are allocated, except for a few `MPWSubData` and `MPWXMLAttributes` objects lingering in their respective caches.

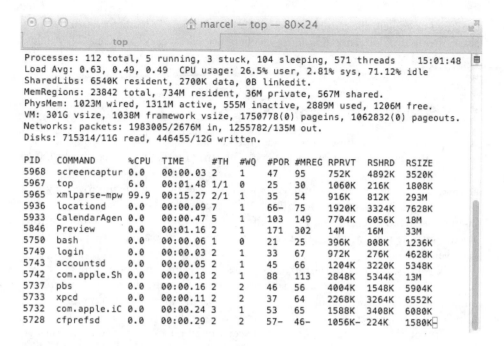

```
○ ○ ○                ⌂ marcel — top — 80×24
         top
Processes: 112 total, 5 running, 3 stuck, 104 sleeping, 571 threads    15:01:48
Load Avg: 0.63, 0.49, 0.49  CPU usage: 26.5% user, 2.81% sys, 71.12% idle
SharedLibs: 6540K resident, 2700K data, 0B linkedit.
MemRegions: 23842 total, 734M resident, 36M private, 567M shared.
PhysMem: 1023M wired, 1311M active, 555M inactive, 2889M used, 1206M free.
VM: 301G vsize, 1038M framework vsize, 1750778(0) pageins, 1062832(0) pageouts.
Networks: packets: 1983005/2676M in, 1255782/135M out.
Disks: 715314/11G read, 446455/12G written.

PID   COMMAND     %CPU  TIME      #TH  #WQ #POR #MREG RPRVT  RSHRD  RSIZE
5968  screencaptur 0.0  00:00.03 2    1   47   95    752K   4892K  3520K
5967  top          6.0  00:01.48 1/1  0   25   30    1060K  216K   1808K
5965  xmlparse-mpw 99.9 00:15.27 2/1  1   35   54    916K   812K   293M
5936  locationd    0.0  00:00.09 7    1   66-  75    1920K  3324K  7628K
5933  CalendarAgen 0.0  00:00.47 5    1   103  149   7704K  6056K  18M
5846  Preview      0.0  00:01.16 2    1   171  302   14M    16M    33M
5750  bash         0.0  00:00.06 1    0   21   25    396K   808K   1236K
5749  login        0.0  00:00.03 2    1   33   67    972K   276K   4628K
5743  accountsd    0.0  00:00.05 2    1   45   66    1204K  3220K  5348K
5742  com.apple.Sh 0.0  00:00.18 2    1   88   113   2848K  5344K  13M
5737  pbs          0.0  00:00.16 2    2   46   56    4004K  1548K  5904K
5733  xpcd         0.0  00:00.11 2    2   37   64    2268K  3264K  6552K
5732  com.apple.iC 0.0  00:00.24 3    1   53   65    1588K  3408K  6080K
5728  cfprefsd     0.0  00:00.29 2    1   57-  46-   1056K- 224K   1580K
```

**Figure 4.6**    top output for MPWXMLParser parsing 291-MB XML file 10 times

| COUNT | BYTES | AVG | CLASS_NAME | TYPE | BINARY |
|---|---|---|---|---|---|
| ===== | ===== | === | ========== | ==== | ====== |
| 1035 | 147440 | 142.5 | non-object | | |
| 90 | 4320 | 48.0 | MPWSubData | ObjC | MPWFoundation |
| 71 | 3408 | 48.0 | OS_xpc_uint64 | ObjC | libxpc.dylib |
| 19 | 3952 | 208.0 | MPWXMLAttributes | ObjC | ObjectiveXML |

# Tune-Ups

Although object caching is a big win, many smaller tweaks also help. For example, the delegate remains constant during parsing, so messages sent to it can be IMP-cached—as can any high-frequency internal message sends, for example, those to the object-cache.

The stack of open tags used to check for well-formedness (close tags match open tags) is internal to the parser and implemented using a C array of structures. The object representing the open tag is cached in that stack and reused for the close tag after it is verified that they match. Finally, note that actual character data is not modified or copied; the parser only ever produces references to the original bytes, also remembering the encoding in case a client actually accesses the data. This yields a "pay as you go" performance cost structure, where actual work is avoided unless and until it is really needed.

# Optimizing the Whole Widget: MAX

XML parsers are typically used to extract useful data from the XML file in question, meaning that user code has to interact with the parse results. As we have seen, DOM and SAX parsers present developers with an uncomfortable trade-off: DOM parsers are reasonably convenient but inherently inefficient, even with the improvements proposed here. They require the entire XML document to be parsed into an in-memory tree representation that requires at least 6 times as much memory as the already verbose textual XML representation, all before application-level processing can even begin.

SAX parsers, on the other hand, can be made very efficient but require fairly sophisticated code for most nontrivial tasks, code that is difficult to get right, and code that is even more difficult to get fast. Example 4.9 gives a small taste of what using a SAX parser actually looks like. Whereas we only handle one particular XML element type, we simulate a more realistic scenario by checking for 10 more, though the file type in question has over 50, which would actually all need to be handled in a similar fashion.

**Example 4.9    Simulating load and parsing abstracts with SAX**

```
@interface MedParser:NSObject
{
        NSMutableString *content;
        NSMutableArray *abstracts;
}
@property (strong,nonatomic) NSMutableString *content;
@property (strong,nonatomic) NSMutableArray *abstracts;
@end
@implementation MedParser


- (void)parser:(NSXMLParser *)parser
    didStartElement:(NSString *)elementName
    namespaceURI:(NSString *)namespaceURI qualifiedName:(NSString *)qName
    attributes:(NSDictionary *)attributeDict
{
   if ( [elementName isEqual:@"AbstractText"] ) {
     [self setContent:[NSMutableString string]];
   } else {
     [self setContent:nil];
   }
}
```

```
- (void)parser:(NSXMLParser *)parser didEndElement:(NSString *)elementName
    namespaceURI:(NSString *)namespaceURI qualifiedName:(NSString *)qName
{
    if ( [elementName isEqual:@"Abstract"] ) {
    } else if ( [elementName isEqual:@"AbstractText"] ) {
                [abstracts addObject:content];
                [self setContent:nil]];
    } else if ( [elementName isEqual:@"Acronym"] ) {
    } else if ( [elementName isEqual:@"Affiliation"] ) {
    } else if ( [elementName isEqual:@"Agency"] ) {
    } else if ( [elementName isEqual:@"Article"] ) {
    } else if ( [elementName isEqual:@"ArticleTitle"] ) {
    } else if ( [elementName isEqual:@"Author"] ) {
    } else if ( [elementName isEqual:@"AuthorList"] ) {
    } else if ( [elementName isEqual:@"Chemical"] ) {
    }
}

- (void)parser:(NSXMLParser *)parser foundCharacters:(NSString *)string
{
    [content appendString:string];
}
```

The XML file in question is a 130-MB database of medical journal articles. It parses in 1.3 s with the basic SAX parser from the "Objects, Cheaply" section of this chapter and in 5.3 s using `NSXMLParser`. Adding the client-side code from Example 4.9 adds 1.7 s to both timings, bringing them to 3.0 and 7.0 s, respectively. Of course, that same 1.7 s represents only a 32% increase in runtime for `NSXMLParser`, whereas it's a 130% increase for our SAX parser, meaning our efficient XML parser is being swamped by client-side processing costs, even when only doing a very limited amount of processing.

The reason, of course, is that the SAX API pretty much requires clients to perform string-comparison and/or lookups in order to dispatch the proper action for a specific XML tag/element, an operation that, as we explored earlier, is quite expensive with `NSString` and `CFString`. Checking with instruments confirms this hypothesis, but can those string comparisons really be eliminated?

The *Messaging API for XML* (MAX) does just that: it leverages the Objective-C runtime and a few tuned objects to turn those string comparisons into message sends. Every XML element encountered is turned into a message of the form `<ElementName>Element:attributes:parser:` that is sent to the parse delegate. The parameters are the sub-elements of this particular element, already processed by the parser, the attributes, and the parser object itself in case the client needs more information. The message is expected to return an object representing that element, which is then presented as an argument to processing messages higher up the element stack.

Example 4.10 shows the MAX client code for the same parser implemented with SAX in Example 4.9. The -AbstractTextElement:attributes:parser: method handles the abstracts and returns nil because we are not building a tree, just getting the abstracts. (Contrary to Cocoa conventions, the message name is capitalized to exactly match the name of the corresponding XML element.) There is no need for managing the accumulator string and no point in trying to simulate additional load as adding empty processing messages adds no overhead. Note that the type information is there purely for documentation purposes: As the message is synthesized at runtime, the compiler never gets to connect the method implementation with the source, and never gets to check the return type.

**Example 4.10    Getting abstracts with MAX**

```
@interface MedParser:NSObject
{
    NSMutableArray *abstracts;
}
@property (strong,nonatomic) NSMutableArray *abstracts;
@end

@implementation MedParser

-AbstractTextElement:(MPWXMLAttributes *)elements
        attributes:(MPWXMLAttributes *)attrs
        parser:(MPWMAXParser *)parser
{
   id text = [elements combinedText];
   [abstracts addObject:text ? text : @""];
   return nil;
}

@end
```

Due to the effort of building a (virtual) tree, MAX is slightly slower than our SAX parser at 1.6 s for the 130-MB database file, but even there more than 3 times faster than NSXMLParser. However, adding the actual client-side processing only adds a minimal 0.1 s (or 6%) to the overall processing time, bringing the total to 1.7 s. That 1.7 s is 70% faster than doing the processing with our SAX parser and 311% faster (4.1 times as fast) as doing the processing using NSXMLParser, while consuming a small fraction of the memory.

# MAX Implementation

It should be obvious from the previous discussion that it is not possible to implement MAX on top of SAX, at least not efficiently, and in fact the SAX parser is implemented on top of MAX instead. MAX takes the character output from the XML scanner callbacks in Example 4.4 and maps these character strings to delegate message sends using a special `MPWSmallStringTable` dictionary that can look up objects by `char* cstr` and `int length`, rather than requiring either a full object or a `NUL`-terminated C-String. The objects it looks up are instances of `MPWFastInvocation`, a replacement for `NSInvocation` that is roughly 50 times faster than `NSInvocation` by only handling object parameters.

Attributes and (sub-)elements are stored in a special XML dictionary/array hybrid that maintains order and allows multiple elements with the same name, as is required for XML. Attributes or elements are efficiently appended to the end of the store and can be retrieved either by index or key.

In the end, the entire stack is tuned so that the least amount of work is performed while parsing, primarily just the scanning, a few lookups of C-Strings, some message sends, and tree manipulations.

You may be wondering where the parallelism is. It is absent, mostly because XML is an inherently sequential file format. For example, you might think that you can parallelize parsing certain subtrees, but can't generically know how deep a specific subtree will be, meaning your partitioning is likely to be off, and furthermore you can't continue to the next element without having parsed the existing subtree. The interface between parser and client is also a tempting target, but the interaction is too high-bandwidth and fine-grained to look very promising.

The only approach of parallelizing XML parsing I have seen that has a chance of working is doing a very quick and dirty scan of the entire document to get the overall structure, and then partitioning the parsing of pieces onto different threads at boundaries that make sense in terms of the document structure.

## Summary

This chapter has presented an XML parser from the beginnings of low-level character processing ideas all the way to creating an efficient object-oriented API using the techniques we looked at in the previous chapter. The XML scanner in question "inspired" the Spotlight XML importer in Leopard, which was the first Spotlight XML importer to be I/O- rather than CPU-bound. The SAX parser was used by Apple's HTML Help Indexer starting in Snow Leopard as a several-times-faster drop-in replacement for the previously used `NSXMLParser`.

So if you ever need fast XML processing, you're now all set! Source code is available at http://github.com/mpw/Objective-XML.

Kidding aside, the techniques presented don't just work with XML, or even just with parsing—they are broadly applicable. For example, the Postscript interpreter I mentioned in Chapter 1 uses the same techniques to outperform Adobe's own C-based implementation on language-oriented tasks (graphics are handled by CoreGraphics). What this means is that if you have a reasonable API, you can *always* create an efficient implementation in Objective-C, mixing and matching high-level and low-level implementation details as needed.

Finally, we also saw that truly great performance means going beyond just creating efficient implementations of existing APIs. The design of the API can be crucial for determining whether the API can be both (a) implemented, and almost more importantly (b) *used* efficiently.

# 5

# Memory: Principles

Memory use is one of the trickiest and least understood areas of performance tuning, but it is arguably also one of the most important. At first glance, it doesn't even seem to be an area for performance at all: either the program fits into memory, or it does not. In fact, that was pretty much exactly how it worked on computers when CPUs were directly connected to memory, before they acquired multilevel memory hierarchies from virtual memory to various CPU caches.

These days, memory is a much more fluid concept. On one hand, virtual memory presents individual processes with isolated address spaces that are multiplexed onto real memory. On the other hand, the CPU can operate at full speed only when accessing a tiny amount of that memory that is built into the CPU itself, with data constantly and mostly transparently flowing between disk, main memory, and the various CPU caches.

## The Memory Hierarchy

System architectures like current Mac hardware or the various iOS devices have several different kinds of memory of different sizes and (vastly) different performance characteristics. Figure 5.1 is a simplified block diagram of one such system, Intel's Core i7-2677M powering my MacBook Air. It shows the CPU with two cores and main memory. Graphics memory will be examined more closely in Chapter 14.

Each core has two Level 1 caches, one for instructions and one for data, each with 32-KB capacity. In addition, each core has a unified Level 2 cache with 256-KB capacity and a single Level 3 cache on the CPU with 4 MB of memory that is shared by both cores. The latencies for the caches are given as 3 cycles for the L1, 8 cycles for the L2, and 21 cycles for the L3 cache.

This information can be gleaned from Apple's specification for the MacBook Air and the Intel processor data sheets, but much of it is also available via the `sysctl` command, with sample output shown in Example 5.1. The `sysctl` output not only confirms the cache sizes (32,768 bytes for the L1, 262,144 bytes for the L2, and 4,194,304 bytes for the L3), it also tells us that the size of a cache line is 64 bytes. All

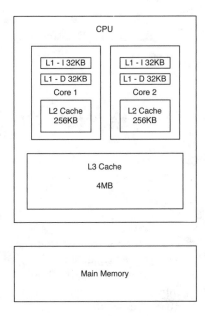

**Figure 5.1**    Core i7 Memory architecture

the caches are organized not by bytes or words, but by lines, so this is the number of bytes that will be transferred from cache to CPU, between caches or between the caches and main memory.

**Example 5.1**    `sysctl` **hardware information**

```
sysctl -a
...
hw.physicalcpu_max: 2
hw.cachelinesize = 64
hw.l1icachesize = 32768
hw.l1dcachesize = 32768
hw.l2settings = 1
hw.l2cachesize = 262144
hw.l3settings = 1
hw.l3cachesize = 4194304
...
machdep.cpu.brand_string: Intel(R) Core(TM) i7-2677M CPU @ 1.80GHz
...
```

Why such a complex arrangement? The short answer is that as of this writing, CPUs are approximately 100 times faster than main memory. The RAM of my trusty

Apple ][+ had access times of around 450 ns, which were state of the art for that time. With the processor running at 1 MHz and accessing at most 1 byte of memory per cycle, memory was actually twice as fast as required for the CPU, allowing Woz to use every other DRAM cycle to refresh the display without the CPU ever noticing. By the time of the first Mac, with the CPU running at 7 MHz and DRAM access times at 250 ns, the addition of video refresh was already having a slight impact on the CPU's access to memory, reducing the effective speed to 6 MHz, despite the puny 512×342 monochrome display. The contemporary Amiga could actually almost completely starve the CPU of memory access cycles due to its higher-resolution color graphics and additional co-processors, prompting the designers to partition its physical memory into *chip memory* that could be accessed by the video logic and *fast memory* that was exclusive the CPU.

Whereas modern CPUs have gotten over 1,000 times faster since the Apple ][+, memory access times have improved only around a factor of 10, to somewhere between 25 and 45 ns. The complex arrangement of caches is designed to hide the difference in latency. At the same time main memory interfaces have been redesigned to provide more data with each access, dramatically increasing the bandwidth while further hurting latencies, all to try and keep the CPU supplied with data for typical programs. Fortunately, all of this complexity is pretty much transparent, mostly even inaccessible to the programmer, who only sees normal memory access instructions. So why bother looking at the cache hierarchy and memory interface?

The data in Figure 5.2 provides an answer to that question: Different memory access patterns have different performance characteristics, varying by a factor of up to 100! The data was obtained by running Example 5.2. This program is designed to create access patterns that are either sequential or random, and either stay within the bounds of a specific cache or require main memory access.

**Example 5.2     Test memory access**

```c
#include <stdio.h>
#include <stdlib.h>
#include <string.h>

#define MBSIZE 16
#define SIZE (MBSIZE  * 1024 * 1024)

#define UNROLL 4
#define COUNT    ( 1000 * 1000)

int main(int argc, char *argv[] )
{
  if (argc > 2) {
    long stride=atol(argv[2]);
    char *ptr=malloc( SIZE + 20 * stride  );
    memset( ptr, 55, SIZE + 10 * stride );
    char *cur=ptr;
```

```
    long curCount=atol(argv[1]) * COUNT/UNROLL;
    long result=0;
    long headroom=UNROLL * stride;
    while ( curCount-- > 0 ) {
      result+=*cur; cur+=stride;
      result+=*cur; cur+=stride;
      result+=*cur; cur+=stride;
      result+=*cur; cur+=stride;
      if ( ((cur-ptr)+headroom) > SIZE ) {
        cur-=(SIZE-headroom);
      }
    }
    printf("result: %ld\n",result);
  } else {
    printf("usage: %s <access-count-in-millions> <stride>\n",argv[0]);
  }
}
```

The inset for Figure 5.2 clearly shows the speed differences between L1, L2, and L3 cache memory. It also shows that this speed difference does not matter for sequential accesses with strides significantly smaller than the cache line size of 64 bytes. Once the stride exceeds the cache line size, though, the access pattern no longer matters. The penalty for random access is virtually nonexistent for accesses within L1, rises to a factor 2 for L2, and to slightly over factor 4 for L3.

The main graph in Figure 5.2 adds the data for main memory access, using the 1-GB buffer size to force the accesses out of the caches. As you can see from the rightmost bar, random access to main memory takes about 38 ns, roughly 100 times the amount to access data in the L1 cache. In fact, the data for the cached accesses, which is repeated in Figure 5.2, has to be scaled down to be almost unreadable in order to accommodate the bar for random main memory access on the page.

However, sequential access (strides 1–2) suffers virtually no slowdown, even when having to plow through a gigabyte of main memory, showing the tremendous bandwidth available with DDR3-1333 memory, but also highlighting the ever increasing gap between latency and bandwidth.

Whereas caches reduce memory access times by a factor of 100 for a small subset of main memory, virtual memory expands addressable memory beyond what is physically installed, but at a potentially huge performance cost. Just how large a difference is shown by the somewhat ridiculous graph in Figure 5.3, which tries to compare the random access time of main memory (36 ns) with the random access time of the fastest available solid-state disks (SSDs) of around 10 $\mu$s. What was by far the longest bar in Figure 5.2 now becomes a barely visible sliver, whereas the SSD access time takes the entire length of the page. The fastest spinning disks, at more than 100 times slower still, won't fit and the times for the CPU caches don't rise visibly above the x-axis.

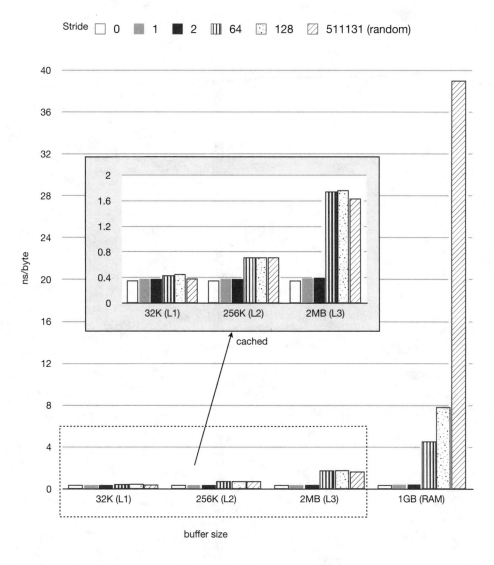

**Figure 5.2**    Memory access

Showing the different parts of the memory hierarchy in a single graph requires using either a log scale (Figure 5.4) or a different book format. The consequences of these numbers should be clear: It really, really pays to stay on the "good" side of the memory hierarchy, and conversely, the performance penalties for getting on the bad side are severe. So if you have essentially random access patterns (as you do with individually allocated objects), you should try very hard to keep your *working set*, the

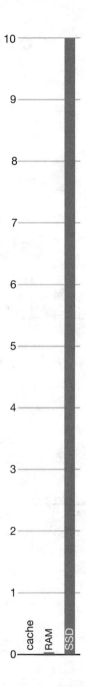

**Figure 5.3**   SSD vs. RAM access times

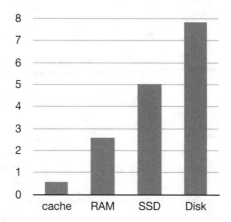

**Figure 5.4**    Memory hierarchy access times, log scale

set of information your program is working with/on in a given time interval, within the caches, preferably L1 or L2. If you have data sets that do not fit within the caches, make sure to access them sequentially—that way you get to take advantage of memory's high bandwidth rather than being stuck with its high latency.

# Mach Virtual Memory

Although the memory hierarchy contains hardware of vastly different types and characteristics, the operating system makes it all appear uniform to the userland developer. The Mach microkernel that OS X is based on does this by separating the concepts of *address space* and *memory*, with the user interacting primarily with address space and the operating system and hardware cooperating to back that address space with different kinds of resources.

Irrespective of the physical memory organization discussed in the previous section, the address space of processes on most modern operating systems is organized into fixed-size *pages*, currently 4,096 bytes on iOS and OS X. You can determine the size yourself using the program in Example 5.3. When your program tries to access memory, it uses a virtual address. This address is translated by the CPU to a physical address by shifting it right by 12 bits to get a page number. That page number is translated to a physical page using page tables maintained by the operating system (with a small cache inside the CPU, the *translation lookaside buffer*, one of the busiest pieces of hardware on a CPU) and the low 12 bits are then used to access memory within the page.

**Example 5.3    Determine VM page size**

```
#include <stdio.h>
#include <mach/vm_page_size.h>

int main() {
 printf("page-size: %ld mask: %lx shift: %d\n",vm_kernel_page_size,
        vm_kernel_page_mask,vm_kernel_page_shift);
 return 0;
}
```

The basic process outlined assumes that real, physical memory is used to back the virtual address being translated. This is not necessarily the case, and in fact address space provided to a process tends to start out not being backed by memory, but rather either *zero filled* or backed by the contents of a disk file.

In either case, the operating system will provide real memory when and if the memory is actually accessed, either zeroed or filled with the data from the disk file.

Whether mapped from disk or allocated from the OS, memory starts out in a *clean* state, meaning it hasn't been written to. Once your process writes to a memory location, that page of virtual memory gets marked as *dirty* by the virtual memory subsystem, meaning it differs from whatever backing store it has.

The reason this distinction is important is that dirty pages are significantly more expensive than clean pages, at least once memory becomes tight, and since the OS is tuned to utilize memory as much as possible, memory essentially always becomes tight, even if you have plenty available.

The OS tries to keep a minimum number of free pages available for allocations, so once free memory drops below a certain threshold, it will start looking for pages in memory that it can evict. Clean pages are easy to evict because all that needs to be done is to change their mapping to point back to the file on disk and the page added to the pool of free memory maintained by the kernel. I/O is only incurred when and if the page is needed again, and then only a read is required. Dirty pages on the other hand must first have their contents written to disk, and they cannot be reused until that I/O has finished.

iOS does not swap to disk, so dirty pages are even more expensive on iDevices. No matter how rarely used, a dirty page can never be written to disk, so the iOS has to even more aggressively swap clean pages (executable code, mapped files) or terminate the process.

# Heap and Stack

"Heap" and "stack" traditionally refer to two distinct regions of dynamically allocated memory. Figure 5.5 shows this traditional arrangement: the static regions of a program, actual program code, initialized global/static data, and uninitialized global/static data are at the bottom of the address space. The rest of the address space

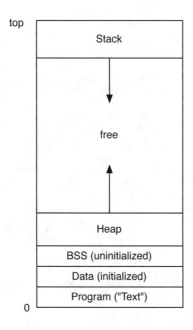

**Figure 5.5**    Traditional Unix memory layout with heap and stack

is available for dynamic allocations, with the program stack starting at the top of free space and growing down and the heap starting at the bottom of free space and growing up, using the `sbrk()` function.[1]

This image of a process's memory layout and the role of "the heap" and the "the stack" is really no longer accurate: There is no single region of memory that is "the heap" and there no longer is a single stack. Instead, "the heap" consists of all the memory (*address space*) allocated from or available for allocation from the operating system, and there are multiple stacks, one for each thread, each one actually allocated from the heap. Address spaces are large and memory mapped files, executable libraries, and "heap" regions are mapped at various locations within this address space. A rough schematic of such a modern memory layout is shown in Figure 5.6.

As you can see, there can be multiple stacks, multiple regions ("zones") from which "heap" memory can be allocated (each zone can be tagged so memory tools can know more about what different allocations are), and multiple places where executables or data files are mapped into the address space. There are also regions of address space (depicted in gray) that are simply unallocated, and unlike the schematic illustration, these sections actually vastly exceed the allocated sections in a 64-bit address space.

---

1. See man `sbrk`.

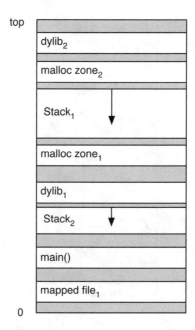

**Figure 5.6**   Mach memory layout: multiple stacks, heap everywhere

## Stack Allocation

However, despite the technical inaccuracy, the terminology has stuck and is close enough to the somewhat more complicated truth. It is now used to distinguish two different types of allocation: *stack allocation* occurs implicitly/automatically when a function or method is invoked by decrementing the stack pointer. All variables local to a function are allocated using this one pointer decrement, so this is extremely quick, as is deallocation: the pointer is incremented again. The sizes are computed by the compiler.

Figure 5.7 illustrates how stack allocation works in the schematic program given in Example 5.4: a `main()` function that has a single `int` variable and calls two functions, the first of which has a single `NSRect` local variable, and the second of which has two more integers. The diagram illustrates another benefit of stack allocation: locality of reference. Since allocation happens by incrementing a single pointer, all the variables are located near each other in memory, which is beneficial for the way caches are organized. All the local variables shown here fit onto a single cache line, and that same cache line is reused for subsequent functions, so all this interaction with stack variables happens within the L1 cache, with infrequent trips to L2 or L3 and only rare interaction with main memory.

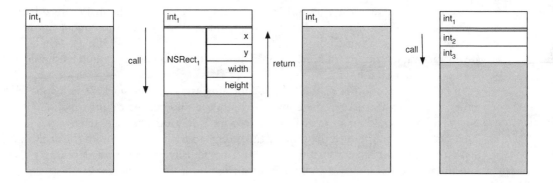

**Figure 5.7**    Stack allocation

**Example 5.4    Three functions to illustrate stack allocation**

```
int function1() {
    NSRect r;
    ...
}
int function2() {
    int a,b;
    ...
}
int main() {
    int a;
    function1();
    function2();
}
```

As usual, this is a simplification, because compilers and platform calling conventions will actually conspire to keep most local variables and function arguments and return values in registers, avoiding even the traffic to L1. However, keeping the current function's variables and arguments in registers means stashing the caller's variables on the stack, so it's close enough.

The downside is that such stack-allocated local variables are, as the name implies, local to that function; they cannot outlive the lifetime of their function. Conceptually, the local variables disappear as soon as the function returns. In reality, the values in memory will persist at that point, meaning that referencing local variables of a just-returned function will sometimes work by accident (when a pointer to such a local variable is returned), but the next function or method call will surely clobber those values, as that function will be using the same space on the stack to store its variables.

In addition, there is a size limit. For example, on my machine the main thread has a limit of 8 MB (see `ulimit -a` for the value on your machine), subsequent threads created by `pthreads` (including `NSThread`) are limited to a 512-KB stack. These are current values, not guarantees, with the upshot that large arrays or buffers should not be allocated on the stack.

In fact, there is another reason for not allocating arrays on the stack: When you return a scalar or a structure, the compiler copies the value to the calling function. Not so for arrays. When an array is referenced in C, it doesn't actually refer to the contents of the array, but to the pointer that points to the first element of the array. So if you return an array from a function, you are actually just returning a pointer into the just deallocated stack frame! Swift solves this problem differently: All collection contents are actually allocated on the heap, always, with a struct referencing the heap-allocated contents.

Stack allocation is closely related to *value semantics*: The actual value or structure is allocated and manipulated. When a value is passed to another function, returned from a function, or stored inside another structure, the actual bits of that variable are copied to the new location.

## Heap Allocation with malloc()

*Heap allocation*, on the other hand, is manual: A function or method (in Swift: constructor) must be called to allocate, and a different function is called to deallocate (there are different ways to automate this, see the "Resource Management" section in this chapter). Heap allocation is necessary if an allocation is to outlive the scope of the function that created it. Heap allocation implies pointers and *reference semantics*, so you can have more than one reference to it. Objective-C and Swift objects have reference semantics and are heap allocated.[2]

User programs usually do not obtain memory (*address space*) directly from the operating system because requiring a system call for every allocation would be too slow and because the smallest allocation would be a 4-KB OS page. Instead, the *malloc* package requests larger (multi-page) pools of memory from the OS and doles them out to the user program in smaller pieces using the functions `malloc`, `calloc`, and `realloc`. It is the user program's job to return memory to those pools using `free`.

Up until version 10.5, OS X used "scalable malloc," an implementation that emphasized memory conservation over raw performance and also required significant amounts of locking. With Snow Leopard, this was replaced by *magazine malloc*, an implementation inspired by the *Hoard* allocator[3] designed specifically for multithreaded applications. In addition to dramatically reducing locking overhead and contention, this implementation also returns contiguous chunks of memory to the operating system, something scalable malloc never even attempted due to the

---

2. Stepstone Objective-C allowed stack-allocated objects, a feature dropped in the NeXT/Apple version.
3. http://www.hoard.org

incorrect assumption that memory fragmentation would always prevent this from happening. So starting with 10.6, heap usage of a process can actually decrease, where previously it would only ever monotonically increase, no matter how much of that heap was unused. Adding insult to injury, such unused memory was usually dirty, so would incur swapping to disk.

Example 5.5 measures the time in nanoseconds it takes to `malloc()` and `free()` a block of memory of a given size, with the sizes increasing by powers of 2, so iteration 9 allocates $2^9 = 512$ bytes.

**Example 5.5    Time memory allocation**

```
#import <Foundation/Foundation.h>

NSTimeInterval mallocTest( long size, long iterations )
{
    NSTimeInterval start=[NSDate timeIntervalSinceReferenceDate];
    for (long i=0;i<iterations;i++) {
        void *ptr=malloc( size );
        free(ptr);
    }
    NSTimeInterval stop=[NSDate timeIntervalSinceReferenceDate];
    return (stop - start) / iterations * (1000000000.0);
}

int main()
{
    printf("log2size , tme (ns) ,   rate (byes/ns)\n");
    for (long log_size=1; log_size <20; log_size++ ) {
        long size = 1<<log_size;
        NSTimeInterval nsPerAlloc=mallocTest( size , 1000000 );
        printf("%10ld , %g ,   %g \n",
        log_size,nsPerAlloc,size/nsPerAlloc);
    }
}
```

The results are plotted in Figure 5.8, again with the x-axis showing powers of 2. As you can see, allocation times are constant at around 45 ns per allocation, up to a size of $2^{17} = 128$ KB (with an unexplained, but for me, reproducible bump at 512 bytes). At 128 KB there is a step function to approximately 280 ns because the allocator switches from allocating a particular request from *malloc-zones* that are obtained in large chunks to allocating each request individual from the operating system. The constant kernel-call overhead dominates for a while until the requests get so large that filling out all the page table entries starts to take noticeable time at around 16 MB.

The fact that allocation takes a constant amount of time for sizes from 1 byte to 128 KB means that allocating a given amount of memory as one large object is far

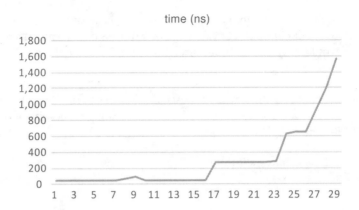

**Figure 5.8**    Time to malloc by power-of-2 sizes ($2^n$)

cheaper to allocate than many small objects. The only question is whether this difference matters, and Figure 5.9 shows that the answer to that question is a resounding "Yes."

Figure 5.9 plots how many bytes you can allocate per nanosecond at different allocation sizes. Unlike the times in Figure 5.8, which were a linear scale, the rates here had to be plotted on a log scale, so at the minimum object size of 8 bytes (one isa pointer and nothing else), we are at an allocation rate of slightly less than 0.1 byte per nanosecond. The straight lines are the rates at which we can *use* the allocated memory on a Skylake processor, 1,400 bytes/ns for the L1 cache, and 18 bytes/ns for main memory.

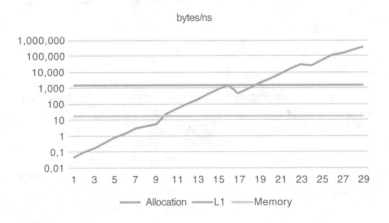

**Figure 5.9**    Malloc rates by power-of-2 sizes ($2^n$)

So for small objects, the heap-allocation vs. use overhead for L1 cache is on the order of a factor 10,000, while for main memory it is still around a factor 100. This is one of the primary reasons why many small temporary objects and high performance don't mix easily, though we will show how it can be done in Chapter 7.

Small temporary objects are absolutely fine for the ≈97% of nonperformance intensive code, and small permanent objects are also fine. This is good, because in many cases, modeling requires objects with identity, and pure value objects just don't fit the required semantics. Reference semantics are also required if you want to construct graphs or need to refer to the same object from multiple different locations for other reasons.

But in general, Objective-C and Swift prefer their objects to be coarser grained and more long-lived than pure(r) object-oriented languages, which tend to have object allocators not based on malloc that can be significantly faster at supporting fine-grained objects.

If you *have* large objects, heap allocation can also be significantly faster than stack allocation because you can simply pass an 8-byte pointer rather than copying the whole object.

At the other end of the scale, you will notice that the allocation overhead becomes extremely small compared to actually using all that memory, and in fact at the high end the operating system hasn't even cleared the memory, it has just lazily provided address space. The more significant cost will come as the program tries to actually use the memory and the operating system provides and clears real memory for the address space initially requested.

# Resource Management

Resources used by a program, such as memory, need to have their life cycle managed somehow: when and how is the resource allocated, when and how deallocated?

One very simple resource management regimen we looked at in the previous section and used in most procedural programming languages, including Objective-C is stack allocation: a variable declared within the scope of a function/method that has **auto** scope and is automatically destroyed once the function/method exits, but continues to exist while other functions are called.

For heap-allocated objects with dynamically determined lifetimes, both Stepstone Objective-C and pre-Foundation NeXTStep had manual memory management, very much like C's **malloc()** and **free()**: An object was created with **+new** and destroyed with **-free**. This works fine in simple cases where there is effectively a single "owner" of an object reference, either because there is only a single reference or there is a discernible "master" reference that determines the lifetime of the object, but it breaks down when multiple independent entities have to coordinate the lifetime of an object.

## Garbage Collection

Fortunately, the problem of determining the lifetime of a reference in nontrivial environments has a long history, with many solutions dating back to at least the early LISP implementations of the 1950s.

There are principally two techniques for garbage collection: tracing the heap to find live objects or using reference counting to find dead objects. As shown in the 2004 OOPSLA paper *A Unified Theory of Garbage Collection* by Bacon, Cheng, and Rajan, these approaches (tracing garbage collection and reference-counting garbage collection) are duals of each other, and optimized versions of each type of collector take on characteristics from the other type.

Early garbage collectors used reference counting, where each time a new reference to an object is created, a count inside the object is increased, and each time a reference disappeared the count is decreased again, all automatically by the runtime system. Once the reference count reaches zero, the object can be released because there are no more references to it.

## Foundation Object Ownership

When OPENSTEP introduced the new Foundation classes still familiar today (NSArray, NSString, NSDictionary, NSNumber, etc.), it also introduced a garbage collection scheme based on reference counting to replace the fully manual resource management scheme of earlier NeXTStep versions.

Although not integrated into the language the way reference-counting collectors are, this mechanism is capable of coexisting with a low-level language like C. Since the reference counting system does not have special access to object internals, it is relatively slow as such systems go. This is compensated by the fact that it generally does not track references in local variables, with the ownership rules only applying to references held in instance variables. This drastically reduces the number of reference-counting operations.

Foundation's ownership-based reference-counting scheme is often referred to as "manual reference counting" (MRC). This is incorrect; reference counting can be, was, and is highly automated by the use of accessors, with those accessors also typically automatically generated, for example, by property definitions. In fact, property definitions in MRC, ARC, and even the tracing collector are essentially indistinguishable.

Figure 5.10 illustrates how reference counts work. The root has a reference to object a, which therefore has a reference count of 1. Object a has a reference to object b, which also has a reference count of 1. If we add a back pointer from object b to object a, object a's reference count increases to 2, with all other reference counts remaining the same.

If the reference from root to object a then goes away, object a's reference count drops back to 1. This example also illustrates a *reference cycle*: objects a and b are no longer referenced from the rest of the program; they should therefore be freed.

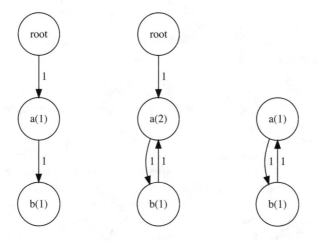

**Figure 5.10**    Creating a retain cycle

However, since they point to each other, their reference counts remain at 1, and therefore reference counting doesn't detect that they should be freed.

The fact that reference counting is implemented using normal message sends allows optimizations such as the object cache described earlier, where we check for a reference count of 1 to indicate whether to evict an object from the cache. It even allows the programmer to elide reference-counting operations altogether in performance-critical sections if it can be proved that the operations are balanced and there is an external reference keeping the object alive for the duration. The fact that reference counting is precise allows the management of expensive resources to be piggybacked on the existing mechanism, although care must be taken to make sure object lifetimes are not unnecessarily extended.

## Tracing GC

As reference counting by itself doesn't deal with cyclical references, those early collectors mentioned above were frequently augmented with a tracing mark-and-sweep collector, which only runs from time to time. In the mark phase, it traces all the live object references from one or more well-known root objects, and in the sweep phase it deallocates all the objects that were not found to be live in the mark-phase, the garbage.

While mark and sweep can also be used by itself, scanning the full heap is quite expensive and also difficult to do concurrently with the program, leading to the phenomenon of *garbage collection pauses*, where the running program is halted while the garbage collection runs. Concurrent garbage collections generally make pauses smaller without completely eliminating them, with additional costs and complexities.

Mark and sweep also interacts poorly with virtual memory, because in a virtual-memory environment it scans address space rather than memory, potentially swapping in large amounts of unused memory from the disk only to discover it is still unused.

Generation-scavenging collectors ameliorate the negative effects of a full scan by taking advantage of temporal cohesion, whereas copying collectors make allocation a cheap "bump pointer" operation, which is why most modern collectors are both copying and generational.

Tracing garbage collection is difficult to implement reliably and efficiently in a language with raw pointers such as Objective-C, where pointers may be hidden, bit patterns may cause false positives, and memory can't be moved.

While workable in special cases, Apple's home-grown tracing garbage collection never achieved the performance and reliability levels to be viable on both OS X and iOS. In the end, it never made it into iOS and was deprecated on OS X after two releases.

## Automatic Reference Counting

With the deprecation of the tracing GC in 10.7, Apple introduced *Automatic Reference Counting* (ARC) as an Objective-C language feature. Probably the biggest advantage over Apple's tracing garbage collection is that ARC code can be mixed with other reference-counting code on a per-source-file basis, unlike the tracing collector, which had to be enabled for an entire process (including any plugins).

ARC doesn't just automate the existing object ownership rules, which are mostly about storing references in instance variables. Instead, the compiler inserts reference-counting operations whenever pointers to Objective-C objects are assigned and passed/returned from/to functions and methods, vastly increasing the number of reference-counting operations, but also closing potential windows of vulnerability and making reference counting more precise.

Despite improvements in the runtime functions supporting reference counting, the overhead of these additional reference-counting operations would be prohibitive, so a special LLVM optimization pass is used to remove as many of these operations as possible. While this additional pass can get rid of the majority of these added reference-counting operations, overall quite a few tend to remain, leading to typical slowdowns in the range of 10% to 100% compared to MRC.

Cycles are still not dealt with automatically, though some mechanisms such as weak zeroing references have been added to make cycle avoidance easier. A weak reference does not count toward the retain count of the object referenced (references that do count are called *strong*), and in addition a back-pointer to the referencing pointer is maintained. When the strong reference count of the object goes to zero and the object is deallocated, all zeroing weak references are tracked down and those pointers set to zero. This avoids dangling references to deallocated objects.

### Process-Level Resource Reclamation

While all the techniques so far work while a program is running, it is important to remember that all temporary resources used by a process will be cleaned up by the operating system at process termination. This resource reclamation is not just essentially perfect, it is also very fast.

# Summary

In this chapter we have seen the tremendous performance range of the different elements in the memory hierarchy, which are all presented as a uniform address space to user programs. In order to optimize performance of memory access, it is necessary to minimize total memory use and optimize memory access patterns so that they take advantage of the (non-linear) capabilities of the hardware.

The following chapters will first show how to measure memory consumption and identify access patterns, and then go on to techniques for tuning memory use.

# 6

# Memory: Measurement and Tools

Memory has many different facets, with no one being primary. Even the seemingly simple question "How much memory is my program using?" does not have a single obviously correct answer. There is the amount of memory your program has obtained from the system via `malloc` and the amount the process (including `malloc`) has obtained from the operating system. Both of these are really address space, not memory, so there is the question of how much of that address space is backed by real memory. In addition, you have mapped files and lots of address space and memory that is shared between processes, mostly by the system.

Furthermore, the operating system is trying its best to optimize memory usage given the current set of running programs, so getting answers is sometimes more akin to outwitting a skilled opponent rather than simply taking a measurement.

In addition, tools that analyze memory consumption generally have to chew through a lot more data than CPU samples, so the impact on the running program is much greater.

## Xcode Gauges

Xcode's "always on" lightweight profiling also includes an overview of memory consumption. Figure 6.1 shows the basic visualizations: circular gauges showing both instantaneous process-specific and overall system memory usage statistics, as well as a timeline showing the process's memory usage over time. While not going into great detail, these do give you a basic overview of what's going on, including a heads up if something is going awry. I personally find the CPU gauge more useful.

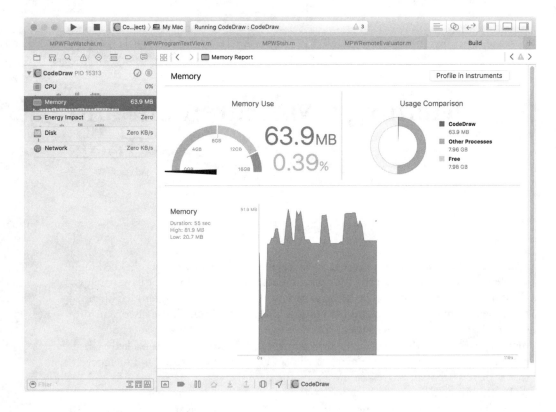

**Figure 6.1**   Xcode built-in memory profiling

# Command-Line Tools

As with CPU performance, the command line offers a number of performance tools that give quick and reasonably detailed information without much overhead or set-up work. Simple shell scripts also allow you to combine multiple commands in order to capture multiple facets at the same time.

## top

We already presented `top` in the "`top`" section of Chapter 2 for CPU measurement and the many of the same benefits are also true for its use in memory analysis. It gives you a continuously updated view of the system as a whole as well as summary information for specific processes.

The summary information that interests me the most is the `PhysMem` line. It shows you how physical memory is actually being used at the system level, with parts `wired`, `active`, `inactive`, and `free`. `Wired` memory is memory that is in use by the kernel and cannot be swapped to disk; it resides permanently in real memory.

Resources that are managed by the kernel, including processes, threads, file descriptors, or even virtual memory pages themselves all take some amount of wired kernel memory for the bookkeeping information maintained by the kernel, in addition to any memory used by the resources themselves.

Free memory is just that, currently unused and immediately available. The kernel usually tries to minimize the amount of free memory in the system, apart from a small reserve, because free memory means that an expensive resource is not being utilized.

The `active` part is also easy; this is memory actually allocated to processes and in, well, active use. It is with `inactive` memory that the kernel manages to minimize free memory: These are old mappings of files and other caches and buffers that the kernel keeps around in case they may be needed again, but can free up in case more `active` memory is required by the processes in the system.

Another number to keep an eye on is the paging rate in the VM line, particularly the pageouts. If the number inside the parentheses is nonzero, your system is currently swapping to disk. If you have sustained pageout activity, you will typically get a noticeable slowdown in your system and hear the disk activity, if you have a spinning hard disk rather than a solid-state drive.

In the per-process lines, I find the RPRVT and VPRVT lines most useful. RPRVT, the *resident memory*, is the actual amount of real memory in use by your process, and in most real-world situations most closely answers the question "How much memory is my program using?" previously discussed. That is, until your process starts swapping, at which point RPRVT can obviously become arbitrarily smaller and thus is no longer good for tracking your memory consumption.

VPRVT shows the amount of address space privately allocated to your process and is a good analog of memory use when swapping. It does not seem to take into account freshly allocated (zero-filled) address space or unread memory mapped files, however. VSIZE captures both of these, but also captures a lot of system-shared address space, which means it is generally only useful as a relative metric.

Figure 6.2 shows the object-allocating version of the integer summing program from Chapter 1 four seconds into its run. It is using 254 MB of real, private memory within 268 MB of virtual address space. But we still have over 2 GB of physical memory available, so there is no danger of swapping (and pageouts are still 0). Figure 6.3 shows the same program 12 s into its run; real memory consumption is now 734 MB, and it still tracks virtual memory, which has increased to 748 MB. We still have free memory, and both pageout counters are still zero. So all in all, we have a program that is rapidly consuming available memory, but within the bounds of the system it is being run on.

## heap

As suggested by the name, the `heap` command takes a snapshot of your application's heap, roughly the memory allocated by `malloc` and its variants. Unlike `top`, it always shows address space and never real memory, in case these two numbers have diverged. On the other hand, it will show you the memory actually allocated by your

```
Terminal — top — 85×25
Processes: 71 total, 3 running, 68 sleeping, 264 threads                    16:58:39
Load Avg: 0.31, 0.25, 0.19  CPU usage: 48.57% user, 4.32% sys, 47.9% idle
SharedLibs: 6212K resident, 6920K data, 0B linkedit.
MemRegions: 9753 total, 667M resident, 19M private, 323M shared.
PhysMem: 563M wired, 964M active, 468M inactive, 1995M used, 2100M free.
VM: 142G vsize, 1037M framework vsize, 84201(0) pageins, 0(0) pageouts.
Networks: packets: 1495/351K in, 2055/411K out.
Disks: 80376/1948M read, 19399/417M written.

PID  COMMAND      %CPU TIME     #TH  #WQ  #POR #MRE RPRVT  RSHRD RSIZE  VPRVT
475- sumintsm     99.6 00:04.22 1/1  0    16   236+ 254M+  240K  254M+  268M+
0-   kernel_task  1.3  01:25.68 62/2 0    2    735  13M    0B    217M+  62M
450  Terminal     1.0  00:13.09 5    1    115  940  27M-   36M   49M-   43M-
457  top          1.0  00:01.70 1/1  0    30+  33   1056K  264K  1632K  17M
60   WindowServer 0.9  00:56.93 4    1    274+ 891+ 8796K+ 113M+ 111M+  44M+
238- Microsoft Wo 0.3  00:29.47 6    1    136  580  35M    49M   89M    105M
204  Quartz Debug 0.2  00:16.32 6    1    111  107  4188K  25M   9452K  32M
118  SystemUIServ 0.1  00:01.63 3    1    253  277  9320K+ 26M   17M    35M-
38   hidd         0.1  00:17.74 4    2    71   49   780K   264K  2056K  22M
52   coreservices 0.0  00:02.81 5    2    311+ 194+ 2656K+ 18M+  19M+   16M+
242- Microsoft Da 0.0  00:01.10 3    1    80   174  2184K  17M   8340K  31M
67-  IPSecuritasD 0.0  00:01.32 6    1    74   72   744K   9928K 1980K  32M
113  launchd      0.0  00:00.46 2    0    210+ 64   508K   500K  1000K  38M
16   distnoted    0.0  00:00.27 3    2    64+  40+  804K+  240K  1264K+ 29M+
206  Preview      0.0  00:02.53 2    1    104  140  9064K  29M   24M    32M
```

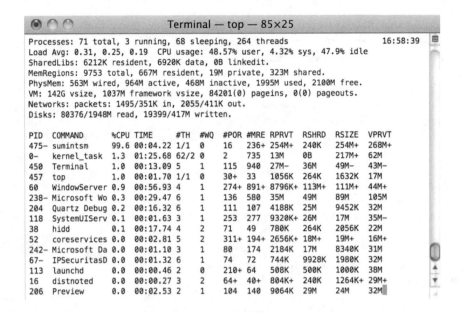

**Figure 6.2** `top` memory parameters

```
Terminal — top — 85×25
Processes: 71 total, 3 running, 68 sleeping, 277 threads                    16:58:47
Load Avg: 0.37, 0.26, 0.19  CPU usage: 48.39% user, 5.44% sys, 46.16% idle
SharedLibs: 6212K resident, 6920K data, 0B linkedit.
MemRegions: 10302 total, 1150M resident, 19M private, 324M shared.
PhysMem: 569M wired, 1446M active, 469M inactive, 2484M used, 1611M free.
VM: 143G vsize, 1037M framework vsize, 84202(1) pageins, 0(0) pageouts.
Networks: packets: 1495/351K in, 2055/411K out.
Disks: 80378/1948M read, 19413/419M written.

PID  COMMAND      %CPU TIME     #TH  #WQ  #POR #MRE RPRVT  RSHRD RSIZE  VPRVT
475- sumintsm     99.5 00:12.25 1/1  0    16   632+ 734M+  240K  735M+  748M+
0-   kernel_task  2.2  01:25.84 62/2 0    2    736  13M    0B    218M+  62M
478  quicklookd   1.0  00:00.08 7    4    79-  82+  2224K- 12M+  6332K+ 43M-
457  top          1.0  00:01.78 1/1  0    30   33   1136K+ 264K  1712K+ 17M
119  Finder       0.7  00:08.73 12   5    203- 348+ 15M+   66M+  37M+   51M+
60   WindowServer 0.3  00:57.02 5    2    267+ 999  10M+   111M- 114M+  54M+
238- Microsoft Wo 0.3  00:29.50 6    1    136  580  35M    49M   89M    105M
450  Terminal     0.3  00:13.11 5    1    115  940  27M    36M   49M    43M
118  SystemUIServ 0.2  00:01.64 3    1    253  277  9456K+ 26M   17M+   35M+
52   coreservices 0.2  00:02.83 5    2    318+ 195  2688K+ 18M   19M+   16M
204  Quartz Debug 0.1  00:16.34 6    1    111  107  4188K  25M   9452K  32M
15   configd      0.1  00:02.28 6    2    246  92   1424K  9164K 3604K  15M
34   mds          0.0  00:21.14 5    4    99   816  119M+  18M   75M+   274M
177  mdworker     0.0  00:08.83 5    2    96   250  12M    12M   62M+   65M
39   fseventsd    0.0  00:00.32 12   2    93+  65+  1076K+ 244K  1600K+ 25M+
```

**Figure 6.3** `top` again

program and will even break that information down by object classes. It is like an X-ray machine for your process, and I find it extremely useful for analyzing program behavior.

To run the heap command, you pass it the process name or process id of the process you want to examine. It then delivers two types of information on stdout. The first part is summary information for each malloc zone it finds. The following shows the summary information for heap running against Xcode. For each zone, it shows both how much the program currently has allocated and how much has been allocated for this zone from the system. Low utilization numbers are usually a sign of fragmentation.

```
marcel@localhost[dyld]heap Xcode
Process 30138: 9 zones
Zone DefaultMallocZone: Overall size: 48343KB; 23809KB (49\% of capacity)
Zone GFXMallocZone: Overall size: 36864KB; for 462KB (1\% of capacity)
Zone auto_zone: Overall size: 8487986KB; 100466KB (1\% of capacity)
Zone DefaultPurgeableMallocZone: Overall size: 4KB; 0KB (0\% of capacity)
[...]
```

For the detailed information shown below, heap tries to figure out the type of object for each block of memory, and in addition to counting those blocks, also add up the total sizes. Any block of memory it cannot associate with a specific object type is lumped into non-object, which is therefore often the largest single category.

```
> heap Xcode -sumObjectFields
[...]
------------------------------------------------------------------------
Zone DefaultMallocZone_0x10c4be000: 81833 nodes (24380320 bytes)

   COUNT     BYTES     AVG    CLASS_NAME                                  TYPE
   =====     =====     ===    ==========                                  ====
   75368  22843232   303.1    non-object
     399     17856    44.8    Security::TypedMetaAttr<Security::UInt32>   C++


------------------------------------------------------------------------
Zone auto_zone_0x10dc91000: 771818 nodes (102876608 bytes)

   COUNT     BYTES     AVG    CLASS_NAME                                  TYPE
   =====     =====     ===    ==========                                  ====
  197047  13455008    68.3    __NSCFString                                ObjC
   36720  26927200   733.3    __NSDictionaryM                             ObjC
   36327   2324928    64.0    XCPropertyMacroExpansionValue               ObjC
   28727   6961184   242.3    __NSCFDictionary                            ObjC
   25560   3004992   117.6    __NSArrayM                                  ObjC
   16772   1073408    64.0    _DVTFilePathAssoc                           ObjC
   14683    958848    65.3    __NSAutoBlock__                             ObjC
   14211    676864    47.6    __NSArrayI                                  ObjC
   13438    430016    32.0    XCPropertySimpleMacroExpansionValue         ObjC
[..]
     228      7296    32.0    IDEOverridingBuildProperties                ObjC
```

```
   226     14464       64.0    RIPData                             CFType
   225   9047136    40209.5    NSConcreteMutableData               ObjC
   221      7072       32.0    CGPath                              CFType
   212     13568       64.0    NSKeyValueContainerClass            ObjC
[..]
```

I always use the -sumObjectFields option, which also takes into account otherwise non-assigned (non-object) pointers emanating from objects already identified—for example, the key and value stores for dictionaries—and adds them to the total sizes for that object category. With this option, heap shows Xcode using around 32 MB for dictionaries and 13 MB for strings (of a RPRVT total of 71 MB). Without -sumObjectFields, 4.1 MB used for dictionaries with the same 13 MB for strings, but 50 MB lumped into the generic non-object category:

```
marcel@localhost[dyld]heap Xcode
[...]
-----------------------------------------------------------------------
Zone auto_zone_0x10dc91000: 773943 nodes (103008096 bytes)

   COUNT     BYTES      AVG   CLASS_NAME                          TYPE
   =====     =====      ===   ==========                          ====
 197211   12928032     65.6   __NSCFString                        ObjC
 164067   55077344    335.7   non-object
  36720    2350080     64.0   __NSDictionaryM                     ObjC
  36327    2324928     64.0   XCPropertyMacroExpansionValue       ObjC
  28759    1840576     64.0   __NSCFDictionary                    ObjC
  25710    1645440     64.0   __NSArrayM                          ObjC
[...]
```

For variable-size objects, the -showSizes option will show objects of the same class but different sizes on separate lines, whereas usually those different sizes are averaged together via the totals.

## leaks and malloc_debug

Even more aptly named than heap, the leaks command will show any leaks in your program. A leak is defined as a heap allocated (malloced) piece of memory that has no pointers pointing to it. Although it can show false positives, it tends to be very accurate. The following output shows the result of running leaks against the program in Example 6.1. It claims 4 leaks for a total of 128 bytes, and then gives details for each of these leaks. If the program was started with MallocStackLogging enabled, leaks will also show backtraces for each allocation.

```
Process:         leaks-cycles [3320]
Path:            /Users/marcel/Documents/test-programs/leaks-cycles
Identifier:      leaks-cycles
Code Type:       X86-64 (Native)

Date/Time:       2012-09-07 12:15:08.208 +0200

Process 3320: 1131 nodes malloced for 111 KB
```

```
Process 3320: 4 leaks for 128 total leaked bytes.
Leak: 0x7fec520430 size=48 zone: DefaultMallocZone_0x102a00 __NSArrayM ObjC
Leak: 0x7fec520460 size=48 zone: DefaultMallocZone_0x102a00 __NSArrayM ObjC
Leak: 0x7fec52b4c0 size=16 zone: DefaultMallocZone_0x102a00
        0x52410460 0x00007fec 0x00000000 0x00000000    `.AR...........
Leak: 0x7fec5240fd50  size=16  zone: DefaultMallocZone_0x102a44000
        0x52410430 0x00007fec 0x00000000 0x00000000    0.AR...........
```

**Example 6.1    Program with leaks**

```objc
#import <Foundation/Foundation.h>

int fn()
{
  NSMutableArray *array1=[NSMutableArray array];
  NSMutableArray *array2=[NSMutableArray array];
  [array1 addObject:array2];
  [array1 addObject:@"constant string"];
  [array2 addObject:array1];
  [array2 addObject:[NSMutableString stringWithString:@"mutable"]];
  return 0;
}

int main(int argc, char *argv[] ) {
    @autoreleasepool {
        fn();
    }
    sleep(20);
    return 0;
}
```

# Internal Measurement

For introspection, the undocumented mstats() function (declared in malloc.h) returns a structure containing information about the memory managed by malloc. Among others, it contains fields for bytes_free, bytes_used, and bytes_total. Note that as usual, these numbers refer to virtual memory, not real memory.

If you need to know what's going on with real memory programmatically, you can get essentially the same summary information top provides on the command line via the Mach vm_statistics_data_t structure that the host_statistics() Mach function will fill out for you when asked for the HOST_VM_INFO info flavor.

While these numbers will tell you how much free, active, and inactive memory there is at a given time, the meaning of those numbers is, as explained earlier, very fluid. For example, if you detect 20 MB of free memory using `host_statistics`, does that mean you have 20 MB to play with? No. On one hand, the OS may make more memory available for you from the inactive list if you ask for it. On the other hand, the 20 MB may be below its threshold free space reserve, and it may start swapping on OS X or sending you memory warnings and/or killing your process at this point on iOS.

# Memory Instruments

As Instruments has slowly gobbled up all other GUI performance tools, it is no surprise that it also has a number of individual instruments for dealing with memory. While somewhat more heavyweight than the command-line tools, it does feature additional capabilities such as tracking usage over time and richer data-analysis options. It also has the ability to run multiple instruments simultaneously, which is useful for capturing the multiple facets of memory. Finally, it is pretty much your only option for iOS devices.

The three main instruments I will look at are the Allocations instrument, the VM Tracker, and the Leaks instrument. In addition, the Counters instrument can give you stats about the effectiveness of the CPU caches, such as cache hits and misses.

## Leaks Instrument

The Leaks instrument is similar to the command-line tool. It finds memory leaks in your application, but provides more detail. Figure 6.4 shows the leaks from Example 6.1, with the call stack in the details pane. An overall call graph with the amount of leaks shown at each node is also available.

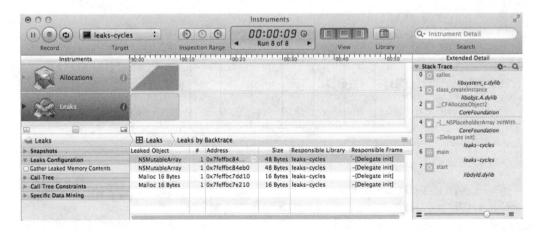

**Figure 6.4**   Leaks instrument showing a list of leaks

If run together with the Allocations instrument, Leaks can also show reference count activity, rather than just the call stack that allocated the object.

For retain cycles such as the one in our example, the Leaks instrument can also show a graphical representation of the cycle in the Roots and Cycles view (Figure 6.5).

## Allocations

It took me a while to get warm with the Allocations instrument, mostly because without more specific configuration, its output is not as easily parsable as the `heap` command-line tool and doesn't give me the quick big picture overview of my allocations. I still find the overview more confusing than `heap` (apart from the summary graph in the track pane), but the options for focused analysis are very comprehensive and allow you to drill down on a specific problem very effectively.

While writing this, I actually noticed what certainly looked like a leak in one of my apps. The summary graph in Figure 6.6 was the trigger for further investigation: It shows total memory consumption while opening and closing the same document three times in a row. While memory goes up when opening the document, it does not drop down at all after closing; instead, it rises monotonically. The Leaks instrument does show a small leak, but nothing near the total of 116 MB.

In order to verify the initial observation, I did a *Heapshot Analysis*.[1] In a Heapshot Analysis, you try to get the system into a steady state and then repeat the action that

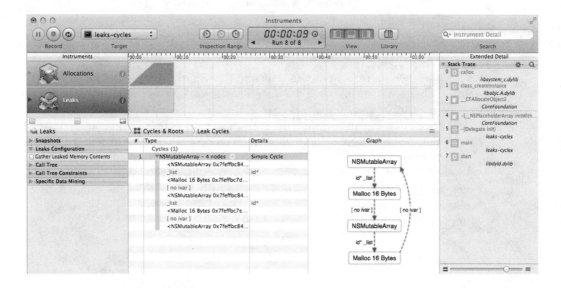

**Figure 6.5**    Leaks instrument visualizing a retain cycle

---

1. This has recently been renamed *generational analysis*, but it works the same way.

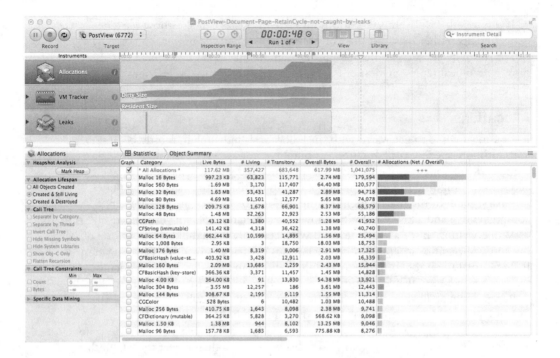

**Figure 6.6**    Noticing memory growth

you are interested in, making sure to return to the original state each time. For example: open a document, close the document again, or insert a paragraph, delete the paragraph again, and so on.

The Allocations instrument supports Heapshot Analysis by allowing you to *mark* a specific state, and it will then compute the differences between subsequent marked states. To view the data generated, switch the details pane into *Heapshot* mode. Once you have several of these marked states, you can see whether there are significant differences. In theory, there should be none; after all, you returned the program to the exact state it was in.

In this case, the scenario is as follows.

1. Open a PDF document.
2. Close the opened PDF document.

Before I start the actual analysis, I run the scenario one or maybe two times in order to get any one-time initializations out of the way. This is necessary because many subsystems use lazy initialization, and therefore general subsystem overhead will be lumped together with the first use of that subsystem. With the warmup out of the way, I click the Mark Heap[2] button, run the scenario, and click the Mark Heap button again, repeating the whole process three times in this instance. The Heapshot view in the details pane, as seen in Figure 6.7 shows a consistent growth of 39.2 MB for each time through the scenario (in the Heap Growth column). However, there isn't really much to go on yet as to where this memory is being allocated or why it isn't being freed, with the expanded Heapshot 2 just showing a `<non-object>` block of 36.34 MB, and the same block showing up in the other heapshots (not shown).

There is simply too much information to make sense of it all, so to get a better idea of what's happening, I limit the Inspection Range to just one time through the scenario and switch to the Call Tree view in the details pane. The call tree shows me how much memory is allocated in each subtree, both in absolute and relative terms. In addition, all the usual call-tree pruning mechanisms are available, so this makes hunting down the source of (large) allocations almost trivial. In Figure 6.8, I have drilled down a bit to a call-tree node that accounts for 96.5% of the total leak. However, the bad news is that this is an internal CoreGraphics function, and

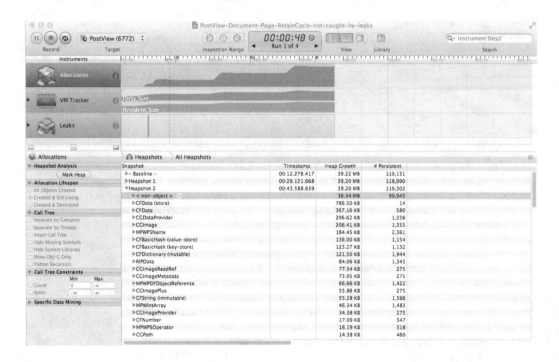

**Figure 6.7**    Initial Heapshot

2. *Mark Generation*

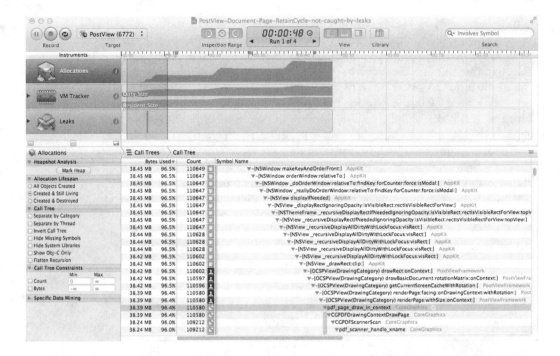

**Figure 6.8**   Call tree

considering the vehemence with which leaks are hunted by the Mac OS X Performance Group, this seems like an extremely unlikely source of the leak.

In order to make sure that the fault is not in CoreGraphics (I could waste a lot of time if it were), I look at memory consumption in Preview opening the same file, and memory use drops after closing the file as expected. So as I suspected, it is my code that is leaking. With the information gathered so far (leaked memory is allocated inside CoreGraphics, while rendering, leaks there unlikely), I am beginning to suspect that my code is leaking either the `CGPDFDocument` or the `CGPDFPage`. While I could try to search through all the objects in either the Summary or the Heapshot views, it would be difficult to make a side-by-side comparison of two runs because of the number of different objects and the fact that they are shown in the same view with disclosure triangles.

An easier approach is to let Instruments look for the PDF objects instead. So I decide to re-run the scenario, this time setting the Allocation instrument's *Recorded Types* (see Figure 6.9) to only record objects that have PDF in their class or type name, making sure to uncheck *Record all types*. (The configure button allows you to set up new kinds of filters.) Notice how the allocations graph in the timeline of Figure 6.9 reflects this selection, is already significantly more rectangular, and also shows some decline.

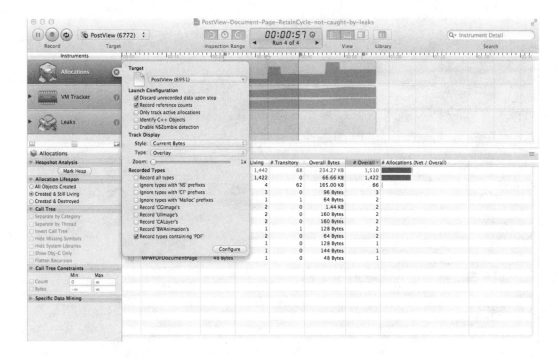

**Figure 6.9**   Look only for PDF objects

The result of heapshotting with that filter in place is shown in Figure 6.10. The drastically reduced number of objects make it easy to actually spot both CGPDFDocument and CGPDFPage in both heapshots, so my hunch was correct that I was leaking at least one of them. The answer to that question is also shown: an instance of OCSPDFDocRep, my NSDocument subclass, also shows up in the trace. And if I am leaking the document object, I am definitely also leaking the PDF resources that go with it. Since I selected only the OCSPDFDocRep for graphing in the Summary view, the timeline graph shows a simple staircase as one new OCSPDFDocRep is allocated in each scenario and not released. Figure 6.10 already has one of the offending object instances selected (Instruments keeps track of every individual instance), and a click on the disclosure arrow will reveal the call history of that object.

Sure enough, the call history of the OCSPDFDocRep at address 0x11205ba0 shown in the details pane of the screenshot in Figure 6.11 shows 7 retains and 1 malloc, but only 7 releases (the autorelease by itself doesn't count because it is only a placeholder for a future release). At this point, the process becomes one of checking the details. The notifications all balance, so those are OK. The retain and the autorelease in PostViewFramework also balance, with the delayed release of the autorelease performed by AppKit a little later. That leaves the

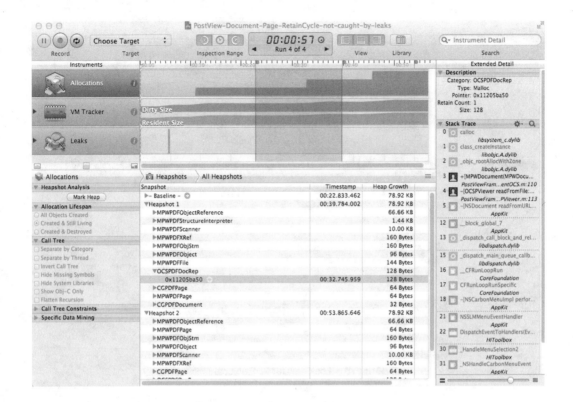

**Figure 6.10**    Heapshots of PDF objects show what we are leaking...

retain in EGOS (Embeddable Graphics Object System) looking suspicious. The call stack in the extended details pane reveals what happened: The `MPWDocumentPage` stores a back pointer to its document and retains that pointer. Since the `OCSPDFDocRep` also maintains a list of its individual pages, I have created a retain cycle. Double clicking on the particular entry in the stack trace takes me directly to the source code, highlighting the offending line in the text.

Breaking this retain cycle by removing the back pointer, making it weak or unretained, fixes the leak, as shown in Figure 6.12. The shape of the graph in the track pane now clearly indicates that most of the memory is getting freed after we close the window. The Heapshot view confirms this initial impression: instead of 41 MB, we are allocating only 500 KB. This is still too much, but much better than before, and now at least some of those allocations appear to be completely inside AppKit and CoreText, without any reference to client code.

There are additional features of the Allocations instrument that we haven't covered; for example, it is possible to show only allocations within a specific size range, or look only at allocations from Objective-C code. However, there are also

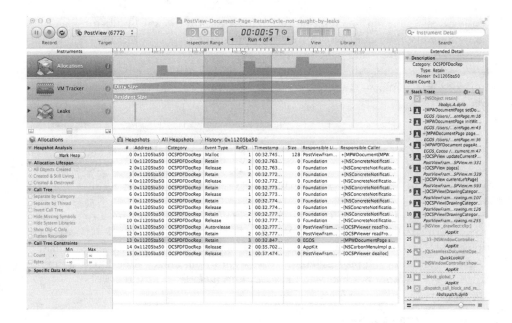

**Figure 6.11**    ...and where we're leaking it

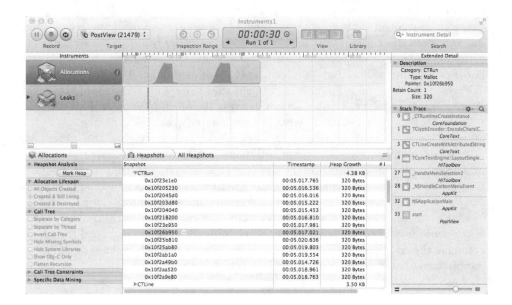

**Figure 6.12**    After fix

some caveats. One big one for a `heap` fan like myself is that the Summary view lacks something like the `-sumObjectFields` option, which means that there are lots of associated allocations cluttering the Summary view.

Another big issue is that, at least on iOS, it doesn't actually capture all allocations, and for some graphics-intensive programs, it captures only a small fraction of all allocations.

## VM Tracker

Fortunately, the VM Tracker instrument does capture these allocations and Instruments not only has the ability to run multiple instruments simultaneously, but by default adds the VM Tracker instrument when you select the Allocations template from the template chooser.

The tool tips in Figure 6.13 show this effect with an iOS application running in the simulator. Only 4.1 MB are tracked by Allocations, but the overall memory used is over 141 MB resident and still over 60 MB dirty, meaning that memory that has been written to by the process (and that we want to minimize). To the best of my knowledge, memory not included in Allocations includes at least the types `CoreAnimation`, *Image IO*, and *CoreGraphics image*.

## Counters/PM Events

The Counters instrument reads out the CPU's performance monitoring registers at regular intervals. These are over 300 different statistics that the CPU keeps, including things like "Cycles the divider is busy" and "Branches executed." I've included the Counters instrument in this chapter on memory because it also includes very detailed statistics about those parts of the memory hierarchy that are managed by the CPU hardware, including the caches, load/store buffers, and memory interface. I don't know of any other way of getting information about memory and cache traffic.

Figure 6.14 shows the Counters instrument after a run with a few counters selected. I inverted the call graph, so it is showing the function with the highest `MISALIGN_MEM_REF.STORES`, which according to the Intel documentation means: "Speculative cache-line split store-address uops dispatched to L1D." Okay.

As you can probably tell, I've never had to use the Performance Counters in anger, or at least I didn't notice that I should have used them, having gotten the information I needed to solve the problem by using other means. At this point, I would like to run into a performance problem that is so deep that it requires a tool this powerful.

One important thing to note about the performance counters is that unlike most instruments, they don't do anything useful out of the box; rather, you need to configure the counters you want in the Record Settings pane by clicking the + button (circled near the bottom of Figure 6.14).

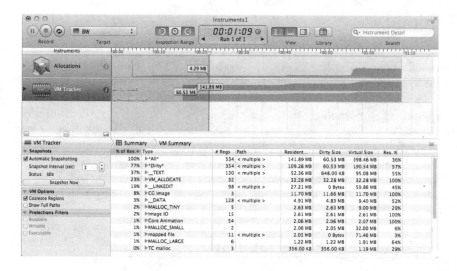

**Figure 6.13**    VM Tracker instrument running with Allocations

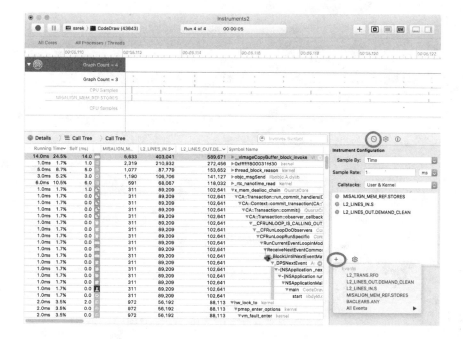

**Figure 6.14**    Counters instrument and configuration

## Summary

Investigating memory use is trickier than CPU consumption, but fortunately we have a number of command-line tools and instruments to help with the task. One thing to always remember is the multifaceted nature of memory—the difference between virtual and real memory as well as clean vs. dirty. Another is that examining memory is expensive. For example, keeping track of every allocation in the Allocations tool at the very least doubles the memory consumption for small allocations, keeping track of stack information increases it further, and tracking reference counting ops increases it dramatically. The Instruments document keeping track of the investigation in the "Allocations" section of this chapter, for example, is 1.3 GB in size, and even `top` spends about 80% of its CPU time in computing memory statistics (`top -d` consumes 1.1% CPU on my system, `top -u` 6.5%).

For this reason, it is recommended that you perform memory analyses either with small data sets or very beefy machines. For iOS, most memory investigations can and should be performed in the simulator, for unlike CPU performance, memory behavior should be very similar, except that the system has more memory and therefore memory warnings have to be triggered manually.

# 7

# Memory: Pitfalls and Techniques

The most common techniques for memory optimization revolve around the use of more compact data structures, and this chapter will definitely discuss that topic. In addition, we will show some pitfalls, especially those common in Objective-C code. (Did you guess that some of them involve use of Foundation objects?)

Of course, we also need to have a look at leak avoidance, and the special role that reference counting plays here for both Objective-C and Swift reference types, as well as the alternative of passing values around instead of references. We will look at Objective-C caching techniques and APIs, as well as APIs for controlling the mapping of address space to real memory.

We will continue our theme of the importance of architectural choices for performance, underscoring the point with a small example highlighting the difference those architectural choices can make. Last but not least, we will look at concurrency issues and the special iOS memory environment.

## Reference Counting

Even after the introduction of Automatic Reference Counting (ARC), one of the first topics in every discussion about Objective-C seems to be the reference-counting mechanism of Apple's Foundation. I have to admit I always find the angst somewhat overblown, as reference counting is both easy to work with and very predictable in its performance characteristics. As the classic reference-counting implementation is provided as library code, it is also amenable to normal factoring techniques for reducing the amount of code involved.

Due to ARC's performance limitations, I still use non-ARC reference counting in performance-critical code. My strategy for dealing with reference counting consists of the following patterns.

1. Always use accessors, except in `dealloc`.
2. Auto-generate all accessors with non-autoreleasing get-accessors or non-atomic properties using automatic accessor synthesis.
3. Always use convenience methods for object creation.

Using these patterns, my own non-ARC code was and is essentially free of reference-counting operations, apart from the `release` messages sent mechanically in `dealloc`. In numbers, I have 230 occurrences of `[... retain]` in 250 KLOC (kilo lines of code, or thousands of lines of code), so slightly below one retain per 1,000 lines of code. The majority of those remaining retains are due either to legacy or "special circumstances," such as (probably premature) optimization. Because of the non-automated `dealloc` methods, occurrences of the `release` message are about 10 times more frequent, but that is still only around 1% of total code.

By reducing the manual memory management code to 1% of total and effectively automating adherence to the Cocoa memory ownership rules, this little code pattern not only almost completely eliminates memory errors, but also eliminates having to think about memory. Conversely, the vast majority of memory errors I have seen has been in code that doesn't follow this sort of pattern. When I see an object being sent a retain in the middle of a method, I get suspicious, and the error is usually not far away.

The 1% figure is also sufficiently tiny that migrating code to ARC is trivial, as it was for garbage collection. However, it also means that the benefits of such a transition are minimal, 1% of code being a far cry from the roughly 50% effort implied by Apple's ARC transition guide.

One potential pitfall to beware of is the default `atomic` modifier for properties we already mentioned previously, which makes property accesses thread safe. Although the fact that everything is auto-generated in Example 7.1 making the code appear clean, it actually has hidden costs, especially for read accesses. If you run it, you will see that every read access incurs a penalty of one pointer's worth of memory, because the `atomic` accessor also implies an autoreleasing accessor, meaning your object is added to the current autorelease pool.

**Example 7.1    Measuring memory overhead of default synthesized read accessor**

```
#import <Foundation/Foundation.h>
#include <malloc/malloc.h>

@interface AtomicTest:NSObject
@property(retain) id myObject;
@end
@implementation AtomicTest
@end


int main(int argc, char *argv[] )
{
    int count=argc>1 ? atoi(argv[1]) : 1;
```

```
[NSAutoreleasePool new];
AtomicTest* obj=[[AtomicTest new] autorelease];
obj.myObject=[NSString stringWithUTF8String:"Hello World"];
struct mstats stats=mstats();
long used_before=stats.bytes_used;
for (int i=0; i< count * 1000 * 1000; i++) {
    [obj myObject];
}
stats=mstats();
long used=stats.bytes_used;
printf("n=%d memory used: %ld\n",count,used);
return 0;
}
```

While this may not seem a lot, read accesses are quite frequent, so this penalty can actually add up in real-world situations, and lots of code expects them to be essentially free. Adding the `nonatomic` keyword to the property declaration drops the memory consumption to the expected amount of zero, and also makes the affected code run up to 10 times faster.

## Avoiding Leaks

With reference counting, there are essentially two ways you can get an object leak: either your retains and releases don't balance, or you have a cycle. When using the rules discussed, your object ownership rules are taken care of automatically, except for the `release` sent from `dealloc`. ARC additionally takes care of automatically generating releases in dealloc. It is a bit unclear why this capability was bundled with ARC, given that a generic dealloc routine is fairly trivial to write. Fortunately, leaks in dealloc are so easy to fix using trivial code inspection (put .h and .m side by side, compare ivar declarations to `dealloc` method) that I've never bothered to actually use a generic/automated `dealloc` method I created in 2001, despite the fact that it worked well and also removed the need for per-class `dealloc` methods. (Generic `dealloc` uses introspection to find the object instance variables and releases them, with an exception list to avoid releasing non-retained references.)

That leaves reference cycles, an issue with reference counting that is neither addressed by the techniques above, nor by ARC (though it provides tools that can help).

A reference cycle is a group of objects that are keeping each other alive despite the fact that they are no longer reachable from outside the cycle. Fortunately, cycles can usually be avoided by the programmer. The common case of a parent link in a structure that is otherwise a tree (for example, the `superview` of the view hierarchy) is handled by making the parent link nonretained, as in Figure 7.1. With the root of the tree retained, the child links are sufficient to keep the objects alive as long as there are references—the programmer just has to remember to set the parent pointer to `nil` when removing a child from the tree.

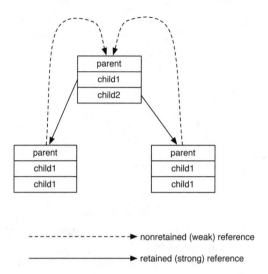

Figure 7.1    Cycle resolved by not retaining parent

ARC helps a little in this case with *zeroing weak references* (`@property (weak)`
`UIView *superview`). These references are just like other nonretained references,
except that they automatically become `nil` when the target object gets deallocated,
saving the programmer from keeping track of these references and making sure there
are no dangling pointers.

Another potential cause for cycles is an object that is composed of different parts,
but the parts need services from the whole. If making the back references nonretained
is not an option, one way to break the cycle is to factor out the functionality into a
separate object and reference that instead, as shown in Figure 7.2.

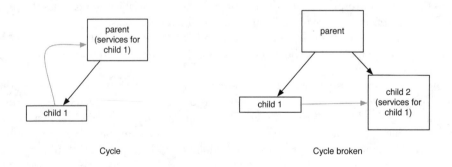

Figure 7.2    Cycle resolved by factoring out functionality

Finally, heap-allocated blocks, especially those used in Grand Central Dispatch, are also prime candidates for cycles, due to the object holding on to the block being referenced non-weakly inside the block. Implicit scope capture makes this an easy mistake to make.

The clang static analyzer can also detect potential leaks, and even though it can show false positives, running it regularly should be part of basic code hygiene.

## Foundation Objects vs. Primitives

We already saw in Chapter 3 that Foundation and CoreFoundation objects, while convenient in some cases, can extract a significant CPU performance penalty, so it shouldn't be surprising that there is a significant memory cost as well.

An `NSNumber` representing a `float` has size of 32 bytes, whereas the `float` itself is only 4 bytes, so an 8-fold expansion. Similar numbers apply to the other primitive wrappers. An exception is `NSNumber` or `CFNumber` objects representing integers on the 64-bit runtime, as we explored in the "Primitive Types" section of Chapter 3. These are encoded in the object pointer itself and so don't take up extra storage.

Speaking of pointers, all the object representations also use up a pointer worth of memory in whatever structure or object is holding onto that reference, so that's another 4 bytes on a 32-bit system or 8 bytes on a 64-bit system. We didn't factor this into our comparison above, so with the pointer, the difference between a direct `float` and an `NSNumber` is actually 4 bytes vs. 40 bytes, and the expansion becomes a factor of 10. Figure 7.3 compares the memory layout of a `Rectangle` object using 4 `real` values or 4 (simplified) `NSNumber` objects. With each box 8 bytes wide, the object using primitives uses 24 bytes total, all of which fit in a single cache line of 64 bytes and therefore can be read in a single memory transaction. Using `NSNumber` objects instead not only increases the basic object size to 40 bytes, it also requires 4 additional `malloced` blocks of memory, each of which will very likely be on a different cache line.

In the "Arrays and Bulk Processing" section of Chapter 3, we saw that a homogenous array of floating pointer numbers was anywhere from 5 to 1,000 times faster than an `NSArray` of `NSNumber` objects. We can now see that it is also 5 to 10 times smaller, depending on the environment (32 or 64 bit) and representation (`float` or `double`). While this difference in size wasn't relevant for the benchmarks in the "Arrays and Bulk Processing" section, because the array was relatively small in size and there was no other activity, it would almost certainly have an additional impact on performance in a real-world scenario. First, the likelihood of an expensive cache miss increases 10 times just from size alone; second, allocating the `NSNumber` object individually means that there is less chance to exploit fast sequential access patterns because each `NSNumber` can be allocated from a different part of the heap.

As you can guess, the numbers get even worse with dictionaries. Let's consider a single mutable `NSDictionary` with a single entry, let's say a `NSKernAttribute Name` with a value of −0.2. In my measurements on a 64-bit system, the dictionary

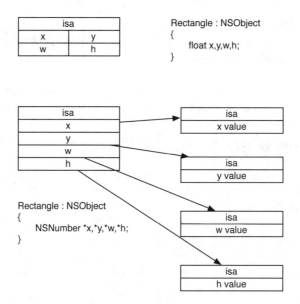

**Figure 7.3**    Memory layout of inlined primitives vs. object pointers

itself takes 112 bytes, with an additional 32 bytes for the NSNumber. I am not counting the NSString key, because it is almost certainly shared, but that's still 144 bytes. If we had an object with a kern float value, our total size would be 12 bytes of actual space, and 32 bytes due to malloc bucketing. Access patterns are also worse; the hash function pretty much guarantees that accesses will be effectively random, and thus incur maximum access-time penalties.

NSDictionary is often seen as a memory-saving device for sparse structures, but it turns out that it is actually very difficult to break even on that large initial space overhead. Figure 7.4 shows just how difficult: The only time NSDictionary breaks even with a straight object representation is with an extremely low 5% or lower utilization and 100 or more total slots. If the utilization rate is higher or the number of slots lower, the object representation is more compact, despite all the seemingly "wasted" slots, and at a utilization of even just 10%, the slope of the graph is also steeper for the NSDictionary-based representation.

# Smaller Structures

Once you've gotten rid of leaks, avoided gratuitous or bulk usage of Foundation objects, and stored bulk data compactly without pointer indirections, finding more compact in-memory representations of your data will help you conserve memory and make your programs go faster. Not only will there be less data to move around, you will also conserve precious cache memory, therefore lessening the chance of a stall

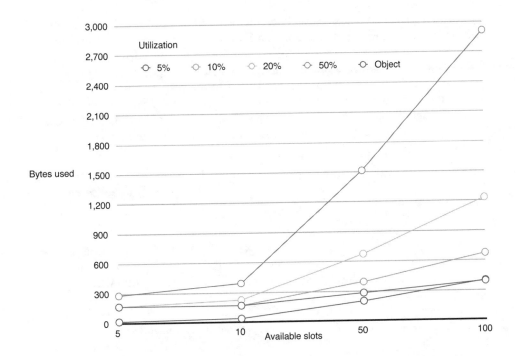

**Figure 7.4**   Memory consumption of sparsely populated dictionaries vs. objects

waiting for main memory, or even worse—a page fault going to secondary storage. Given the realities of today's machines, the size/speed trade-off is really no longer a trade-off; smaller sizes will almost always also translate into faster execution.

The first thing to do is not to waste space gratuitously, but sadly, wasting space is both easy and extremely common. An example is the date representation in Example 7.2, which was taken from a real-life calendaring application that ships on millions of machines. Even having standard 32-bit integers for values with a range from 0 to 24, 0 to 31, or 0 to 60 is already amazingly wasteful, but the authors either automatically or at least unthinkingly made the situation much worse by following the advice to replace `unsigned ints` with `NSUInteger`. As it stands, this will take $6 \times 8 = 48$ bytes of memory, and you can expect a lot of dates to exist in a calendaring app.

**Example 7.2   Gratuitous 64-bit integers in a date representation**

```
typedef struct {
    NSUInteger year,month,day;
    NSUInteger hour,minute,second;
} date_time;
```

This can trivially be replaced with the bit-field representation in Example 7.3 without any loss of required precision, except for being limited to dates a couple of million years into the future. This representation is 48 bits or 6 bytes in size, which is 8 times smaller. Since the compiler will in all likelihood pad this out to at least 8 bytes, we could conceivably add another 16 bits to the year, making the year range 128 billion years, which should tide us over until the next software update. This simple change shaved a couple of megabytes off the memory footprint of the app, and multiplying that by a couple of million users makes for a whopping terabyte of memory savings.

**Example 7.3    More compact date representation**

```
typedef struct {
  unsigned long year:21,month:5, day:5, hour:5, minute:6, second:6;
} date_time;
```

Another pitfall to avoid is gratuitous subclassing. The same calendaring app's main model object was the event, but for some reason lost in history, this model object was a subclass of NSView. Simply replacing the superclass with NSObject saved another several megabytes.

With the 64-bit transition, many data types have been expanded from 32 to 64 bit; for example, NSUInteger and NSInteger, but also CGFloat. For temporary variables and message parameters, this is generally OK, but it probably makes sense to verify how much range and precision are really needed for instance variables. As a counterexample, CGColor is defined to have CGFloat components, which are now 64-bit C double floating point numbers. Considering the fact that human color vision is able to distinguish at most around 10 million colors ($10^7$), representable in 24 bits, having 64 bits per color component (so a total of 192 bits for RGB, or $10^{38}$ combinations) seems a bit excessive.

## But What About Y2K?

You may recall the year 2000 (Y2K) scare that was due to many programs using only 2 digits to represent date, so for example, the year 1982 was represented as the string 82, with the century prefix 19 implied. This would obviously stop working come New Year's Day 2000, which these programs would interpret as 1900, and potentially charge interest for −99 years, compute speeds incorrectly, and so on.

While the original developers had assumed that their programs would have been replaced long before this particular hack ever became relevant, the software in question turned out to be much more long-lived than anticipated, resulting in a worldwide, multi-billion-dollar cleanup effort, lots of crossed fingers, and much overtime on New Year's Day 2000 and fortunately very little damage. So, don't the recommendations here potentially have the same pitfalls?

I think the answer to that is "No." First, the recommendation is to optimize field sizes within objects, behind those fantastic encapsulation boundaries that we try to make fast without optimizing them away. For message interfaces (parameters and return values), using the full width of the machine (32-/64-bit integers and floats/doubles) is both recommended and essentially free, because a full register will typically be taken no matter what. Second, even the slightly optimized representations presented here still have enormous amounts of headroom. So if our software lasts a couple of billion years longer than we expected or humans evolve to be several quadrillion times more color sensitive, all we will need is a minor update of a localized component, with all interfaces remaining the same.

## Compression

Compression is an obvious space-saving measure, and many of the techniques for saving memory, such as the bit-field discussed above, can be viewed as specialized forms of compression.

These types of compression have the feature that they are directly usable in their compressed state. General-purpose compression algorithms tend to not have this characteristic, so the data needs to be decompressed before it can be used. This means that both the uncompressed and the compressed representation are now in memory, with at least the uncompressed version also being dirty. An uncompressed representation can therefore paradoxically often be both faster and more memory efficient than one that is compressed.

## Purgeable Memory

One way of alleviating the memory pressure of dirty decompressed versions of data, or any other data that can be recomputed from a more compact representation, is *purgeable memory*. Marking memory as purgeable indicates to the operating system that when there is memory pressure, it can discard this memory just like clean memory despite the fact that it is known to be dirty, instead of having to swap it to disk.

Apple provides both a low-level interface using flags to the mmap() system call, as well as the much higher-level and more convenient NSPurgeableData class, which wraps a NSMutableData compatible interface around purgeable data and also implements the NSDiscardableContent protocol.

The beginContentAccess and endContentAccess messages of the protocol must be used to lock and unlock the actual contents, respectively; data can only be accessed while locked and only purged while unlocked.

The discardContentIfPossible message will purge the data unless it is currently locked, and this can also be done by the system if there is memory pressure. Once the data has been purged, beginContentAccess returns "NO" and access methods like bytes or mutableBytes will throw if used without a successful lock using beginContentAccess. It is important to not keep pointers to the data around, as accessing data via these pointers will cause the process to be killed if the data has been purged.

One thing to note about purgeable memory is how it is accounted for by the tools. For example, in top: when locked, it appears in the RSHRD column (rather than

RPRVT), and when unlocked it actually doesn't appear at all! The rationale is probably that the system can reclaim that memory at any point, but that's slightly misleading, because purgeable memory still produces memory pressure, even when unlocked. In my experience, and depending on the global situation, the system can and will prefer paging out other memory rather than releasing a purgeable memory segment.

# Memory and Concurrency

With the large discrepancy between CPU and memory speeds even for a single core, it shouldn't come as a surprise that managing memory bandwidth and latency is one of the primary concerns in writing high-performance multicore software.

If you want to keep multiple cores busy, they need to be able to work out of their private caches the majority of the time. *Cache aware* programs specifically take the known size of the caches into account, for example, splitting work into blocks of 16K or some other size. As the name suggests, they tend to be parametrized by the specific cache size and characteristics, so they are either hardware dependent or at least need to be parametrized at runtime.

*Cache-oblivious* algorithms use a recursive subdivision strategy and typically work on trees or tree-like structures, with most of the detailed work done near the leaves. The team behind the experimental and now defunct Fortress numerical computing language (intended to be a safe successor to FORTRAN, hence the name) has many good presentations[1] on the Web on this topic.

Another case of *cache pollution* can occur when a thread streams through memory, forcing other threads' data out of the caches. Special instructions in multimedia instruction sets such as SSE allow reading data from main memory without going through the caches. Since streaming performance of main memory is much higher than random access speeds, this can be sufficient for actual streaming algorithms. Apple's vDSP and vImage already take advantage of these instructions, so they can be a good option.

Contention occurs when two threads are trying to access the same piece of data. Since data in CPUs is organized in cache lines of typically 64 bytes, *false sharing* can occur when two threads access data that is actually at different locations, but those two locations lie on the same cache line. In this case, the CPU has to keep shuffling the data between the two cores, dramatically lowering throughput. If you find you have false sharing between threads, adding enough padding between the pieces of data that are causing the sharing to put them on different cache lines can dramatically improve performance.

If multiple threads work on the same data by handing it off between themselves, it makes sense to use the `thread affinity` APIs to pin them to the same core. Conversely, two concurrently running threads working on different data sets should

---

1. https://web.archive.org/web/http://research.sun.com/projects/plrg/Publications/

be scheduled on different cores in order to avoid having them fight over who owns the CPU-specific L1 cache.

# Architectural Considerations

We already saw some effects of architectural style in the difference between SAX and DOM parsers in Chapter 4. Whereas stream-oriented SAX parsers use effectively constant memory,[2] DOM parsers use memory proportional to the total file size. However, the effects of architectural style can be even more pronounced than that, as we will see.

Example 7.4 should print out the description of an NSArray with a single member, another NSArray. This final description would be something along the lines of " ( ( ) )," and take on the order of a couple of bytes, but because the two arrays are nested in each other, the program crashes. On my system, it actually runs out of stack space before running out of total memory, but it would eventually run out of memory as well.

**Example 7.4   Crashing using two NSMutableArrays and description**

```
import Foundation

var a=NSMutableArray()
var b=NSMutableArray()
a.addObject(b)
b.addObject(a)
print(a.description)
```

You might be wondering what this result has to do with software architecture. Isn't it just a bug in NSArray or description? Not really. Example 7.5 simply nests arrays, without the mutual recursion. Now, instead of a crash, we get the $n^2$ memory consumption curve for temporary objects shown in Figure 7.5. The actual size of the description grows linearly and is shown for comparison.

**Example 7.5   Measuring memory consumption for description of nested NSArrays**

```
import Foundation

let numArrays=Int(Process.arguments[1])!
let before=mstats();
var base:NSMutableArray=["Hello World"]
for i in 1...numArrays {
    base=[base]
```

---

2. More precisely: linear with the height of the tree.

```
}
let b=base.description
let after=mstats();
print("memory used: \( after.bytes_used - before.bytes_used)")
```

The graph only shows memory use up to a nesting level of 50, because after that the $n^2$ allocations curve becomes sufficiently large that the description size becomes effectively pinned to the x-axis when shown at the same scale. With 750 nested NSArrays, memory consumption grows to 500 MB and CPU time to 78 ms. Doubling to 1,500 nested NSArrays, both memory and CPU use quadruple to 2 GB and 306 ms, respectively. I've actually managed to run out of address space at times with a couple of thousand nested NSArray instances …on a 64-bit machine!

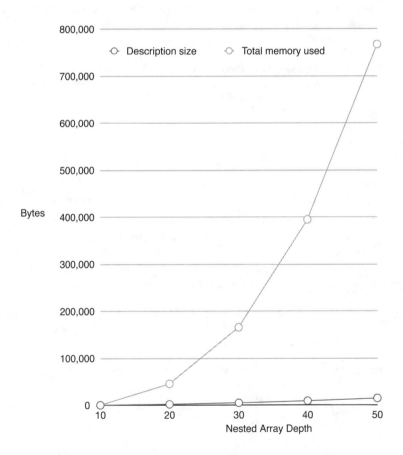

**Figure 7.5**   Quadratic memory consumptions for description of nested NSArrays

(If you really want to try this yourself, be prepared to wait a long time and at the very least reboot your machine to clean up swap space afterward. You may also actually run out of swap space and induce a kernel panic, so I don't recommend this. Save your work, back up your system beforehand, and don't say you weren't warned!)

The reason for this memory growth is not an implementation flaw in the `description` method, it is a fundamental characteristic of the *call-and-return* architectural style. In this style, you *call* a function or method *and* it *returns* a result.[3] Since that is the entire interaction, the result that is returned has to be complete; there is no real concept of a partial result.

When we need to compose these intermediate results into a final result, it means we need to first completely build all of the partial results, then allocate enough memory to hold the combined results, and then copy the partial results into the final result. Repeat this at each nesting level and you get a total complexity of $O(m \times n)$, where $m$ is the nesting depth and $n$ is the total size. In the (admittedly slightly pathological) example given here that has the nesting depth equal the total size ($m = n$), that gives us the $n^2$ result that we measured.

Fortunately, there is a fairly simple solution using a streaming approach, similar to what we saw with SAX for XML parsing, but simpler because we are generating instead of parsing. Instead of constructing complete partial results, we accumulate partial results into a shared buffer allocated once at the start, passing that buffer in to our methods instead of returning the result from the methods. The `describeOn:` method in Example 7.6 implements this accumulator-based streaming design for `NSArray`. The remainder of the code integrates it with the current description protocol and exposes a `fastDescription` method that encapsulates setting up the accumulator.

**Example 7.6    Streaming a description with `describeOn:`**

```
#import <Foundation/Foundation.h>

@implementation NSArray(describeOn)

-(void)describeOn:(NSMutableString*)description
{
  [description appendString:@"( "];
  NSString *separator=@"";
  for (id obj in self ) {
    @autorelease {
      [obj appendString:separator];
      [obj describeOn:description];
      separator=@", ";
    }
```

---

3. In Objective-C, we'd typically prefer the terminology *send a message*.

```
   }
   [description appendString:@")"];
}
@end

@implementation NSObject(describeOn)
- (void)describeOn:(NSMutableString*)description
{
   [description appendString:[self description]];
}
- (NSString*)fastDescription {
   NSMutableString *s=[NSMutableString string];
   [self describeOn:s];
   return s;
}
@end
```

Changing Example 7.5 to use `fastDescription` instead of `description` yields the dramatically different results shown in Figure 7.6. Not only does the total memory graph stay relatively flat and very close to the final size of the description, but notice that the x-axis starts at a nesting depth of 5,000, which is 100 times the last value given in Figure 7.5. Total memory consumed at the 5,000-object mark is around 20 KB. Where the $n^2$ algorithm required 2 GB for 1,500 items, we can get the description for ten times the number of items using just 60K of memory, so the accumulative algorithm is 35,000 times more memory efficient at this point.

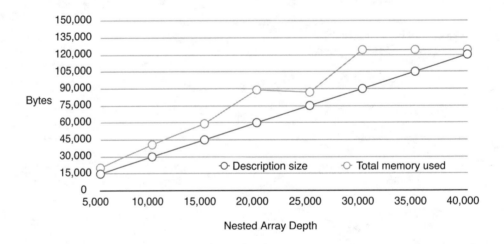

**Figure 7.6**   Linear memory consumption for `describeOn:` of nested `NSArrays`

While this was obviously an extreme example, the general principle holds that large data sets with partial results are difficult to handle with a *call-return* architectural style, and even medium-sized data sets with nesting will suffer from the need to have full partial results recomputed and the $m \times n$ space/time complexity inherent for nested structures in the style. Objective-C suffers more from this style than other languages would, due to the cost of object creation and the associated `autorelease` handling needed when returning a newly created object from a method. Just adding data to an already existing object is much cheaper.

So when designing a processing API, try to make it fundamentally streaming capable, for example, by passing some sort of accumulator that can accept results incrementally. Examples of this type of object abound—for example, the CoreGraphics `CGContextRef` object for talking to the display or perhaps more famously the Unix file descriptor *fd* or the *stdio* `FILE` object for I/O. In fact, Unix is probably the poster boy for streaming, with its *pipes-and-filters* architectural style, and most Unix filters will work on arbitrary-length data without any degradation.

As shown in Example 7.6, adding a call-return convenience method that encapsulates the streaming mechanism is usually easy, whereas converting a call-return API to streaming tends to be difficult to impossible without a rewrite.

Once we have an accumulator, an obvious extension is to make the accumulator smarter than just a simple `NSMutableString`. We will look a little more closely at a family of such classes in the next chapter, which will also take care of the infinite recursion in Example 7.4.

# Temporary Allocations and Object Caching

As we've seen here and in the "Object Creation and Caching" section of Chapter 3, temporary objects can be a serious challenge for Objective-C programs. The buildup of temporary objects is both expensive in itself and can lead to considerable heap growth, even if we've taken care not to build $n^2$ algorithms.

Heap growth can be controlled with nested autorelease pools or with the new `@autoreleasepool` compiler directive. The `describeOn:` method in Example 7.6 demonstrates this method by wrapping every iteration of the loop that describes the contents of the array in a nested pool. This cleans up any temporary objects that are no longer needed, especially those of the recursive send of `describeOn:`.

Even if we manage to avoid excessive heap growth by cleaning up regularly, temporary objects still present a performance problem because they are expensive to create and destroy. This is due to the fact that NeXT/Apple Objective-C and Swift require objects to be heap allocated; they do not allow the objects themselves to be allocated on the stack like other temporary variables. From a performance point of view, this limitation is unfortunate because stack allocation is essentially free: A single addition to the stack pointer "allocates" all the stack variables for a given function.

Of course, the fact that we're talking about a true C superset means that just because something is not allowed does not actually imply that you *can't* do it, just that you probably really should not. Example 7.7 shows how you can allocate Objective-C objects on the stack, if you really want to.

1. Get the class and the instance size of the class.[4]
2. Allocate and zero memory on the stack for the object using `alloca()` and `bzero()`.
3. Set the class.
4. Use within the block scope and no further.

**Example 7.7    Stack allocation of an Objective-C object**

```
#import <MPWFoundation/MPWInteger.h>
#include <stdlib.h>
#include <objc/runtime.h>

int main(int argc, char *argv[]) {
        Class mpwint=[MPWInteger class];
        size_t instance_size=class_getInstanceSize( mpwint );
        id a=alloca( instance_size );
        bzero(a, instance_size );
        object_setClass(a, mpwint);
        [a setIntValue:43];
        NSLog(@"a=%@",a);
        return 0;
}
```

While I have seen this done in production code at a certain Cupertino-based consumer electronics company, I have to admit to cringing, and I myself have never needed it in a good quarter century of performance-obsessed Objective-C hacking. With advances such as non-fragile instance variables, the already enormous chances of not just shooting yourself in the foot but actually blowing your entire leg off have increased even further, so I strongly recommend against this.

At the very least, you'd need to create a subclass that throws exceptions on any attempt to `retain` the object in question, make sure that it doesn't get stashed away anywhere without a retain, obviously make sure you're not returning it from your method/function, and don't even think of using this with ARC.

The object cache we introduced in the "Mutability and Caching" section of Chapter 3 solves both the problem of heap growth and allocation/destruction cost for short-lived objects in one fell swoop. Instead of allocating a fresh temporary object every time and then hoping it will get destroyed in time, or allocating an object on

---

4. Foundation objects often lie about their size and so aren't suitable for this.

the stack and hoping it doesn't escape and cause the world to blow up, we just reuse already allocated objects at the expense of a couple of function calls.

# NSCache and libcache

A somewhat different type of cache was introduced by Apple in Snow Leopard, with the Cocoa NSCache class and the lower-level libcache library it is built on. NSCache is a key-value store similar to NSMutableDictionary, except that contents may be evicted from this dictionary if the system detects memory pressure. NSCache allows you to aggressively use as much available memory as possible for caching, while minimizing the chance of degrading system performance with that memory use—for example, causing undue memory pressure or in the worst case paging the caches to and from slow secondary storage.

Note that *evicted* here just means that the object is removed from the cache (sent a release), not that the object is deallocated. This happens according to the normal memory management rules, so the object will only be deallocated if the NSCache was holding the last reference—in essence, if no one else was using it.

With a few minor caveats, you can use NSCache just like a NSMutable Dictionary. Since objects can disappear, you need to retain the object you get until you're done with it, preferably by stashing it in an instance variable with a proper accessor. Conversely, just because an object is removed from an NSCache does not mean it will be released as it may be retained elsewhere.

Since the eviction occurs asynchronously and that includes the time after you requested it but before you can store it yourself, the object is protected in transit using the retain + autorelease combination known from atomic read accessors. Unlike NSMutableDictionary, NSCache is thread safe and doesn't copy its keys.

Although you can use NSCache as simply a drop-in replacement, it also allows you to exercise more control if you so desire. If you have a cost-function for your objects, you can specify a maximum cost of the objects in the cache (for example, bytes used). If your cost function is "1," you can limit the number of objects in the cache.

NSCache can also interact with its content objects via the NSDiscardable Content protocol (as implemented by the NSPurgeableData we discussed earlier), essentially a separate reference counting protocol that was probably necessary to make NSCache work with the tracing collector that was also introduced with version 10.6.

# Memory-Mapped Files

Although memory mapping a file has to do with reading that file into a memory, a memory-mapped file can also be regarded as a special case of purgeable memory (ignoring the fact that memory-mapped files predate purgeable memory by a number of years). Like purgeable memory, a mapped file's memory can be reclaimed by the system at any time, but unlike purgeable memory this is completely transparent to the user. Since we provide the system with a data source for the memory (the underlying file), the system can automatically restore the contents of memory from that data source whenever we access it. Since it can do this at any time, it doesn't even need to actually read any data from the file until and if we actually do access the memory.

Using flags for the `NSData` method `dataWithContentsOfURL:options:error:` (either `NSDataReadingMappedIfSafe` or `NSDataReadingMapped Always`), we can completely change what those methods do, although the end result is semantically (largely) indistinguishable.

Without the mapping flag (see Example 7.8), these functions allocate memory and then use system calls to read the data from disk, returning after the data has been read. Since we have written into allocated memory, that memory is now marked as dirty.

**Example 7.8    Reading a file**

```
NSData *data;
data=[NSData dataWithContentsOfFile:@"documentation.pdf"
              options:0
              error:nil];
```

With the mapping flags, shown in Example 7.9, all that happens during the call is that address space is created and that address space is marked as being backed by the file in question. The difference is illustrated in Figure 7.7. No actual physical memory is allocated or I/O performed during the call; the manipulation was purely of virtual address space. Actual I/O is only performed if and when those mapped addresses are referenced. If only parts of the file are accessed, only those parts are read (though the system may elect to speculatively read more than was requested). What's more, since the process hasn't written to those pages, they remain clean. They even remain clean once the system does the I/O to fill them with data from the file because there is no difference between the data in memory and the file backing that memory.

**Example 7.9    Mapping a file**

```
NSData *mapped;
mapped=[NSData dataWithContentsOfFile:@"documentation.pdf"
              options:NSDataReadingMappedAlways
              error:nil];
```

The difference between the clean and dirty pages becomes noticeable when we have memory pressure and the system wants to free some memory. With parts of the mapped file actually read into memory, the system can simply undo the mapping, pointing that particular address space back at the original file. With the file read using Unix I/O, the system cannot do this, so if it wants to reuse that memory it first has to stash its contents in the swap file. For large files exceeding physical RAM, this can

```
[NSData dataWithContentsOfURL:@"file:documentation.pdf"
       options:0  error:nil];
```

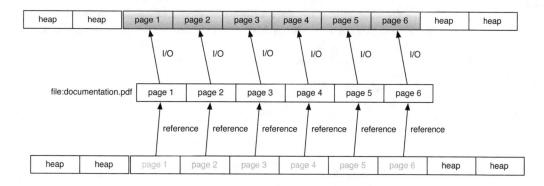

```
[NSData dataWithContentsOfURL:@"file:documentation.pdf"
       options:NSDataReadingMappedAlways  error:nil];
```

**Figure 7.7**    Reading a file vs. mapping a file

lead to the situation of having the data read from disk, swapped back out to swap and read back in from swap, possibly multiple times. On iOS, of course, no swapping takes place so dirty pages cannot be reclaimed by the OS. That leaves two options: either the process has to reclaim the memory in response to a memory warning or the OS has to kill the process.

So with memory mapping, potentially less memory is used in the first place. It can be reclaimed quickly and efficiently when needed, and I/O and processing can in many cases be interleaved, rather than having to do all I/O upfront before starting processing. So file access should essentially always be using memory-mapped files.

There is one main caveat to using memory-mapped files: with the I/O being done lazily, there may be I/O problems in code not expecting it. At its simplest, this may simply be I/O latency for an operation where we're expecting at most memory access costs, but that can also happen when swapping, so we're not really worse off. At its worst, however, this latency could reach infinity if the physical volume is removed—for example, if the network connection to a mounted volume is interrupted or an external hard disk removed. If that happens, the failure will result in a segmentation violation for the memory access. While this Unix signal can in theory be handled, in practice it will crash the program. When specifying the NSData ReadingMappedIfSafe flag, the system will therefore only map the file if the volume it is on is considered safe from sudden disappearance acts (for example, the boot volume).

One way to mitigate this issue is to preread the mapped data: For example, a so-called *page walker* running in its own thread simply touches every page of the mapped file, causing it to be read into memory. A very simple page walker is shown in Example 7.10. It assumes the page size is 4,096 bytes and reads exactly 1 byte from each page in the NSData argument. More sophisticated versions can be paced to stay only a little ahead of the main computational thread, for example, when sequentially processing a large memory-mapped file.

**Example 7.10   Page walker**

```
int pageWalker( NSData *data )
{
    int dummyResult=0;
    const char *bytes=[data bytes];
    for ( int i=0, max=[data length]; i<max; i+=4096 ) {
        dummyResult+=bytes[i];
    }
    return dummyResult;
}
```

# madvise

Although page walking does not affect the semantics of a program, it improves performance by essentially causing the I/O for a piece of the mapped file to occur before the processing that will actually need that data reaches it. Another way to achieve this effect is with the madvise system call, which allows you to give hints ("advice") to the system about your future plans with specific pieces of address space.

One hint you can give is MADV_WILLNEED. This should have the effect of paging any data that's not in memory yet—similar to the page walker, but simpler. Once you're done with a piece of memory, you can also tell the system this, using MADV_DONTNEED, which will make those pages eligible for eviction before others. If you are simply accessing contents sequentially, MADV_SEQUENTIAL the system will effectively do read-ahead and free-behind for you.

Going back to the discussion in the "Architectural Considerations" section of this chapter, what memory mapping in general and MADV_SEQUENTIAL in particular allow you to do is program in the easy *call-return* style while at the same time enjoying the performance advantages of a *streaming* style, with the additional flexibility of being able to break out of that style when necessary without jumping through hoops.

The MADV_FREE is like MADV_DONTNEED except that you are saying you don't actually care about the content of the memory in question, meaning that the system can discard it. (Dirty memory with MADV_DONTNEED still needs to be paged out.) The malloc update in Snow Leopard applies MADV_FREE to heap memory that's been freed, in order to avoid swapping memory to disk that no longer contains useful data.

When used wisely, the different `madvise` options can have a huge impact on your memory footprint and performance. Two caveats to watch out for are, first, that all advice given with `madvise` is advisory only; the kernel has no obligation to follow the advice (and until Leopard, most options were in fact ignored). Second, advice tends to be global, so it is possible to interfere with other processes' use of memory when dealing with shared mappings.

## iOS Considerations

As we've noted a number of times, the lack of a swapfile on iOS makes a significant difference: Instead of performance degrading gradually, you hit a brick wall. What doesn't change, however, is the fluid nature of the memory subsystem, and together these make for a challenging environment.

On one hand, your process will get killed if you are too aggressive or quick about requesting memory from the system, or too slow in giving up when requested. On the other hand, the system still has enough uses for memory that checking memory status and using only what is available will often not allow your app to function properly either.

Memory warnings, for example, get delivered on the main thread. This means that if your app is busy on the main thread (whether allocating or not) while a memory warning is pending, your app is likely to get marked as unresponsive and get killed. On the other hand, just moving your allocations onto a background thread is also not the answer: I have seen apps getting killed because the background thread was happily allocating large chunks of memory while the foreground thread was trying to process a memory warning.

One solution I have found is for background threads with high allocation requirements is to "ping" the main thread a "do-nothing" message. (using the `performSelector:onMainThread:` class of messages with the `waitUntil Done` flag set to `YES`). If a memory warning is being processed on the main thread, this will block the background thread behind that processing and allow memory to be freed before proceeding.

Speaking of memory warnings, when you receive a memory warning, pretty much drop everything else you're doing and start freeing memory.

The inability to swap dirty pages out to disk means that keeping your memory clean, for example by mapping, is even more important on iOS than on OS X. Although the system can't swap, it can still force all those clean pages out of memory, requiring the system to read them back in when next required, so the system can be slowed down by memory pressure just like OS X.

## Optimizing ARC

When we were working on the Wunderlist 3.0 release, we suddenly ran into a crash in the `NSOutlineView` delegate method shown in Example 7.11.

**Example 7.11    Method that returns 0**

```
- (BOOL)outlineView:(NSOutlineView *)outlineView isGroupItem:(id)item
{
    return NO;
}
```

This was surprising to say the least, because there is nothing there that could possibly crash. We were expecting the assembly code to be roughly something like Example 7.12, only manipulating registers. In fact, I would have been happy with just the xorl %eax,%eax, retq, but setting up the frame pointer doesn't really add much overhead and this was a debug build.

**Example 7.12    Non-ARC-generated assembly for method that returns 0**

```
-[WLTaskListsDataSource outlineView:isGroupItem:]:
01000e958a        pushq    %rbp
01000e958b        movq     %rsp, %rbp
01000e958e        xorl     %eax, %eax
01000e9590        popq     %rbp
01000e9591        retq
```

However, what we actually got was the code in Example 7.13. All of the arguments are retained indirectly via calls to objc_storeStrong(), and then released again by also calling objc_storeStrong(), but this time clearing the local variable. The crasher appeared to be caused by the NSOutlineView passing us an invalid object, which was also surprising considering this was (a) ARC, where that sort of thing isn't supposed to happen, and (b) Apple's code.

**Example 7.13    ARC-generated assembly for method that returns 0**

```
-[SomeOutlineViewDelegeate outlineView:isGroupItem:]:
01001bfdb0    pushq    %rbp
01001bfdb1    movq     %rsp, %rbp
01001bfdb4    subq     $0x30, %rsp
01001bfdb8    leaq     -0x18(%rbp), %rax
01001bfdbc    movq     %rdi, -0x8(%rbp)
01001bfdc0    movq     %rsi, -0x10(%rbp)
01001bfdc4    movq     $0x0, -0x18(%rbp)
01001bfdcc    movq     %rax, %rdi
01001bfdcf    movq     %rdx, %rsi
01001bfdd2    movq     %rcx, -0x30(%rbp)
01001bfdd6    callq    0x10027dbaa          ##  _objc_storeStrong
01001bfddb    leaq     -0x20(%rbp), %rdi
01001bfddf    movq     $0x0, -0x20(%rbp)
01001bfde7    movq     -0x30(%rbp), %rsi
```

```
01001bfdeb    callq     0x10027dbaa          ##  _objc_storeStrong
01001bfdf0    leaq      -0x20(%rbp), %rdi
01001bfdf4    movabsq   $0x0, %rsi
01001bfdfe    movl      $0x1, -0x24(%rbp)
01001bfe05    callq     0x10027dbaa          ##  _objc_storeStrong
01001bfe0a    movabsq   $0x0, %rsi
01001bfe14    leaq      -0x18(%rbp), %rax
01001bfe18    movq      %rax, %rdi
01001bfe1b    callq     0x10027dbaa          ##  _objc_storeStrong
01001bfe20    movb      $0x0, %r8b
01001bfe23    movsbl    %r8b, %eax
01001bfe27    addq      $0x30, %rsp
01001bfe2b    popq      %rbp
01001bfe2c    retq
```

While we were eventually able to find and remove the crasher, measurements also indicated that the ARC code was roughly 26 times slower than the non-ARC code. That's more than an order of magnitude difference between optimized and non-optimized code.

Why were we running non-optimized code? The default build settings that ship with Xcode (shown in Figure 7.8) specify that optimizations be off for debug builds, meaning virtually all development builds.

We didn't notice this slowdown of 26 times because the method was in the 97% non-performance-critical part of the code, and the experience really drove home the message of the very strong split between performance-critical and non-critical code.

While in this case the optimizer saved us (just leaving the issue of potentially unusably slow debug builds), this is not always the case. A little further inspection showed that many even very simple methods produced a lot of non-obvious calls to objc_storeStrong() even with optimizations on, overwhelming the useful work done in the method. The two ways to deal with this are to either move the performance-critical code to a file not compiled with ARC, or to add __unsafe_unretained attributes where necessary until the extra retains go away. Example 7.14 compiles to code without any extraneous retains, even with optimizations turned off.

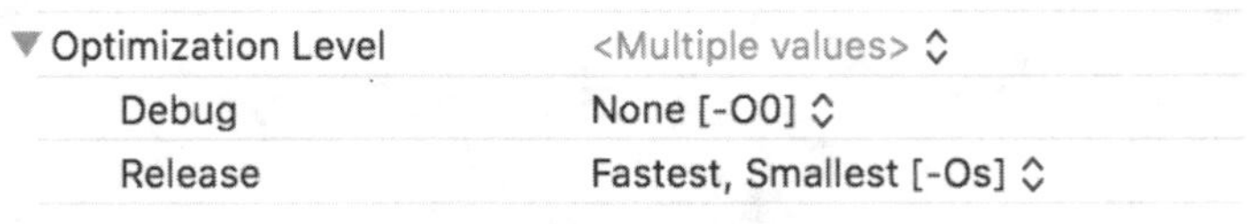

| ▼ Optimization Level | <Multiple values> ◇ |
|---|---|
| Debug | None [-O0] ◇ |
| Release | Fastest, Smallest [-Os] ◇ |

**Figure 7.8**  Default build configuration for new projects

**Example 7.14    Method that returns 0 without retaining its arguments**

```
- (BOOL)outlineView:(__unsafe_unretained NSOutlineView *)outlineView
        isGroupItem:(__unsafe_unretained id)item
{
    return NO;
}
```

I personally prefer keeping performance-sensitive code completely out of ARC, relying on ARC/non-ARC interoperability instead. For example, the object-cache in the "Object Creation and Caching" section of Chapter 3 cannot be expressed with ARC active; it has to be in a separate file. In addition, I am slightly uncomfortable with declaring that "I know what I am doing" when in ARC mode, because I am not sure I do. The interactions with the compiler have on many occasions been surprising.

# Summary

This chapter introduced a number of techniques both for keeping down the memory footprint of your application and making sure you use that memory as effectively as possible. As usual with Objective-C, you want to leverage coarse-grained objects filled with primitive types whenever possible, and we have seen how that coarse-grain structure interacts well with the cache-line-oriented nature of modern CPU-memory interfaces.

Basic data-structure tuning is also important, though not really Objective-C or Cocoa specific, unlike reference counting and cycle-breaking techniques or the specific object caches. Some of these caching mechanisms even have private interfaces to the virtual memory subsystem that allow them to adapt caching behavior to the system environment, while other VM APIs allow programs to optimize their use of non-cached resources.

Both iOS memory management techniques and the streaming architectural style are important topics that we will cover in more depth using the examples in the next chapter.

# 8

# Memory Example: FilterStreams

We've touched on streaming approaches before, for example, when looking at the effects of memory mapping or when comparing DOM-based XML parsers to those based on SAX or MAX.

In the preceding chapter, we showed how to drastically lower memory consumption by changing the `description` method that returns an `NSString` to a streaming `describeOn:` method that updates an `NSMutableString` passed into it as an argument.

However, having the argument be an `NSMutableString` seems to somewhat contradict our advice of having semantically rich objects, and also doesn't solve the initial problem of an infinite recursion causing a crash. So it shouldn't come as a surprise that we can do better. In fact, we will briefly introduce an entire hierarchy of *FilterStreams*, which combine aspects of the Unix pipes-and-filters architectural style with object-oriented concepts such as polymorphism, incidentally also solving the problem of infinite recursion in `-description`.

## Unix Pipes and Filters

The Unix pipes and filters architecture is probably the best known streaming architecture. It has at least two very desirable properties: the filter components are interchangeable and data can be processed incrementally, reading partial inputs and writing partial outputs until processing is complete, as long as the semantics of the operation make it possible. It is also concurrent, with each filter processing data in its own process, highly optimized, and unityped (everything is a stream of bytes). A graphical representation of a two-stage pipeline is shown in Figure 8.1: the output from *Filter 1* is connected to the input of *Filter 2*. In addition, the whole pipeline again has one input and one output, meaning the composed pipeline can act as a filter in another pipeline.

However, the data operated on by Unix filters are characters, which have to be parsed into meaningful units on input and regenerated from any internal

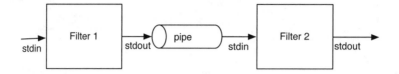

**Figure 8.1**   Two Unix filters connected by a pipe

representation on output for every step in the pipeline. In addition, communication is via fairly heavyweight inter-process communication.

Example 10.1 in Chapter 10 is a simple Unix filter that capitalizes the first character of every line it reads. It looks a little more complex than necessary because it eschews the library routines for buffering and extracting lines of text, illustrating the problem of having to parse meaningful structures out of the byte stream—a fundamental problem of Unix style filters.

Example 8.1 takes advantage of buffering and the built-in libraries for dealing with lines of text, making the code much simpler and around 250 times faster than Example 10.1.

**Example 8.1    Upcase filter using line-oriented I/O**

```
#include <stdio.h>
#include <ctype.h>

#define MAXLENGTH 8192

int main(int argc, char *argv[] ) {
  char buf[MAXLENGTH];
  while (fgets(buf,MAXLENGTH,stdin)) {
    buf[0]=toupper(buf[0]);
    fputs(buf,stdout);
  }
  return 0;
}
```

Integrating data object types other than streams of bytes or lines of text requires coming up with a byte-serialization format, libraries for parsing and serializing those objects from and to byte streams. Passing object pointers seems easier, especially for complex, hierarchical, or large data structures. Additionally, whereas filters can be reused via composition, specializing an existing filter to do something slightly different is not supported.

# Object-Oriented Filters

Stepping back from the particulars of the Unix implementation, we see that the fundamental characteristic of the pipes and filters architectural style are the uniformity of its interface and the forwarding of results to a target rather then returning them the caller. We can achieve the same or very similar effects using objects as filters and objects as the data that is exchanged between filters. FilterStreams reduce the two elements (pipes and filters) to a single element, the FilterStream object. Figure 8.2 shows the structure of a FilterStream, with a `writeObject:` method and a `target` instance variable into which the results are accumulated or which points to another FilterStream.

Example 8.2 shows the Objective-C code for the "null" FilterStream, which just passes its input unchanged to its `target` filter, similar to the Unix `cat` command. (The example elides boilerplate code such as the accessors, `dealloc`, and initialization method.)

**Example 8.2    Null Filterstream**

```
@protocol Streaming
-(void)writeObject:anObject;
@end

@interface MPWFilterStream : NSObject<Streaming>
{
  id   <Streaming> target;
}
@end
@implementation MPWFilterStream

-(void)writeObject:anObject
{
  [target writeObject:anObject];
}
@end
```

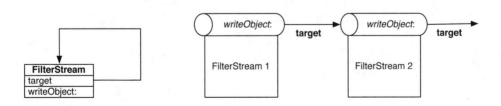

**Figure 8.2**    FilterStreams

The null filter isn't very interesting of course, but it sets the stage for filters that actually do something by overriding the `writeObject:` method with actual processing.

# DescriptionStream

Recasting `description` as a FilterStream results in a `DescriptionStream`, which accepts arbitrary objects as arguments to its `writeObject:` method and writes a description of those objects to its target. The simplest implementation of this specification is to simply send the `description` message as shown in Example 8.3, but this isn't very useful because it doesn't actually stream the result.

**Example 8.3    Simple but inefficient DescriptionStream**

```
@interface MPWDescriptionStream : MPWFilterStream
@end
@implementation MPWDescriptionStream

-(void)writeObject:anObject
{
   [target writeObject:[anObject description]];
}
@end
```

In order to actually get the streaming behavior we want, we need to at least distinguish between arrays and other objects, breaking up the arrays and writing them incrementally as shown in Example 8.4. The `writeObject:` method checks whether the argument is an `NSArray`, and if this is the case it describes the individual elements surrounded by round parenthesis and separated by commas. Describing the individual elements of the array is handled recursively by writing them to the stream itself.

**Example 8.4    DescriptionStream with case analysis**

```
-(void)writeObject:anObject
{
   if ( [anObject isKindOfClass:[NSArray class]] ) {
      BOOL first=YES;
      [target writeObject:@"( "];
      for ( id content in anObject ) {
         if ( !first) {
            [target writeObject:@", "];
         } else {
            first=NO;
         }
```

```
      [self writeObject:content];
    }
    [target writeObject:@") "];
  } else {
    [target writeObject:[anObject description]];
  }
}
```

Having the filter self-contained as in Example 8.4 is in line with the Unix tradition, but the case analysis is a code smell that begs for a more object-oriented solution. Instead of checking the class in question, Example 8.5 uses *double dispatch*[1] to bounce the problem back to the object in question while encoding the type of stream using the message name `describeOn:`. In addition, the stream makes API available for the client objects to actually write the description.

**Example 8.5     DescriptionStream with double dispatch**

```
@implementation DescriptionStream
-(void)writeObject:anObject
{
    [anObject describeOn:self];
}
-(void)writeDescription:(NSString*)partialDescription
{
  [target writeObject:partialDescription];
}
@end

@implementation NSArray(describe)

-(void)describeOn:(MPWDescriptionStream*)aStream
{
  [aStream writeDescription:@"( "];
  BOOL first=YES;
  for (id obj in self ) {
    if (first) {
      first=NO;
    } else {
      [aStream writeDescription:@", "];
    }
    @autoreleasepool {
      [aStream writeObject:obj];
    }
  }
```

---

1. http://en.wikipedia.org/wiki/Double_dispatch

```
   [aStream writeDescription:@")"];
}
@end

@implementation NSObject(describe)
-(void)describeOn:(MPWDescriptionStream*)aStream
{
   [aStream writeDescription:[self description]];
}
@end
```

Using double dispatch removes the case analysis and makes the code ready for future extension. For example, we don't have to modify any existing code in order to accommodate NSDictionary objects, we just need to implement describeOn: on NSDictionary. On the other hand, we have moved much of the logic of the filter out of the filter itself into the client objects, requiring categories, and tangled that code with filter-specific logic such as writing the description parts.

One way to move the code back into the filter is to dispatch back to the filter again, this time encoding the kind of object to process; for example, writeArray: for NSArray. If we do this, we actually don't need to encode the kind of stream in the first dispatch because the stream that we finally bounce the message back to knows what it is. Although the code shown in Example 8.6 also uses categories, these categories are purely behind-the-scenes plumbing that not only can be given clash-resistant names, but can in fact be generated from blocks using imp_implementationWithBlock().

### Example 8.6    DescriptionStream with triple dispatch

```
@implementation DescriptionStream
-(void)writeObject:anObject {
   [anObject writeOnStream:self];
}
-(void)writeDescription:(NSString*)partialDescription {
   [target writeObject:partialDescription];
}
-(void)writeNSObject:(NSObject*)anObject  {
  [self writeDescription:[anObject description];
}

-(void)writeNSArray:(NSArray*)array
{
  [self writeDescription:@"( "];
  BOOL first=YES;
  for (id obj in array ) {
    if (first) {
      first=NO;
```

```
    } else {
      [self writeDescription:@", "];
    }
    @autoreleasepool {
      [self writeObject:obj];
    }
  }
  [self writeDescription:@")"];
}

@end

@implementation NSArray(StreamWriting)

-(void)writeOnStream:(MPWFilterStream*)aStream {
  [aStream writeNSArray:self];
}

@end

@implementation NSObject(StreamWriting)

-(void)writeOnStream:(MPWFilterStream*)aStream {
  [aStream writeNSObject:self];
}

@end
```

Each object gets written to the stream using the `writeObject:` message that represents the stream interface. The stream then asks the object to write itself using the `writeOnStream:` message, with the object responding by sending a message encoding its class to the stream (see Figure 8.3). While this may seem like a lot of

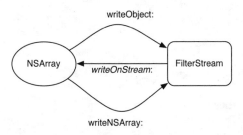

**Figure 8.3**    FilterStream interacting with an NSArray written to it

messages, remember that messages are comparatively cheap, compared to having to allocate temporary memory and unpack/repack intermediate results.

The NSMutableString is now hidden behind the target of the DescriptionStream, so we can actually replace it with an object that outputs directly to *stdout*, *stderr*, or a file, instead of accumulating the entire description in memory before outputting it. This makes memory consumption for the description effectively constant, so $O(1)$, down from $O(n^2)$ for the original description method and $O(n)$ for the improved describeOn:.

## Eliminating the Infinite Recursion from description

With the stream object that interacts with the object graph to produce the description, we now also have a place to keep enough state for catching infinite recursions in our data structures—for example, the mutually recursive NSArray objects from Example 7.4.

When we encounter an object that we are already in the process of describing, we don't want to describe it again. So in order to avoid this, we need to keep track of the objects we are currently describing and bail if we encounter it again. The MPWDescriptionStream of Example 8.7 has an NSMapTable to keep track of the objects that are in the process of being described, as well as taking on the NSMutableString that was the direct argument of describeOn: previously. The writeObject method defined in Example 8.8 implements the strategy just described: first put an object in the table, then describe it if it is not already in the table, and finally remove it again. If the object is already in the table in step 2, we just write a pseudo description.

**Example 8.7    Description Stream definition**

```
#import "MPWFilterStream.h"

@interface MPWDescriptionStream : MPWFilterStream
{
  NSMapTable *alreadySeen;
}
@property (nonatomic,retain) NSMapTable *alreadySeen;
-(void)writeObject:anObject;
-(void)writeArray:(NSArray *)anArray;
-(void)describeObject:anObject;
@end
```

**Example 8.8    Description Stream implementation**

```
@implementation MPWDescriptionStream
#define OPAQUEPTR    NSPointerFunctionsOpaquePersonality
```

```
-(instancetype)init
{
  id table=[NSMapTable mapTableWithKeyOptions:OPAQUEPTR
                            valueOptions:OPAQUEPTR];
  self=[super init];
  [self setAlreadySeen:table];
  return self;
}

-(void)writeObject:anObject
{
  if ( [alreadySeen objectForKey:anObject] ) {
    [self appendDescriptionFormat:@"<already saw: %p>",anObject];
  } else {
    [alreadySeen setObject:anObject forKey:anObject];
    [super writeObject:anObject];
    [alreadySeen removeObjectForKey:anObject];
  }
}
// ... rest as before
@end
```

The procedure described that removes the described object avoids the infinite recursion and no more. More generally, if you want to not repeat objects in the output, just leave the described objects in the table. At that point, you've effectively built an object-graph serializer and also a detector for potential retain cycles!

Add in the glue code from Example 8.9, and running last chapter's Example 7.4 no longer crashes, but outputs something along the lines of a1: ( ( <already saw: 0x7fa0fb40a880> ) ). The example is obviously incomplete; for example, it would at the very least require a writeDictionary method, and preferably all objects would implement describeOn: instead of description so they also acquire this protection.

**Example 8.9    Description Stream glue code**

```
@implementation NSObject(describeOn)

-(void)describeOn:(MPWDescriptionStream *)aStream
{
  [aStream describeObject:self];
}

-(NSString*)fastDescription
{
  MPWDescriptionStream *s=[MPWDescriptionStream stream];
  [s writeObject:self];
```

```
    return [s target];
}
@end

@implementation NSArray(describeOn)

- (void)describeOn:(MPWDescriptionStream *)aStream
{
    [aStream describeArray:self];
}

@end
```

## Stream Hierarchy

The sum of these transformations now gives us polymorphic, subclassable, and composable streams that can process data incrementally. Instead of writing directly to a NSMutableString as did our solution to the description problem in the previous chapter, we now write to the stream.

A subclass of MPWDescriptionStream can easily override writeArray: to output a JSON-formatted string instead of the NeXT-style property list format that description creates.

All in all, I have implemented well over two dozen types of FilterStream in my MPWFoundation framework[2] since I started using FilterStreams in 1998, a small subset of which is shown in Figure 8.4. They have served me well, especially in byte encoding or transformation roles such as compression and encoding, with commonalities between encodings captured and output easily directed to a buffer, the network, or a file.

The Byte Stream subtree generalizes what you can do with Unix filters, and in fact includes a class that invokes Unix filters. The dataflow paradigm means that URL Fetch Stream can handle the asynchrony inherent in network operations with ease and without callback hell; we've been using it in Wunderlist to great effect. The reason is that call-and-return requires a return value immediately, whereas dataflow just requires a result to be passed on to the next filter without being too particular about when that happens. In fact, it isn't just not particular about the timing of the results, but also about the number. A filter can write multiple results to its target or zero, for example, when there is an error, making it possible to keep error handling out of the "happy path" and centralize it instead.

The actual implementations are only a little bit more involved than shown here. For example, the initial message that writeObject: sends is not fixed but specified

---

2. http://github.com/mpw/MPWFoundation

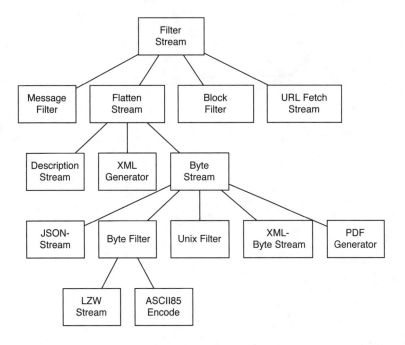

**Figure 8.4**    FilterStream hierarchy

as a parameter of the FilterStream in question, in order to enable objects to respond
to specific kinds of stream, but with a hook so that common behavior can be shared.

Convenience methods adapt the streaming architectural style to call-and-return.
For example, the +process: message defined on the root FilterStream class
initializes the stream, writes the object to the stream, and returns the result.

# Summary

In this chapter, we've looked at expanding the idea of using streaming approaches
from the previous chapter into an entire library of components that implement the
*Pipes and Filters* architectural style. With this library, streaming is baked into the
substrate, making it trivial to implement computations in a way that is not just
memory efficient but also easy to make asynchronous.

# 9

# Swift

Introduced to great fanfare at WWDC 2014, Swift is Apple's new programming language, billed as "Objective-C without the C." This was an interesting marketing slogan, considering the fact that we know Objective-C was created by adding most of Smalltalk to C (Equation 9.1).

$$\text{Objective-C} = \text{C} + \text{Smalltalk} \tag{9.1}$$

According to the rules of Algebra I learned in high school, subtracting C from both sides of the equation (Equation 9.2) does not yield Swift, and in fact Swift seems much more closely related to C# or C++ than Smalltalk or, for that matter, Objective-C.

$$\text{Objective-C} - \text{C} = \text{Smalltalk} \tag{9.2}$$

Minor marketing issues aside, Swift has been a hugely popular success, with many articles, books, and conferences dedicated to the topic.

## Swift Performance: Claims

From the very beginning, Apple has been heavily promoting Swift's performance, right down to the name: Swift. In the Platforms State of the Union, performance of the new language was a key focus, for example, with the performance comparison shown in Figure 9.1.

It is an impressive display, with Swift being 3.9 times faster than...exactly what? Python. You might wonder what Python is doing in this comparison, considering that it is an interpreted scripting language that is not intended for performance-intensive work at all and has effectively no relevance to OS X and iOS development.

It turns out that when you compare only the Objective-C and Swift columns, 2.6 vs. 3.9 is just a factor 1.4 difference, and when you plot *that* and make the colors the same as one another, as shown in Figure 9.2, that's not a particularly impressive slide.

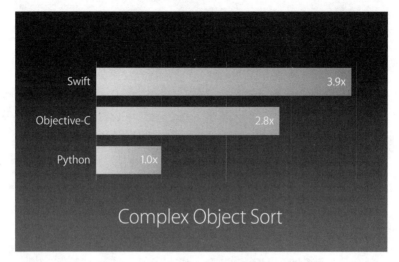

**Figure 9.1**    WWDC 2014 State of the Union slide comparing Swift to Python

Bringing Python into the mix simply makes the Swift number look much more impressive; 3.9 sounds a lot better than 1.4. Even among developers, few are going to exert the mental effort required to get the more relevant Objective-C vs. Swift number, and certainly not when slides are flying by in a keynote address.

Another thing that might leave you scratching your head is just how *bad* those numbers are. After all, Python is an interpreted scripting language, with most comparisons I've seen rating it around 2 times slower than even Ruby.

Two years after the introduction, the Swift language section of Apple's main site (see Figure 9.3) still uses Python as a comparison, now with Swift 8.4 times faster than Python.

The fact that Python is still used as a comparison doesn't exactly instill confidence, and neither does the "up to" wording. Though better than before, these numbers are both still odd and still pretty bad. Being only around 8 times faster than Python with

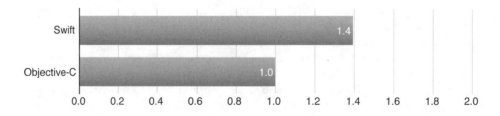

**Figure 9.2**    Leaving out Python

## Better performance equals better apps.

Swift apps more than live up to the name.
For instance, a common search algorithm
completes much faster using Swift.

Up to

2.6x

faster than
Objective-C

Up to

8.4x

faster than
Python 2.7

10,000 integers found in a graph
using depth-first search algorithm*

**Figure 9.3**    Performance claims on http://apple.com/swift

a compiled language would be disappointing, and Objective-C code that's only around 2.5 times faster than Python code is downright disturbing.

Although not particularly convincing upon closer examination, Apple's Swift performance marketing has been extremely effective. The idea that Swift is very, well, *swift* is now an accepted fact in the Apple developer community.

## Language Characteristics

Although Apple hasn't given us any solid evidence *of* Swift's performance, it has given us reasons *for* amazing Swift performance.

- Swift's design is much more static than Objective-C's, meaning there is much more information available at compile time for the compiler to use in optimization.
- Specifically, dynamic dispatch is drastically reduced, with most "native" Swift methods being dispatched statically.

  Objective-C's dynamic dispatch is an absolute barrier to compiler awareness, which was always a thorn in the side of the compiler and runtime team. Just-in-time (JIT) compilers can resolve this at runtime, but there are many reasons not to rely on JIT technology for performance.[1]

---

1. See *Jitterdämmerung* (http://blog.metaobject.com/2015/10/jitterdammerung.html).

- The greater use of value semantics (see the "Stack Allocation" section of Chapter 5) using structs is supposed to free us from the cost of heap allocation and reference counting, especially ARC (see the "Reference Counting" section in Chapter 7), and it is true that dealing with references is particularly expensive in Swift, much more so than in Objective-C.

- Primitives and objects are much more closely integrated, so whereas a Foundation NSArray can only contain object references, a Swift Array can contain primitives, structs, or object references. Primitive numbers are easily boxed and unboxed, often automatically, when used in object contexts.

- Generics allow specialization to be applied, so for example the generic sort method of an array can be specialized by an integer-comparison function to yield an optimized integer-sorting function without indirection through function pointers or message sends.

All of this is good stuff, and certainly it gives opportunities for a compiler to optimize. Having a more unified syntax instead of two separate systems bolted together and held together with duct tape is also certainly welcome.

However, all of these mechanisms only *might* lead to better performance; there is no guarantee that they actually *do*, and they are available to Objective-C programmers as well. For example, Objective-C makes heavy use of value semantics for all primitive types such as integers and floating point numbers and structs such as NSPoint, CGPoint, NSRect, NSRange, and so on.

Making their use slightly more convenient is not a bad thing per se, but it also doesn't actually do much for performance, especially since Apple recommends and expects most modeling to be done using classes:

> "In all other cases, define a class, and create instances of that class to be managed
> and passed by reference. *In practice, this means that most custom data constructs should be
> classes, not structures.*"
>                    Apple Inc., 2014. *The Swift Programming Language (Swift 3).* iBooks.

This recommendation to use classes is sound, as we know that micro-optimizations such as this won't matter for 97% or more of the code. However, it is in direct conflict with Apple's performance recommendations for Swift, which are to vastly prefer structs unless there is a compelling reason not to do so.

The problem is that both recommendations are correct, and the inherent conflict flies in the face of the collected wisdom regarding performance tuning collected over the last 40 years or so: Model the domain first, appropriately; apply targeted optimizations afterward. With Swift, you are supposed to make this performance choice at the modeling stage of your application.

Objective-C also had and still has this problem, but as the previous chapters showed there were mechanisms that allow the developer to apply targeted optimizations for much better performance, such as IMP-caching, object-caching, or use of basic C data types like char* instead of String. These mechanisms frequently allow you to have and keep your modeling cake while simultaneously munching down on some delicious performance chow, but they have been either curtailed or eliminated outright in Swift.

Instead, the programmer is supposed to structure her programs in such a way as to give as much information to the compiler as possible. That way it is easy for the compiler to understand the whole program and then rely on the optimizer to actually figure out how to most efficiently map the high-level abstractions to efficient/optimal machine implementations.

I call this approach *compiler-oriented development* (COD) because it seems to be more focused on making life easy for the compiler rather than the developer.

It is very different from the hybrid model represented by Objective-C that we talked about a bit in the "The Power of Hybrids" section in Chapter 1: The compiler mostly gets out of the way, and the language provides simple and understandable abstractions. It is the developer's job to spot hotspots and fix them using the many tools provided.

## Benchmarks

This is a short section.

While Apple has provided slides and headline comparison numbers, it hasn't provided the benchmarks those numbers are based on or even just detailed results. Requests to provide the source code to those benchmarks were met with silence.

In short, Apple has provided no usable empirical data regarding Swift's performance.

# Assessing Swift Performance

With Apple not being forthcoming on Swift's actual performance characteristics, we have to take a look ourselves, as tuning without at least some idea of what those characteristics are in practice is meaningless. In the following, I will give an overview and an analysis of the current state of Swift performance and look at the highly compiler-centric model of optimization championed.

## Basic Performance Characteristics

We already saw some basic Swift performance characteristics in Chapter 1, for example, the integer summation code in Examples 1.5 and 1.6.

Performance when computing with primitives and basic control flow is not too dissimilar to basic Objective-C, with an approximate 50% performance penalty, rising to roughly 300% when objects were involved. To find out what the cause of this penalty was, I compiled the primitive version in Example 1.5 (integer summation) and then examined the generated machine code with `otool -Vt`. The result is shown in Example 9.1.

**Example 9.1    Assembly code for Swift summation**

```
0000000100000d5f cmpq    $0x3b9aca00, -0x8(%rbp) ## imm = 0x3B9ACA00
0000000100000d67 jg      0x100000db0
0000000100000d69 movq    -0x8(%rbp), %rax
0000000100000d6d addq    __Tv10swiftbench1aSi(%rip), %rax

0000000100000d74 seto    %cl
0000000100000d77 movq    %rax, -0x18(%rbp)
0000000100000d7b movb    %cl, -0x19(%rbp)
0000000100000d7e jo      0x100000eda

0000000100000d84 movq    -0x18(%rbp), %rax
0000000100000d88 movq    %rax, __Tv10swiftbench1aSi(%rip)
0000000100000d8f movq    -0x8(%rbp), %rcx
0000000100000d93 incq    %rcx

0000000100000d96 seto    %dl
0000000100000d99 movq    %rcx, -0x28(%rbp)
0000000100000d9d movb    %dl, -0x29(%rbp)
0000000100000da0 jo      0x100000edc

0000000100000da6 movq    -0x28(%rbp), %rax
0000000100000daa movq    %rax, -0x8(%rbp)
0000000100000dae jmp     0x100000d5f
```

For reference, the assembly output of the respective Objective-C example is shown in Example 9.2. I have to admit that I expected the code to be, apart from the overflow checks, a lot more similar than it turned out to be.

**Example 9.2    Assembly code for Objective-C summation**

```
0000000100000f16 cmpl    $0x3b9aca00, -0x8(%rbp) ## imm = 0x3B9ACA00
0000000100000f1d jg      0x100000f45
0000000100000f23 movslq  -0x8(%rbp), %rax
0000000100000f27 addq    _a(%rip), %rax
0000000100000f2e movq    %rax, _a(%rip)
0000000100000f35 movl    -0x8(%rbp), %eax
0000000100000f38 addl    $0x1, %eax
0000000100000f3d movl    %eax, -0x8(%rbp)
0000000100000f40 jmp     0x100000f16
```

The basic structure of the code actually is similar, with a cmp instruction at the top of the loop and a jump (jg) to outside the loop if the counter now exceeds the

**Table 9.1   Swift and C summing with different optimization levels**

| Settings | Swift | Objective-C | Ratio |
|---|---|---|---|
| No optimization | 3.7 | 2.0 | 1.85 |
| -0 / -Os | 0.903 | 0.009 | 100 |
| -Ounchecked / -O3 | 0.016 | 0.009 | 1.77 |

maximum value `0x3b9aca00`, hex for the decimal number 1000000000. At the bottom of the loop, there is a `jmp` back to the loop entry.

In the middle, between the comparison/exit the jump back to the top of the loop, is the actual meat: incrementing the loop counter, in the Objective-C case using an `addl` instruction, in the Swift case an `incq` and the addition of the counter to the summation. However, the Swift code appears to do a lot more additional bookkeeping. It also checks for overflow using `jo` instructions and makes sure to set the overflow flag.

Overflow checking can be eliminated using either the `-Ounchecked` compiler flag (not recommended, because it changes Swift source code semantics) or judicious use of the unchecked arithmetic operators such as `&+`, `&-`, and so on. Table 9.1 shows the results of the different options, compared to equivalent Objective-C code and optimization levels.

I didn't do a comprehensive survey of all of Swift's primitive operations, but overall they seem to generally be a little behind C but in the same ballpark, which isn't too surprising considering they are using the same LLVM back end.

## Collections

We already looked a bit at array access times in the "Arrays and Bulk Processing" section of Chapter 3. The setup was dealing with an array of floating-point numbers, a typical application for bulk processing, with a custom floating point array class `MPWRealArray` introduced in Chapter 3.

Example 9.3 shows how one might populate and sum an array of floating point numbers in Swift.

**Example 9.3   Sum floats with Swift arrays**

```
extension Collection where Iterator.Element == Float {
  func sum() -> Float {
    return reduce(0, +)
  }
}
var a:Float = 0
var someFloats = [Float]()
```

```
someFloats += stride( from:1.0, through:1000000.0, by:1.0 )
for i in 0..<Int(CommandLine.arguments[1])!  {
  a += someFloats.sum()
}
print("a = \(a)")
```

The code first creates an extension to `Collection` that uses the `reduce` higher-order function to sum the elements of the array. What's neat is that even though `reduce` takes a function argument, you can just pass it the + operator because in Swift operators are just functions. There is obviously some magic where the function gets resolved (otherwise there'd be an infinite recursion of functions), but that is hidden.

You might be wondering about the definition of the `sum()` extension when `reduce(0,+)` doesn't seem much longer. One reason is that the `reduce()` is not intention revealing—the name doesn't describe the intended effect, but the implementation used to achieve that effect. This makes the code much more difficult to read and understand, as the reader has to infer the intended result from the implementation provided. It also means clients are tied to this specific repeated implementation, for example, not benefiting from the improved implementation of `sum()` based on `vDSP_sve()` that we present later. Last but not least, the generic `reduce()` function also induces significant compile-time cost, a cost that's better to have just once in the `sum()` definition.

Foundation does not have a `reduce` method or function built in, so we must add our own to `MPWRealArray`, shown in Example 9.4. It then goes on to define the `sum` method in terms of `reduce:`.

**Example 9.4    Reduce using a block in Objective-C**

```
-(float)reduce:(float(^)(float,float))reduceFun
{
    float result=0,*my_reals=[self reals];
    for ( long i=0,max=[self count];i<max;i++) {
        result=reduceFun( result, my_reals[i]);
    }
    return result;
}
-(float)sum
{
    return [self reduce:^(float a,float b){ return a+b }];
}
```

As before, the full `MPWRealArray` implementation is not shown. The driver program for the Objective-C tests is shown in Example 9.5.

**Example 9.5    Objective-C driver program using `MPWRealArray`**

```
#import <MPWFoundation/MPWRealArray.h>

int main(int argc, char *argv[])
{
  MPWRealArray *array=[MPWRealArray start:1 end:10000 step:1.0];
  float sum=0;
  for (int i=0,max=atoi(argv[1]); i<=max; i++) {
    sum+=[array sum];
  }
  NSLog(@"sum:   %g",sum);
}
```

The `reduce:` method takes a block with two arguments that returns a single value; the `sum` method uses a block that just adds the two arguments. The results are shown in Table 9.2.

As usual, Swift without optimizations is catastrophically bad, 68 times slower than Objective-C without optimizations and 322 times slower than Swift with optimizations. With optimizations, Swift does well; the example code is roughly 2 times faster than the Objective-C code we used here.

The reason for this is fairly clear: The Objective-C code has to call the argument block for every pair of elements, and that function call overhead is much larger than the cost of the actual + operator.

With optimizations, Swift does generics specializations, combining the `reduce` function with the + operator, creating a single function that just adds the elements without any additional function calls.

However, the block-based code in Example 9.4 is not the code that is actually in `MPWRealArray`, because it is perfectly obvious that it would be slow; I only added it for this chapter in order to check what the performance would be.

The reason this code is slow is that in Objective-C, the + operator is not a first–class object, meaning that among other things, you cannot pass it directly to a function or method as a parameter.

**Table 9.2    Array summation via reduce and blocks**

| Settings | Swift | Objective-C | Relative % |
|---|---|---|---|
| No optimization | 261.80 | 3.83 | 6837 |
| -O | 0.82 | 1.57 | 52 |
| -Ounchecked / -O3 | 0.78 | 1.42 | 55 |

The way to solve this problem in Objective-C is to use the preprocessor. Example 9.6 defines REDUCE as a macro, or more precisely REDUCE_METHOD, which creates a method based on reducing with a specific operator.

**Example 9.6    Reduce as a C macro**

```
#define REDUCE_METHOD( name, operator  )\
-(float)name\
{\
    float *my_reals=[self reals],result=my_reals[0];\
    for ( long i=1,max=[self count];i<max;i++) {\
      result=result operator my_reals[i];\
    }\
    return result;\
}\
REDUCE_METHOD( product, *  )
REDUCE_METHOD( differences, - )
REDUCE_METHOD( sum, + )
```

Swift has no preprocessor, so the way to implement a generic operation like this is to use higher-order functions as we did earlier. There are many advantages to that approach, but you don't have control over the code that is generated, or how it is transformed by the optimizer. With the macro from Example 9.6, the code that will be generated is very obvious (see Example 9.7).

**Example 9.7    Reduce macro expanded for sum**

```
-(float)sum
{
    float *my_reals = [self reals], result = my_reals[0];
    for (long i = 1, max = [self count]; i < max; i++) {
      result = result + my_reals[i];
    }
    return result;
}
```

The results are shown in Table 9.3, with the Swift numbers just replicated because there is no equivalent. I did try expanding the reduce() function manually, but that made no difference to the result.

Without any optimizations, the macro-based code is actually a little bit smaller than the block-based code, but still around 50 times faster than Swift without optimizations. With basic optimizations, Swift and Objective-C are neck and neck, and with aggressive optimizations, the macro-based code is now more than 6 times faster than Swift at the same level of optimization, and 2,000 times faster than unoptimized Swift.

Table 9.3     **Array summation via macro**

| Settings | Swift | Objective-C | Relative % |
|----------|-------|-------------|-----------|
| No optimization | 261.80 | 5.31 | 4893 |
| -O | 0.82 | 0.78 | 105 |
| -Ounchecked / -O3 | 0.78 | 0.12 | 645 |

However, that's still not really ideal. For optimized bulk operations on various numeric types, including `float` numbers, Apple provides the Accelerate framework, with the `vDSP_sve()` function for summing an array of floating pointer numbers. Example 9.8 shows how to extend `Array[Float]` with a vectorized summation method.

Example 9.8     **Vectorized sums with Swift arrays**

```
import Accelerate

extension Collection where Iterator.Element == Float {
  func vecsum()->Float {
    var sum:Float=0
    vDSP_sve(self as! [Float], 1, &sum, UInt(self.count.toIntMax()))
    return sum
  }
}
```

This is the simplest way I found of achieving the desired effect. Strangely, it isn't possible to just extend `Array[Float]`; the extension has to be on `Collection` with a type-constraint to `Float`, and then inside the method `self` has to be cast to a `[Float]` type. If that cast fails, the program crashes.

The Objective-C code in Example 9.9, which is just part of the `MPWRealArray` class, seems simpler. It passes the `floatStart` instance variable, which points to the array of `float` values, and the `count` instance variable, which holds the current number of elements.

Example 9.9     **Vectorized sums with MPWRealArray**

```
@import Accelerate;

-(float)vecsum
{
    float theSum=0;
    vDSP_sve ( floatStart, 1, &theSum, count );
    return theSum;
}
```

**Table 9.4**    **Array summation via Accelerate framework**

| Settings | Swift | Objective-C | Relative % |
|---|---|---|---|
| No optimization | 0.261 | 0.113 | 231 |
| -O / -Os | 0.132 | 0.099 | 133 |
| -Ounchecked / -O3 | 0.130 | 0.099 | 131 |

The results are shown in Table 9.4. This is an interesting table. All of the times are essentially the same, except for unoptimized Swift, which manages to be 2 times slower. The times are the same because we are calling an optimized routine with a lot of data (a million floating point numbers), so what we do outside that routine has very little impact.

In fact, what the code outside vDSP_sve does is of so little consequence that calling it from the Objective-Smalltalk script in Example 9.10 only brings the time to 0.160 s.

**Example 9.10**    **Vectorized sums from an Objective-Smalltalk script**

```
#!/usr/local/bin/stsh
#-<float>sum:<int>iterations
array := MPWRealArray start:1.0 end:1000000 step:1.0.
sum:=0.
1 to:iterations do:[ sum := sum + array vecsum ].
sum.
```

Why an interpreted script in "the world's slowest scripting language" is faster than unoptimized Swift is an interesting question. First, the Swift code is filling the array itself, element by element, whereas both the Objective-C code and the Smalltalk code are calling an optimized Objective-C routine to fill the array.

However, the summation code is called 1,000 times, whereas filling the array is done just once. However, the unoptimized Swift code is so incredibly slow that even running it 0.1% of the time (1 iteration vs. 1,000) causes a more than 100% performance regression.

While I have mentioned this before, I can't stress the importance of these relations enough. Performance differences of a factor of 1,000 are so far outside the normal bounds that they are no longer just quantitative, they become qualitative.

For example, a car may travel at 100 km/h with two passengers. If you slow it down by a factor of 1,000, it will travel 100 meters per hour. That's no longer a car; two people can easily carry a *sofa* 100 meters in an hour.

So why is Swift array processing so incredibly slow when not optimized? Figure 9.4 is the Instruments profile that shows us the reasons.

In short, the Swift code adds tremendous amounts of abstractions and indirection—so much that the profile simply doesn't appear to reflect the code from

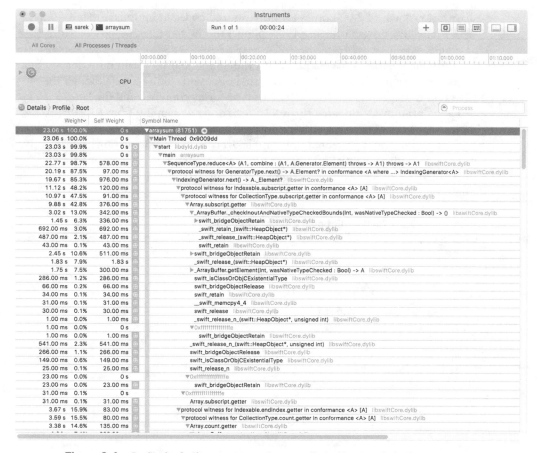

**Figure 9.4**    Profile for Swift array summation compiled without optimizations

Example 9.3 whatsoever, just like the car that's slowed down by a factor of 1,000 is more like a sofa than an automobile.

The code we are trying to run is being totally overwhelmed with compiler-inserted bookkeeping, both in terms of visible code and execution time. Just one instance of `swift_bridgeObjectRetain` takes several times the entire running time of our `MPWRealArray`-based code, and there are a number of these. And why are we retaining and releasing objects in the inner loop of this thing in the first place, when we are dealing purely with arrays of primitive types, and maybe a closure?

With this level of base performance, the claim that "Swift is designed for speed" is a bit hard to swallow: The abstractions that are used exact tremendous performance penalties and require an optimizer that is 100% perfect all the time in order to get rid of them. And I really mean 100%. As we saw with the vectorized code, when you have a slowdown of 2,000 times for unoptimized code, an optimizer that is "only" 99.9% effective instead of being 100% perfect means we still get a slowdown of 2 times!

With dictionaries, I tried a case that I thought would be a slam dunk for Swift: a dictionary mapping from `String` to `Int`, both Swift value types (although the `String` is backed by a hidden reference type for its contents) and the latter a machine primitive, compared to an `NSDictionary` mapping from `NSString` objects to `NSNumber` objects, both slow reference types.

The Swift code is presented in Example 9.11. It creates the dictionary from a fixed set of keys with sequential values for those keys. It then fetches the value for a particular key chosen from the original list of keys 10 million times and sums those values.

**Example 9.11    Testing dictionary access in Swift**

```swift
func getBench( n:Int, dict:[String:Int], key:String ) -> Int
{
  var sum = 0
  for _ in 0..<n {
    if let value = dict[key] {
      sum += value
    }
  }
  return sum
}

let which = Int(CommandLine.arguments[1])!
let keys = ["ABC", "DU", "ASDASD", "24323423423", "DUasdfasdf",
            "HZSasdfasdfdasdfasdf", "ASDasdfasdfdasdfasdfd",
            "ASDASasdfD", "asdff24323423423",
            "11111111111111111111222222222222222222", "1"]
let s = keys[which]
var dict = [String:Int]()
var i:Int
for i in 0..<keys.count {
  dict[keys[i]]=i
}
let sum = getBench( n:10_000_000, dict: dict, key:s )
print("sum: \(sum)")
```

The index of the key to use is passed on the command line. If none is provided, the program crashes due to the use of force-unwrapping for the parameter. As usual, the result is printed so the optimizer doesn't have an excuse to eliminate all of the code. Although it could in theory figure out that looping is not necessary, currently the benchmark still works.

The Objective-C version in Example 9.12 is a straight transliteration of the Swift code.

**Example 9.12    Testing dictionary access in Objective-C**

```
#import <Foundation/Foundation.h>

long getBench( int iterations, NSDictionary *dict , NSString *key )
{
  long sum = 0;
  for (int i=0;i<iterations;i++) {
    id value=dict[key];
    if ( value ) {
      sum += [value intValue];
    }
  }
  return sum;
}

int main( int argc, char *argv[] )
{
  int which=atoi(argv[1]);
  NSArray * keys=@[ @"ABC" ,   @"DU", @"ASDASD",
                    @"24323423423"  ,@"DUasdfasdf",
                    @"HZSasdfasdfdasdfasdf",
                    @"ASDasdfasdfdasdfasdfd" , @"ASDASasdfD",
                    @"asdff24323423423",
                    @"11111111111111112222222222222222",@"1" ];
  NSString *s=keys[which];
  NSMutableDictionary * dict=[NSMutableDictionary dictionary];
  for (int i=0;i<keys.count;i++) {
    dict[keys[i]]=@(i);
  }
  long sum = getBench( 10000000, dict,s );
  printf("sum: %ld\n",sum);
  return 0;
}
```

The results of running these two programs are presented in Table 9.5, and again, the results are surprising. Far from being faster due to value types, primitives, and specializable generics, the Swift code is consistently 80% to 250% slower than NSDictionary. (While still not great, these numbers for Swift 3.0 are significantly better than Swift 2.x, which was 4 to 6 times slower than Objective-C on the same test.)

**Table 9.5    Swift and Objective-C dictionary access times**

| Settings | Swift | Objective-C | Ratio |
|---|---|---|---|
| No optimization | 1.46 | 0.43 | 3.5 |
| -O | 0.75 | 0.41 | 1.8 |
| -Ounchecked | 0.73 | 0.40 | 1.8 |

Of course, we saw in Chapter 3 that `NSDictionary` is not exactly a speed demon, and a specialized Objective-C dictionary that maps strings to objects (`MPWSmallStringTable`) can easily be 3 times faster.

# Larger Examples

The examples in the previous section are obviously microbenchmarks that may or may not be indicative of real-world performance in larger projects. With the language being as young and still-in-flux as it is, the number of real-world projects with performance numbers is limited. At work, we've only had one Swift project so far, which we had to rewrite in Objective-C due to compatibility restrictions. For these reasons, I have to rely more on outside sources for larger examples of Swift projects that actually measured performance.

## nginx HTTP Parser

One such project was a port of the C HTTP parser included in the popular nginx HTTP server to Swift[2] by Helge Hess, another former Apple employee. Despite the fact that performance was not the main purpose of the port, I expressed curiosity as to how the performance of the Swift port compared to the original due to the fact that performance is nginx's main selling point.

Helge had done as straightforward and close to a 1:1 transliteration of the code as possible, though various features such as macros and `goto` statements could not be mapped directly. Our expectation was that performance would be similar.

Instead, it was 10 times slower.

Some fairly heavy-handed optimization using `@inline{_always}` and `UnsafeMutablePointer` instead of `Array` improved performance to "only" 3 times slower, with most of the gains due to inlining, and most of the problems (both original and remaining) due to ARC.

This was using Swift 2.x; the 3.0 Swift betas were significantly slower.

---

2. https://github.com/helje5/http-c-vs-swift

## Freddy JSON Parser

Another real-world example is the Big Nerd Ranch's *Freddy* JSON parser written in pure Swift.[3] Unlike most of the Swift JSON parsers out there, this one is not a wrapper around `NSJSONSerialization`, and the reason given is performance: switching on the `AnyType` returned to Swift by `NSJSONSerialization` apparently incurs a performance overhead of 25 times, 6.29 s vs. just 0.25 s for the basic parse on a 16-MB sample data set that they provide.

Freddy improves that total time to 2.08 s for the complete JSON to Swift structs conversion, with 0.75 s of that being the basic parse. That's a nice overall improvement, but the basic parse got 3 times slower than `NSJSONSerialization`, and the overall parse + conversion time for `NSJSONSerialization` and Objective-C objects was just 0.58 s, so almost 4 times faster than the complete conversion to Swift structs.

And once again, `NSJSONSerialization`, though one of the faster Apple-provided serialization mechanisms (see the "Serialization Summary" section in Chapter 12), is several times slower than methods such as MAX from Chapter 4 that avoid the "generic intermediate representation" pitfall (see the discussion in the "Pitfall: Generic (Intermediate) Representations" section of Chapter 3).

## Image Processing

David Owens II has been documenting his attempts at getting image processing code working with reasonable performance in Swift over the last couple of years.[4] The basic idea is to have a `Pixel` struct with `red`, `green`, `blue`, and `alpha` components and do some pixel processing on an image 960×540 pixels in size.

For C, times ranged from 30 ms per operation for an unoptimized build to 2.3 ms with the setting `-Ofast`. For Swift, the story was more complex. Keeping the `Pixel` abstraction and organizing those Pixels in `Array` collections, times ranged from 2,400 ms for unoptimized builds to 18 ms for optimized (`-O`). Getting better performance required (1) dropping the `Pixel` structure in favor of just modeling the pixels as unsigned integers, (2) dropping the `Array` abstraction in favor of `UnsafeMutablePointer` using the `withUnsafeMutablePointer` construct, (3) turning off all compiler checks with `-Ounchecked`, and finally (4) adding vector instructions (SIMD).

With *all* of these in place, Swift managed a time of 3.04 ms, only a respectable 30% slower than C. (For some reason, explicitly using SIMD instructions made this particular C code slower, so maybe the code auto-vectorized well or there is some

---

3. https://github.com/bignerdranch/Freddy/wiki/JSONParser
4. https://github.com/owensd/swift-perf

further improvement to be had on the C side.) Note that all of this had to be done just so; for example, just using `UnsafeMutablePointer` without the `withUnsafeMutablePointer` was 2 times slower. Keeping the `struct Pixel` abstraction in the Swift code always had a penalty of at least 6 times for times around 18 ms.

The irony here is that Swift is supposed to allow us to write more domain-centric, less machine-specific code and have the compiler cut through those abstractions, but in reality the opposite was the case. With Swift, not only did the `Array` abstraction have to be ditched for what are basically C pointers, even the `Pixel` abstraction with which C managed quite well had to be abandoned in favor of modeling the pixels as integers.

Of course, it is always possible to leave the heavy lifting to Objective-C code and bridge to it from Swift.

## Observations

Finally, the benchmark game[5] shows Swift programs benchmarking consistently 5 to 30 times slower than equivalent C programs. Just to be certain that these results were not outliers, I cross-checked by comparing Swift with Java. Here, Swift was typically 5 times slower than Java, with the range being 20% to 8 times slower.

Although any one of these results is easy to dismiss as an outlier, the pattern is really too consistent for that: 3 to 10 times slower with "reasonable" code. Heroic manual optimizations and a bit of luck are required to take that to somewhere between 3 times slower and almost parity, depending on the type of code in question. With Swift evolving as quickly as it does, all of these specific timings will probably be obsolete by the time this book is in print, but again the overall pattern seems hard to break.

Conversely, when I see claims of Swift beating C/Objective-C in performance, the claims are typically not backed with data, instead justified either not at all or with "well, it should, because, er, *reasons.*" In the rare cases that there is data, the data is at best dubious and at worst outright false, with non-robust benchmarks being optimized away, operations on primitive integers compared to operations on objects, or non-optimized but easily optimizable C code compared to highly optimized Swift code.

The one case I have seen that is somewhat legitimate is that of sorting integers, for the same reasons that we saw for summation: the Swift `Array.sort()` methods are generic on the type to be sorted, and can specialize for that type at compile time rather than having to do it at runtime using either function pointers for `qsort()` or message sends for `NSArray` sorting. However, the effect was small, maxing out at around 20% faster for an array of integers, and could easily be overcome by replacing these generic routines with a specific one for integers.

---

5. http://benchmarksgame.alioth.debian.org/u64q/swift.html

# Compile Times

Swift leans on the compiler quite heavily, much more so than Objective-C, and more similar to C++, which also has compile times typically far longer than C or Objective-C. My experience is that there is a base overhead of about 2 times relative to C/Objective-C, with at least 4 times when optimizing. This is reflected in the compile times of the integer summing benchmark we looked at earlier, which are shown in Table 9.6.

As with many other aspects of performance, C and Objective-C compilers are not the benchmark for fast compilation speeds. The legacy of file-inclusion-based modularity with header files poses a huge challenge for any C-based language, even though precompiled headers or modules help a lot. Languages such as Go that were specifically designed to avoid that type of problem can be compiled much more quickly, and development systems like Smalltalk compile individual methods instantaneously.

As with other aspects of Swift performance, it is therefore somewhat surprising that performance levels of the compilation process don't even meet, let alone exceed, the low bar set by C and Objective-C. As soon as you start going into more advanced language features such as sophisticated optimizations, generics, or type inference, performance is impacted further.

## Type Inference

Type inference is a great feature for reducing clutter and developer overhead; it allows us to write something like let a = [ "hello" ] and let the compiler figure out that a is an array of strings. However, like most good things, there is a cost. First, it can yield surprising results, especially because in Swift both sides can be indefinite (left-hand side completely undefined, right-hand side polymorphic). In these cases, figuring out the most appropriate type is hard, both intrinsically and computationally.

At my university, we were introduced to type inference with a functional language called Miranda. As long as it could figure out the types, it was amazing. But when it failed, the error messages were long and completely inscrutable.

Another issue is that the type that is inferred can be surprising. The inferencer is looking for the most specific type that is compatible with the information presented, otherwise it could call everything AnyType and be done with it.

**Table 9.6    Swift and C compile times for integer summing benchmarks**

| Settings | Swift | Objective-C | Ratio |
|---|---|---|---|
| No optimization | 0.079 | 0.044 | 1.80 |
| -O | 0.203 | 0.050 | 4.06 |
| -Ounchecked | 0.223 | 0.050 | 4.46 |

In the early betas, Swift's type inferencer was very insistent about inferring that most specific type, so `var a = 255` would not infer the type `Int`, but the type `UInt8` for a, which was probably not what you expected—especially since it would trap if you later incremented a. Nowadays, this seems to be among a whole range of special-case exemptions to the "most specific applicable" rule in the compiler.

Performance is also a problem, as type inference is inherently expensive and many innocuous-looking cases can run into exponential running times. For example, the simple declaration in Example 9.13 was exponential for *n* in Swift 2.x, reaching a time of half an *hour* for $n = 20$.

**Example 9.13    Exponential collection literals**

```
let a = [  "level1": [  [ 1 ],  [ 2 ],  ... ,  [ n ]]
```

This is not a bug per se, but it is indicative of the inherent complexity of type-inference algorithms. For example, Scala's creator Martin Odersky explains that Scala's notoriously slow compile times are largely due to type inference.

This is also not a new problem. I remember reading about early attempts to improve the performance of the Self dynamic prototype-based language using compile-time type inferencing. The running times were so bad, in the minutes for small expressions, that the Self team had to turn to a different approach. Instead of figuring out the types at compile time, they just logged the types at runtime, which in fact they were already doing in their *polymorphic inline caches*. Using that type information gathered at runtime they then optimized the code, a technique that led in a straight line to the advanced JITs of today such as Java's HotSpot.

Fortunately, it is often possible to special-case specific egregiously bad cases, and this particular problem was "fixed" in Swift 3: compile times for that particular construct are now "only" quadratic with *n*, so you need to have $n = 200$ to reach half a minute of compile time.

A similar issue that has not been fixed as of this writing is shown in Example 9.14. This will terminate with a compiler error about expressions that are too complex to be solved after around 3 s.

**Example 9.14    Expression too complex to be solved in reasonable time**

```
let a = String(1) + String(2) + String(3) + String(4)
```

In fact, the problem seems to be more general and not dependent on the type inference having to infer a type for the variable or on `String` involvement. In Example 9.15, all the types seem to be spelled out, yet the result is the same compiler error, after around 5 s.

**Example 9.15    Expression still too complex to be solved in reasonable time**

```
let a:[Int] = [1] + [2] + [3] + [4] + [5] + [6]
```

Reducing the number of components to 5 lets the expression compile in 2.7 s. Reducing it to 4 components reduces the compile time to 0.26 s.

## Generics Specialization

In the "Observations" section of this chapter, we saw that one of the Swift features that can actually improve performance beyond what is easily achievable in C is generic specialization (taken from C++ template instantiation). Instead of dispatching to specialized routines at runtime via messaging or function pointers, the parameterized routines are specialized at compile time, with a completely new function generated that contains no external calls or message sends. Example 9.16 illustrates the problem.

**Example 9.16    Specializing array sort**

```
let a           = [54, 32, 1, 2, 4, 5]
let b:[Float]   = [54, 32, 1, 2, 4, 5, 23]
let c:[Double]  = [74, 32 ,1 ,2 ,4, 5, 23]
let d:[String]  = ["Hello", "World"]
let e           = [[ "hello": 1 ], [ "world": 2]]

print(a.sorted())
print(b.sorted())
print(c.sorted())
print(d.sorted())
print(e.sorted( by: { ( a,b ) -> Bool in  return true }))
```

We first create arrays with five different kinds of content: integers, floats, doubles, strings, and dictionaries. Then we sort each of those arrays. With optimizations enabled, this causes the Swift compiler to generate a specific version of the generic sort() function specialized to each of the specific array types. Although Apple isn't telling, I am assuming that something along these lines, though certainly more sophisticated, was the "Complex Object Sort" benchmark touted at WWDC 2014.

The effect on compile times can be seen in Figure 9.5, with the x-axis showing the number of specializations performed. (I commented out print(x.sorted()) lines to get the right number of specializations.)

Whereas both Objective-C (regardless of optimization) and unoptimized Swift show constant compile times no matter how many different types of arrays are defined and used, optimized Swift compile times are linear with the number of different Array sort() methods that have to be generated, with the cost being around 250 ms per specialization on my machine. For reference, the Objective-C NSArray code is shown in Example 9.17.

**Example 9.17    NSArray sort**

```
@import Foundation;

int main()
```

```
{
  NSArray* a=@[ @(54) , @(32) ,@(1) ,@(2) ,@(4) , @(5) ];
  NSArray* b=@[ @(54.0) , @(32),@(1) ,@(2) ,@(4) , @(5), @(23) ];
  NSArray* c=@[ @(74.0) , @(32),@(1) ,@(2) ,@(4) , @(5), @(23) ];
  NSArray *d=@[ @"Hello", @"World" ];
  NSArray *e=@[ @{ @"hello": @(1) } , @{ @"world": @(2)} ];

  NSLog(@"a: %@",[a sortedArrayUsingSelector:@selector(compare:)]);
  NSLog(@"b: %@",[b sortedArrayUsingSelector:@selector(compare:)]);
  NSLog(@"c: %@",[c sortedArrayUsingSelector:@selector(compare:)]);
  NSLog(@"d: %@",[d sortedArrayUsingSelector:@selector(compare:)]);
  NSLog(@"e: %@",[e sortedArrayUsingSelector:@selector(compare:)]);
}
```

## Whole-Module Optimization

When you think about it, the generics specialization mechanism discussed in the previous section is quite a feat. It reaches across compilation units to extract a definition from a previously compiled file and then instantiate the definition in the current compilation unit, apply arguments, and compile the result.

In the C/Objective-C/C++ world, this simply isn't possible. The only way to access definitions from another file is to physically include the source text of those definitions into the currently compiling unit using an include. That included file can contain either macro definitions, inline function definitions, or C++ templates.

*Whole-module optimization* takes this concept a step further by completely eliminating the idea of separate compilation. Instead, all of the program files are compiled together at once, with all definitions and uses visible to the compiler.

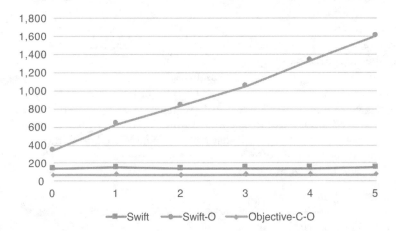

**Figure 9.5**    Compile times for specialized generic sort routines in milliseconds

Of course, this means that compile times, in particular recompile times after making small changes to one or a few sources files, are now dependent on the total size of the project rather than the size of an individual file. Considering that compile times are not all that great to begin with, that could lead to real problems down the road for larger projects.

On the other hand, considering the whole program at once can actually speed up compile times when the whole module is being recompiled anyway. One reason for this is specialization: if multiple files contain a specific specialization (for example, sorting integer arrays), then a whole-module compilation only has to create the specialized version once, instead of once for every file. The trade-offs are non-obvious.

### Controlling Compile Times

You can check for slow compile times using the compiler option `-Xfrontend -debug-time-function-bodies`. This should output the time the compiler needed for each function (or method) compiled. I tried out this feature by placing all of Example 9.16 into a function and leaving only a call to that function at the top level. The compiler claimed that this function, the only one in the file, took only 17.6 ms to compile, despite the entire compilation taking 1.8 s, with the rest (the majority) of the time simply not accounted for.

The reason for this discrepancy seems to be that the per-function times are taken before the Swift Intermediate Language (SIL) optimization passes are run. Possibly these are run for the whole compilation unit without attribution to a specific function. I saw the bulk of this time spent between the `-emit-silgen` and `-emit-sib` phases.

In summary, I find Swift compile times to be generally unpredictable because the compiler is not only capricious but the holes it can fall into almost arbitrarily deep, with quadratics or exponentials lurking behind many innocuous-looking constructs. In general, generic specialization will probably always be expensive, as will type inference, particularly with literals. Optionals also appear to be expensive because the type-checking path splits into two at each optional.

While some specific problems will almost certainly be addressed, the problem with compile times is not an accident of a young language implementation, but a necessary consequence of design decisions that were made.

# Optimizer-Oriented Programming

One reason that Swift is currently slow is almost certainly that it is a young implementation of a young language. Things have improved and are likely to improve further. However, the rate of improvement appears to have already slowed, and we are still very far away from reaching parity with Objective-C, never mind going beyond.

The other, and in my estimation the primary reason is that Swift's model is what I call *optimizer-oriented programming*, a style that has basic constructs that are very distant from any machine model and rely almost exclusively on the optimizer to figure out the relationship between these abstractions and efficient machine implementations. Importantly, the resulting code is not really usable without optimization (remember car vs. sofa).

We already saw an example of this approach in the "Optimizing ARC" section of Chapter 7 when discussing the performance of Objective-C ARC. The results of the optimizer-centric approach to performance are at best mixed: yes, the optimizer can remove most of the performance penalty most of the time, but the initial penalty is so large and so unpredictable that even a small rest has a significant performance impact.

Despite the mixed results, Swift doubles down on this approach. ARC is no longer optional and abstractions have been introduced that, as we saw, can have a performance penalty of three orders of magnitude or more!

That's just the tip of the iceberg, though. There are actually optimization passes that run even with -Onone. For example, all local variables are allocated on the heap by the Swift compiler, as explained by Chris Lattner and Joe Groff at LLVM Meetup 2015 (Figure 9.6).

An additional optimization pass promotes variables that aren't captured by closures in specific ways to the stack (and then later optimization passes can promote them to registers).

This is by all means a very clever approach to the problem of local variables with nonlocal lifetimes. Instead of making stack allocation the base mechanism and then

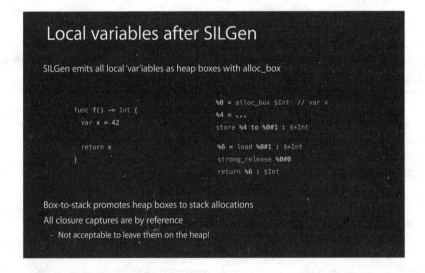

**Figure 9.6**   Local variables on heap

having to deal with potentially incorrect code (crashes) when lifetime requirements for stack variables are not met (and/or having to introduce different mechanisms for local variables with nonlocal lifetimes), we instead treat all variables as having the more expensive nonlocal (heap) lifetimes and then try to figure out which can be optimized by putting them on the stack because we can prove that their lifetimes are more constrained.

This level of reliance on the optimizer to create code of reasonable (i.e., not ludicrously awful) quality is something new I haven't seen before, as it changes the role of compiler optimizations from "nice to have" to "must have."

However, this dramatic change in the importance of the optimizer has not led to a similar change in the level of control over the optimizer or its results: all we can say is that we would like optimizations and hope for the best. We have no way of forcing certain optimizations to be performed and no way of checking whether they have been performed.

# A Sufficiently Smart Compiler

In essence, the Swift compiler team is claiming to be building the *sufficiently smart compiler* (SSC), a compiler that can see perfectly through arbitrary layers of abstraction in order to find optimal implementations for those abstractions. The Swift marketing team, of course, is claiming that they have already succeeded.

The problem with the SSC is that it is a legend, a myth that has been floating around in computer science circles for many decades, although the name was coined around 2003 or 2004 on the C2 wiki. No such compilers exist, and people have been trying (and claiming success!) for a long time.

Although optimizers can be pretty smart, they aren't nearly as smart as the SSC would like or need them to be, and progress in optimization technology is also on the slow side. Whereas *Moore's Law* has given us a doubling of hardware performance every 18 months, *Proebsting's Law* states that optimization technology gives us a doubling of performance every 18 *years*. More recent research has shown that, if anything, Proebsting erred on the side of optimism; actual progress has been somewhat slower.

Swift actually manages to break Proebsting's Law. The relative performance difference of 1,000 times that is achieved by the optimizer relative to unoptimized code is equivalent to roughly 180 years of progress according to Proebsting's Law.

Alas, Swift has made this progress in the wrong direction, as shown in Figure 9.7. Instead of pushing optimized performance forward, it has further pessimized unoptimized performance.

This is not a coincidence or an isolated case; in fact, a 2015 study[6] by Anton Ertl of the Technical University Vienna showed that the current trend by compiler writers

---

6. A.M. Ertl. "What every compiler writer should know about programmers or 'Optimization' based on undefined behaviour hurts performance," *Proceedings Kolloquium Programmiersprachen* (2015), Technical University of Wien.

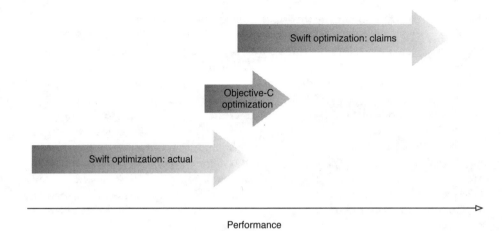

**Figure 9.7**   Range of optimization

to exploit undefined behavior in the C standards for optimization actually hurts performance rather than helping it. The modifications required to currently working efficient code to make it conform to these compilers' changed ideas of correctness causes a larger regression in performance than the gains from the additional optimizations that are enabled.

Swift's design and implementation are a further step in this direction than current C compilers, and so the results are similar, but more extreme. Yes, many of the features help the *optimizer* produce greater relative optimizations, but they don't necessarily help programmers write faster programs. In many cases they actually hurt much more than they help. If you look at the examples, you will see that the best way to get Swift to perform is to manually remove levels of abstraction, sometimes more of them than in an equivalent C program.

Furthermore, the study showed that most modern C compilers did not implement a set of straightforward semantics–preserving source-level optimizations from a 33-year-old optimization example by Jon Bentley. To put it more bluntly, no optimizing compiler will change a bubble sort to a merge sort or a quick sort. In fact, it probably shouldn't do that, but in order to be sufficiently smart it would have to be able to operate at that level, if not do that specific transformation.

So compilers aren't "sufficiently smart" by a wide margin; they leave a lot of straightforward optimizations on the table. Punching through deep layers of abstraction to reach an optimal machine representation can and does work, but so far it has only ever been shown to work for very specific and limited cases.

What's worse, the biggest problem with SSCs is not that they don't work—the real problems actually materialize when such a compiler *does* work as advertised, because performance becomes much, much less predictable and controllable than it is today: you write your code and hope that the optimizer will figure it out.

When the optimizer can't figure it out, you are stuck. This is especially bad when the optimizer did figure it out yesterday and can no longer figure it out today, for example, because you made a minor change in your code base that you don't think of as significant but the compiler does, or because the compiler or a library changed. As there are no diagnostics, good luck trying to figure it out!

## The Death of Optimizing Compilers

The type of performance model underlying the quest for the SSC was useful when computers were generally slower and we just wanted them to be a bit faster (or a lot faster—but that rarely worked out, see Proebsting's Law).

Today, computers are generally fast, and therefore large parts of most programs are not performance critical. In fact, what started out as the Pareto rule for performance-critical code (20% of the code accounts for 80% of the performance and vice versa) had already moved to a 97:3 rule in 1974 when Knuth made his famous remarks about small efficiencies, and nowadays it is even more skewed.

The overwhelming majority of code in most programs, and especially in interactive programs, is not just not hot, it is ice cold. Therefore, its performance is largely irrelevant. (At least unless you have factors of a thousand and more involved: even code that is used 1% of the time becomes a significant factor if it runs 1,000 times slower!)

I think the Cocoa community provides ample evidence that this is true. Just look at our own surprise at the ARC code in the "Optimizing ARC" section of Chapter 7: the code in non-optimized debug builds was over an order of magnitude slower than release, yet we didn't notice. I am pretty sure that the same goes for most Swift code used in iOS or Mac development. Yes, it is being compiled in debug mode (no optimization), and yes, it is an order of magnitude or more slower than release mode (optimized), but no, nobody notices. This also explains Swift's reputation for speed that is strongly contradicted by just about every bit of empirical data I could find.

As a consequence, one might think that *performance* is becoming increasingly irrelevant, but that turns out to be an incorrect conclusion. Performance is actually getting *more* important, not less. As computers become faster, users are using them to process more data, often dramatically more. With more data, the innermost loops of our programs are becoming significantly *more* performance relevant, not less, even as the rest of the program becomes less and less relevant.

At the same, demands on performance are increasing. Initially, computer jobs were submitted to a data center and could take a day or two to be run. With interactive terminals, response times in the seconds became the norm, and later those expectations rose to "immediate," meaning less than 100 ms. Nowadays, significant parts of our computations have to be able to run at animation speeds, 60 frames per second or 16.66 ms per frame, with stuttering not permitted. So, predictability and worst-case performance are essential.

In his 2015 talk "The death of optimizing compilers,"[7] `qmail` author and security researcher Daniel Bernstein argued that these developments meant that whereas performance is still as important as ever, optimizing compilers are becoming increasingly irrelevant because there is very little of use that they can contribute.

Optimizing compilers are being squeezed from both ends, as seen in Figure 9.8. On one hand, ever larger parts of our programs don't need to be optimized; on the other hand, the performance-critical parts of our programs that are so important are usually also so small that optimizing compilers aren't sufficient, therefore this code needs to be hand-optimized.

We saw this effect firsthand in the "Collections" section of this chapter: the best solution was to use one of the hand-optimized `vDSP` routines, which even when used from a scripting language was several times faster than Swift's Heldenoptimizer at its best.

Erlang creator Joe Armstrong goes one step further, saying that our inner loops are moving into hardware, and there is also ample evidence of this trend: iPhones have dedicated hardware decoders for JPEG images, x264 encoded movies and most widely used audio formats, not to mention the GPU for graphics acceleration.

No optimizing compiler is going to help you integrate these hardware resources and their trade-offs (we look at hardware/software trade-offs for image decoding in the "Beautiful Weather App" section of Chapter 17), or optimize moving larger amounts of data from the OS to those hardware resources, or rearrange code so your animation doesn't stutter.

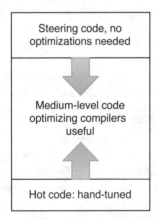 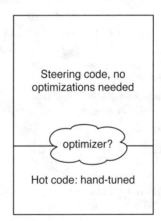

**Figure 9.8**    Optimization trends

---

7. Daniel Bernstein. "The death of optimizing compilers," European Joint Conferences on Theory and Practice of Software (2015), Queen Mary University of London.

Even worse, optimizing compilers make performance less predictable, and Swift in particular has appalling worst-case performance, which is much more important these days than best-case or even average performance.

## Practical Advice

In practical terms, the only reliable option you have for performance-intensive code is to code it in C/Objective-C and call that from Swift. We've already seen how to write fast code in Objective-C in the previous chapters, so I won't rehash that information. Information on interfacing Swift and Objective-C can be found in the Swift book[8] and Apple's developer documentation.

IBM's *Kitura* Swift Web framework uses this approach, with the HTTP parser itself taken from *node.js* and written in C, and the higher-level routines in Swift, with very good performance results. The mix is around 15% C code and 85% Swift code. In the end, most of Cocoa also uses that approach, and in this chapter we saw it work well with calling the vDSP function.

Although Kitura and vDSP use pure C, as that is what the underlying libraries provide, the most straightforward way to interact with your performance-sensitive code is to place it in an Objective-C class and use message sending to interact with it from Swift.

This way, you can heed Apple's Swift modeling advice and make the most of your Swift code classes. On the other hand, you can ignore Apple's contradictory Swift performance advice to make everything structs and statically dispatch where possible, because if you need performance Swift won't get you there.

## Alternatives

I have to admit that I was more than puzzled by Apple's Swift announcement, especially from a performance perspective. As you can read here, Objective-C has essentially all the mechanisms in place for producing great high-performance code, and for exploiting the hybrid nature of performance today.

I therefore would have expected a language that banks these capabilities and then improves on them. Some easy changes that would make the mechanics of optimizing Objective-C code simpler include the following.

1. Compiler assistance for IMP caching. Not automation, but a simple way of indicating to the compiler that you would like IMP caching to take place, by treating a receiver as constant. The compiler can then create the code to obtain and cache the IMP, and if useful, hoist that code out of loops as a strength-reduction optimization.

---

8. Currently in the chapter called "Using Swift with Cocoa and Objective-C," *The Swift Programming Language (Swift 3)* (Apple Inc. iBooks, 2014).

Caching could be extended to an entire protocol for instance variables, so the compiler allocates IMP pointers for the protocol and automatically updates them when the object instance variable changes.

Extensions of this approach would be "always-static" dispatch and/or inlining, with the important distinction being that these features need to be controlled by the call site, not the definition, though the definition might have to indicate whether static dispatch and inlining are *allowed*.

2.  Reenable stack allocation for Objective-C objects. This was a feature of the Stepstone compilers, and while integrating stack allocation with reference-counting semantics is challenging, it seems quite doable.

3.  Closely related to stack allocation is bulk allocation of objects for homogenous, packed collections.

None of the mechanisms mentioned present anything that hasn't been done before, but having slightly better compiler support would help.

Another approach would have been to use existing languages that offer a systems-programming approach to replace the C part of Objective-C, for example, D or Rust. Maybe Objective-D or Objective-Rust? Adding the Objective part to other languages was always part of the plan.

In fact, Apple acknowledges that there are deficiencies in Swift's memory model in terms of performance and predictability, and has specifically called out to Rust for inspiration:

> Memory ownership model: Adding an (opt-in) Cyclone/Rust inspired memory ownership model to Swift is highly desired by systems programmers and folks who want predictable and deterministic performance (for example, in real time audio processing code).
>
> "Looking back on Swift 3 and ahead to Swift 4,"<br>Swift Evolution Mailing List[9]

A more ambitious approach would be to take the "Objective-C without the C" idea seriously: Instead of adding Smalltalk-style messaging to C, use Smalltalk as the base language and add one of the optional type systems available for Smalltalk (Strongtalk, Typed Smalltalk, SmallType, etc.).

Cocoa has enough support for tagged pointers and other optimizations of the object system such as a super-fast `objc_msgSend()` implementation that pure objects are perfectly viable for the steering part of our programs, the 99% or more that aren't particularly performance sensitive.

Example 9.18 shows how a scripting-like flavor is achieved by simply leaving out type annotations.

---

9.  C. Lattner. 2016. "Looking back on Swift 3 and ahead to Swift 4." July 29. Accessed at https://lists.swift.org/pipermail/swift-evolution/Week-of-Mon-20160725/025676.html.

**Example 9.18     Dynamically typed object addition in Objective-Smalltalk**

```
| a |
a := 3 + 4.
```

In this case, the variable `a` is an object, the declaration being comparable to `id a` in Objective-C and the + "operator" being a binary message send dispatched via `objc_msgSend()`. As the number literals are used in an object context and sufficiently small to fit, they are generated directly as tagged object pointers taking a single cycle each (see Example 3.2).

Example 9.19 shows how optional typing can be added. It is equivalent to the Objective-C code `NSNumber *a`.

**Example 9.19     Statically typed object addition in Objective-Smalltalk**

```
| <Number> a |
a := 3 + 4.
```

Just as in Objective-C, the actual code generated for the addition could be identical to the case of `id` objects, the static declaration only being for machine-checked documentation.

Alternately, the compiler could emit special case instructions for adding two tagged numbers similar to the code in Example 3.2, with a fallback to messaging if the objects in question are not tagged integers. This small change would make it feasible to use number objects in virtually all use-cases, and with real objects you can build a real numeric tower so that small integers overflow gracefully into a multiword representation that never loses accuracy.

Example 9.20 dramatically changes the code that is generated, despite the minor syntactic change. This time the type is a C primitive type, and therefore the code that is generated is the same for the Objective-C primitives.

**Example 9.20     Primitive addition in Objective-Smalltalk**

```
| <int> b |
b := 3 + 4.
```

This would keep the familiar Objective-C keyword syntax used throughout the entire Mac OS X software stack, without the troubles of integrating two language syntaxes as in Objective-C and without the integration difficulties Swift has had and continues to have with keywords. Somewhat surprisingly (or not, if you've read the rest of this chapter), even a bytecode interpreter for the pure object parts would have performance superior to unoptimized Swift.

Bytecode is typically much more compact than machine code, meaning less memory pressure, as long as you don't try to JIT-compile. Performance-sensitive parts can optionally be compiled to machine code, and with the right type-annotations directly to C-like machine code.

A huge benefit of such an approach would be instantaneous compile times, as code can be compiled a method at a time without interference and the Smalltalk-to-bytecode compilation step is very simple and fast. (The fact that Swift is usable at all in playgrounds is a testament to the power of modern machines; it is hard to conceive of a language less well-suited to the task.)

The *Objective-Smalltalk*[10] project I have mentioned occasionally has exactly these optimizations in mind, but it is currently exclusively focused on expanding expressiveness, not the optimization aspects.

## Summary

Early editions of Aaron Hillegass's seminal book *Cocoa Programming for Mac OS X* included a chapter on the Cocoa-Java bridge. It consisted of a single sentence that basically read, "Don't use it." As you can probably tell, that is the chapter I would have wanted to write on Swift performance. Due to the success of Apple's marketing campaign regarding Swift's performance, that sentence would not have elicited the same knowing chuckle as Aaron's chapter-sentence did, but I hope to have shown why I think it is equally justified.

Swift is not only extremely slow to compile but also slow to execute and, worst of all for modern performance, quite unpredictable and hard to control. Don't use it for performance-intensive code. In fact, it can be so incredibly slow that even using it for code that appears to be noncritical can suddenly have a noticeable performance impact.

Instead, code your performance-sensitive code in Objective-C using the techniques discussed here, and use that code from Swift. It's what Apple does, and it's what IBM does.

If you have no choice, there is not all that much advice I can give; you are mostly in the hands of the compiler and particularly the optimizer. Apart from that, you will probably have to do all the premature optimization recommended by Apple, such as using structs instead of classes throughout (but careful about large structures!), aiming for static dispatch where possible, and leaving any heavy lifting to Objective-C if you can.

---

10. http://objective.st

# I/O: Principles

When Apple introduced the PowerMac G4, it was billed it as the world's first desktop supercomputer. Ken Bachter once quipped that "a supercomputer is a device for turning compute-bound problems into I/O-bound problems." In a sense, all computers are supercomputers now, with today's iPhones vastly outpacing a PowerMac G4, and with compute performance vastly outpacing I/O performance. In addition, the difference between access times (latency) and transfer speeds (bandwidth) that we saw with memory access is even more pronounced with I/O devices. Whereas the difference between latency and throughput is around 1:100 with memory, it is 1:100,000 and more with I/O devices.

## Hardware

The fundamental performance characteristics of different types of I/O hardware are both significant and not something that can be abstracted away, unlike different access mechanisms, which are hidden behind uniform APIs. Storage tends to be provided either by rotating magnetic disk drives or solid-state flash disks, whereas connectivity is provided by different types of networks, from high-speed switched Ethernet to packet switched radio.

### Disk Drives

Although *solid-state disks* (SSD) are becoming increasingly popular, rotating media still has a large role in providing persistent storage for computer systems. A schematic of a disk is shown in Figure 10.1: a round magnetic platter is divided into concentric circles called *tracks*, which are in turn divided into *sectors*.

A disk head is positioned over a particular track in order to read or write the data on that track. Transfer speed is a simple function of the rotational speed of the disk and the density of the recorded information, so in order to speed up a disk's transfer speed, you either need to spin it faster or increase the recording density so that more information gets written or read during a revolution.

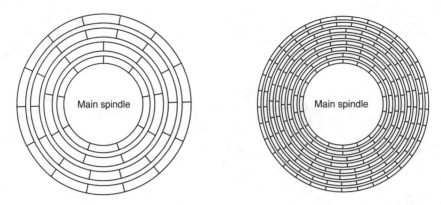

**Figure 10.1**   Schematic disk with tracks and sectors, original (left) and with density doubled (right)

The first microcomputer hard disks spun at 3,600 revolutions per minute (rpm) and had fixed-size sectors that provided a transfer speed of 5 MBit/s (625 KByte/s). Today's disk drives don't spin much faster, with speeds from 4,200 to at most 7,200 rpm for laptop and desktop drives and up to 15,000 rpm for server-class drives where power consumption, heat, and noise are less of an issue. Table 10.1 relates rotational speed to the time it takes to read a track.

The other factor controlling transfer speed is density, and this has gone up significantly as ever more clever ways of encoding the bits on the magnetic media have been found: putting tracks closer together with servo motors homing in on the exact track, recording bits vertically into the medium, getting more sensitive heads, heating the platter right before a head, and so on. However, due to the fact that the disk is a 2D platter, but the read/write operations are of a linear track, density increases always produce a linear increase in transfer speed but a quadratic increase in storage capacity.

Increases in transfer speeds of hard disks therefore always lag behind increases in storage capacity, due to simple math. Considering the seeming inexorable fact that the amount of data stored tends to increase with available storage capacity, this means that disks, while getting nominally slightly faster, in fact are growing increasingly

**Table 10.1    Rotational speed**

| Rotational Speed (rpm) | Time to Read a Track (µs) |
|:---:|:---:|
| 3,600 | 278 |
| 4,200 | 238 |
| 5,400 | 185 |
| 7,200 | 138 |
| 15,000 | 66.7 |

slower relative to the work we are asking them to do, and also ever slower relative to the computers they are hooked up to.

The Apple II's ProDrive had a transfer speed of 5 MBit/s, which was actually *faster* than the Apple's 6502 processor could handle at a 1-MHz clock speed and several clocks per instruction. It could transfer its 5-MByte capacity in around 10 s, not counting seeks. Today's hard drives transfer around 100 MByte/s, so around 10 ns per byte. In those 10 ns, our laptop CPU can execute well over 30 instructions, if it isn't blocked on memory. The contents of a typical consumer drive with 1-terabyte capacity would take 10,000 s, or almost 3 hours to transfer.

If that weren't enough bad news, access times, while also getting slightly faster over time, are getting faster at an even slower rate than transfer speeds. Access speeds are determined by the ability to quickly move and then stop a mass (the seeking disk head) and rotational delays. Both are largely questions of physics; those physics haven't changed and likely aren't going to change, with engineering advances in moving and stopping these masses coming much more slowly. In addition, moving masses quickly is associated with noise, so demand for quieter disk drives has actually led to decreases in seek performance.

The ever-increasing spread between transfer speed and seek performance has led to the phrase "Disk is the new tape."

## Solid-State Disks

SSDs lift many of the physically induced limitations of rotating disks, due to the fact that they have no moving parts. Especially the initial access times ("seek") are much improved, but as we saw in the last chapter, they still are slow compared to main memory. There are also physical limitations, for example, increases in capacity such as multilevel cells have as their trade-off not just decreased reliability, but also slower read and write speeds.

Writing in general is problematic, as an entire section of flash has to be bulk-erased (which takes some time) before any information can be written. Batching becomes even more important than on hard drives because lots of small writes will not only be slow, but they will also wear out the cells ahead of time.

So while SSDs represent an improvement, and are the easiest way to improve things like application start-up performance or server-side databases (especially if read-mostly), they are not a panacea. In fact, a 2012 study[1] of smartphone Web-browser performance found that it was not limited by processor speeds or even slow cellular networks, but instead by the combination of SQLite and slow flash memory speeds!

---

1. H. Kim, N. Agrawal, and C. Ungureanu. "Revisiting Storage for Smartphones," *10th USENIX Conference on File and Storage Technologies* (2012). https://www.usenix.org/conference/fast12/revisiting-storage-smartphones-0.

## Network

Physics also plays a large factor in network I/O, largely in the form of the speed of light, which determines the minimum time for a round-trip. This speed is not expected to change anytime soon, and we are already close enough to those limits that we can't expect much change. In addition, network protocols such as TCP require several round-trips to negotiate a connection.

So while we are able to increase bandwidth, with Ethernet having gone from 10 MBit/s to 10 GBit/s, latencies are going to remain constant. Additionally, we now have cellular networks to deal with, with much reduced bandwidth and also high latencies, sometimes in the multisecond range.

# Operating System

The operating system always plays an important role in allocating the resources that programs wish to use. However, whereas in the case of CPU and memory, the OS is involved in parceling out some resource and then lets the program go about its business. With I/O, every access is mediated via the OS. So although fundamental hardware capabilities are, well, fundamental, the OS plays a much larger role.

One of the functions of the OS is to provide a uniform interface for diverse hardware. For example, it simply doesn't matter to the application program whether a "disk" is an actual rotating magnetic platter, several platters stacked on top of each other, an RAID array of such devices, or solid-state flash memory—apart from the performance characteristics, that is. In addition to providing a uniform interface, the OS tries to improve I/O performance, primarily by caching, buffering, and batching I/O requests. Finally, it extends the uniform interface to interprocess communication such as networking using TCP/IP protocol.

## Abstraction: Byte Streams

The abstraction that the Unix operating system Mac OS X is based on is that of a *stream of bytes*. This abstraction is usually not exactly what the program needs, which may deal with database records, lines of texts, or rows of pixels, to name few, nor is it what the hardware provides, which will often be disk sectors or network packets.

The basic methods for accessing these streams of bytes are the `read()` and `write()` system calls, which use integers called *file descriptors* to identify the particular byte stream to access. File descriptors for disks or devices are obtained using the `open()` system call, for interprocess communication using the `pipe()` system call, and for network communications using some combination of the `socket()`, `accept()`, `bind()`, and `connect()` calls.

The services and abstractions of the operating system come at a cost; for example, the user-space/kernel transition. Example 10.1 is a case in point.

**Example 10.1    Upcase: A simple Unix filter using the kernel API for byte I/O**

```c
#include <stdio.h>
#include <ctype.h>

int main(int argc, char *argv[] ) {
  int first=1;
  int eof=0;
  do {
    char buffer;
    if ( read(0,&buffer,1)==1) {
      if ( first ) {
        buffer=toupper(buffer);
        first=0;
      }
      write(1,&buffer,1);
      if ( buffer=='\n' ) {
        first=1;
      }
    } else {
      eof=1;
    }
  } while (!eof);
  return 0;
}
```

This code performs the same function as the code in Example 8.1, but reads and writes every byte individually using the read() and write() system calls. At 2 min 25 s for a 145-MB file, it is around 200 times slower than Example 8.1 (0.69 s), with 1 min 56 s or 80% of that time spent in the kernel, whereas Example 8.1 spent only 0.068 s (10% of its much lower running time) in the kernel, less than 1/1,000th of Example 10.1's kernel time.

The samples that follow confirm that the time is spent in the read() and write() system calls. Although this cost of around 500 ns per read or write call already makes the huge difference we just saw, this is just the overhead of calling into the kernel. As we saw in the "Hardware" section in this chapter, actual I/O transactions can take on the order of milliseconds, or many thousands time longer. At such rates, processing a 145-MB file would take several days.

```
8958 start  (in libdyld.dylib)
   4827 main  (in upcase-single-char)
   + 4827 read  (in libsystem_kernel.dylib)
   3919 main  (in upcase-single-char)
   + 3919 write  (in libsystem_kernel.dylib)
```

```
185 main   (in upcase-single-char)
10 main   (in upcase-single-char)
+ 9 toupper   (in upcase-single-char)
```

We already saw before what the solution to high transaction costs is: *batching*, or in this case, *buffering*. Instead of incurring these transaction costs for every single byte, we get a whole buffer's worth of bytes from the kernel, which we then process without bothering the kernel. Then we batch the processed bytes up in an output buffer and write the whole batch to the kernel.

While this processing does make code more complicated than Example 10.1, the Unix *stdio* library takes care of most of the complications for us, especially for line-oriented processing, making Example 8.1 actually less code. However, client code that does not deal with lines of text (`fgets()`) or fixed-length records (`fread()`) will have to deal with all the problems of buffer sizes not matching logical sizes, such as partial input and buffer stitching, on their own. I am so used to I/O being presented using batching APIs that it actually took me a while to realize that a call like `read()` is, in fact, a batching API. The actual unit of communication is the byte, not the buffer. But in order for performance to be acceptable, we need to deal with bytes in bulk, in buffers.

## File I/O

Files in Unix are also just streams of bytes, with the addition of metadata such as a name (more precisely, zero or more names), an owner, and access permissions as well as access dates. Filesystems manage the mapping of a hierarchy of these abstract files onto concrete sectors on a hardware device, and the kernel manages moving data between the disk (via device drivers) and the unified buffer cache (UBC) and clients such as user programs or other parts of the kernel. As with the basic API, buffering plays a crucial role in making the abstraction perform acceptably.

Figure 10.2 shows a rough approximation of how a filesystem maps both a hierarchical namespace to streams of data and both the directories of the hierarchical namespace and the data itself to blocks on a storage medium.

Getting to the file `/mach_kernel` means reading the directory `/`, looking for the `mach_kernel` entry in that directory, and then looking up the data blocks for that file there.[2] Accessing a file deeper in the hierarchy such as `/Users/marcel/Documents/Hi` means starting again at the `/` directory, finding the `Users` entry in that directory, finding the data block(s) for the `Users` directory, reading those data blocks, finding the `marcel` entry, and so forth.

The OS must obviously cache as much of this information in memory as possible, otherwise every access to a particular "file" abstraction would require multiple discrete disk accesses, each involving an expensive seek, because the data accessed is

---

2. Although complicated enough as is, Figure 10.2 leaves out the extra Unix indirection of *inodes* that map directory entries to files.

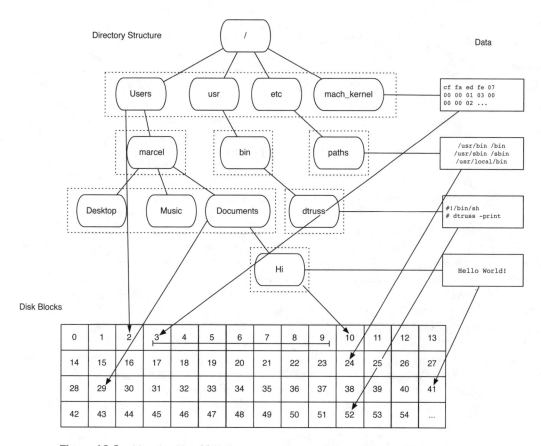

**Figure 10.2**    Mapping Mac OS X directory structure and file data to disk blocks

part of different files and not laid out together on disk. Fortunately, this is the case, and in fact there is even a special *namei cache* that essentially duplicates the hierarchical dictionary structure and maps directly from complete path names to data blocks. These caches work very well in the general case, but as with all caches, they only affect best- and average-case behavior, and it is always possible to get hit with the worst case. They also involve additional processing on actual I/O, as data is copied first into the buffers and then supplied to the client that made the request.

Traditionally, Unix operating systems reserved a special section of memory as a *buffer cache* for buffering recent disk I/O, so a client `read()` request would cause data to be read into those buffers and then copied into the client's address space, and a `write()` request would write to the buffer cache and be flushed to the disk later. The separate *page cache* was used for the virtual memory used by processes, which had a separate path to the disk to enable swapping, often to special regions of the disk.

Although this separation between virtual memory and (wired) buffers for file I/O initially seemed sensible, it had a number of drawbacks. First, the buffer cache's size was usually fixed, so as main memories got larger you frequently had large amounts of unused RAM that could have been used for disk buffering. Second, with the introduction of the `mmap()` system call for mapping files directly into a process's address space without `read()`, the distinction that was so clear before became blurrier. And moving data from the buffer cache to virtual memory not just incurred an extra copy, it could also lead to the same data residing in multiple caches, leading to more wasted space and extra copy operations.

The solution arrived at by all Unix distributions was the UBC, shown in Figure 10.3 along with the old pre-UBC state.

With the UBC, the distinction between virtual memory operations and file I/O is erased. All buffered file I/O, both via `mmap()` and `read()` and `write()` goes via the virtual memory subsystem: first, the kernel creates a mapping from the filesystem object (usually a disk file) to a set of virtual memory pages. This set of pages is then either mapped directly into the address space of the process in question in the case of `mmap()`, with actual I/O operations initiated when those pages are accessed, or in case of a `read()` the kernel immediately initiates I/O and copies the data into the calling process's address space once it arrives.

The advantages of the UBC are that it can and does use all available RAM for buffering file I/O, and it eliminates duplicate copies in the case of memory-mapped files. These benefits are usually transparent, but the unified nature of the cache can and does cause problems at times. Since the UBC doesn't really distinguish between file I/O and application paging, heavy file activity can cause the system to start

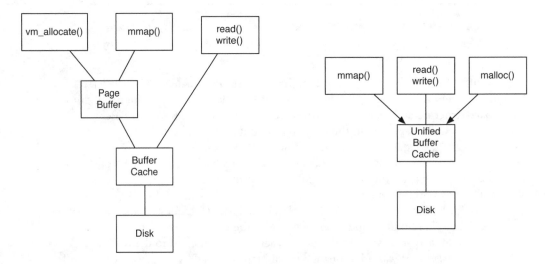

**Figure 10.3**   Non-unified (left) and unified (right) buffer cache

swapping despite the fact that there is plenty of RAM to keep all programs in memory—a problem that showed up with Spotlight, for example.

Fortunately, this tends to be more of a problem for system services and can also be mitigated by using uncached/unbuffered I/O and/or explicitly controlling the allocation strategies with the madvse() system call we saw in the "madvise" section of Chapter 7.

In addition to caching previous reads in case the same data is read again in the future, the disk subsystem also speculatively reads data that it believes will be requested in the future, so-called read-ahead.

The UBC doesn't just cache reads, it also buffers writes. When a program writes data to a file using the write() system call, that data is not actually written to disk; it is copied to the UBC. The sync() system call globally writes pending changes to disk. It is executed every 30 s by the launchd daemon (earlier OS versions had a separate update daemon for the same task). Delaying the writes decouples the application from the slower I/O devices and allows the system to group I/O together in larger batches, optimizing the I/O in the process, combining writes to a single flash block, or sorting requests to minimize disk seeks.

Again, this buffering behavior is crucial to general system performance, an earlier version of Unix that used synchronous writes had around 3% to 5% the write throughput of systems with write buffering, and similar slowdowns can be observed when manually forcing writes to be synchronous. The main cost of delayed writes is that data may not be consistent on disk even though the application has written it and can be lost if there is a power failure or system crash between the time that the application wrote the data and the time of the failure. In addition, there is an in-memory copy operation.

## The Network Stack

The main network stack on OS X and iOS deals with TCP/IP, the Transmission Control Protocol/Internet Protocol. Basic IP is packet oriented like most of the network hardware, but the widely used TCP provides the "stream of bytes" abstraction used throughout the rest of the Unix kernel. Most of the high-level protocols in use over the Internet today such as HTTP and FTP are built on top of TCP's stream abstraction, with the packet-oriented, unreliable User Datagram Protocol more widely used as the basis for broadcast and media applications.

A naïve implementation of a reliable, stream-oriented transport would be performance limited by the latency of the network, because receipt of packets has to be acknowledged. Fortunately, TCP is a very sophisticated protocol paired with equally sophisticated implementations. Significant amounts of buffering, sliding receipt windows, flow control, out-of-order retransmission, and so on, help TCP achieve throughput close to the available bandwidth in many situations without much help from the application programmer.

However, establishing TCP connections *is* limited by network latency, and actually takes several round-trips, so care should be taken to minimize the number of connections, preferring instead to reuse an existing connection. FTP, for example, uses a single control connection for an entire session but requires a new data connection for every new transfer, making it ill-suited for transferring a large number of smaller files. HTTP also suffers from being fundamentally connectionless, although later versions of the specification have allowed reusing connections for multiple transfers.

## Summary

In this chapter, we've seen that I/O performance over time follows a very specific pattern: capacity increases more than bandwidth, which increases more than latency, even with occasional jumps like the move to SSDs.

In practice, this means that good performance can best be achieved by making requests as large as possible; reading or writing a single byte is practically as expensive as reading or writing many kilobytes. Unless absolutely necessary, I avoid writing parts of files, instead taking a page from the Amoeba operating system[3] and treating files as immutable, only ever reading and writing entire files at a time, and ideally avoiding small files. If I want to read parts of a large file, I use memory mapping in order to still only deal with the whole file logically, leaving any partial access to the OS. If I need to incrementally generate a large file, I only append to it and only allow reading once the file has finished writing.

We will take a close look at these sorts of techniques and the problems with partial file reads and updates, especially in the context of databases, in Chapter 12.

---

3. http://fsd-amoeba.sourceforge.net/amoeba.html
https://en.wikipedia.org/wiki/Amoeba_(operating_system)

# 11

# I/O: Measurement and Tools

Measuring I/O is even harder than measuring memory consumption. Most of the time, interesting events will be those where nothing is happening; the system is simply waiting for some external event such as the hard disk head moving to the right location. In addition, the whole operating system is designed purposely to make I/O measurement nonrepeatable—er, I mean, to *optimize* I/O, with lots of global shared state such as caches and disk layout. Even worse, while there are techniques for controlling these variables, they usually also lead to nonrepresentative measurements because the optimizations are absolutely necessary for normal operations.

To illustrate, we will use the short program from Example 11.1 that just reads a file into `NSData` and then computes a checksum of the bytes in the file.

**Example 11.1**   `datamapping` **test program: reads a file and computes an xor-checksum**

```
#import <Foundation/Foundation.h>

int main(int argc, char *argv[] ) {
  NSURL *url=[NSURL fileURLWithPath:@(argv[1])];
  NSData *d=[NSData dataWithContentsOfURL:url options:0 error:nil];
  char result=0;
  const char *bytes=[d bytes];
  const char *end=bytes+[d length];
  for (const char *cur=bytes; cur < end; cur++ ) {
  result ^= *cur;
 }
 printf("result: \%x\n",result);
}
```

Example 11.1 does a computation on the file contents and prints out those results to make sure data is actually read and the `printf` ensures the compiler can't just optimize the computation away as dead code.

# Negative Space: `top` and `time`

Our friends `time` and `top` are useful in detecting that I/O is happening and blocking our process, though mostly by using the concept of `negative space`: if we notice time that is not accounted for otherwise, or CPU utilization significantly below 100%, there is a strong suspicion that I/O may be to blame. For example, running the command `time ./datamapping test_file` yields the result shown:

```
> time ./datamapping  testfile_3gb
real    0m10.669s
user    0m0.305s
sys     0m1.613s
```

Note the large discrepancy between `real` and `user` time, with user time only being 0.3 s, but the actual real time being more than 10 s. The `sys` time only adds 1.6 s of kernel CPU time, for a total of just under 2 s of time using the CPU. The other 8 s are missing, meaning only about 20% CPU utilization and 80% idle time. This could have been other processes preempting this one, but because scheduling is usually fair it would have to have been several processes or one running at significant higher priority, for example, a real-time process. Another reason would have been that the process decided to de-schedule itself by using the `sleep()` system call or similar calls to wait for some specified amount of time.

The most likely explanation, especially in our case, is that the process was I/O bound, meaning it was synchronously waiting for an external device to perform some I/O—in this case, to deliver data.

Assuming you have enough memory for keeping the file in RAM, doing a second timing run of the program will yield the very different results shown below: it is much faster, and `user` and `sys` times add up almost exactly to the `real` time measured.

```
> time ./datamapping  testfile_3gb
real    0m1.937s
user    0m0.305s
sys     0m1.613s
```

This is the result of the buffer cache we discussed in the last section. The entire file has been cached in memory, and instead of doing I/O from disk, the OS just copies the data from the buffer to the program, making repeatable I/O testing difficult.

The `purge` command empties the entire buffer cache and returns the system to roughly the same state it was in after a cold boot (from power-off). After a `purge`, the OS will be forced to read from disk again. The `purge` command's effects are global and also cause changes to be written to disk, so expect significant degradation in system performance for a while. Also, wait for the system to settle and page in its basic necessities before performing your measurements.

You can also see symptoms of an I/O bound process in the `top` screenshot Figure 11.1, with `top` showing the `datamapping` process at 17.7% CPU

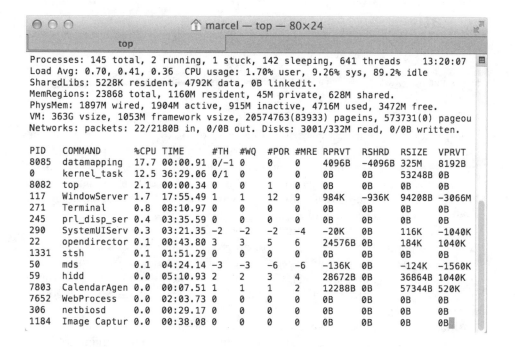

**Figure 11.1**   top showing an I/O-bound task

utilization. The `top` output also confirms that the reason is not CPU contention, because the CPU has over 80% idle time and there are no other processes that have high CPU usage statistics. Finally, `top` also has an indicator that I/O is taking place with the `read` and `written` fields in the statistics section.

# Summary Information: `iostat` and `netstat`

Whereas with `time` and `top`, I/O activity was mostly detectable indirectly, the aptly named `iostat` command gives a direct measure of I/O activity. `iostat` gives summary information of I/O happening in the system, either as a snapshot or continuously if given a time interval on the command line.

The following is output during a run of the `datamapping` command.

```
> iostat 1
          disk0          cpu      load average
   KB/t tps  MB/s    us sy id   1m   5m   15m
   6.00    2  0.01     2  3 95  0.61 0.50 0.51
 421.13  430 176.94    2  9 89  0.61 0.50 0.51
 417.56 1104 450.26    1 15 84  0.61 0.50 0.51
 426.35 1071 445.95    2 15 83  0.72 0.52 0.52
```

```
454.21 999 443.28    2 16 82   0.72 0.52 0.52
407.63 1038 413.29   2 14 84   0.72 0.52 0.52
422.73 1057 436.50   1 14 85   0.72 0.52 0.52
493.48 929 447.48    2 20 77   0.72 0.52 0.52
491.08 186 89.07    21  6 74   0.83 0.54 0.53
 11.33   6  0.07    25  1 73   0.83 0.54 0.53
 20.40  10  0.20     3  8 89   0.83 0.54 0.53
```

The first three columns display the I/O activity on disk0, in this case the built-in SSD of my MacBook Pro and the only disk attached to the system. I personally find the third column (MB/s) most relevant, most of the time. The first two just break this total number down into average kilobytes per transaction (KB/t) and transactions per second (tps), which can be useful if you are trying to determine if you are doing too many small and possibly random I/Os.

For this run, we see the system initially essentially idle (two transactions, total of 12 KB transferred). Once the `datamapping` program starts, we quickly ramp to 400 MB/s, the sequential transfer speed of the built-in SSD and finally drop down again once the program is done. The misalignment of the columns during the run shows the age of the program: the formatting didn't anticipate transfer speeds going into the triple digits!

Although `iostat` paints with a very broad brush—it only provides summary information combining all I/O going to particular devices—I often find it not just useful to verify that what I think should be happening is in fact really happening, but also sufficient to see what is happening with a particular process if I manage to keep the rest of the system quiet enough.

The `netstat` command performs a very similar function as `iostat` when given a time interval on the command line, printing out aggregate network activity in bytes and packets for the specified interval, though it can also give much more detailed information.

## Instruments

Needless to say, Instruments has tools to help us with I/O performance measurement. For example, we can use our trusty *Time Profiler* as shown in Figure 11.2.

One thing to notice is that CPU utilization shown in the graph is only at 100% near the end; in the first part of the graph, it stays at much less than 100%. This is another example of the *negative space* we discussed earlier: the fact that we have less than 100% utilization indicates that the program is waiting for something—in this case, reading data from disk using Unix I/O, which despite reading from an SSD at around 400 MB/s does keep the CPU waiting for most of the time. After the I/O is done and everything is read into memory, utilization shoots up to around 100%.

However, if we look closely, we also notice a couple of problems. First, the times do not match: the graph shows 7 s of usage, but the tree view only accounts for 4.7 s. Second, the tree view claims that just 44% of the time is spent reading the file, but we

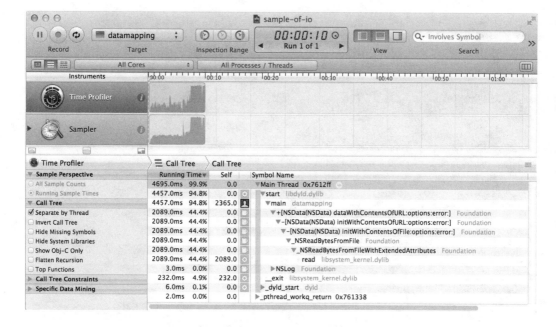

**Figure 11.2**   Time Profile of Unix I/O

both know and can see that it's close to three-quarters of the time. The reason for this discrepancy is that the Time Profiler instrument by default only accounts for CPU time; it does not account for time waiting for I/O. In order to also account for time waiting for I/O, we need to check the *Record Waiting Times* checkbox in the inspector.

With the Record Waiting Times checkbox selected, we get a result like the one you can see in Figure 11.3.

However, recording all time is also confusing: our `main` function, which we know is the only thing really doing work, is now shown as just taking slightly more than 25% of the time, with almost 50% taken by `start_wqthread` and its descendants, which bottom out at `_workq_kernreturn`, and another 25% in `_dispatch_mgr_thread`. What we are seeing are three helper threads that are sitting idle, but Instruments can't tell the difference between idleness waiting for something we are interested in, such as the result of `read()`, and idleness due to being parked, so all threads that are around for the time of the process will show up with equal weight, and our total sample count will be *threads × total − time*.

Fortunately, we have data-mining tools that can help us, as illustrated in Figure 11.4.

We need to focus on our `main` function, after which we get what we were looking for. Although we no longer get running time in milliseconds in the tree view,

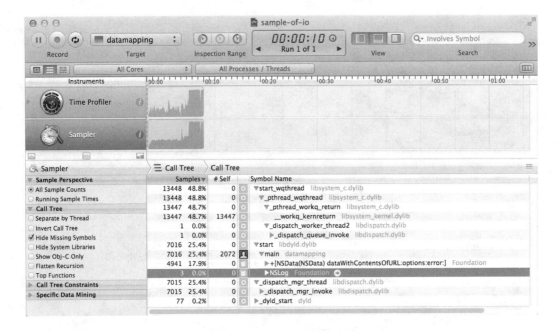

**Figure 11.3**    Time Profile of Unix I/O sampler tool, all states

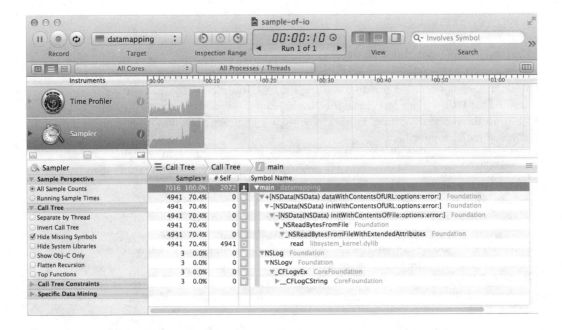

**Figure 11.4**    Sampler Instrument of Unix I/O, all states and focused

we do still get samples and were sampling at a rate of 1 per ms. The 7,000 odd samples we got correspond to the real time taken, and the `read()` is now shown as taking 70% of the total.

Note that the profile no longer directed us to the most important part of the program; we had to have that knowledge and use it to actually get at the information we need.

Although there are other, much more I/O-specific instruments available, I haven't had much use for them. The basic command-line tools give me a better overview, the Sample instrument gives me a better overview of how I/O fits into the rest of the program, and `fs_usage` discussed in the next section gives me all the detail I would want. Figure 11.5 shows the Reads/Writes instrument. Although it does keep track of bytes read and written, it only graphs this information, allowing only a rough qualitative evaluation. The call graph only shows the number of calls, which is less useful.

# Detailed Tracing: `fs_usage`

The `fs_usage` tool provides much more detailed information, recording effectively all I/O activity. Beware, though, that it is potentially a firehose, especially when output is not restricted. On my system just 6 s of `fs_usage` amounted to 1,255 lines of output, despite the system being ostensibly idle!

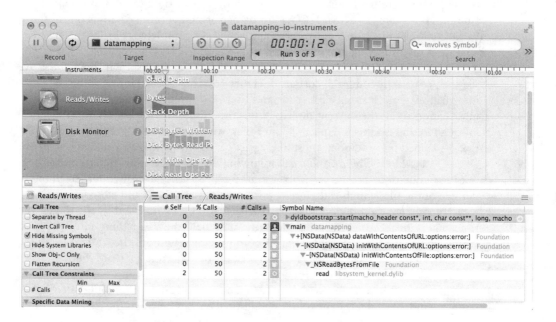

**Figure 11.5**    Reads/Writes instrument

Data can be limited to certain types of output via the −f flag and to a specific process by adding the process name or process identifier on the command line. The output below shows monitoring the datamapping process using fs_usage:

```
> sudo fs_usage -f filesys datamapping
15:20:29  open              .                0.000025    datamapping
15:20:29  fstat64                            0.000005    datamapping
15:20:29  fcntl                              0.000007    datamapping
15:20:29  stat64            ook/test-programs 0.000015   datamapping
15:20:29  PAGE_IN_FILE                       0.000005    datamapping
15:20:29  open              rams/testfile_3gb 0.000019   datamapping
15:20:29  fstat64                            0.000004    datamapping
15:20:34  read                               5.184634 W  datamapping
15:20:36  read                               5.025971 W  datamapping
15:20:36  close                              0.000010    datamapping
15:20:36  write                              0.000012    datamapping
```

Each line of the output indicates a single I/O event. The first column is a timestamp, and the second column indicates the operation—for example, the system call (lstat64, open, read, close). The center portion has additional information if such information exists—for example, filenames. Following this is a number indicating the time the operation took, in seconds. The number of digits after the decimal is chosen so that the digits show microseconds (0.000025 seconds = 25 microseconds). If the process had to be *scheduled out*, the time is followed by the letter W, otherwise there is a blank. Scheduling out means that the process was no longer running. For example, actual I/O had to be performed because data was not in the cache, and the process was put to sleep until the I/O completed. Finally, the last column is the process name, which in this case is always datamapping.

With this in mind, we can interpret the trace in the output shown above. First, we see the program opening the current directory (open(".")), getting some information about it using fstat(), and later using stat() to get some more information about the current directory, this time using the full path. Cocoa does a lot of statting, so this is expected. After that, we get a page-fault serviced from a file that is mapped into memory, most likely part of the executable or a shared library (PAGE_IN_FILE). The open() call following the page-fault initiates access to the test file in question, testfile_3gb. fstat64() is most likely used to determine the size of the file, which is then read using two read() calls and closed. The two read() calls are the only ones that needed actual I/O, as indicated by the W after the time. They are also the only ones where the time field shows anything substantial, which isn't a coincidence: calls serviced from memory (without the W) tend to finish in a few microseconds at most. The final write is our printf() that's there so compiler doesn't eliminate the xor-loop due to the result not being used.

When I ran this same test with less free memory (not enough to hold the complete file in memory at once), I saw a lot of additional entries between the read() calls and the close() call of type PAGE_IN_ANON, meaning swapping in data that isn't backed by a user-defined file, but rather anonymous memory that is backed only by the swapfile. This meant that data was read from the data file, swapped to the swap file, and then paged back into memory from the swap file, which is somewhat insane but can happen when using Unix I/O. The page-out events corresponding to the page-ins observed do not show up when looking at a particular process because paging to disk is handled by the kernel task. It does show up in a global trace.

One caveat of specifying a process to monitor is that `fs_usage` expects the process to already exist and will terminate with an error message if it doesn't. There is no equivalent of `sample`'s `-wait` flag that will wait for such a process to come into existence. If that is a problem, an alternative is to keep the `fs_usage` itself unconstrained (global) and filter the output using grep: `sudo fs_usage -e | grep datamapping`. The output is shown here:

```
14:32:42   open                 .              0.000012   datamapping
14:32:42   fstat64                             0.000003   datamapping
14:32:42   fcntl                               0.000005   datamapping
14:32:42   close                               0.000005   datamapping
14:32:42   stat64            ../test-programs  0.000009   datamapping
14:32:42   PAGE_IN_FILE                        0.000004   datamapping
14:32:42   PAGE_IN_FILE                        0.000012   datamapping
14:32:42   PAGE_IN_FILE                        0.000003   datamapping
14:32:42   PAGE_IN_FILE                        0.000003   datamapping
14:32:42   open              ../testfile_3gb   0.000016   datamapping
14:32:42   fstat64                             0.000003   datamapping
14:32:42     RdData[A]                         0.000868 W datamapping
14:32:42     RdData[A]                         0.000826 W datamapping
14:32:42     RdData[A]                         0.000366 W datamapping
14:32:42     RdData[A]                         0.000722 W datamapping
14:32:42     RdData[A]                         0.000791 W datamapping
14:32:42     RdData[A]                         0.000954 W datamapping
14:32:42     RdData[A]                         0.000470 W datamapping
...
```

This approach to filtering generates significantly more output: we see many lower-level `RdData[A]` events. A *lot* more: I got around 13K lines of output. It helps to redirect to a file! My current understanding is that the lower-level events are part of the kernel event stream and therefore do not show up when filtering directly by process.

The `fs_usage` command is very versatile. For example, I was also able to confirm that the job that used to be done by the `update` daemon (calling `sync()` every 30 s) is now performed by `launchd` instead, as the following output shows. As of version 10.8.3, the `sync(2)` man page still refers to `update(8)`, despite that man page having been removed.

```
> sudo fs_usage -f  launchd  | grep sync
12:08:44   sync                                0.051223 W launchd
12:09:14   sync                                0.057016 W launchd
12:09:44   sync                                0.055366 W launchd
```

```
12:10:14  sync                        0.062487 W launchd
12:10:44  sync                        0.049468 W launchd
12:11:14  sync                        0.057325 W launchd
```

Apart from being a firehose, another drawback of fs_usage is that it is flat. There is no call graph, so correlating activity and doing data mining can be arduous. An instrument with the capabilities of fs_usage would be really useful.

## Summary

This chapter introduced some of the major tools for measuring I/O performance. Unlike CPU and memory tools, however, they tend to not be enough to pinpoint exact locations of I/O performance problems, never mind root causes. Fortunately, they don't have to; all we need is evidence that I/O is causing problems and enough information to form a usable working hypothesis.

With a working hypothesis, we can create an experiment (i.e., make a code change) and then verify or reject the hypothesis by measuring the running time of the modified program. Rinse and repeat. We will see that method in action in the next chapter.

# 12

# I/O: Pitfalls and Techniques

Despite the fact that I/O performance has increased more slowly than the improvements in other parts of the system, it still is fast enough for low-rate or reasonably small I/O...in computer terms. In human terms, that is still incredibly fast. For example, the Project Gutenberg version of a reasonably large novel such as *Moby Dick* is just 1.2 MB in size. On my SSD–equipped MacBook Pro, I can copy this file 280 times per second using a shell script. The fastest typist in the world, on the other hand, types less than 20 characters per second, so in case we were working on our *Moby Dick*-sized novel, we would be able to save the entire novel on every keystroke and have plenty of time left for other tasks. For many I/O tasks today, brute force is a reasonable implementation strategy.

## Pushing Bytes with NSData

The `NSData` method `dataWithContentsOfURL:options:error:` is the most basic Foundation method for reading bytes into memory. Figure 12.1 looks at the performance effects of the different *options* that can be passed when reading a file from disk. The *mapped* bars refer to the option `NSDataReadingMappedAlways`, with *mapped + used* actually touching the memory that was mapped. The *read* bar refers to passing no option (or option 0), which means that the file will be read using the Unix `read()` system call, and *read+uncached* refers to the option `NSData ReadingUncached`, which also implies Unix I/O but using uncached reads. Each variant is timed in two environments: one with the data already residing in the operating system's buffer cache (*cached*), and one with actual I/O from disk ensured by issuing a `purge` command beforehand.

As you can see, simply mapping the 300-MB file into memory is by far the fastest operation, taking only 0.03 s in the cached case and 0.007 s in the uncached case (apparently, creating virtual memory mappings to a disk file is quicker than creating mappings to resident pages). Of course, that number is only partly useful because as we saw earlier, real I/O only happens when the mapped pages are actually used by the program (*mapped+used*). If we actually use the data, a comparison with the

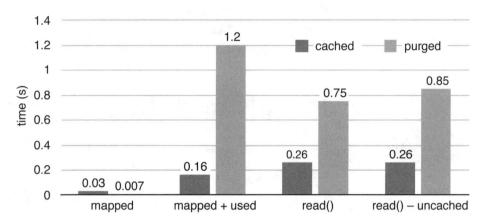

**Figure 12.1**   Mapping and reading a 300-MB file into memory via NSData

read() option is more mixed: mapping is 57% faster if the data is already in the buffer cache ( 0.16s vs. 0.26s), but read() is 60% faster than mapping if the data has to be read from disk. Uncached reads are no faster than cached reads.

Using Instruments quickly illuminates why memory mapping is faster than read() in the cached case—the former just remaps the virtual pages, whereas the latter actually copies data using the kernel version of bcopy(), and a bcopy() of 300 MB does take around 160 ms. The case of actual I/O is a little more mysterious. One suspicion is that the page-fault handling and remapping work is greater for mapped pages than actual data movement for copied ones. However, the fact that remapping is significantly faster than copying in the cached case makes this unlikely, and in fact, the difference between the uncached read() and mapped cases is greater than the total time for remapping in the cached/mapped case.

The iosnoop tool provides what looks like the answer: in the read() case, data is read in 512-KB chunks, when memory mapping the chunk size is only 128 KB. At first blush, this seems understandable; the page-fault handler has no information about future access patterns, whereas we told the NSData that we wanted to read the entire file, so a larger read-ahead seems sensible for that case. However, neither using our own Unix code with significantly smaller chunks nor giving the virtual memory subsystem using madvise() with MADV_SEQUENTIAL or MADV_WILLNEED changes the behavior significantly. So at this point, this seems to be a true kernel (performance) bug or maybe just a misconfiguration, with the read-ahead for mapped files set at 1/4th the size of that for read() system calls, with reduced performance as a result.

## A Memory-Mapping Anomaly

The preceding measurements and results were the result of a large number of experiments at different sizes and with varying access patterns. At file sizes above

2 GB, we saw a nonlinear increase in execution times for mapped files—for example, scanning through a 3-GB file that was resident in memory took 4 s, 2.5 times more than the 10-times increase we would expect over the 300-MB file case.

Despite many experiments, an explanation—or better yet, a *fix*—was not forthcoming, until almost by accident I tried varying the stride with which I access memory in order to cause actual I/O to happen on the mapped file. The usual stride was 4,096, the size of a virtual memory page, making sure that every page mapped is actually accessed and paged into memory. Paging in only every second page by changing the stride to 8,192 caused a decrease in running time, which is to be expected, but the decrease was rather high. Closer inspection revealed the data shown in Figure 12.2: even changing the stride from 4,096 to 4,097 bytes caused a performance improvement of around a factor of 2.5. This can't be explained by having less data to page in, because the number of pages read only drops by 0.02%.

The only explanation I have for this behavior is that the kernel logic that tries to detect sequential access patterns in memory-mapped files has a bug that causes it to chew up extra CPU time once the file size is larger than will fit in a 32-bit signed integer. The bug doesn't manifest itself if your access pattern is even very slightly nonsequential. Another way to fix the problem is the `madvise()` system call with the `MADV_SEQUENTIAL` flag for the memory in question. The result of applying this flag is shown in Figure 12.3.

However, when you apply the `MADV_SEQUENTIAL` flag, you must absolutely ensure that access will be 100% perfectly sequential, otherwise the performance

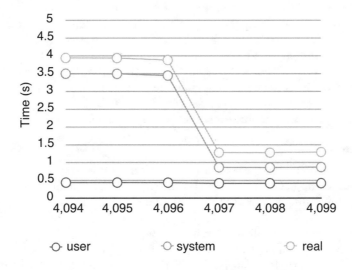

**Figure 12.2**   Sequential mapped I/O performance by stride, no flags

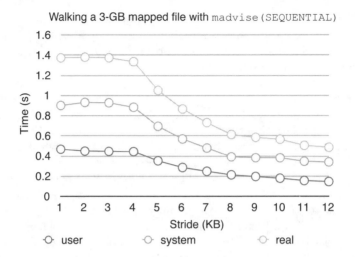

**Figure 12.3**   Sequential mapped I/O performance by stride, `madvise(SEQ)`

penalties can yield up to a factor of 10 worse performance, especially when having to do actual I/O. Figure 12.4 compares the times for actual I/O with different strides.

I was able to confirm this behavior on Mac OS X versions 10.6 to 10.9, but no longer in 10.11, so I would still recommend memory-mapped I/O for most applications. However, I do also recommend that you keep a lookout for this type of behavior.

The two biggest factors in favor of mapping are the fact that it reduces memory pressure significantly and that it allows for lazy loading of data pretty much automatically, meaning the application isn't unresponsive while data is being loaded. This point is actually present in Figure 12.1, if maybe a little hidden. For the `read()` times, the time shown in Figure 12.1 is essentially the duration of `NSData`'s `dataWithContentsOfURL:options:error:` method and the calling thread is blocked during that time. Using mapping, the time spent in `dataWithContentsOfURL:options:error:` is that shown in the first bar; after that the application can perform other tasks such as interacting with the user.

## How Chunky?

While we were preparing for the release of Leopard, I was tasked, among other things, with looking at program launch performance. For launch, we distinguish between a *warm* launch where the data required is already mostly present in the buffer cache and the less common *cold* launch requiring all code, resources, and data to be read from disk, which usually only happens after system boot.

On a then high-end PowerMac G5 with a fast 35-MB/s hard disk and plenty of RAM, Pages.app took less than 1 s (less than one dock bounce) on a warm start, but over 6 s during a cold start. Profiling the I/O operations revealed that around 10 MB

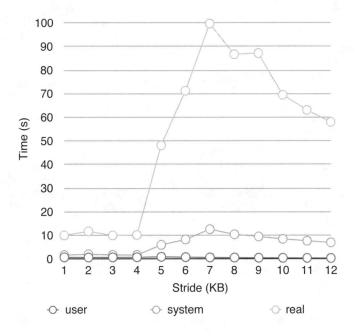

**Figure 12.4**   Nonsequential mapped I/O performance by stride, `madvise(SEQ)`

of data were being read, and the fact that a warm launch was so much quicker strongly suggested that I/O was to blame.

At the same time, I was experimenting with the Squeak Smalltalk system, and when I measured its cold launch performance for kicks, I was surprised by the result: Despite the fact that it was reading an image file of well over 10 MB, it cold-launched in less than a second!

The reason for the discrepancy, with Pages taking almost an order of magnitude more time to read the same amount of data, was that the Squeak Smalltalk image is a single file that is read into memory all at once, whereas the Pages resources required at launch (nib files, images, string tables, libraries, etc.) were scattered across a large number of small files.

Figure 12.5 shows this effect on modern hardware, the SSD-equipped MacBook Pro with Retina Display that many of these tests were run on. All of the timings are for reading 1 GB of data, but distributed in chunks of 100 MB down to 10 KB each, with the number of individual files rising correspondingly from 10 to 100,000.

Despite the fast-seeking SSD, the difference is striking. Reading the same amount of data takes about 10 times longer with the smallest file size and the largest number of files. Figure 12.6 shows why we didn't go to the next step, 1 million files of 1K each. File-writing times increase even more dramatically, and writing 100K small files is almost 50 times slower than the same amount of data distributed over 10 large files.

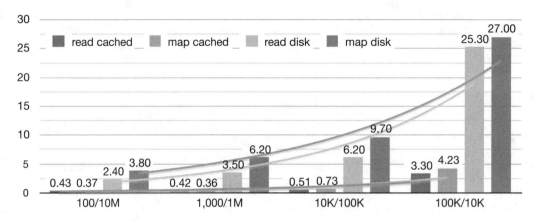

**Figure 12.5**    Time to read 1 GB of data at different granularity

# Unixy I/O

Of course, we don't have to use `NSData` to read bytes; we can also use the lower-level Unix functions such as `read()` and `mmap()`. From a performance point of view, this makes no difference, at least if they are used the same way: if I `malloc()` a buffer the size of the file and then `read()` the file, it takes the same amount of time as using `NSData` without any options, and if I `mmap()` the file it takes the same amount of time as `NSData` with the mapping options.

What does make a difference, however, is using the streaming I/O style we showed earlier, where instead of reading or mapping the whole file into memory at once, you

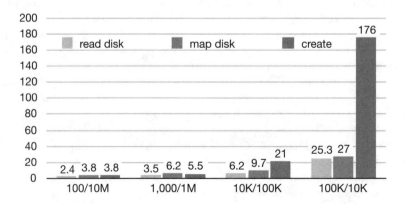

**Figure 12.6**    Time to read and write 1 GB of data at different granularity

continuously read parts of the file into a small fixed buffer. Example 12.1 shows this technique using a buffer size of 64 KB.

**Example 12.1    Unix file reading with fixed buffer size**

```
#include <stdlib.h>
#include <fcntl.h>
#include <unistd.h>

int main( int argc, char *argv[] ) {
  char *filename=argv[1];
  size_t size=64 *1024;
  char *buffer=malloc(size);
  int fd=open( filename, O_RDONLY );
  while ( size ) {
    size=read(fd,buffer,size);
  }
  close(fd);
}
```

For the 300-MB sample file we used earlier, this approach proves to be the quickest of all, taking only 65 ms to read the entire file when file-cache resident and 880 ms when it needs to be read from disk. For the cached case, this is actually faster than memory mapping, which in turn was faster than instructing NSData to use read(), seemingly contradicting my earlier claim that using Unix system calls didn't make a difference compared to NSData.

The small but crucial difference that explains and removes the apparent contradiction is the time it takes to allocate memory. Allocating and populating a 300-MB buffer, whether using NSData or malloc(), actually trumps the cost of bcopy()ing the memory into those buffers. One thing that does *not* make much of a difference, on the other hand, is the actual buffer size used in the read() system call, unless you go down so small that the system call overhead starts to byte: the OS recognizes a sequential read() access pattern and start reading large clusters (512K per chunk on my system) into memory in single I/O operations, regardless of the actual size requested in the read() call. The part not requested by the process simply goes into the buffer cache. I also couldn't detect a significant difference when using the buffered *stdio* library calls, so use whichever is more practical in your application.

So why not use streaming Unix I/O all the time? For one, it is of no use if you actually need to keep whole file contents in memory. In that case, your data will be in memory twice—once in the buffer cache and once in dirty application memory that will be swapped out if memory gets tight—rather than simply unmapped in case of mapped memory. Alternately, you can implement your own buffering scheme, moving subsets of the full data into and out of memory programmatically. However, this means having separate code paths for data that fits into memory and data that does not, as well as having to manage the data movement without much if any feedback from the OS regarding total memory pressure and eviction preferences. Finally, you won't be able to take advantage of buffered memory as quickly; data that remains mapped is simply a normal memory access away, whereas you need to at least issue a `read()` system call and copy data into your address space when managing your own buffers.

A better use-case is when you are parsing external data into a different internal format, but even that is not without problems. Unless you have fixed-size data elements and take those into account when reading, there will be elements of interest straddling buffer boundaries, as shown in Figure 12.7.

Handling this case usually requires *buffer stitching*. First, remember the start of incomplete elements as you are parsing, then recognize that an element was an incomplete element while parsing *buffer 1*. You then need to copy the remainder of *buffer 1* containing the incomplete element into a new buffer and finally append the newly read contents (*buffer 2*) to that rump and restart the parse. Repeat at each buffer boundary. Not just is this logic complicated, it requires additional copies, which also impact performance. If the data is truly use-once, the additional logic can be worth it, however, and it may even be worth disabling caching. Of course, you may not have a choice in the matter, for example, if you're parsing data produced incrementally by another program or from the network.

# Network I/O

A couple of years ago, I was contacted by a newspaper that was having problems with the performance of their iOS reader. They had read about my XML parser, and since their reader was based on RSS and HTML, they thought I might be able to help them. A first look at the app confirmed that it was unusably slow. After launch or after a refresh it would just hang there for several minutes and then finally display some information.

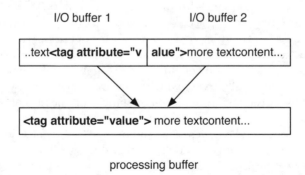

**Figure 12.7**   Buffer stitching when element of interest straddles buffers

Of course, XML had nothing to do with it, but I was able to help them in the end. Their app was designed for offline reading, so during an update it was loading their entire feed, starting with the master list of categories, RSS feeds for each category, and finally thumbnail images, article text, and images for each article. The algorithm used was a depth-first traversal of the feeds, and looked as follows:

1. Fetch and parse the overall feed directory using `NSXMLParser`'s `-initWithContentsOfURL:`.
2. For each feed encountered:
   a. Fetch and parse the RSS for that particular feed using `NSXMLParser`'s `-initWithContentsOfURL:`.
   b. As you are parsing, for each news story in the RSS feed:
      - Fetch the thumbnail associated to show next to each feed entry synchronously, this time using `NSData`'s `-initWithContentsOfURL:`.
      - Fetch the story's HTML content synchronously the same way.
      - Fetch all the images for the story's HTML content synchronously the same way.

If you squint, you can recognize this as a variant of the problem of applying the call-return architectural style inappropriately, though this time the symptom is not explosive memory consumption. By treating network access using `-initWithContentsOfURL:` like any other synchronous message send, therefore waiting for a result before proceeding, we were limiting performance to the *latency* of the network, rather than its potential sequential *throughput*, at least for the small- and medium-sized files we were requesting.

When using synchronous request/response, throughput is bounded by the response time, so for example with a network round-trip time of 45 ms and a request size of 1,400 bytes, we can achieve a maximum transfer speed of 1,400/45 bytes/ms, or around 31 KB/s, irrespective of the bandwidth of the network. The reason TCP can achieve much higher transfer speeds with roughly those network characteristics is that although it presents a synchronous API to its clients, it actually works somewhat asynchronously, allowing multiple requests to be in flight at the same time.

## Overlapping Transfers

Allowing multiple requests to be in flight at the same time is exactly the same strategy we needed to employ, except in this case at the HTTP-request level. Fortunately, the `NSURL` loading system makes it possible to load HTTP requests asynchronously using the `NSURLSession` and `NSURLSessionTask` classes. Figure 12.8 shows the effects of having multiple requests in flight on download performance, and they are quite dramatic: up to about four simultaneous requests, throughput increases almost linearly, with the initial time of 41.6 s dropping four-fold to 11.4 s. After four simultaneous requests, the curve starts to flatten and after about six requests there is

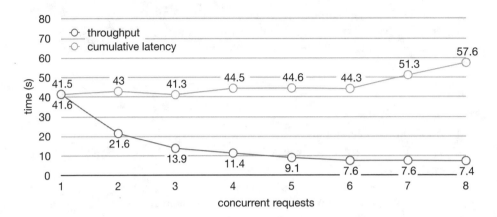

**Figure 12.8**   Time to complete 100 HTTP requests over WAN with varying concurrency levels

no further improvement in throughput on that particular connection with the request size used in the test.

In fact, we see that after six simultaneous requests, the *cumulative latency* starts to slowly increase, whereas it held steady before. The cumulative latency is the sum of the times of all the individual requests, so that means that individual requests are starting to take longer, even if the total time is still decreasing slightly. This is a sign that the network between the client and server has filled to capacity and is now congested, with the individual requests now competing for bandwidth.

Figure 12.9 demonstrates how piling more simultaneous transfers on a saturated channel does nothing to increase throughput; in the best case it only serves to lengthen the individual request times. An application tends to be more responsive when 10% of its requests have completed than when all of its requests are at 10% complete.

In addition, bombarding a server with many simultaneous transfers ties up per-request resources on the server, potentially causing resource starvation, dropped requests, or even resource exhaustion and crashes on the server. On a slow network, you can also run into connection timeouts.

## Throttling Requests

So you actually don't want unconstrained asynchronous network operations because you *really* do not want to overwhelm the channel.

TCP itself provides automated congestion control for single channels by monitoring dropped packets, but HTTP doesn't have such a facility; you have to manage congestion caused by multiple simultaneous HTTP requests yourself. The HTTP/1.1 specification does require limiting the number of simultaneous persistent connections to two per client, but that does not directly correlate with the number of

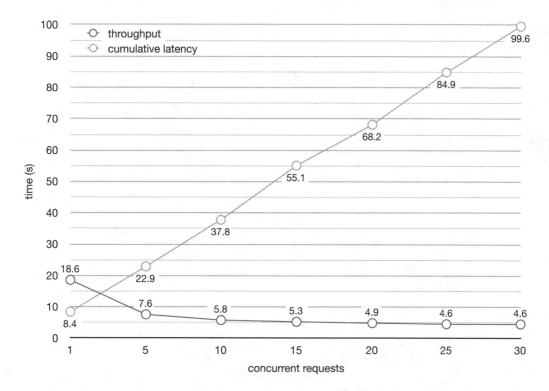

**Figure 12.9**  Time to complete 10,000 HTTP requests locally with varying concurrency levels

simultaneous requests and is only a requirement imposed on clients, not something enforceable by the protocol.

The main way to accomplish this is to limit the number of simultaneous requests. You don't have to get that number perfectly right; TCP's congestion control will ensure that the data is delivered, and the performance effects only become significant when the channel capacity is exceeded significantly. HTTP/2 manages its transfers via a single persistent and multiplexed connection, possibly benefitting much more from the underlying TCP protocol.

Although this aspect is not documented, both my testing and the complaints from the server team(s) indicate that now deprecated NSURLConnection class does not limit the number of connections. In fact, just creating a NSURLConnection instance will start the transfer. In order to work around this limitation, I had to create a small bit of infrastructure that would queue incoming download requests and only start a few of them at a time.

The NSURLSession URL-loading system introduced in iOS 7 and Mac OS X 10.9 fortunately makes much of this infrastructure unnecessary. For example,

NSURLSessionTask instances controlling a particular download start off suspended; you have to explicitly -resume them to start the download. Furthermore, the NSURLSessionConfiguration class that configures a NSURL Session and all its NSURLSessionTasks comes with the HTTPMaximum ConnectionsPerHost property that at least allows limiting the number of connections going to a specific host, at the very least avoiding overloading a particular host with simultaneous connections.

The default value for HTTPMaximumConnectionsPerHost varies to be appropriate for the current environment. For example, it is 6 on my MacBook Pro and 4 on my iPhone, but on the iPhone it does not seem to vary with the active network type. These values are good generic defaults for average requests that closely match the data seen in Figure 12.8, but you may have to tweak them yourself—for example, limiting large downloads to a smaller number—as these can saturate the network all by themselves. The HTTPShouldUsePipelining flag is turned off by default; if your server supports pipelining, then turning on this flag can significantly increase throughput.

## Data Handling

In addition to not utilizing network bandwidth, another problem with the initWithContentsOfURL: approach is data handling and memory consumption. Each individual file is loaded into memory completely before processing begins, which can be a problem if the amount of data is large.

There are two basic ways of dealing with this problem. The first is to process data immediately and incrementally as it arrives. This approach works well if the amount of incoming data per file is large, can be processed incrementally, and will be reduced substantially in processing. It does mean that the processing logic has to be able to process data in small chunks, probably dealing with buffer stitching (see above) and partial results, and also be able to report those partial results to the UI.

For this particular feed-handling application we chose the second approach, which is to download the files to disk instead of to memory and then map those disk files into memory. This gives us the advantages of memory mapping and the simplicity of dealing with complete files. It was feasible because the individual feed files were relatively small; we just had a lot of them.

By downloading to disk, we also more or less automatically had our own URL cache. Unlike the system-wide URL cache, we could control the lifetime of objects in our cache and therefore also use it for offline reading and quick start-up, starting the application from the cache and updating the data incrementally from the server if available.

The final problem with the news application was that not only was all this network activity synchronous, and therefore slow, it was also being done on the main thread, and therefore it blocked the application until complete. Although the NSURLConnection (and NSURLSession) system runs asynchronously on an NSRunLoop, and could therefore in theory have been managed from the main thread without blocking on-network operations, there was still enough other work being done (checking caches, writing data to disk, loading the downloaded data from disk and processing it, initiating transfers, etc.) that it was beneficial to have a separate thread with its own `NSRunLoop` manage all of the I/O, reporting to the main thread only when data had been processed and the UI was ready to be updated.

The final feed update algorithm looked as follows:

1. Fetch the overall feed directory either from the caches or from the Web.
2. For each feed in the directory:
    a. Fetch the RSS feed, either cached or from the Web.
    b. Parse thumbnail, article content, and image URLs from the feed.
    c. Submit all of the thumbnail URLs for fetching.
    d. Submit all of the article content (HTML) URLs for fetching.
    e. Submit all of the article image URLs for fetching.

Notice that the first two levels of fetching are actually synchronous. This not only keeps the code compact and easy to follow, more importantly it also minimizes the time until the first news feed can be displayed. So until the first feed is available, we minimize latency; only after the first feed is downloaded (and can be displayed to the user) do we start submitting multiple simultaneous requests and optimize for overall bandwidth rather than individual latency. We also submit the requests in the order that they will most likely be needed.

With these changes in place, the application went from being unusably slow to being highly responsive, with instant start-up and feeds and stories popping up almost immediately after an empty start or a refresh.

In experiments running over the loopback interface, the Cocoa network stack used here was capable of managing 1,000 requests per second for small requests and an over 300 MB/s transfer speed for large requests, both vastly exceeding typical client needs or (wide-area) network capabilities. So although higher-performance models for network I/O exist, the basic Cocoa networking stack is more than sufficient for client networking needs.

## Asynchronous I/O

As a matter of fact, I want to briefly digress on a bit of over-engineering in the name of alleged performance improvements, particularly the use of asynchronous I/O primitives and techniques built on top of them.

Most of the Unix system calls have asynchronous variants that do not block their calling thread until the I/O is done, but rather use different mechanisms for signaling completion. In theory, this is a good idea because having a larger number of potential I/O operations to schedule together gives the OS greater opportunities to optimize the actual I/O.

In practice, the asynchronous POSIX functions are actually not that useful: For example, "synchronous" file writes are already asynchronous by default, going to memory first and only being flushed later by the OS, "synchronous" file reads use lots of read-ahead to have a similar effect. In fact, the creator of the reference BitTorrent implementation `libtorrent` documented in a blog post[1] how his experiments with asynchronous APIs led him to adopt a strategy similar to the one in the previous section with a single I/O service thread, though this time for disk I/O.

This is a variant of the basic *evented* network architecture that has also been adopted by high-performance Web servers in response the *C10K problem*[2] presented in 1999 by Dan Kegel. It posited that hardware at that time had become capable of handling 10,000 simultaneous Web clients, but limitations of the software stack were preventing high-concurrency Web servers from functioning.

Of the options presented, using one thread per connection and normal-blocking (synchronous) I/O is presented as problematic because some OSes "have trouble handling more than a few hundred threads." It should be obvious that this does not present a problem when you are dealing with typically six or maybe up to a dozen network connections rather than tens of thousands. For a typical networking client communicating with servers over the public Internet, synchronous I/O is more than adequate from a performance point of view; there is no need to use asynchronous APIs for performance reasons.

This advice also applies Apple's *Grand Central Dispatch* (`dispatch_io`) and higher-level libraries built on top (`NSStream` comes to mind). If you find that these APIs make your code easier than a simple `read()` or `write()` loop, by all means go ahead. Just don't expect to reap any measurable performance gains, unless you were performing that I/O on the main thread. This doesn't mean that, for example, GCD isn't a good implementation of those concepts, it's just that the effects that `GCD`-like architectures address don't appear until you reach concurrency levels that are several orders of magnitude higher than a typical client, and are absolutely dwarfed by other effects as we will see in the next section.

## HTTP Serving

Like many Mac developers with a NeXT background, I miss the old Objective-C WebObjects framework. Being able to share code between a front end and back end is an enticing feature, so much so that developers have started using JavaScript on the server, for example, in the form of *node.js*. Objective-C is a good combination of high performance for scalable Web services and good expressiveness for rapid development. In principle, it should be able to save start-ups from initially implementing their services using Ruby on Rails and then having to move them to Java or Go when the services start failing under load.

Unfortunately, I never had an excuse to look at this problem in earnest until I had to embed a small HTTP server into a Cocoa desktop program, to vend Atom feeds

---

1. http://blog.libtorrent.org/2012/10/asynchronous-disk-io/
2. http://www.kegel.com/c10k.html

and calendar information in a peer-to-peer setting. I initially tried Cocoa HTTP, but I found it surprisingly difficult to modify to serve dynamic content, so I quickly switched to GNU libmicrohttpd. Looking at this in a server context shows how networking code looks when actually pushed hard, which we saw doesn't really happen in most client code.

Even after I wrapped libmicrohttpd somewhat inexpertly with an Objective-C class that maps different HTTP verbs to messages, I found performance to be remarkably good. Figure 12.10 shows request handling performance for small requests compared both to Cocoa embeddable libraries such as the GCD-based *CocoaHTTPServer* and the *OCFWebServer* that serves as the basis of a Cocoa-based Web-hosting service, but also the *Sinatra* Ruby micro-framework, the champion of high-performance non-blocking JavaScript serving *node.js*. The static servers *Apache* and *nginx* are included for reference only; they were serving files while the other servers were all serving from memory.

All the results were gathered using the *wrk* stress-testing tool via the loopback interface using a command such as `wrk -r 10000 -c 100 http://localhost:8081/`. The loopback interface was used in order to test the server code rather than the network hardware, with the obvious drawback that the load generator and the server are running on the same host. This actually caused problems when it turned out that both *apache bench (ab)* and *httperf* were not fast enough to keep up with the faster servers under test, but *wrk* solved that particular issue.

What's striking about Figure 12.10 is that even after wrapping, libmicrohttpd manages about 4 to 6 times the throughput of other Cocoa-based embedded Web-servers, despite using old-fashioned techniques such as `select()`-based polling with a thread pool or even spawning a thread per connection and using blocking I/O, rather than modern techniques such as GCD-based I/O.

The reason for this is that, just as I wrote above when discussing asynchronous I/O, differences in thread-scheduling or work-crew management, though they do matter, clearly matter far less than other factors. Looking at an Instruments inverted call tree for both *CocoaHTTPServer* (Figure 12.11) and libmicrohttpd (Figure 12.12) shows this en-détail.

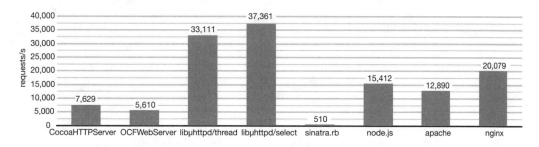

**Figure 12.10**   Web server request handling performance

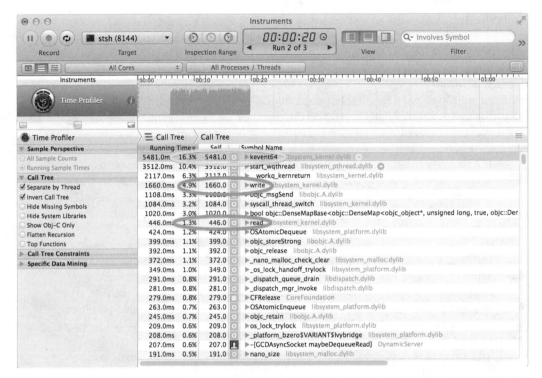

**Figure 12.11**    Trace for Cocoa HTTPServer. Functions doing useful network I/O work are circled in green (the two bottom circles). Overhead is circled in yellow (the top-most circle).

In both traces, the functions doing useful network I/O work are circled in green (the two bottom circles). These are the top functions in the libmicrohttpd trace (Figure 12.12), but occur much further down in the *CocoaHTTPServer* (Figure 12.11), which is dominated by overhead, circled in yellow (the top-most circle). For example, messaging overhead is several times higher relative to useful work, as is memory allocation. The special GCD features that are supposed to guarantee efficiency also contribute, with the kevent() function that is supposed to be a more scalable replacement for select() actually taking around 16 times longer relative to the network I/O being performed.

Of course, Sinatra performance is almost comically bad, clocking in at 10% of the embedded Cocoa servers and less than 2% of libmicrohttpd. *node.js*, being based on libev, is actually quite efficient for the simple static data serving task but utilizes only one core on this two-core system. The libmicrohttpd architecture allows it to take advantage of multiple cores and also handle a thread blocking, for example, because of a virtual memory fault requiring some memory to be swapped in from disk.

For completeness, Figure 12.13 shows the throughput of these same Web servers, again using the loopback interface. As throughput is dominated by the kernel's

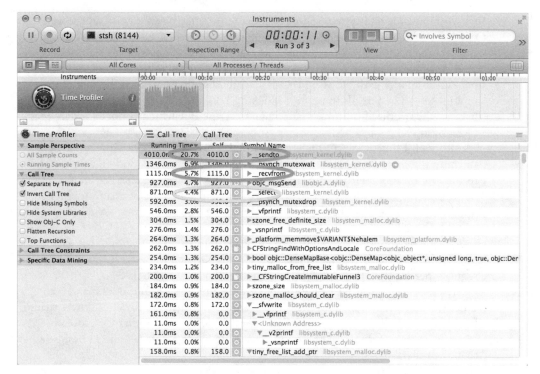

**Figure 12.12**  Trace for libmicrohttpd. Functions doing useful network I/O work are circled in green (the two top circles). Overhead is circled in yellow (the bottom-most circle).

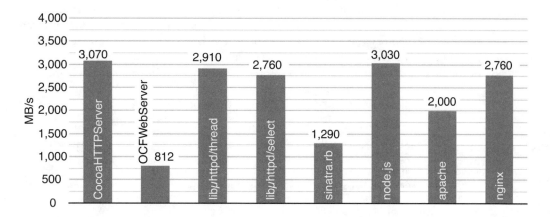

**Figure 12.13**  Web-server throughput for large files

networking code and system call interface, the variance between different servers is much less. All of these servers would be able to saturate a 1 Gbit/s network interface, and all except *OCFWebServer*[3] would also saturate a 10-Gbit/s link.[4]

A small data point to note is that in throughput, libmicrohttpd connection-per-thread model with blocking I/O is actually slightly faster than the model that multiplexes a few threads using non-blocking I/O and `select()`, presumably because the overhead of using `select()` to figure out which connections are ready is removed.

Although I don't expect Objective-C to take over the Web-serving world by storm in the immediate future, it is good to know that, given good libraries, it is up to the job. Pushing performance in a server setting also reveals that the basic optimization guidelines we discussed in earlier chapters have a dramatically higher impact on performance than complex technologies for performing asynchronous and non-blocking I/O.

I also tested a number of Swift HTTP server frameworks. The one that gave the most convincing showing was Dynamo,[5] clocking in at a respectable 8,000 to 9,000 requests per second. That is faster than Sinatra, CocoaHTTPServer, or OCFWebServer, but slower than the big guns node, apache, and nginx, and 3 to 4 times slower than wrapped libmicrohttp. Swifter[6] was around 10 times slower than Dynamo and tended to crash. I couldn't get Taylor, Perfect, Kitura, or vapor to compile, as they were all relying on intermediate Swift 3.0 development builds rather than the official betas.

## Serialization

Although `NSData` and raw Unix I/O are good for moving bytes between memory and devices, Objective-C applications will typically want to load and save documents or other structured data that is represented in memory as Objective-C objects. In principle, there are two options for accomplishing this: You can simply dump and load the internal memory representation, or you can serialize the internal representation into an extern format. You can either serialize the data yourself, or you can use one of the mechanisms built into Cocoa: property list serialization or object archiving.[7]

In order to compare these approaches, we will look at saving and loading objects of the very simple `SampleObject` class shown in Example 12.2.

---

3. *OCFWebServer* by default used `NSString` as response data, dropping throughput to 426 MB/s. The test was performed with an `NSData` object instead.

4. Sinatra required very large request sizes not to be limited by the low request throughput. For example, a 1-MB request would have limited Sinatra to 500-MB/s throughput.

5. https://github.com/johnno1962/Dynamo

6. https://github.com/httpswift/swifter

7. The Apple documentation incorrectly uses the term *serialization* only for types of serialization that do not preserve object identities and relationships. We will use the more widely accepted definition in which archiving is a special case to serialization, not an alternative to it.

**Example 12.2   Sample object for archiving comparisons**

```
@interface SampleObject : NSObject
{
    int retainCount;
    int a;
    float b;
    NSString *name;
    NSArray  *children;
}
```

Because this is a book on performance, we will be looking at roughly 1 million objects taking around 60 MB of memory when resident. The `SampleObject` instances are arranged in the tree shown schematically in Figure 12.14.

The tree has a depth of three, with the top-level object pointing to 1,000 second-level objects, which in turn point to 1,000 leaf objects each. Each object has instance variables of the primitive `float` and `int` types; interior nodes also have an `NSArray` containing their children whereas leaf nodes have an `NSString`.

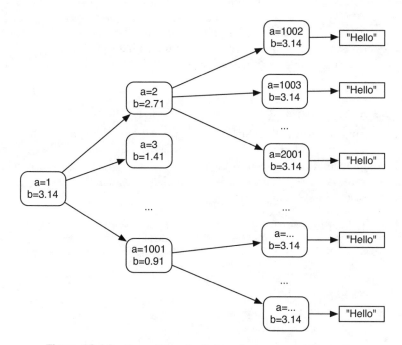

**Figure 12.14**   Tree of `SampleObject` instances used for testing

## Memory Dumps

The conceptually simplest and potentially fastest technique for saving state is to do a memory dump. Just take the base address of the data you save and either `write()` it out or wrap it in an `NSData` for writing with one of the `writeTo...` methods, making sure to use the non-copying initializer (`initWithBytesNoCopy:...`).

This technique used to be quite popular. The early Microsoft Office formats such as `.doc` and `.xls` were effectively dumps of the (fairly complicated) internal data structures. This was great for performance, but is somewhat less than stellar for interoperability, as you would need to either have or reverse-engineer Microsoft Office's internal data structures in order to read and write the file format. This becomes tricky as internal data representation changes, for example, due to different structure padding, endianness, and the move from 16 to 32 to 64 bits.

The Squeak system I mentioned earlier solves most of these issues. It uses an *image* file as primary storage, which is simply a memory dump of the internal object store. Memory is kept contiguous by the copying garbage collector, the address of a saved image is stored, and on load it tries to use the same address or it adjusts all pointers in the image if it cannot allocate memory at the same address. Endianness is also reversed if necessary.

The results are quite good. The default Squeak image has around 1.2 million objects, it only takes 200 ms to save those to a 23-MB image file, and adding our 1 million `SampleObject` instances increases the space to 46 MB and the time to only 500 ms.

However, the one problem they haven't solved is interoperability. Only other Squeak systems can interpret image files, and an image has to save as a whole, so I can only save my `SampleObject` instances by saving the entire image containing those objects.

## A Simple XML Format

One of the things we can do is create our own format, and following in the steps of the new Office (MS and Open) and iWork file formats, let's make it XML. A trivial example of the format can be seen in Example 12.3: the object gets translated to an `S` element, with the `a` and `b` instance variables translated to attributes and the `c` attribute translated to element content.

**Example 12.3    Sample raw XML**

```
<S a="100" b="100.12">
  <S a="0" b="0">
    <S a="0" b="0">hello world</S>
    <S a="0" b="1">hello world</S>
    <S a="0" b="2">hello world</S>
    <S a="0" b="3">hello world</S>
...
```

We will use the fast XML parser from Chapter 4 to read the file and a simple XML writer based on the *FilterStreams* concept from Chapter 8 to write, shown in Example 12.4.

**Example 12.4    Raw XML encoding**

```
-(void)generateXMLOn:(MPWXmlGeneratorStream*)stream
{
  [stream writeElementName:"S"
          attributeBlock:^(MPWXmlGeneratorStream *s) {
            [s writeCStrAttribute:"a" intValue:a];
            [s writeCStrAttribute:"b" doubleValue:b];
            [s writeCStrAttribute:"name" value:name];
          } contentBlock:^(MPWXmlGeneratorStream *s) {
            for ( SampleObject *o in children ) {
              [o generateXMLOn:s];
            }
        }];
}
```

The serialization code uses the `MPWXmlGeneratorStream`'s block-based method `writeElementName:attributeBlock:contentBlock:` to actually generate the XML representation. The methods `writeCStrAttribute:intValue:` and `writeCStrAttribute:doubleValue:` make it possible to write the primitive attributes without requiring object conversion of either the key or the value, and the block for the content of the element manages the recursive structure, again without requiring translation to an intermediate object form. The whole method is very similar to using `printf()` calls to generate the XML, but with the generator stream ensuring correct XML syntax.

The parsing code shown in Example 12.5 uses a block to handle the S element. The a and b attributes are obtained from the attributes using `objectFor UniqueKey:`, and the children are presumed to already be decoded.

**Example 12.5    Raw XML parsing**

```
+(instancetype)parseFromXML:(NSData*)xmlData
{
  MPWMAXParser *parser= [MPWMAXParser parser];
    [parser setHandler:self forElements:[NSArray arrayWithObject:@"S"]
           inNamespace:nil prefix:@"" map:nil];
    [parser handleElement:@"S"
               withBlock:^(id elements,id attrs, id parser) {
        id children;
        if ( [elements count] == 1 ) {
          children=[elements lastObject];
        } else {
          children=[elements allObjects];
```

```
        }
        return [[self alloc]
                    initWithA:[[attrs objectForUniqueKey:@"a"] intValue]
                           b:[[attrs objectForUniqueKey:@"b"] floatValue]
                           c:children];
    }];
  }
  return [parser parsedData:xmlData];
}
```

Both saving and loading the 1 million `SampleObject` instance object graph takes slightly less than a second on my MacBook Pro, 0.4 s for generating and 0.7 s for parsing the XML representation. This takes 50 MB on disk, which is around twice the size of the Squeak memory dump and takes not quite twice as long, but with a file format that is human readable and accessible to other programs and tools.

The performance of our XML serialization routines translates to a little over 100 MB/s for writing and a little less for reading, so near the sequential write performance of modern hard disks and around one fourth of a reasonably fast SSD. Can we do better?

Since we need to convert number to ASCII and XML is a somewhat verbose format, a compact binary representation might be advantageous.

## Property Lists

Both OS X and iOS have deep system-level support for property lists, which have both an XML and a binary storage format. Property lists have been around for a long time—they come from NeXTStep—and are pervasive, being used not just in everything from the user defaults database to Xcode project files and bundle Info.plist files, but also in third-party file formats such as Omni Graffle and Aquaminds NoteShare. It stands to reason that there has been plenty of time and motivation for Apple to optimize them.

Property lists consist of trees containing instances of the classes `NSArray`, `NSDictionary`, `NSString`, `NSData`, `NSDate`, and `NSNumber`, with the latter split into real numbers, integers, and Boolean values.

Converting between a serialized and an object representation of a property list is a one-step process using the aptly named `NSPropertyListSerialization` class's class methods: `[NSPropertyListSerialization dataWithProperty List:plist format:NSPropertyListXMLFormat_v1_0 options:0 error:nil]` gets you a serialized representation of a property list in XML format, changing the `format:` parameter allows you to create an optimized binary representation instead. Mac OS X 10.7 Lion and iOS 5 added support for JavaScript

Object Notation (*JSON*[8]), which shares almost exactly the same object model and even very closely matches the original NeXTStep property list syntax.

However, our object graph does not contain objects of the requisite classes, it contains `SampleObject` instances. So, we first need to convert our tree into that format. Example 12.6 shows how this conversion might look, turning an instance of the `SampleObject` class into an `NSDictionary`, the `float` and `int` parameters into `NSNumber` instances. We also define `asPlist` to return itself for `NSString`, because `NSString` is already a property list, and `NSArray` converts its contents to dictionaries.

Running this code yields surprising results. The highly optimized binary property list format is not faster than our simple ASCII-based XML scheme, but at 6.6 s to serialize and 2.79 s to deserialize, it is significantly slower for a file that at 61 MB is around 20% larger than our XML representation. To be precise, saving is more than ten times slower and reading is three times slower.

How come? The problem does not seem to be a bug in Foundation or in the binary property list format, as CoreFoundation's `CFPropertyListCreateData()` function takes exactly the same amount of time and changing the format to XML almost doubles the serialization and deserialization times over the binary format.

Thinking back to the "Architectural Considerations" section of Chapter 7 suggests that requiring the entire intermediate representation to be present in memory might be a problem, and checking with Instruments shows that, indeed, memory overhead for creating the binary plist is over 300 MB, more than 7 times the size of the on-disk representation and still 5 times the size of our object graph in memory. (The XML generator has negligible memory overhead.) The reason this is so big is, of course, that the intermediate representation we have to provide is made up of `NSDictionary`, `NSNumber`, and friends, which we already saw are highly inefficient ways to store data.

Example 12.7 shows the verbosity of the XML property list representation: Instead of our specific `S` tag, we have generic tags such as `key`, `string`, and `integer`. Indeed, the entire XML tag vocabulary is used for meta-modeling, with our actual model relegated to content inside the various tags along with the actual data. In memory, the instance variable `a` is represented by 4 bytes of memory containing a binary representation of the value, with metadata about the value such as its name and type stored separately and shared by all instances of the class. In the raw XML representation, the same integer was represented as the string `a="100"`, in the plist representation, the representation expands to `<key>a</key><integer>100</integer>`. Despite this massive expansion, the plist representation actually contains less information; the `dict` element is generic without any indication that this particular `dict` is linked to the `SampleObject` class.

---

8. http://www.json.org/

**Example 12.6    Convert SampleObject to and from property list**

```
-processCArrayFromPlist:someC {
  if ( [someC isKindOfClass:[NSArray class]] ) {
    NSMutableArray *r=[NSMutableArray arrayWithCapacity:[someC count]];
    for ( NSDictionary *d in someC ){
      [r addObject:[[[[self class] alloc] initWithPlist:d] autorelease]];
    }
    someC=r;
  }
  return someC;
}

-(instancetype)initWithPlist:(NSDictionary*)aPlist
{
  return [self initWithA:[[aPlist objectForKey:@"a"] intValue]
          b:[[aPlist objectForKey:@"b"] floatValue]
          c:[self processCArrayFromPlist:[aPlist objectForKey:@"c"]]];
}

-(NSDictionary*)asPlist
{
  NSMutableDictionary *dict=[NSMutableDictionary dictionary];
  [dict setObject:@(a) forKey:@"a"];
  [dict setObject:@(b) forKey:@"b"];
  [dict setObject:[c asPlist] forKey:@"c"];
  return dict;
}
@implementation NSString(asPlist)

-(NSDictionary*)asPlist { return self; }

@end

@implementation NSArray(asPlist)

-(NSDictionary*)asPlist {
  NSMutableArray *plist=[NSMutableArray array];
  for (id a in self ) {
    [plist addObject:[a asPlist]];
  }
  return plist;
}
@end
```

**Example 12.7    Sample XML property list (incomplete)**

```
<plist version="1.0">
<dict>
        <key>a</key>
        <integer>100</integer>
        <key>b</key>
        <real>100.12000274658203</real>
        <key>c</key>
        <array>
  ...
                                <dict>
                                        <key>a</key>
                                        <integer>0</integer>
                                        <key>b</key>
                                        <real>0.0</real>
                                        <key>c</key>
                                        <string>hello world</string>
                                </dict>
  ...
```

So it seems we should be able to do better with a serialization method whose API does not require us to provide a complete intermediate representation, and especially not one composed largely of NSDictionary instances. In fact, Apple's *Property List Programming Guide* advises us that if "you need a way to store large, complex graphs of objects, . . . , use *archiving*."

## Archiving

Whereas property lists are restricted to trees of the special property list classes, archiving can serialize arbitrary object graphs and data within those graphs. The NSCoding protocol is also incremental in the way we saw in Chapter 7; you get to archive one object and one attribute at a time. Although any class can implement the NSCoding protocol, Apple has only two: the older NSArchiver using binary typed streams inherited from NeXTStep and the NSKeyedArchiver that is recommended by Apple for Cocoa since its introduction in Mac OS X 10.2 and is the only Apple-provided archiver available on iOS.

Example 12.8 shows the methods for archiving and unarchiving our sample objects. It uses simple macros that expand to the code shown in comments but avoid having to duplicate the variable names and keys. As you can see, the code is somewhat simpler than above, and the methods produce their results incrementally.

**Example 12.8    Archiving and unarchiving an object**

```
-(void)encodeWithCoder:(NSCoder*)aCoder
{
  encodeVar( aCoder, a );          // [aCoder writeInt:a forKey:@"a"];
  encodeVar( aCoder, b );
  encodeVar( aCoder, c );
}

- (id)initWithCoder:(NSCoder *)aCoder {
     if (self = [super init]) {
        decodeVar( aCoder, a ); // a=[aCoder decodeIntForKey:@"a"];
        decodeVar( aCoder, b );
        decodeVar( aCoder, c );
     }
   return self;
}
```

An actual archive is created either in memory using the `archivedDataWith`
`RootObject:` method returning an `NSData` or directly on disk/to a file using
`archiveRootObject:toFile:`, each taking the root of our `SampleObject`
tree as its primary argument. However, runtimes were disappointing: 9.1 s to save and
2.6 s to load, so even slower to serialize than property lists (by a factor of 2), and no
faster reading. Memory use is dramatically worse: 819-MB overhead for an archive
that takes 77 MB on disk.

Why does keyed archiving perform so badly? One potential theory is the fact that
archiving does something that serialization does not: It maintains object relationships,
and therefore has to do a little more work in maintaining those relationships.
However, Apple's "old-style" archiver also does this work and is much faster: 2.12 s
to archive and 0.81 s to unarchive. Also, as we will see in the next chapter, the binary
property list format actually also has facilities for uniquing. So maintaining
relationships is not the problem.

Apple's primary recommendation for improving keyed archiving performance is to
leave out keys that only contain default data, but even leaving out *all* the data from
our object graph except for the structural parts (so no integers, doubles, or string)
improves serialization and deserialization speeds only marginally to 6.0 s and 2.06 s,
respectively.

A little investigation shows that the reason for keyed archiving's poor performance
is that it does not actually stream results, despite the nice streaming API. Instead, it
builds a property list behind the scenes, and as Example 12.9 shows, this property list
contains several additional levels of indirection and is even larger than the direct
property list we created in the previous section.

**Example 12.9    Keyed archive property list (incomplete, converted to XML)**

```
<dict>
        <key>$archiver</key>
        <string>NSKeyedArchiver</string>
        <key>$objects</key>
        <array>
                <string>$null</string>
                <dict>
                        <key>$0</key>
                        <integer>100</integer>
                        <key>$1</key>
                        <real>100.12000274658203</real>
                        <key>$2</key>
                        <dict>
                                <key>CF$UID</key>
                                <integer>2</integer>
                        </dict>
                        <key>$class</key>
                        <dict>
                                <key>CF$UID</key>
                                <integer>7</integer>
                        </dict>
                </dict>
                <dict>
                        <key>$class</key>
                        <dict>
                                <key>CF$UID</key>
                                <integer>1007</integer>
                        </dict>
                        <key>NS.objects</key>
                        <array>
                                <dict>
                                        <key>CF$UID</key>
                                        <integer>3</integer>
                                </dict>
                                <dict>
                                        <key>CF$UID</key>
                                        <integer>1008</integer>
                                </dict>
                                <dict>
                                        <key>CF$UID</key>
...
```

It is not entirely clear why Apple chose such an inefficient format, where every object is represented not just by one but by multiple dictionaries, and these dictionaries are actually manifested in one gigantic object tree before that tree is finally serialized.

## Serialization Summary

Figure 12.15 summarizes how the different serialization mechanisms performed: of the Apple-provided mechanisms, the old-style archiver did the best, closely followed by all the property list–based mechanisms, with the new JSON (de-)serializer leading the pack, trailed by the keyed archiver. However, all except the old-style archiver were beaten handily by our little XML serializer, and none of them came close to matching the hardware.

Figure 12.16 shows the sizes of the serialized representations, along with the peak memory usage during serialization. The difference in memory consumption between the different serialization methods is even more pronounced than just the timings, whereas the on–disk size differs by around a factor of 2 at most.

When dealing with large data sets, especially large numbers of objects, Apple currently does not have an adequate serialization mechanism, and the mechanism that Apple recommends most for large data sets is actually the one that is least suitable both in terms of time and memory used. The discrepancy is less bad for deserialization than it is for serialization, with the argument being that files are read a lot more than they are written. With auto-save and versions, this may no longer be the case.

It should be noted that Apple themselves do not use any of these standard mechanisms for their Apple Productivity Apps Pages, Numbers, and Keynote (formerly known as *iWork*). Previous versions used an XML format via `libxml2`, but since iWork '13 the format was switched to Google protocol buffers via a private framework.

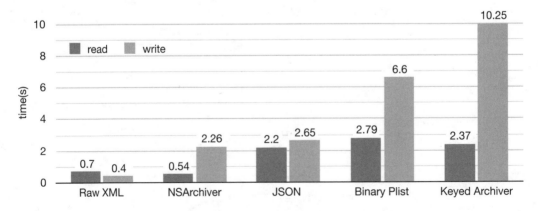

**Figure 12.15** Time to read and write 1M objects

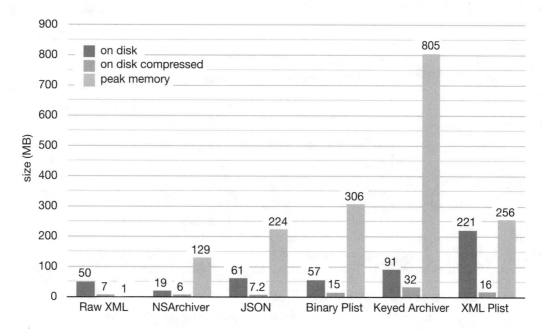

**Figure 12.16**    Disk and memory space required for serializing 1M objects

# CoreData

For high performance with large data sets, Apple recommends CoreData, as a "highly optimized" solution that has the "best memory scalability of any competing solution." According to the documentation, "you could spend a long time carefully crafting your own solution optimized for a particular problem domain, and not gain any performance advantage over what Core Data offers for free."

In light of these hopeful remarks, let's apply CoreData to our sample task: create and save our tree of roughly 1 million `SampleObject` instances and find ways to optimally fetch them for in-memory processing. In order to do this, we need to make `SampleObject` a subclass of `NSManagedObject`, which can then automatically synthesize the special setters and getters required for CoreData attributes (see Example 12.10). As a slight simplification, we leave out the root object, so starting with what used to be the second level of 1,000 objects, each with 1,000 child objects.

**Example 12.10    `SampleObjects` as a CoreData class**

```
@interface SampleObject : NSManagedObject

@property (nonatomic,assign) NSInteger a;
@property (nonatomic,assign) float b;
```

```
@property (nonatomic,assign) NSString *c;
@property (nonatomic,strong) NSSet *children;
@property (nonatomic,assign) SampleObject *parent;

@end

@implementation SampleObject

@dynamic a,b,c,children,parent;

@end
```

In addition, we need to create a NSManagedObjectModel, either in approximately 60 lines of code or using the Xcode data modeler. Once we have that, we obtain an NSManagedObjectContext and another 30 lines of code, and we are then ready to create some objects and save them to an SQLite store. Fortunately, iOS 10 and OS X 10.12 simplify this using the NSPersistentContainer class.

## Create and Update in Batches

The results of creating our 1 million objects and saving them the way we did before are somewhat disappointing: The whole process takes 34.4 s, roughly 3 times what our previous slowest mechanism, NSKeyedArchiver, required. At slightly over 1 GB, it also manages to increase memory overhead slightly over NSKeyedArchiver, despite the actual on-disk store being pretty small at only 44 MB. What's also surprising is that just creating the objects in memory already takes 12 s, with the remainder in the save. For reference, creating our SampleObject graph made of plain objects rather than NSManagedObject subclasses only took 350 *milliseconds*, so 1/30th of the time, and as we recall from Chapter 1, allocating objects is one of the slower operations we deal with.

Using an XML store instead of SQLite takes a minute and a half and more than 4.5 GB of memory to produce a 399-MB on-disk result, with the binary store almost the same, so atomic stores aren't the solution. Even the in-memory store takes 20 s, so I/O is not really the problem. Figure 12.17 shows the timings, with Figure 12.18 showing memory consumption and on-disk sizes.

Apple's CoreData documentation strongly suggests splitting such operations and operating in batches, which is great if your data model supports it. Our model supports it sufficiently to run some tests with different batch sizes, from 10 elements (meaning 100,000 batches) all the way to 1 batch of a million objects. We are assuming completely independent batches that allow us to reset the NSManagedObjectContext, which completely purges the objects from memory.

The results are in Figure 12.19, plotting both performance and memory by batch size. For performance, there is a sweet spot right in the middle, with a batch size of 1,000 objects. Smaller batch sizes start incurring the higher I/O overhead of small writes, real time as shown by significant time command increases, whereas larger

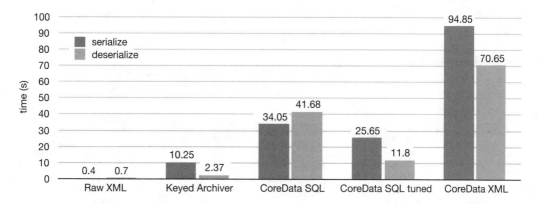

**Figure 12.17**    Time to read and write 1M objects, including databases

batch sizes incur higher CPU loads. Apparently there are data structures or algorithms that have a slightly worse than linear scaling. Memory, on the other hand, is strictly linear, taking 1 KB of memory per saved or modified object, with a lower bound of 14.7 MB. If you cannot `reset` the `NSManagedObjectContext` between batches, memory consumption will be around 600 MB for the 1 million objects.

Please note that we have now adapted our program structure, and possibly our data model, to work around the limitations of CoreData. In fact, it is more specific than that, because the batching strategy described only improves performance with the SQLite store; it makes things catastrophically worse with atomic stores. The reason is that atomic stores have to re-read all previous data in order to process each batch, the size of which increases linearly, turning the problem from an $O(n)$ complexity with a high constant factor making it slow to $O(n^2)$ complexity with the same high constant factor.

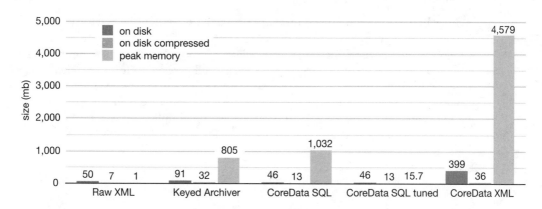

**Figure 12.18**    Disk and memory space for 1M objects with CoreData

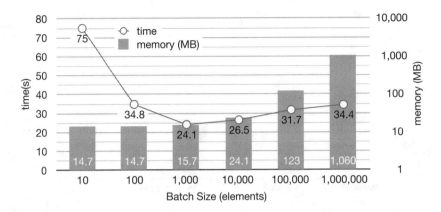

**Figure 12.19**   CoreData time/space trade-off for writing (by batch size)

Using the batch size of 1,000 that proved optimal for the SQLite store, the first iteration saved its batch of 1,000 objects in 0.1 s. By the 50th iteration, the time for saving a batch had already increased to 1 s and that linear trend continued, adding another second to the per-batch save time every 50 batches. I interrupted the process after 10 minutes at batch 250 (of 1,000), with per-batch save times having already increased to 5 s. Extrapolating the $O(n^2)$ curve shows that using the batch technique would have taken around 2 hours 48 minutes with the XML store.

Modifying an object graph has essentially identical performance characteristics both in time and space, meaning that CoreData is unsuited for any tasks requiring bulk creation or modification of large data sets.

## Fetch and Fault Techniques

My first experiments with fetching results left me highly impressed, fetching the top-level 1,000 objects for later traversal took less than a half second, and even fetching all the 1 million objects took less than a full second. Of course, I had fallen into the classic benchmarking trap of not using the results of my computation that we had already seen in the CPU chapters: Just like the compiler eliminates computations of unused results, CoreData does not necessarily pull in the data for the fetched objects, especially objects accessed via relationships like the parent–child relationship in our object graph. So in order to test the actual performance, I added the sumB method shown in Example 12.11, which, as the name implies, sums the value of the b attributes of all the objects in the tree.[9]

---

9. I will come to the reason for adding the b attribute 10 times in the "Object Interaction" section later in this chapter.

**Example 12.11    Computing with the `SampleObject` object graph**

```
-(double)sumB
{
    double result=0;
    for (int i=0;i<10;i++ ) {
      result+=[self b];
    }
    for ( SampleObject *s in [self children] ) {
        result+=[s sumB];
    }
    return result;
}
```

The first time I traverse the object graph, CoreData faults in all the values it needs, and takes almost 42 s doing it. The second traversal is essentially instantaneous at 0.3 s. The results for this and other fetch variants are shown in Figure 12.20.

The problem is that each time a relationship is accessed, a fault fires independently, triggering another separate round-trip to the database. Naïve faulting like this was also one of the major problems in using CoreData's predecessor, *Enterprise Object Framework*. For example, a system I was tasked to replace at the BBC was fetching a tree of sport competitions (for example, *FIFA World Cup → Quarter Final*) by iterating over each level of the tree independently in Objective-C code. This caused several hundred round-trips to the database, essentially one for each object in the tree. Explicitly fetching the tree levels reduced those round-trips to three and the time from over 40 s to less than 1 s.

Of course, "round-trip to the database" means something very different in enterprise applications than it does with CoreData: In an enterprise setting, you have to serialize your query, then send it off over the wire to your database server machine.

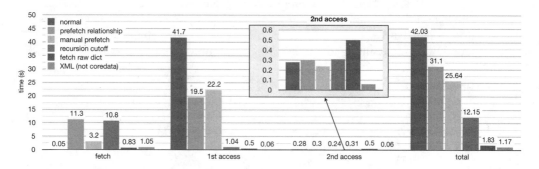

**Figure 12.20**    Timing for CoreData fetch and prefetch variations

Although the database server is a powerful machine with lots of RAM, a high-power CPU, and high-speed disks, the round-trip latencies will destroy your performance, closely followed by the amount of data you are sending over the network. In such an environment, putting business logic on the database server and very carefully selecting the data you send or receive is crucial for minimizing network latency and throughput.

In CoreData, however, the "database server" and the client are usually the same computer (until recently it was the only configuration supported). Furthermore, my experience with object graphs encoded in relational databases is that acceptable performance is usually only achieved when the database resides in RAM (either in the OS's buffer cache or in the database's buffers).

Even with the database files in the buffer cache, the relationships are the major performance drain in this test, but I had a hard time convincing CoreData that I really wanted to fetch the targets of those relationships. My first attempt was `NSManagedObjectContext`'s aptly named `setRelationshipKeyPaths ForPrefetching:` method, asking it to fetch the `children` relationship. That did not make a discernible difference in total time (though it did shift some of the total to the initial fetch), and neither did `setReturnsObjectsAsFaults:NO`. I finally figured out that I had to specify the attributes at the end of the relationship as well, or those would not get read in, so `children`, `children.a`, and `children.b`. With these keys to prefetch, we finally got the results labeled *prefetch relationships*.

However, despite the fact that I was now ostensibly prefetching all the data needed to compute the result, I was still getting significant delays during the first graph traversal, suggesting that there was more faulting going on. Another suggestion for resolving relationship faults is manually fetching the relationships using a separate `NSFetchRequest` with a predicate of the form `@"parent IN %@"`, `fetchedArray`, where `fetchedArray` is the result of the initial fetch. This *manual prefetch* improved things a little by allowing the initial fetch to complete in 3.2 s instead of 11.3 s, but did not change the first time traversal time of 19.5 s.

I finally realized that what CoreData was trying to fetch were the nonexistent children of the leaf objects. Alas, my attempt at being smart and prefetching those using a prefetch key of `@"children.children"` wasn't smiled on by the CoreData gods, resulting in the following error message:

```
CoreData: error: (1) I/O error for database at db.db.
    SQLite error code:1, 'too many SQL variables'
Core Data: error: -executeRequest: encountered exception = I/O error
        for database at db.db.
  SQLite error code:1, 'too many SQL variables' with userInfo = {
    NSFilePath = "db.db";
    NSSQLiteErrorDomain = 1;
}
```

Instead, the only way I found to deal with the situation was to adjust the computation and the object model to include an explicit flag for leaf objects that is not computed by counting the children. With this modified computation shown in Example 12.12, I finally managed to get all required data in the fetch, taking 10.8 s, but no more fetching in the first-time traversal, which now took only slightly over 1 s for the best overall CoreData managed object time of 12.15 s (label *prefetch cut recursion*). Of course, there now is additional overhead in keeping this flag synchronized with the `children` relationship.

**Example 12.12    Cutting off the `SampleObject` object graph traversal**

```
-(double) sumB
{
    double result=0;
    for (int i=0;i<10;i++ ) {
      result+=[self b];
    }
    if ( ![self isLeaf] ) {
      for ( SampleObject *s in [self children] ) {
            result+=[s sumB];
      }
    }
    return result;
}
```

All of these times were measured with a database that had indexes on the keys that are being queried; the same queries without those indexes were generally a few percent slower throughout.

One intriguing optimization suggestion is the setting `NSDictionaryResult Type resultType` in the `NSFetchSpecification`. Instead of returning `NSManagedObject` instances, this will return only `NSDictionary` instances with the attributes specified in the fetch specification. The results are shown in Figure 12.20 with the *fetch raw dict* label, and they are quite astounding: 0.8 s for the fetch! We learned earlier that `NSDictionary` is not usually associated with high performance, so what's going on here?

There are actually a number of things going on here. First, it turns out that the CoreData performance is not limited by SQLite; the dictionary fetches show that getting data from SQLite to Cocoa can be extremely quick. CoreData turning those fetched results into objects, and particularly managing the relationships, is where the performance goes. Second, raw dictionary fetches are limited; they do not handle any relationships. So, for example, our object tree is not available, only a flat array of dictionaries. Third, we cannot modify and save raw dictionaries. Finally, the relative performance of dictionaries compared to "normal" objects is still as we expect, as shown in the inset *2nd fetch*.

The last set of results in Figure 12.20, *XML (not coredata)* shows the times for "fetching" our object graph via the XML deserialization mechanism we looked at in the previous section, with the initial fetch representing the time to deserialize the object graph, and both first and second access being normal object graph traversals using plain Objective-C message sends to retrieve attributes. Accessing instance variables via message sends is still roughly ten times faster than using dictionary access, which is why the total for XML is slightly faster than the raw dictionary fetch, despite the raw dictionary having the faster initial fetch.

## Object Interaction

The *2nd access* times highlight another aspect of CoreData performance that is sometimes neglected: the overhead of retrieving data from an `NSManagedObject` subclass or a dictionary once it has been fetched. The overhead for the former appears to be around 6x compared to a plain object, the latter 10x. We already saw the overhead for writing attributes, which is several orders of magnitude higher. Although CoreData uses special dictionaries and highly optimized dictionary-like access methods for `NSManagedObject` instances, the cost of interacting with attributes is still several times greater than that of interacting with regular objects.

## Subsetting

Where CoreData shines is in dealing with subsets of a large data set, because when connected to an incremental store like SQLite, it is capable of querying subsets, modifying those subsets, and storing them without having to deal with the rest of the data that wasn't touched. While *cost* per element is high (one or more orders of magnitude higher than the simple brute-force techniques we looked at earlier), we can still achieve good or at least reasonable performance for overall performance (*number* * *cost*) if we can push the *number* of elements down.

Reading and writing a single object or one small subset that can be retrieved via index will be quick with CoreData, whereas with the serialization mechanisms we looked at earlier we have to load the entire object graph even if we only need one object, and save the entire object graph even if we only modified a single object.

This ability to deal with subsets is offset by the fact that subsetting is also a hard requirement: You absolutely *must* subset your data, and be absolutely certain that you *always* can find sufficiently small subsets, or performance will blow up in your face. As we saw, CoreData simply can't adequately deal with those large data sets, so you need to make sure your working set is always sufficiently small.

For example, adjusting the query to only fetch 1,000 objects instead of the whole million reduces the fetch time to 10 ms, which is sufficient for many applications but does require not fetching relationships and having an index on the key that we're fetching. Without the index, SQLite has to do a table scan and times increase to around 1.5 s for this data set, which will at the very least be a noticeable delay. Modifying those 1,000 objects in memory takes 31 ms and saving them 144 ms, which is at the edge of interactive performance. For reference, our 1,000 objects are 1/1,000th the 46 MB total file size, so 46 KB, giving us a data rate of 4.4 MB/s for reading and 250 KB/s for writing, which is around 1% or 0.25% of the capabilities of the underlying SSD hardware, respectively.

To really get interactive performance levels for a read/modify/write cycle requires dropping down to around 100 objects on the Mac: 3 ms to read, 4 ms to modify, and around 40 ms to save the results. Again, this requires having an index on the attribute and not fetching relationships. If we start fetching a significant percentage of the relationships, either by faulting or by prefetching, performance once again drops remarkably.

### Analysis

Apple has plenty of other recommendations for optimizing CoreData: tweak the data model to use external storage for large binary data blobs (this is always a good idea; see also the "Segregated Stores" section in this chapter), de-normalize your data model to avoid cross-relationship fetches, experiment with batch sizes in data import tasks, put numeric predicates first in fetch specifications, because those evaluate more quickly, and so on.

However, all of these recommendations are indicative more of overcoming a weakness than showing off a strength. If CoreData has such great performance, why do I have to spend so much effort tuning, getting my fetch specifications to be just the right size, not too large, not too small? These recommendations would make a lot more sense if we actually had the client/server model that CoreData is patterned after, because minimizing traffic across the network is almost always a good idea. When the "server" is not just on the same machine, but actually a library sitting in the same process just a function call away, preserving communications bandwidth to that server doesn't have the same weight.

# SQLite

If CoreData doesn't work for you and you also don't want to hold the entire object graph in memory as required by the serialization techniques presented thus far, another option is talking directly to some sort of database. SQLite is popular for this application on OS X and iOS because it comes as a library that is embedded in your application rather than a separate database server application. It also ships with both OSes and is widely used by Apple themselves, not least in CoreData.

The SQLite C API is somewhat verbose, so I used the lightweight *fmdb* wrapper.[10] Unlike CoreData, fmdb does not handle relationships automatically, so we have to add both an object id and a parent id to our data model, which we then need to populate and resolve as we interact with the database.

Performance was overall much better than with CoreData, for example, 6.7 s to insert the 1M objects instead of 26 to 36 s, with only around 16 MB of constant

---

10. GRDB is a similar wrapper for Swift (https://github.com/groue/GRDB.swift).

memory overhead on top of the size of the object tree itself. An option that helped was enabling prepared statements; runtime without them was 3 to 4 s higher. With fmdb, this is just a flag; the library then manages the prepared statements, looking them up by the string that's sent as a query.

Somewhat more important, the loop that inserted the 1M objects was wrapped in a transaction using [db beginTransaction] and [db endTransaction]. Without an explicit transaction, SQLite wraps every statement in its own individual transaction. For inserting our 1M objects, that increased the total write time to a staggering 11 minutes 43 seconds, roughly 100 times slower than with an explicit transaction! So use explicit transactions for any bulk updates, unless that bulk update can be expressed in a single statement.

Fetching our 1M objects back from the database was also pleasant, taking around 3.6 s for creating the objects from the FMResultSet. As noted above, relationships had to be resolved manually with a NSMapTable mapping database ids to objects. This added another 700 ms, taking the total to 4.3 s for a fully constituted object graph. As the API uses keyed access [rs intForColumn:@"a"], [rs doubleForColumn:@"b"], whereas the low-level SQLite API uses column indexes, I wondered whether this was a problem. A quick check with Instruments revealed that things were as expected and the conversion from string keys to column indexes was taking almost 50% of the time. Adding a little patch practically removed that overhead, reducing fetch times to 2.1 s, including relationship resolution.

So for basic serialization and deserialization of object graphs, direct SQLite access is competitive with most of the serialization mechanisms presented earlier in this chapter. In addition, SQL allows bulk modification of the data on disk without having to first fetch objects, modify them in memory, and finally write them back out again. For example, all SampleObject rows in the database can be have their b attribute set to the value 42 using the following SQL statement: UPDATE SampleObject set b=42. This statement executes in about 1.5 s on my machine, generally quicker than a read/modify/write cycle with serialized objects. Of course, you need to make sure that any objects in memory are either also updated or invalidated; there is no automatic change tracking helping you out.

Like CoreData and unlike basic serialization mechanisms, SQLite direct access can also efficiently fetch and update subsets of your object graph. Restricting to bulk UPDATE we did above to 1,000 objects with a WHERE clause reduces the update time to 90 ms, and fetches of 1,000 objects can be accomplished in 13 ms (all times with index; not having the index adds around 260-ms table-scan time with the database file in the buffer cache).

This was with *write-ahead logging* (*WAL*), enabled in SQLite using the command PRAGMA journal_mode=wal. WAL dramatically improves update performance by sequentializing disk access and is enabled by default for CoreData since iOS 7 and Mac OS X 10.9. Instead of updating data in place in the database file, seeking to the right position for each change, updates are appended sequentially to a log. Reads first look in the log for data and only after that in the main database file.

## Relational and Other Databases

These somewhat tepid results for SQLite and CoreData run contrary to the common perception of relational databases as the pinnacle of I/O optimization and performance, but this perception was never well founded historically, theoretically, or practically.

In my personal experience, relational databases have typically been around an order of magnitude slower than even fairly simplistic nonrelational storage and query strategies. For example, when I was conducting my investigation into Mail.app performance, I was stunned to find out that querying the metadata of a mailbox with approximately 20K messages took SQLite well over a second, whereas doing a simple brute-force linear search of an mbox format version of that mailbox (essentially a concatenation of all the messages in a single file) using the grep command-line utility took a few tens of milliseconds. So the most naïve possible brute-force algorithm was orders of magnitude faster than a sophisticated SQL database!

Jamie Zawinski tells a similar story about the Netscape mailbox summary files: Netscape versions 2.0 and 3.0 used a custom binary format that had 2% space overhead and was able to open a mailbox with 15K messages in under a second on a Pentium/266 class machine (so, roughly the same amount of data and same performance as Mail.app on a 2.5-GHz PowerMac G5). A rewrite dropped in a "proper" database, increasing space overhead by more than an order of magnitude to 30% and dropping performance by an order of magnitude.[11]

One reason, of course, is that relational databases are general-purpose tools that were never designed with performance as their primary goal. Instead, they were meant to allow multiple clients access to normalized enterprise data sets and to permit ad-hoc queries. It took many years of engineering work in the 1970s to 1980s for relational database management systems to at least catch up in performance with their competitors. Many of the implementation strategies for coping with the hardware environment of the times, such as on-disk B-Trees, multi-threading to hide disk latency, and explicit buffer management don't match today's hardware well, and removing them improves database performance by an order of magnitude or more.[12]

In fact, Turing Award winner and general database guru Michael Stonebraker (Ingres, Postgres) has published a series of papers, first declaring the end of the "one size fits all" use of relational databases for specialized applications,[13] and later the "end of an era," casting doubt even on the use of traditional databases in their core application of online transaction processing (OLTP).[14]

---

11. http://www.jwz.org/doc/mailsum.html
12. S. Harizopoulos, D.J. Abadi, S. Madden, and M. Stonebraker. "OLTP through the looking glass, and what we found there," *Proceedings of the 2008 ACM SIGMOD International Conference on Management of Data.* (2008) ACM, pp. 981–92.
13. M. Stonebraker. "Technical perspective—one size fits all: An idea whose time has come and gone," *ACM Communications* (2008).
14. M. Stonebraker, S. Madden, D.J. Abadi, S. Harizopoulos, N. Hachem, and P. Helland. "The end of an architectural era (it's time for a complete rewrite)," *VLDB Proceedings* (2007), pp. 1150–60.

# Event Posting

One interesting alternative to (relational) databases is an architectural pattern known as *Event Poster*,[15] where instead of modifying a persistent store, you store deltas that are applied to an in-memory representation of your data. Coming back to our example of saving *Moby Dick* on every keystroke, imagine just writing the list of keystrokes instead of (a) storing the entire file or (b) trying to modify the file in-place as it is edited.

It should be obvious that this approach can work very efficiently for saving data: Instead of writing $O(n)$ items on every save as we would when writing the entire file, we write just $O(1)$. Updating an on-disk data structure such as a B-Tree would take $O(\log n)$ for each update, though that likely understates the relative cost because the operations would tend to be expensive seeks and possibly moves, whereas events can usually be efficiently appended to a file sequentially. For $n$ operations, that makes the complexity $O(n^2)$ for the full save, $O(n \log n)$ for update-in-place, and $O(n)$ for event posting.

In the pure form of the pattern, the event log is the only storage, the in-memory state is reconstructed on load by replaying the entire event log. This can be a surprisingly simple and effective strategy, as I discovered when implementing the replacement[16] for the problematic BBC feeds processing application mentioned before. Once we had written the feed ingest logic, we noticed that all we needed for persistence was to remove the code that deleted those incoming feed files (which we already wanted to do for auditing purposes). Having a well-optimized ingest processor meant we could simplify the rest of the system: Performance begets simplicity begets performance, a virtuous cycle that I have witnessed numerous times.

## Hybrid Forms

Issues with the pure Event Poster pattern are that it requires all data to fit in main memory and that the event log can get very large, potentially growing without bounds, irrespective of the size of the currently active data (think of rewriting every sentence in *Moby Dick* ten times: the log will be ten times larger with the size of the book hardly changed). For this reason, the Event Poster pattern is usually not applied in its pure form, but instead combined with other forms of storage.

One such hybrid is a checkpoint of the current store: write the state of the system at specific checkpoints, for example, using a fast memory dump. On reads, first attempt to read the checkpoint file, reverting to replaying the log if the checkpoint file does not read correctly. This was the strategy we used with the feeds processing system, in addition to occasionally pruning the log to eliminate entries that were no longer relevant, for example, because they were overwritten by later entries (this needs to be done carefully if you want to keep the log for audit purposes).

---

15. http://martinfowler.com/bliki/EventPoster.html
16. M. Weiher and C. Dowie. "In-process rest at the BBC," *REST: Advanced research topics and practical applications* (2014). Eds. C. Pautasso, E. Wilde, and R. Alarcon.

Another hybrid form is utilized by the *LevelDB* key-value store, an open-source rewrite of Google's *BigTable* data store. Its basic store comprises *Sorted String Tables*, which are read-only lists of strings with an index. Writability is provided using a *Log Structured Merge Tree*: all changes are appended to a log, which is kept in memory and on disk. Reads are satisfied first from the recent changes stored in memory and then from the sorted read-only tables on disk, for example, by having those tables mapped into memory. This means that writes are always fast and reads are always fast, with the cost of having to occasionally rewrite the sorted tables from the log, operations that can then be performed using large batches, and sequential reads and writes.

LevelDB still provides a classic Create Read Update Delete (CRUD) interface to the data, but oftentimes the applications themselves exhibit the characteristics of an Event Poster, RSS feeds, chat or social networking applications, and even e-mail. Such systems can really take advantage of the (time-based) structure of their data: e-mail messages received the last day are usually more frequently accessed than those received last week, which are in turn more frequently accessed than those of the last month, and so on. On the other hand, many people, myself included, never actually delete mail. A relational database like SQLite treats all elements in a table equally, so over time performance deteriorates for all messages, even though the actual working set remains the same.

If I were to write a storage back end for e-mail, I would structure it in a way similar to LevelDB: keep the most recent messages in memory and in a local store that is quick to access and quick to modify in memory. Every once in a while, I would write older messages to read-only chunks (maybe per-month) with extensive summary, indexing, threading, and other metadata information so that most operations would only ever have to look at the summaries. This way accessing the working set would remain the same speed regardless of the size of the mailbox, with older storage only accessed for searches and then performed in large batches at optimal sequential access speeds. However, I would not actually use LevelDB, because its limitation to only strings and no indexes would be too restrictive.

# Segregated Stores

The mail store I just described is really an example of a segregated store. The idea of a segregated store is to keep pieces of data with different sizes, access requirements, and life cycles separate from each other—for example, old messages from new messages.

One example of this idea standing in for other media-rich applications is Apple's Keynote presentation program. In its pre '13 file format, all object layout information was contained in a single XML file called `index.apxl`, either in a directory wrapper or in a zip file. Media data such as images or movies are kept separate from this index file, so even presentations with up to 100 pages and a total size of over 1 Gigabyte had an `index.apxl` file size of less than 2 MB.

In addition, the contents of the `index.apxl` file change effectively with every edit, whereas the media files are immutable once they are imported; they only change if a new version of the media file is imported.

Directory wrappers are ideal for this sort of situation because they allow you to store the large, infrequently changing data separately from the frequently changing smaller data. When saving, make sure you keep a reference to the original data on disk, possibly via its `NSFileWrapper`. Cocoa will only write out the bits that have changed, even performing hard links to unchanged bits on disk if you use the `atomic` version of the file wrapper saving methods.

The zip file versions of the file iWork file formats diminish the advantages of this setup a little because the different components end up in the same zip file. However, just copying bits from one file to a new file is still often much quicker than serializing the data anew, as we saw earlier.

In the current version of the iWork file formats, Apple added another dimension to keeping data separate: each page is a separate entry in the zip file. For saving to disk this probably makes very little difference; instead, it is probably a feature for keeping changes isolated in order to make iCould syncing work.

## Summary

In this chapter, we looked first at basic disk and network I/O, and then at higher-level strategies for serialization, including the built-in serializers, databases, and CoreData and alternative strategies such as XML and the Event Poster pattern.

Alas, we have also seen a lot of pitfalls, many of which involve problems we have encountered before such as overuse of dictionaries and verbose intermediate representations. In short, Cocoa and Objective-C don't have a really good data persistence option, only a bunch of marginally useful ones.

# 13

# I/O: Examples

Having looked at the performance characteristics of some of the I/O and serialization APIs in the previous chapter, we'll now look at some practical examples of making I/O faster. *Significantly* faster.

We start out with a simple word list for a game and work our way up through Apple's binary property list format, which we speed up significantly for many practical purposes. Finally, we throw in some fast comma-separated value (CSV) parsing and design a compact file format for public transport data that beats CoreData by orders of magnitude.

## iPhone Game Dictionary

This particular quest was kicked off by a message from Miles on Apple's cocoa-dev mailing list.[1] Miles wanted to load about 2 MB of text as a dictionary of words for an iPhone game, with the words separated by newlines.

The interface of the class is given in Example 13.1 and illustrates the basic features of the StringTable: initializing with a file and determining whether a specific string is contained within the table.

**Example 13.1   Naïve string table class**

```
#import <Foundation/Foundation.h>

@interface StringTable : NSObject

-(instancetype)initWithContentsOfFile:(NSString*)filename;
-(BOOL)containsString:(NSString*)str;

@end
```

---

1. http://www.mail-archive.com/cocoa-dev@lists.apple.com/msg33602.html

His first attempt saw him taking 0.5 s to read the file, and another 13 s to split the file into lines using [fileContents componentsSeparatedByString: @"\n"] on an iPhone 3G or 3GS class device. Needless to say, he thought this was a bit too long, and I would tend to agree with him.

It is actually worth following the thread as the usual suspects are rolled out: binary property lists, specialized trie data structures, and even SQLite. Binary property lists actually helped a little bit, taking the time from 13.5 s to anywhere from 5 to 8 s, which was still way too slow.

Example 13.2 shows the naïve implementation of that interface that took 13 s using Foundation objects and methods (the declaration and implementation of the words property is not shown).

**Example 13.2    Initializing and searching in the naïve string table**

```
-(instancetype)initWithContentsOfFile:(NSString*)filename
{
  self=[super init];
  NSString *wordList=[NSString stringWithContentsOfFile:filename];
  [self setWords:[wordList componentsSeparatedByString:@"\n"]];
  return self;
}
-(BOOL)containsString:(NSString*)searchStr
{
    return [[self words] indexOfObject:searchString] != NSNotFound;
}
```

In addition to the substantial time, this approach also takes quite a bit of heap memory because first the NSString is allocated, filled with contents from disk, and then each individual word string is allocated. All this memory is of the "dirty" kind, meaning it cannot be reclaimed on iOS without killing the process.

The approach I suggested[2] was to map the file into memory using -[NSData dataWithContentsOfMappedFile:], then *not* convert the words to individual objects but instead tokenize by keeping offsets to the words in a separate integer array, staying with the strategy of annotating data whenever possible rather than converting it.

We can keep the external interface from Example 13.1 changing only the implementation to use this more optimized representation. Tokenization, shown in Example 13.3, is straightforward: go through the bytes, and when we find a newline, add the current offset to the offsets table. The offsets table is an instance of MPWIntArray, which works like an NSArray, just for int values instead of objects. The implementation uses direct instance variable access.

---

2. http://www.mail-archive.com/cocoa-dev@lists.apple.com/msg33602.html

**Example 13.3    Initializing the faster StringTable**

```
@implementation StringTable {
    NSData     *words;
    MPWIntArray *offsets;
}

-(void)tokenizeWords
{
  const char *bytes =[words bytes];
  const char *cur =bytes;
  const char *end=bytes + [words length];
  [offsets addInteger:0];
  while ( cur < end ) {
    if ( *cur++ == '\n' ) {
      [offsets addInteger:(int)(cur-bytes)];
    }
  }
  [offsets addInteger:end-bytes];
}
-(instancetype)initWithContentsOfFile:(NSString*)filename
{
  if ( (self=[super init] ) ) {
    offsets=[[MPWIntArray alloc] init];
    words=[[NSData alloc] initWithContentsOfMappedFile:filename];
    [self tokenizeWords];
  }
  return self;
}
```

The search method shown in Example 13.4 is also straightforward: For each offset, compare the bytes at that offset to the bytes of the search string. Most of the code in Example 13.4 is just boilerplate getting the various parameters into a form usable by the central search algorithm, which in itself is made slightly more complicated by the fact that the string-table we are searching does not have NULL terminated strings; the bounds are only defined by the next offset.

**Example 13.4    Searching within the StringTable**

```
-(BOOL)containsString:(NSString*)needleStr
{
  const char *bytes =[words bytes];
  const char *searchStr=[str UTF8String];
  long maxLen=[str length];
  int *offsetsp=[offsets integers];
  int max=[self count];
  for (int i=0;i<max;i++) {
```

```
    int len=offsetsp[i+1] - offsetsp[i]-1;
    if (len==maxLen && !strncasecmp(bytes+offsetsp[i],searchStr,len)) {
      return YES;
    }
  }
  return NO;
}
```

When I added this implementation to the test program kindly provided by one of the participants in the thread, the time to load the file (load + tokenize in this implementation) dropped to 0.084 s, down 160 times from the 13.5 s of the original implementation, and still more than 80 times faster than the solutions based on binary property lists. It should be noted that this simple method doesn't handle all the complexities of Unicode, but that wasn't a requirement.

Hardware and software have changed significantly since that time, and Apple has worked hard to improve the implementation of -componentsSeparatedBy Strings:. However, as Figure 13.1 shows, the basic differences still hold up for an iPhone 4S and iOS 7: Splitting the strings using -componentsSeparatedBy String: is still slowest, the property list–based methods around 2 times faster and our StringTable is still around 30 times faster than NSString-splitting and 20 times faster than property lists. I expect relative performance to remain roughly the same even as hardware gets faster.

Lest you think that the message is: "just use C," I've also included the *stdio strings* entry. This implementation uses the fgets() function to read the words into individually allocated C-String buffers. Although it is somewhat faster than property lists or NSString-splitting, that method is 10 times slower than using a single buffer with offsets, and of course it also suffers from the disadvantage of heap-allocated, non-mapped, and therefore dirty memory.

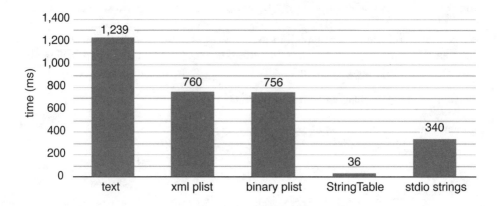

**Figure 13.1**    Different methods for loading a 2-MB word list on an iPhone 4S

As we saw in the previous chapter, Foundation overhead vastly overwhelmed actual I/O overhead. Expanding the abstraction barrier from the single word (an `NSArray` of `NSString` objects) to the whole word-list mitigates and largely eliminates this overhead, while also providing a better interface.

# Fun with Property Lists

Just in case you thought I was kidding when I wrote that that the message is *not* "just use C," we're now going to look at making things faster by recasting from C to Objective-C.

Although the StringTable from the previous sections solves the problem the original poster was having, it is a bit of a one-trick pony, only handling the case of a flat list of strings. I was reminded of the need for a more general solution by a student in one of my performance courses. He had several iPhone apps that were basically viewers for static, pre-loaded information. At any one time, only at most a dozen items would be visible, but loading the entire data set took just a little too long on start-up and the data model was a little more complex than a list of strings.

For the static data to be loaded, the student had chosen a property list, which was quite sufficient for encoding his data structure. In theory, the property list should also be fast enough for completely interactive performance. The previous chapter saw decoding speeds of around 300K objects per second on OS X, so even assuming a performance penalty of 10 times for iPhone hardware, we would still be able to do the 30 objects visible at any one time in 1 ms, 16 times faster than required for 60 Hz animation performance (and that's still a very conservative measure as we wouldn't need to swap out all objects on every frame).

The obvious problem is that despite only needing a maximum of around 30 objects at a time, we have to read the entire property list before we can display even a single item. If you have a large data set, this can quickly become prohibitive. Although CoreData might be an option in this case, this was rejected by both the original poster and my student as too complex for the applications at hand, an assessment I would agree with.

The obvious solution to the obvious problem is a lazy-loading property list, so only the elements that get accessed are decoded. A good place would be the decoding of arrays: instead of decoding the array immediately, return an object that decodes its elements on-demand. With an actual object-oriented implementation of a property list reader we could probably just override the implementation of `-decodeArray` or some equivalent method, but Apple's Foundation implements property list reading in terms of CoreFoundation's C API for property lists, so there are no extension points. You get whatever `CFPropertyListCreateWithData()` gives you, and you will like it.

## A Binary Property List Reader

So before we can make modifications to property list reading semantics, we first have to create our own reader, in Objective-C, with the ability to override functionality in subclasses. There is no official specification of the binary property list format, but Apple's implementation is published as open source[3] and not only contains code, but also a lengthy comment describing the format in sufficient detail to allow an alternate implementation.

Figure 13.2 is a rough schematic of the structure of a binary property list file extracted from the comment in `CFBinaryPlist.c`.

There are two main sections: the *object table* containing variable-length encodings of the actual objects and the *offset table* with indexes into the object table. All references to objects go through the offset table. Surrounding the two central sections are a header and a trailer, with information such as the root object index, the location of the offset table, and the sizes of various offsets.

A few of the most relevant object encodings are also shown in Figure 13.2. The object type is encoded into the top nibble of the first byte, with the second nibble either encoding a subtype or a length of 0 to 15. A length of 15 is a flag indicating that the actual length will be encoded as an integer word following the initial byte.

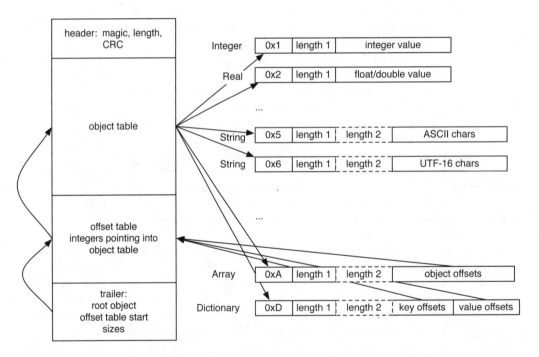

**Figure 13.2** Schematic representation of binary property list format

---

3. For example, see https://github.com/opensource-apple/CF/blob/master/CFBinaryPList.c.

The algorithm for parsing a binary property list is basic recursive descent.

1. Start with the root index.
2. Read object at an index *n*.
3. If the object has already been parsed, return it.
4. If the object has not been parsed, parse it:
    a. Get offset of encoded object via offset table.
    b. Decode object at offset.
    c. For any embedded object with index *m*, read object at this index.
    d. Return the parsed object.

The `parseObjectAtIndex:` method that encodes the core of this algorithm is shown in Example 13.5. It reads the top nibble of the first byte and then switches on the object type encoded in that nibble, dispatching the decoding of the different object types to individual methods. Code typically does not parse objects directly but indirects through the `objectAtIndex:` method (also in Example 13.5), which implements a cache for objects already read.

**Example 13.5    Parse an object from a binary property list**

```
-parseObjectAtIndex:(long)anIndex
{
  long offset=offsets[anIndex];
  int topNibble=(bytes[offset] & 0xf0) >> 4;
  id result=nil;
  switch ( topNibble) {
    case 0x1:
      result = [self readIntegerNumberAtIndex:anIndex];
      break;
    case 0x2:
      result = [self readRealNumberAtIndex:anIndex];
      break;
    case 0x5:
      result = [self readASCIIStringAtIndex:anIndex];
      break;
    case 0x6:
      result = [self readUTF16StringAtIndex:anIndex];
      break;
    case 0xa:
      result = [self readArrayAtIndex:anIndex];
      break;
    case 0xd:
      result = [self readDictAtIndex:anIndex];
      break;
    default:
      [NSException raise:@"unsupported"
```

```
                  format:@"unsupported data in bplist: %x",topNibble];
      break;
    }
    return result;
}

-objectAtIndex:(NSUInteger)anIndex
{
  id result=objects[anIndex];
  if ( !result ){
    result=[self parseObjectAtIndex:anIndex];
    objects[anIndex]=[result retain];
  }
  return result;
}
```

The code for parsing a simple integer is shown in Example 13.6. The basic parsing code in the `readIntegerOfSizeAt` function just shifts the number of bytes indicated from the file, which is defined to be in big-endian byte order, into a `long` integer, no matter what the byte order of the target architecture. It is implemented as an inline function instead of within the `readIntegerNumberAtIndex:` method because the bplist format actually has a number of different places where integers are read (for example, the offset table), all with slight variations on the basic theme.

**Example 13.6**   **Parse an integer from a binary property list**

```
static inline long readIntegerOfSizeAt( const unsigned char *bytes,
                                        long offset, int numBytes
)
{
  long result=0;
  for (int i=0;i<numBytes;i++) {
    result=(result<<8) | bytes[offset+i];
  }
  return result;
}
- (NSNumber*) readIntegerNumberAtIndex:(long)anIndex
{
  long offset=offsets[anIndex];
  int bottomNibble=bytes[offset] & 0x0f;
  return @(readIntegerOfSizeAt(bytes, offset+1, 1<<bottomNibble));
}
```

Integer parsing is also frequent enough (the offset table) that turning that code from a method into an inline function had a measurable impact. Fortunately, that conversion is purely mechanical. One oddity in the format is that the length of the integer (in bytes) is encoded as the $\log_2$ of the length, despite the fact that we have 4 bits to encode the length. This encoding means that we can only encode integers with a length of 1, 2, 4, 8, ... bytes, no values in between, but can encode integers up to 32 bytes in length, equivalent to 142 decimal digits.

Other primitive types such as floats, doubles, or Booleans are encoded similarly.

Parsing of a complex object with embedded objects is shown in Example 13.7, which deals with parsing arrays. The lengthForNibbleAtOffset() inline function handles the encoded length, which may be encoded in the bottom nibble or an extension integer.

**Example 13.7    Parse an array from a binary property list**

```
static inline int lengthForNibbleAtOffset( int length,
                const unsigned char *bytes, long *offsetPtr )
{
  long offset = *offsetPtr;
  if ( length == 0xf ) {
    int nextHeader = bytes[offset++];
    int byteLen = 1<<(nextHeader&0xf);
    length = readIntegerOfSizeAt( bytes, offset, byteLen ) ;
    offset += byteLen;
    *offsetPtr = offset;
  }
  return length;
}
-(long)parseArrayAtIndex:(long)anIndex
            usingBlock:(ArrayElementBlock)block
{
  long offset=offsets[anIndex];
  int topNibble=(bytes[offset] & 0xf0) >> 4;
  int length=bytes[offset] & 0x0f;
  offset++;
  if ( topNibble == 0xa ){
    [self pushCurrentObjectNo];
    length = lengthForNibbleAtOffset( length, bytes,  &offset );
    for (long i=0;i<length;i++) {
      long nextIndex = [self readIntegerOfSize:offsetRefSize
                        atOffset:offset];
      currentObjectNo=nextIndex;
      block( self, nextIndex, i);
      offset+=offsetRefSize;
    }
    [self popObjectNo];
  } else {
    [NSException raise:@"unsupported"
                format:@"bplist expected array (0xa), got %x",
```

```
                    topNibble];
  }
  return length;
}
-(NSArray*)readArrayAtIndex:(long)anIndex
{
  NSMutableArray *array=[NSMutableArray array];
  [self parseArrayAtIndex:anIndex
            usingBlock:^(MPWBinaryPlist *plist,
            long offset, long anIndex) {
    [array addObject:[plist objectAtIndex:offset]];
  }];
  return array;
}
```

The `parseArrayAtIndex:usingBlock:` is the workhorse for array parsing, with the `for`-loop reading encoded integer object indexes and calling the argument block for every index read. The indexes are offsets into the offset table, which then yields actual object offsets.

Finally, the `-readArrayAtIndex:` method constructs a result `NSArray` and fills it by calling the `parseArrayAtIndex:usingBlock:` method with a block that parses the object at the index that is passed to the block and adds the parsed object to the array (it actually uses `objectAtIndex:` instead of `parseObject AtIndex:` so it doesn't have to parse objects twice).

Parsing dictionaries is similar, except that we have two parallel lists of indexes and add key-value pairs to a `NSMutableDictionary` instead of just objects to a `NSMutableArray`. Most of the rest of the parser follows the same patterns and is otherwise fairly straightforward.

## Lazy Reading

With a truly object-oriented binary property list parser, adding lazy loading becomes a fairly simple matter. We create a subclass that overrides the `readArrayAtIndex:` method to create a `MPWLazyBListArray` instead of an `NSArray`, as shown in Example 13.8. Instead of creating individual objects, we store the object indexes (using an `MPWIntArray`) which we then use to create the `MPWLazyBListArray`.

**Example 13.8    Creating the lazy array**

```
-(NSArray*)readArrayAtIndex:(long)anIndex
{
  MPWIntArray *offsets=[MPWIntArray array];
  [self parseArrayAtIndex:anIndex
            usingBlock:^(MPWBinaryPlist *plist,
                    long arrayIndex,
                    long anIndex) {
```

```
        [arrayOffsets addInteger:arrayIndex];
    }];
    return [[MPWLazyBListArray arrayWithPlist:self offsets:offsets];
}
```

The definition and implementation of the `MPWLazyBListArray` class is shown in Example 13.9. It is an `NSArray` subclass that keeps a reference to the binary plist in question and knows about the offsets of its encoded objects in that plist.

**Example 13.9   Lazy NSArray definition**

```
@interface MPWLazyBListArray : NSArray
{
    NSUInteger count;
    MPWBinaryPlist      *plist;
    MPWIntArray         *offsets;
    id  *objs;

}
@end
```

Example 13.10 shows the lazy implementation of `objectAtIndex:`. When an object is requested with `objectAtIndex:`, it first tries to retrieve it from its objects, and parses it if it's not already there.

**Example 13.10   Lazy NSArray implementation**

```
-initWithPlist:newPlist offsets:(MPWIntArray*)newOffsets
{
    self=[super init];
    if (self ) {
        count=[newOffsets count];
        objs=calloc( count , sizeof *objs);
        offsets=[newOffsets retain];
        plist=[newPlist retain];
    }
    return self;
}
-objectAtIndex:(NSUInteger)anIndex
{
    id obj=nil;
    if ( anIndex < count) {
        obj=objs[anIndex];
        if ( obj == nil)  {
            obj = [plist objectAtIndex:[offsets integerAtIndex:anIndex]];
            objs[anIndex]=[obj retain];
```

```
    }
  } else {
    [NSException raise:@"outofbounds"
    format:@"index %tu out of bounds",anIndex];
  }
  return obj;
}
```

Although it may seem that Swift's built-in `lazy` collections may obviate the need for custom code, that turns out not to be the case: Swift's standard library does not implement actual lazy behavior, which caches the result once it is computed. Instead, it recomputes on every access unless the entire collection is converted to a non-lazy collection at once, which is exactly what we are trying to avoid.

The effect of applying the example to our word-list example is significant: time to initialize the word from a property list drops from 756 ms to 26 ms, an improvement of 29 times that makes this variant faster to initialize than even the word list we used before. Figure 13.3 shows all the times.

We do have to be slightly more careful with the lazy variant though, because if we do a linear search, for example, all that laziness disappears as the entire list is retrieved and the 700+ ms spent at a time when we aren't expecting it. In order to avoid this, we need to switch our search from a simple linear search with `indexOfObject:` to a binary search using `indexOfObject:inSortedRange:options:usingComparator:` with the option `NSBinarySearchingFirstEqual`.

The binary search will only load log *n* of the items during every search, so for the 26K word list mentioned, it would be around 15 items decoded per search.

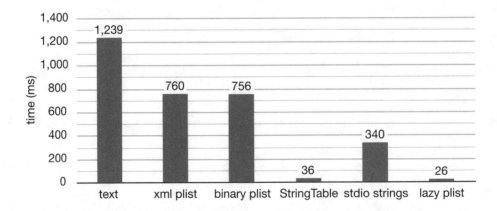

**Figure 13.3**   Including lazy property lists in iPhone game dictionary loading comparison

## Avoiding Intermediate Representations

Now that we have our own property list reader, another problem from Chapter 12 comes to mind: property list reading was slow and memory intensive partly because we had to create a temporary but complete in-memory representation of our object graph as dictionaries and arrays and Foundation number objects.

With our own reader, could we avoid this intermediate representation and initialize our object graph directly from the binary property list? The answer, of course, is "Yes, we can!"

The code for unarchiving a `SampleObject` from our own property list is shown in Example 13.11.

**Example 13.11    Unarchiving from a plist without intermediate representation**

```
-(instancetype)initWithBinaryPlist:(MPWBinaryPlist*)aPlist
{
  if (self=[super init]) {
    [aPlist parseDictUsingContentBlock:^(MPWBinaryPlist *plist) {
      a=[plist readIntegerForKey:@"a"];
      b=[plist readRealForKey:@"b"];
      name=[plist readObjectForKey:@"name"];
      NSMutableArray *array=[NSMutableArray array];
      [plist parseArrayAtKey:@"children"
                 usingBlock:^(MPWBinaryPlist *plist) {
        id obj= addObject:[[[self class] alloc] initWithBinaryPlist:plist];
        [array addObject:[obj autorelease]];
      }];
      children=[array retain];
    }];
  }
  return self;
}
```

It is very similar to keyed archiving code, except that the code to decode compound objects like dictionaries and arrays is wrapped inside blocks. The reason for this difference is that, unlike a keyed archive, a plain property list does not store any information about object classes. In archiving, the class information is stored in the archive and used by the unarchiver to instantiate objects of the right class and send them the `initWithCoder:` message. We instead have to pass the knowledge for decoding a specific dictionary or array into the method that decodes that dictionary or array, and blocks make this easy.

Can we do the same for serializing a binary property list as we did for deserializing? Sure, the streaming architectural style introduced in Chapter 8 is just the ticket. Implementing a binary plist serializer as a kind of FilterStream makes it possible to produce (most of) the binary property list incrementally.

I won't show the implementation here because it is too long and quite straightforward, mostly dealing with two concerns: creating encoded objects and recording the offsets of those objects. For compound objects, it also has to record the indexes of their child objects.

Example 13.12 shows how such a binary property list writer is used to encode `SampleObject` instances. Blocks can be used a little less because objects are recursively encoded using the `writeOnPropertyList:` message, with an array simply sending `writeOnPropertyList:` to all its elements.

**Example 13.12    Archiving directly to a plist**

```
-(void)writeOnPropertyList:aWriter
{
  [aWriter writeDictionaryLikeObject:self
                   withContentBlock:^(id writer,id anObject){
    [writer writeInt:a forKey:@"a"];
    [writer writeFloat:b forKey:@"b"];
    [writer writeObject:name forKey:@"name"];
    [writer writeObject:children forKey:@"children"];
  }];
}
```

Figure 13.4 shows the impact that not creating a temporary representation has on performance: an improvement of 5 times in both serialization and deserialization times. In other words, 80% of the original binary property list times were due to generating the generic intermediate representation!

The last set of bars shows the performance impact of using the custom property list serializer and deserializer with the intermediate representation: The performance impact is minimal, the custom versions barely a few percent faster than the ones built into (Core)Foundation. This clearly shows that the major impact was the architectural one.

As you might have guessed, the impact on memory consumption of avoiding the temporary representation is even more pronounced: Figure 13.5 shows a factor of 50

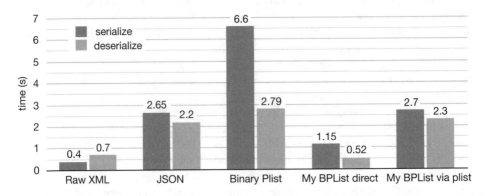

**Figure 13.4**    Time to read and write 1M objects with custom plist reader/writer

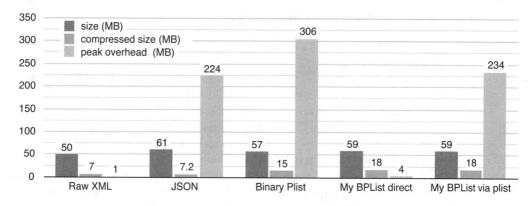

**Figure 13.5**    Sizes with custom plist reader/writer

to 70 less peak memory usage compared to generating the intermediate representation and then serializing it. The reason it does show 4 MB of peak memory usage is that although we can serialize the objects on the fly, we do have to keep track of the offsets in memory, only flushing them out to disk at the very end.

When I started this exploration into binary property list encoding, I had no idea where it would go, and frankly I wasn't expecting much. After all, the format has been in use for well over a decade and is an Apple workhorse, so has been optimized heavily during that time. I have to admit that I am very happy with the way it turned out. Not only does this example show the principles and techniques I discussed earlier at work, it has tangible practical results that can be applied immediately. With lazy loading, property lists can now be used for very large data sets, potentially greatly simplifying a certain class of applications that need lots of data. Using direct reading/writing removes 80% of the time and over 99% of the memory overhead.

The large magnitude of these results were obtained not by looking in Instruments and removing hotspots, but by looking at architectural issues such as the non-overridable API and the call/return semantics requiring a fully formed argument.

That said, more could be done: write performance could be improved further by optimizing the handling of object offsets or even allowing them to be eliminated entirely by adding inline objects for primitive types. The same API could be extended to also cover XML and JSON property lists.

In addition, you might have noticed that the API is now very close to keyed archiving. Add to that the fact that binary property lists can actually handle at least acyclic object graphs, and you see that the only thing missing from a keyed archive is a way to encode object classes for dictionaries, for example, in a section after the object table, the format has room for it. Alternately, it seems likely that the performance overhead of keyed archiving would be significantly reduced if the additional nested dictionaries were not materialized in memory.

# Comma-Separated Values

Another option that my student and I considered for encoding start-up data was CSV, but we never got around to it because we already got good results with the lazy property list. It was only a good while later that I was confronted with CSV files in earnest, in the form of a 25-MB database dump of 16,000 records provided by a client for formatting into a printed telephone directory.[4] With high-quality PDF generation built into Mac OS X, such database publishing jobs can now be performed using Cocoa programs instead of having to go through large and slow third-party apps such as Adobe InDesign or Quark XPress.

A normal compile-link-debug cycle, however, is not interactive enough to handle graphical fine-tuning, so I wanted to access these data from a live-programming environment I had written. In a live-programming environment, the display is updated after every keystroke, so the program has to evaluate in substantially less than 100 ms to keep the experience interactive. However, the NSScanner-based code I was using[5] was taking 4.8 s to parse the file. Waiting 4.8 s between keystrokes makes the experience decidedly non-live, so that wasn't an option.

Looking back at the game dictionary example from the beginning of the chapter, we saw that splitting a file into lines was very quick if we did it using basic C-String processing, and once we have the line-indexes we can access the individual lines in any order, rather than having to process them all sequentially. With that and the fundamental performance equation *items * cost* we have the solution: only read the *items* required to display the part of the directory that's visible, a page or maybe two, rather than all 16,000 entries.

This particular data set was simple enough that componentsSeparatedBy String: was sufficient to parse the individual rows and turn them into dictionaries (see Example 13.13). The total time only dropped to 1.55 s for all 16,000 entries—still way too slow, but with the time per entry at 98 $\mu$s and only around 200 entries per page, that was only 20 ms for data reading—more than fast enough, both overall and because reading time was dwarfed by rendering time.

**Example 13.13**   **Simplistic CSV reader**

```
-(NSString*)lineAtIndex:(int)anIndex
{
    int *offsets=[[self lineOffsets] integers];
    int offset=offsets[anIndex];
    int nextOffset=offsets[anIndex+1];
    int len = nextOffset-offset-[self eolLength];
    return [self subdataWithStart:bytes+offset length:len ];
}
```

---

4. The records are large: 133 fields and an average of 1.3 KB per record.
5. http://www.cocoawithlove.com/2009/11/writing-parser-using-nsscanner-csv.html

```
-(NSDictionary*)dictionaryAtIndex:(int)anIndex
{
    return [NSDictionary
            dictionaryWithObjects:[[self lineAtIndex:anIndex]
                componentsSeparatedByString:fieldDelimiter]
            forKeys:[self headerKeys]];
}
```

The fact that we got slightly faster processing was largely irrelevant; the important part was providing random access so we could parse only the *items* we needed.

# Public Transport Schedule Data

A somewhat larger problem reading CSVs presented itself in the form of the public transport schedule data, in order to answer the question, "What are my nearby travel options using public transport?" The data required for this includes the location of nearby stops and the departure times for different lines from these stops. Berlin's main public transportation company, Berliner Verkehrsbetriebe (BVG), provides this data in Google's General Transit Feed Specification (GTFS) format.[6] A GTFS feed consists of a zip containing CSV files; the ones for the BVG feed are shown in Table 13.1. They represent such concepts as the stops that are serviced, the lines that exist, and all the individual times that stops are serviced by particular lines.

For the problem at hand, the data of interest is provided in the stops.txt and stop_times.txt files, extracts of which are shown in Example 13.14. As you can imagine (and verify in Table 13.1), by far the largest data set is the one describing all the individual stop times; it weighs in at 118 MB and over 3 million entries.

**Example 13.14    Stop and stop time data**

```
stop_id,stop_code,stop_name,stop_desc,stop_lat,stop_lon,...
9003101,,U Hansaplatz (Berlin),,52.5181110,13.3421650,...
9003102,,S Bellevue (Berlin),,52.5197640,13.3469160,...
9003103,,S Tiergarten (Berlin),,52.5144000,13.3364690,...
9003104,,U Turmstr. (Berlin),,52.5258370,13.3424010,...
...
trip_id,arrival_time,departure_time,stop_id,stop_sequence,...
1,18:16:00,18:16:00,9096310,...
1,18:18:00,18:18:00,9096364,...
1,18:19:00,18:19:00,9096311,...
1,18:21:00,18:21:00,9096365,...
```

---

6. https://developers.google.com/transit/gtfs/reference

**Table 13.1**    **Main GTFS files for Berlin**

| File | Contents | Size | Rows |
|---|---|---|---|
| routes.txt | Bus, tram, and subway routes | 37 KB | 1.3K |
| stops.txt | List of stop locations | 775 KB | 13K |
| stop_times.txt | Times of all routes at the stops they serve | 118 MB | 3M |
| transfers.txt | Stops that allow transfer between routes | 330 KB | 13K |
| trips.txt | Each route may have several different kinds of trips | 7.5 MB | 152K |

Issue 4 of the online developer magazine *objc.io*[7] provided a solution to this for iOS using CoreData on the device and an importer module to prepopulate an SQLite database offline from the GTFS CSV files. The sample iOS program displays the time for pure location search and location + time search (in ms): 3.63, 3.26, 3.25, 3.27 (location), 388, 417, 653, 679 (location + time ). Around 3 to 4 ms per location-only search is fine for interactive performance, but about 1/2 s for the location + time search isn't really; we would like immediate feedback (100 ms or less) if possible.

In addition, the offline importer takes more than 22 minutes on a MacBook Pro to convert the GTFS `stops.txt` and `stop_times.txt` files into an SQLite database. The database is more than 120 MB in size, which makes for a somewhat unwieldy app or data download, depending on whether the data is included with the app. Let's see if we can do better.

## Stops

The stops file only contains 13,000 entries, so we can fairly easily read the CSV into memory at start-up into a `StopList`, which contains an array of `BusStops`. Each `BusStop` instance has a latitude and longitude read from the file, as well as a name and an id. Reading the CSV is fast enough that we can just keep the file as is without converting to some other format, especially with some of the enhancements to CSV reading that we will introduce a little later.

We use a `CoreLocation` to get the precise distance comparison via `CLLocation`'s `distanceFromLocation:`, but although that method is very accurate, it is fairly slow at 13.3 ms per search and is also memory intensive, as it requires instantiating a `CLLocation` for every stop for every search. We could use sophisticated 2D data structures such as k-d trees to optimize the lookup, but a simple sorted index on latitude (or longitude, it doesn't really matter) that can prune the results with a binary search reduces the result set sufficiently for search times to drop to around 45 $\mu$s on the device, after which optimizing further is probably pointless.

The index is a simple array of structs containing a floating point number and an integer pointing into the `BusStop` array: `typedef struct { float`

---

7. http://www.objc.io/issue-4

latitude; int anIndex; } LatIndex;. After initializing from the BusStop instance, we sort it using the block-based qsort_b() function. We do have to use a custom binary search because the one in the standard library requires exact match, whereas with latitudes and longitudes we are happy to find the closest entry.

## Stop Time Lookup

The stop times are a bit more challenging simply because there are a lot more of them, around three million. We also won't be able to read the 118-MB data file at start-up, even with a fairly fast CSV parser. We also can't search the CSV file on the fly because the entries are not sorted by stop time, but rather by trip-id. Finally, adding the times to the search increased search time roughly 100 times in the CoreData implementation, and it would be nice if that wasn't the case here.

Fortunately, the data for the stop times are very simple: an hour, a minute, and an id. Since hours have a nominal range of 0 to 23 (0 to 31 in the data, as they allow times to wrap-around) and minutes a range of 0 to 59, we can represent them with integers of 5 and 6 bits, respectively. We will map the stop id to an index into our array of around 13K stops, so 20 bits are plenty. In total, we now have 31 bits to represent each stop time, or 4 bytes for the structure shown in Example 13.15. For 3 million stops, that will be an array of about 12 MB, so approximately one tenth of either the CSV or SQLite representations.

**Example 13.15    Efficient binary encoding of a stop time**

```
typedef struct {
    unsigned int    stopIndex:20;
    unsigned int    hour:5,minute:6;
} StopTime;
```

The fact that our lookup parameter "time" is encoded as two rather small integers also makes lookup extremely simple. Segment the array of stop times into buckets for each hour and minute in the day and use a 2D array indexed by hour and minute to point to those buckets. This bucket index is shown in Example 13.16, along with a structure combining the stop times themselves and the bucket index.

**Example 13.16    Index structure**

```
typedef struct {
    int bytime[32][60];          //  hour, minute
} Buckets;

typedef struct {
    Buckets bucketOffsets;
    StopTime times[];
} AllTimes;
```

With this structure mapped into memory, lookup by time becomes quite efficient, only taking around 53.4 $\mu$s per lookup, roughly a factor of 8,000 faster than the same operation using CoreData. I mentioned in Chapter 12 that mapped binary representation is the way to go for best performance; this is an example of that concept. You might expect that replacing a database query with two in-memory structures exacts a memory penalty for our performance improvements, but instead I observed a slight drop in memory consumption, around 4 MB vs. 5 MB for the CoreData solution. In addition, due to the fact that the structure is mapped, the memory used remains clean and thus contributes only marginally to memory pressure, with the system always capable of evicting parts of it without having to send memory warnings.

I experimented with a few different algorithms for combining the two search results (location and time). What ended up being fastest was a simple doubly nested loop, first filtering by location and then searching for the stops that were found in the buckets for the relevant time interval.

## Stop Time Import

So how do we get the stop times from GTFS file into the efficient binary format that we can use? Once we have an array of StopTime structures, we need to sort it and create the bucket indexing that makes access so fast. Since we are sorting by small integers, we can use an efficient bucket sort, one of the few (non–general) sorts that run in $O(n)$ rather than the theoretical lower bound of $O(n \log n)$ for general sorts based on comparison and item exchange. Example 13.17 shows the code; the algorithm is as follows.

1. Size the individual buckets, incrementing the bucket count for every instance of a particular count.
2. Offsets must take the sizes of all the previous buckets into account, so accumulate the sizes.
3. Create a temporary copy of the StopTimes.
4. Do the actual bucket sort:
   a. Place the stop time into its bucket based on hour and minute.
   b. Increment the bucket offset of the current bucket.
5. Finally, sort the stop offsets within each bucket using a conventional merge sort.

**Example 13.17    Efficiently sorting stops first by time and then by stop id**

```
-(void)sort
{
    StopTime *sorted=calloc( count+20, sizeof(StopTime));
    Buckets bucketSizes,bucketOffsets;
    bzero( &bucketSizes, sizeof bucketSizes );
    bzero( &bucketOffsets, sizeof bucketOffsets );
```

```
    //--- size the buckets
    for (int i=0;i<count;i++) {
        StopTime current=times->times[i];
        if ( current.hour < 31 || current.minute < 60 ) {
            bucketSizes.bytime[current.hour][current.minute]++;
        }
    }
    //--- accumulate counts into offsets
    int currentOffset=0;
    for (int h=0;h<30;h++) {
        for (int m=0;m<60;m++) {
            bucketOffsets.bytime[h][m]=currentOffset;
            currentOffset+=bucketSizes.bytime[h][m];
        }
    }
    memcpy( &times->bucketOffsets, &bucketOffsets,
            sizeof times->bucketOffsets );
    //--- bucket-sort by time
    for (int i=0;i<count;i++) {
        StopTime t=times->times[i];
        sorted[bucketOffsets.bytime[t.hour][t.minute]]=current;
        bucketOffsets.bytime[t.hour][t.minute]++;
    }
    //--- regular sort of stop within a bucket by stop-index
    for (int h=0;h<29;h++) {
        for (int m=0;m<60;m++) {
          int offset=bucketOffsets.bytime[h][m];
          int numElements=bucketOffsets.bytime[h][m+1]-offset;
          mergesort_b(sorted+offset, numElements, sizeof(StopTime),
                      ^int(const void *va , const void *vb ) {
                StopTime *a=va;
                StopTime *b=vb;
                return a->stopIndex - b->stopIndex;
          });
        }
    }
    memcpy(times->times, sorted, count * sizeof(StopTime) );
}
```

How long does this take? All of 280 ms, including the fwrite() that writes the AllTimes structure to disk, with the sorted StopTimes and the Buckets that act as the index. The CoreData solution took more than 22 minutes, of which 19 minutes are spent in -[NSManagedObjectContext save], so the binary file format is not just 8,000 times faster reading, it is also 4,000 times faster writing.

# Faster CSV Parsing

Of the remaining 3 minutes of the CoreData solution not spent in -[NSManaged ObjectContext save], 2 minutes 15 seconds are taken by CoreData setter implementations, with the remaining 45 s spread between initializing NSDate (18 s) instances, splitting fields using componentsSeparatedByString: (also 18 s), and miscellaneous object housekeeping (9 s). Our simplistic CSV parser in Example 13.13 also takes around 15 s, so the times for CSV parsing are actually pretty comparable, after subtracting the CoreData overhead and the NSDate creation that we don't need because we use hours and minutes as indexes.

However, whereas 15 or 18 s don't really register when dealing with 21 minutes of CoreData overhead, they do stick out when compared to 280 ms, taking over 98% of the total processing time and reducing the overall speed advantage of our solution from 4,000 to only 88 times. We clearly need a faster CSV parser!

Unlike some of the optimization tasks in this chapter, which required outside-the-box thinking, this is a straightforward optimization task: identify what is slow, optimize or remove it, repeat.

## Object Allocation

We know that object allocation is expensive, so creating a new NSString for every field value with componentsSeparatedByString: is definitely going to be at the top of the list. Replacing componentsSeparatedByString: with the code in Example 13.18 that uses C-String processing to parse the fields and uses MPWSubData objects that are re-used via an MPWObjectCache yields a speedup of 3 to 4 times, by far the largest impact of any single measure here. (The code also removes the temporary NSArray instance, instead reading the parsed fields into an id array allocated on the stack, for another 47% speedup.)

The code in Example 13.18 also handles some (but not all) of the quoting required by the Internet Engineering Task Force (IETF) Request for Comments 4180,[8] the IETF standard for CSVs.

**Example 13.18    Getting data for fields of interest in a row**

```
-(long)dataAtIndex:(int)anIndex
            into:(id*)elements
          mapper:(int*)mapper
             max:(int)maxElements
{
  MPWSubData *lineData=(MPWSubData*)[self lineAtIndex:anIndex+1];
  const char *start=[lineData bytes];
  const char *cur=start;
  int delimLength=[[self fieldDelimiter] length];
```

---

8. Shafranovich, Y. 2005. Common Format and MIME Type for Comma-Separated Values (CSV) Files. Request for Comments 4180, Network Working Group. http://tools.ietf.org/html/rfc4180.

```
const char *end =start+[lineData length];
int elemNo=0;
int mappedElemNo=0;
while ( cur < end && mappedElemNo < maxElements ) {
  BOOL quoted=NO;
  const char *next=cur;
  if ( *next == '"') {
    quoted=YES;
    next++;
    while ( *next != '"' && next < end ) {
      next++;
    }
  }
  next=strchr(next, fieldDelimiterBytes[0]);
  if ( !next)  {
    next=end;
  }
  if ( next && (elemNo == mapper[mappedElemNo] )) {
    int len=next-cur;
    if ( quoted ) {
      cur++;
      len--;
    }
    elements[mappedElemNo++]=[self subdataWithStart:cur length:len];
  }
  cur=next+delimLength;
  elemNo++;
}
return mappedElemNo;
}
```

## Push vs. Pull

Allocating a new NSDictionary object for every row only to discard it immediately is also wasteful, so we change the API to pass a block into the parser to parse each row rather than returning an NSDictionary for each row from it: -(void)do:(void(^)(NSDictionary* theDict, int anIndex)) block. The block in turn gets the parsed dictionary for the row passed to it, as well as the row number. With this API change, we can reuse the dictionary and just fill it with new values. This helps a little, but not very much, because clearing entries out of an NSDictionary is quite expensive, even when using the shared key dictionaries introduced in iOS 6 and Mac OS X 10.8.

However, the MPWSmallStringTable subclass of NSDictionary that's also used by the XML parser of Chapter 4 does efficiently support static key sets with varying values. For example, you can create the hashes once and access the values by index afterward, so we don't have to rehash the same keys over and over again. It also features fast C-String based lookup that's not based on hashing. Both measures together yield around another 30%.

## Keys of Interest

Another feature that yields 30% is the ability for the client to specify keys of interest. The insight here is that many clients only look at a subset of the keys, yet the parser expends the parsing effort on all keys, whether they will be used or not.

A general solution to this would be lazy evaluation, triggering parsing only when the value is requested. The overhead for managing the lazy evaluation can easily outweigh the savings, especially for the relatively simple operations we're using here. In addition, complexity also increases significantly in languages such as Swift or Objective-C that do not have comprehensive built-in support for lazy evaluation.

So instead of lazy evaluation, we let the client specify the keys that they are interested in, and the parser will then only parse field values for those keys. The code in Example 13.18 already incorporates support for keys of interest using the mapper parameter, which maps field indexes in the file into field indexes in the result set. After the boundaries of the field are determined, a new MPWSubData is only created if there is an entry in the mapper array.

## Parallelization

The optimizations so far get us to the client code in Example 13.19: it first sets up the keys of interest (only departure_time and stop_id), parses the departure_time into an hour and a minute (assuming 2 digits for each), and turns the stop_id into a stop index using a lookup table we set up earlier while parsing the stops.txt file.

**Example 13.19   CSV to packed binary structure**

```
[timeTable setKeysOfInterest:@[ @"departure_time", @"stop_id"]];
[timeTable do:^( MPWSmallStringTable *d, int i ){
  StopTime time;
  NSString *arrival=[d objectForCString:"departure_time"];
  if ( [arrival length]==8 ) {
    const char *buffer=[(NSData*)arrival bytes];
    time.hour=twoDigitsAt(buffer);
    time.minute=twoDigitsAt(buffer+3);
    NSNumber *stopID=@([[d objectForCString:"stop_id"] intValue]);
    time.stopIndex=[[stopToNumber objectForKey:stopID] intValue];
    localTimes[i]=time;
  }
}];
```

Including sorting and writing of the StopTime array, this code runs in 2.1 s, more than 7 times faster than when we started optimizing CSV parser. It was now roughly 600 times faster than the CoreData code and pretty much done in terms of low-hanging optimization targets—and I probably should have called it a day. The official justification is that fast CSV reading is generally useful, particularly because

CSV files tend to be used when there is lots of data. However, I admit that at that point I just wanted to get to 1,000x.

So I started experimenting with multithreading this code. In theory this should be possible, because the initial indexing step we've retained from the string table at the start of the chapter means that we are not limited to sequentially processing lines as they come in. We can partition the table in the middle and let two threads work on each part, minimizing the thread-creation overhead. That's one reason the block argument of the do: method gets the row-index passed to it: The block can potentially be called with nonsequential rows.

However, I immediately ran into problems with the object cache. Whereas the rest of the object is immutable at that point, and therefore thread-safe, the object cache gets mutated many times for each row. Putting locks or @synchronized sections around the cache did not work at all: not only was the multithreaded code many times slower than the single-threaded variant, the locks by themselves did not solve the problem.

Foregoing the object cache altogether did solve the problem, but once again the multithreaded code was many times slower than the single-threaded code with the object cache. I then tried having an object-cache per thread, somehow indexing into a collection of object caches via the thread id. This may have been feasible, but the complexity just kept increasing and with the additional overheads I was at best close to breaking even, at least on my machine with two real cores.

Only after giving up did I finally realize that the solution was actually very simple: one object per thread, so create new objects for the new threads! More specifically, create copies of the entire CSV reader object, using the cloneForThreading method shown in Example 13.20.

**Example 13.20    Cloning a CSV reader for multithreaded reading**

```
-(instancetype)cloneForThreading
{
  MPWDelimitedTable *clone=[[[self class] alloc] initWithData:data
                                 delimiter:fieldDelimiter];
  [clone setLineOffsets:[self lineOffsets]];
  [clone setHeaderKeys:[self headerKeys]];
  [clone setKeysOfInterest:[self keysOfInterest]];
  return   [clone autorelease];
}
```

The mistake that I had made was one that I have seen a lot: mistaking the cost of an object with the cost of the object graph that it fronts. The cost of allocating a new instance of the CSV reader is the same as allocating a new NSString or a new NSNumber, it's just the actual NSData and offset array, and so on, that are expensive. So if we do a shallow copy of the CSV reader, instantiating the clone with references to our instance variables *except* the object cache, then we get a fresh object cache per thread at very little cost.

With the cloned copies, we can now spawn separate threads to work on the results, using a `parallelDo:` method similar to the `parallelCollect:` shown in Example 13.21.

**Example 13.21    Parallel CSV reading**

```
-(NSArray*)parallelCollect:(id(^)(id theDict))block
{
  int numParts=4;

  int partLen=[self count]/numParts + 1;
  NSMutableArray *partialResults=[NSMutableArray array];
  for (int i=0;i<[self count];i+=partLen) {
    int thisPartLen=MIN( partLen, [self count]-i);
    MPWDelimitedTable *threadClone=[self cloneForThreading];
    NSRange thisRange = NSMakeRange(i, thisPartLen);
    NSArray *partialResult=[[threadClone future] inRange:thisRange
                                                  collect:block ];
    [partialResults addObject:partialResult];
  }
  NSMutableArray *results=[NSMutableArray array];
  for (NSArray *temp in partialResults) {
    [results addObjectsFromArray:temp];   // blocks on the future
  }
  return results;    // final array has no more futures
}
```

The `collect:` and corresponding `parallelCollect:` methods are similar to `do:` and `parallelDo:` except that for each row they return a result that is collected in an `NSArray`. I am using the `parallelCollect:` example because `parallelDo:` has some additional wrinkles that distract from the essential features of the code.

First, we decide how many parts we want to process in parallel. In this case, that number is hardcoded to 4; in real code, it should depend on the size of each chunk (large enough to make the overhead of parallelization worthwhile) and possibly the number of available cores. For each part, we create a clone using the `cloneForThreading` method shown in Example 13.20. Finally, we use the `future` Higher Order Message (discussed in Chapter 3) to spawn the thread. As discussed there, `future` returns a proxy for the result that will block waiting for the result of the asynchronous message as soon as the result is used, but placing it in an array does not trigger that process.

After all the threads have been spawned, we combine the results into a single array in order. At that point, the calling thread will block if necessary to wait for the result to be computed.

For the client, the only thing they have to do is replace the message name `collect:` with `parcollect:`, or in our case `do:` with `pardo:`. The interface is otherwise exactly the same. The result for our stop times parsing is another 61% speedup, bringing the time down from just under 2.1 s to slightly less than 1.3 s. More importantly, the speedup compared to the 22 minutes taken by the CoreData based importer is now ever so slightly greater than factor 1,000.

This faster CSV parser also works well with the 25-MB database from the "Comma-Separated Values" section in this chapter: processing time per row goes down from 98 $\mu$s to 20 $\mu$s for the entire row, or down to 2 $\mu$s when using the keys of interest feature to only select 1 of the 133 fields. This means that the entire file can be parsed in anywhere from 34 to 340 ms, depending on how many fields we are interested in. So in this case we managed to address the *items* $*$ *cost* equation from both ends, with either variant sufficient to get us to interactive performance, and the combination even better.

# Summary

This chapter began with the fairly trivial example of making a word list faster, but we then picked up some speed and extended that example to a lazy and flexible property list parser, finishing with an ultra-fast parser for comma-separated files and memory-mapped binary data representation for public transportation data.

Very similar to what we saw in earlier chapters, we found that primitive data can be much more efficiently represented by C data types rather than Foundation objects. On the other hand, messaging provides flexibility that is not easily achievable with C structures and function calls. This flexibility makes it possible for the object-oriented property list parser to cooperate with its client to directly create target objects, avoiding costly temporary representations and making the architecture more stream oriented. The improvements are around 4x in memory and CPU time for both parsing and generation.

Having an object-oriented parser also made it possible to create a subclass of the parser that creates arrays lazily. Lazy loading does not actually increase speed, but it makes it possible to use property lists with almost arbitrarily large data sets without having to load the entire property list at once.

Finally, the public transportation example made good on our claim from Chapter 12 that binary representations that can be mapped into memory are the tool of choice if you want to go fast. How fast? Over a thousand times faster than an equivalent CoreData-based program for both querying and generating the data, with a roughly 10 times smaller on-disk footprint.

Although these examples are obviously not applicable everywhere, and some may be overkill, they should certainly be a good starting point for getting your I/O into shape.

# 14

# Graphics and UI: Principles

Now that we've looked at the performance of several lower-level subsystems, the CPU, memory, and the I/O subsystem, it's time to put the parts together to build high-performance user interfaces. That means both drawing those user interfaces quickly, and also putting everything together so the application reacts quickly to user requests.

## Responsiveness

When we speak of a high-performance user interface, we usually mean one that is *responsive*, meaning it responds quickly to a user action. How quickly? Well, in general as quickly as possible, but there are actually specific perceptual thresholds that delineate qualitative differences in user perception. These limits are shown in Table 14.1.

The times that are probably most relevant are the 100 ms for feedback to user requests and 60 Hz/16(2/3) ms for smooth animation. Both are important for creating the illusion of directly manipulating objects on the screen, rather than giving commands to a computer that then does something on the screen a little later. The 25-Hz (often also quoted as 30-Hz) figure is the one used, for example, for analog film reproduction, but it relies on integration effects such as motion blur that are

**Table 14.1    Response time limits**

| Response Time Limit | Effect |
| ---: | --- |
| 10 s | Keep user's attention |
| 1 s | User stays in flow |
| 100 ms | User is manipulating object directly |
| 40 ms (25 Hz) | Multiple frames fuse into motion |
| 16(2/3) ms (60 Hz) | Motion becomes smooth |
| 1 ms | Fast-moving hand is tracked* |

* See http://www.youtube.com/watch?v=vOvQCPLkPt4.

automatically provided by the analog medium for smoothness. For animations on digital screens, 60 Hz should be the goal.

The 60-Hz figure is also a fairly tough goal: 16.67 ms is not a lot of time when we compare it to some of the other times we saw earlier. Basic CPU-bound operations on a bound number of objects are OK, but even one disk seek of 7 ms probably means you have already blown your budget when taking into account that you probably have other things to do and your graphics subsystem is also going to take a little time.

So is 60 Hz the limit? Actually, given current hardware and software constraints, the answer to that question is yes, the last entry of Table 14.1 notwithstanding. However, even though animation is smooth at that point, there is actually still room for improvement. For example, if you are drawing or writing and your pen or stylus is moving at 5 cm/s (roughly 2 in/s), it will move almost a millimeter in the 16.7 ms it takes the screen to refresh at 60 Hz. That is a very noticeable distance for the "ink" to be behind the pen and will result in a "laggy" feel. The same goes for dragging an object on the screen. If you move your pointing device (finger, mouse, . . .) quickly, the system can't really keep up with precision.

Fortunately, something like the mouse cursor is small enough that you can't actually locate it precisely enough while it is moving this quickly, so the lag isn't really all that noticeable, but drag a larger object and you will notice that it doesn't track precisely. Exploiting the limits of human perception, or simply fooling the observer, is a common technique for keeping up the appearance of responsiveness even when an actual answer or other result cannot actually be supplied in time.

## Software and APIs

On Mac OS X and iOS, user interaction is largely mediated by high-level frameworks, `UIKit` for iOS and `AppKit` for Mac OS X. These kits read user input from different input devices, translate them into events delivered to client code, and organize drawing the user interface. A high-level overview of the graphics APIs is shown in Figure 14.1.

The high-level toolkits provide a fairly large number of ready-made widgets such as buttons, checkboxes, tables, and text editors. With a few exceptions, the widgets are both sufficiently self-contained and sufficiently fast for responding within the thresholds discussed earlier, so performance is generally not a problem.

These widgets are built with a user-extensible view hierarchy based on the class `NSView` on OS X and `UIView` on iOS. A view generally describes a rectangular area on the screen that it renders, usually using the `drawRect:` method and for which it gets to handle use input events. These high-level toolkits do their drawing primarily via the general-purpose graphics API CoreGraphics, aka Quartz.

Another major graphics API is OpenGL, which is primarily intended for 3D graphics applications such as games, but which is also used by other APIs due to its privileged access to accelerated graphics hardware. Additionally, there are APIs for image or video processing such as CoreImage and CoreVideo, and media playback

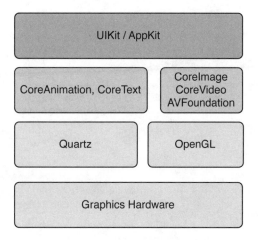

**Figure 14.1**    Graphic API block diagram

using AVFoundation or QuickTime X. Newer additions include SpriteKit for 2D games and SceneKit as a high-level retained 3D graphics API.

This distinction between *retained-* and *immediate-*mode graphics is one that is a defining characteristic of graphics APIs since the very beginning, when display lists were retained by the graphics subsystem and used to directly drive the vector cathode ray tubes (CRTs). In an immediate-mode API, the client sends drawing commands, and these are executed and leave some effect, be it on a display or a piece of paper. In a retained-mode API, the API creates objects of some sort or another that are then maintained by the API and can, for example, be moved later.

Figure 14.2 illustrates the difference with an example of three geometric shapes. In the retained-mode API on top, the client first creates the three shapes and then these are maintained by the API in a data structure or database of some sort. To change the position of the rectangle, the client must remember the rectangle in question and tell the API to move that object. The API is then responsible for refreshing the scene. With the immediate-mode API at the bottom, the scene is simply drawn twice, once with the rectangle having the old coordinates and once with the new.

The primary graphics APIs Quartz and OpenGL are both immediate-mode APIs; you issue drawing commands and these are executed. OpenGL distinguishes between its own immediate and retained modes, but these are both immediate mode in the general sense. SceneKit and SpriteKit on the other hand are retained-mode APIs; you create nodes that are added to some sort of scene and then managed by the API.

Retained-mode graphics APIs at first appear simpler, especially if the graphical object hierarchy matches what the application needs. In many cases, a simple graphical editor can be implemented as a thin wrapper on top of the API. However, most realistic applications have their own, domain-specific data model, with graphical primitives generated algorithmically from domain-model descriptions. In this case,

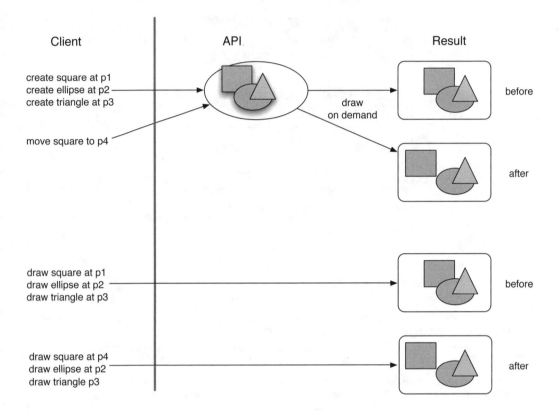

**Figure 14.2**   Retained (top) vs. immediate (bottom) mode

you either need complex algorithms to create diffs to the retained model, or you start throwing the retained model away on each update cycle, having thus created an expensive immediate-mode API.

UIKit/AppKit are hybrids: the views themselves are retained, but they draw themselves via the immediate-mode -drawRect: method. This allows you to define views once and the system takes care of maintaining a consistent overall display of your image as views are moved, scaled, or modified, with your code being asked to redraw parts of its view as necessary—but you retain the flexibility of modeling in domain-specific terms. The three geometric shapes of Figure 14.2 could be individual views (retained) or drawn by a single drawRect: method (immediate).

Core Animation also straddles the line, but in a different manner that will be discussed later.

# Quartz and the PostScript Imaging Model

Like so much of our current computing environment, Quartz traces back to the Xerox Palo Alto Research Center (PARC) as the *Bravo* system, which later became the PostScript page description language for printers and typesetters and via NeXT's DisplayPostScript client server-based windowing and drawing system and Adobe's PDF, PostScript without the programmability, turned into Mac OS X's Quartz.

One of the unique features of the PostScript page description language on which PDF and Quartz are based is that it has a precisely defined imaging model. The target is defined as a raster image, with the source being three distinct primitive types:

1. Raster images
2. Paths, either filled or stroked
3. Text

These three primitives can be transformed by arbitrary affine transformations, clipped by arbitrary paths and filled with a color, and in later versions of the model a gradient or other type of non-constant shading. The original formulation of the imaging model defines the Painter's Algorithm for rasterization, meaning that the last primitive to write a particular pixel defines the shade, replacing whatever is there. Quartz and current versions of PDF use a newer formulation that includes alpha-blending, meaning that previous values can contribute to new values. Anti-aliasing depends on this sort of blending operation, because partial coverage of a pixel by a primitive is simulated by blending the color of the rendered primitive with the background color already present at that pixel.

What's important is that the final value of every pixel is defined precisely by the model and not up to vagaries of the implementation, and Apple has been very consistent in applying this quality perspective.

In the imaging model, all the primitives above turn into one: the filled path. Text characters are mapped to glyphs via encodings and then turned into paths via font programs. Stroked paths ("outlines") are converted ("stroked") into two outlines with the area in-between filled; join and end-cap elements are also added as geometry to this path to be filled. Curves are converted to straight line segments ("flattened") at high enough resolution and then rasterized.

Even raster images are defined as grids of rectangles that can be scaled and rotated just like any other rectangles. For example, drawing a 256-pixel-wide and 1-pixel-high raster image with values ranging from 0 to 255 is defined to have exactly the same result as drawing 256 rectangles with gray values from 0 to 1, and the raster image method was in fact the recommended emulation of gradients before gradients became an intrinsic: Set the shape you want drawn as a clip path and then draw an image that represents the gradient, scaled to fill the shape.

Figure 14.3 illustrates these different representations using the example of the lowercase "a," rendered in the *Times Roman* font.

**Figure 14.3**    Letter "a" with control points, flattened, and on a raster

Notice that at each step of the conversion the amount of data increases, sometimes significantly. The letter itself can be expressed in a single byte, the ASCII character 97. The glyph is also either a number specific to the font or a name. The outline, however, consists of 3 straight and 34 curved path segments, for a total of 210 floating point coordinates, and flattening the curves into straight line segments can easily cause the number of coordinates to double or more, depending on the resolution (484 coordinates in my test). Finally, rasterization of this glyph at 24-point size and retina resolution results in around 2 KB of raster data in monochrome and 8 KB of full-color raster data with alpha. If you are using super-sampling for anti-aliasing purposes, the amount of raster data increases even further.

While actual implementations don't have to implement the mappings this way, and as a matter of fact usually do not, both text and raster images would be too slow otherwise. The defined imaging model means that the results have to be indistinguishable from the accurate but expensive formulation.

# OpenGL

The second fundamental graphics API in Mac OS X is the 3D OpenGL API (OpenGL ES on iOS). OpenGL is a language-independent and cross-platform 3D graphics API originally developed by Silicon Graphics but later turned into an open standard. It surpassed the existing open-standard PHIGS largely because, like Postscript and Quartz, it was an immediate-mode graphics library that was considered much easier to program than the retained-mode PHIGS.

The graphics model and the primitives supported are very different from Quartz. OpenGL has vertex arrays that can be accessed by polygon meshes, polylines, or point clouds. Images are not supported directly, but rather as textures applied to surfaces. Text isn't supported at all, so libraries have to be used to convert text to polygons or bitmaps.

Although drawing is immediate mode, OpenGL supports uploading resources such as textures or vertex arrays to the graphics hardware that can be referenced later multiple times. In OpenGL terminology, this is called retained mode, to distinguish from a separate mode where all data is specified incrementally.

One issue with OpenGL is that it provides a procedural/call–return API, which is not a good match for the actual interface to modern graphics hardware, which is more batch oriented. The mismatch means that code that looks "natural" for the API is very inefficient, whereas efficient code is extremely unnatural and hard to get right.

## Metal

The *Metal* API is Apple's answer to the mismatch between the OpenGL API and actual hardware interfaces. Like the similar *Vulcan* API from the Khronos group, Metal is a lower-level API that does not try to hide the underlying hardware interface.

Instead of a call to the API corresponding to some specific state change or drawing command, the application manages command buffers that it then sends to the GPU.

## Graphics Hardware and Acceleration

Although some terms in computer graphics such as "Display List" recall the days when we still had actual vector displays (where an electron beam was moved to specific points on a CRT in order to draw precise lines), virtually all displays today are raster displays. A raster display defines a rectangular grid of picture elements (pixels), just like a raster image does on the input side.

With modern solid-state displays such as LCDs, OLEDs or plasma screens, the actual pixel grid is also predefined by the hardware: There are actual individual picture elements in the hardware for each pixel represented in the frame buffer.

One result of this is that there is a fairly stable environment in terms of the actual number of pixels that we have to provide, at least once we take the jump to retina displays into account. An iPhone screen is going to have between 700K and 2M pixels, an iPad in the vicinity of 3M pixels, and an iPad Pro or a laptop up to 5M pixels. So no matter how complex your application is, that is the maximum number of pixels you have to modify to completely change the entire screen on every refresh. In Big-O notation, the complexity is $O(k)$.

Despite the number of pixels being a constant, and therefore negligible in terms of algorithmic complexity, this constant is actually quite large and therefore anything but negligible in practice. In many cases, producing graphics is the most computationally intensive task in modern non-server computers.

Over time, this has led to different configurations of hardware support for graphics operations, some of the most common of which are shown in Figure 14.4. The simplest configuration (1) is that there is no extra hardware support; it is just the CPU drawing into main memory, and main memory is also used as the frame buffer to refresh the screen.

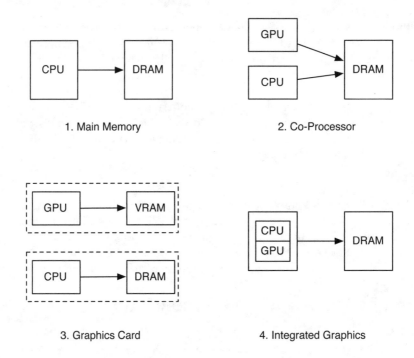

**Figure 14.4**    Graphics hardware configurations

This CPU–drawing model has the advantage that it is the most simple and most general. It was used with great success in machines ranging from the Xerox Alto to the Apple II and the original Macintosh and NeXT machines. It is also the model used by Quartz, that is, in general, Quartz draws using the CPU into main memory.

Graphics co-processors (graphics processing units, GPUs) can assist with various parts of the graphics pipeline, from geometry calculations to pushing pixels in memory. The separate GPU attached to the same main memory as the CPU (2) was popular in home computers in the 1980s and 1990s, but seems to have fallen into disuse.

Today, most graphics hardware falls into the categories of discrete GPU with its own high-speed video RAM, usually on a separate graphics card (3), or *integrated graphics* with the GPU combined with the CPU on the same chip and accessing the same RAM over a common bus interface (4).

Note that this development is somewhat circular, with specialized hardware assisting general-purpose hardware, but the specialized hardware then becoming more general, with modern GPU cards being used for general-purpose computation with OpenCL and, for example, Intel's "Larrabee" graphics card architecture consisting of a large number of reasonably general-purpose x86 core. Finally, the integrated

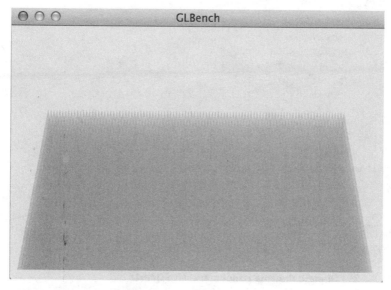

**Figure 14.5**   Triangle bench result

graphics architecture looks a lot like the original CPU-only configuration, and could be considered a variant of the former.

Despite the fact that these variants look very similar architecturally, they still perform very differently. For example, I tested drawing 2D triangles yielding the not particularly well-designed picture in Figure 14.5 on a 13-inch MacBook Pro with Retina Display and (integrated) Intel HD Graphics 4000.

First I tried this with OpenGL, and therefore utilizing the graphics hardware; see Example 14.1.

**Example 14.1    Triangle drawing benchmark with OpenGL**

```
-(void)drawRect:(NSRect)dirtyRect
{
    int iterations=10000;
    glClearColor(1.0, 0.5, 0.5, 0.5);
    glEnable (GL_BLEND);
    glBlendFunc (GL_SRC_ALPHA, GL_ONE_MINUS_SRC_ALPHA);
    glPushMatrix();
    glScalef(0.4, 0.4, 1.0);
    for (int i=0;i<iterations;i++) {
        float a = -0.5 + (float)i / (float)iterations;
        glColor4f(1.0f, 0.85f, 0.35f + a,0.4);

        glBegin(GL_POLYGON);
```

```
        {
            a*=2;
            glVertex3f(  0.0 + a,   0.6, 0.0);
            glVertex3f( -0.2 + a,  -0.3, 0.0);
            glVertex3f(  0.2 + a , -0.3 ,0.0);
            glVertex3f(  0.0 + a,   0.6, 0.0);
        }
        glEnd();
    }
    glPopMatrix();
    glFinish();
}
```

This OpenGL example was more than 10 times faster than doing effectively the same drawing via the Quartz code shown in Example 14.2. I saw a comparable result on a 2007 Mac Pro with a discrete graphics card.

**Example 14.2    Triangle drawing benchmark with Quartz**

```
-(void)drawRect:(NSRect)dirtyRect
{
  int iterations=10000;
  CGContextRef context=[[NSGraphicsContext currentContext]
  graphicsPort];
  CGContextSetRGBFillColor(context, 1.0,0.5,0.5,1.0 );
  CGContextAddRect( context, dirtyRect);
  CGContextFillPath( context );
  CGContextScaleCTM( context, [self frame].size.width,
  [self frame].size.height );
  CGContextTranslateCTM( context, 0.25 , 0.5);
  CGContextScaleCTM( context,0.2, 0.2);

  for (int i=0;i<iterations;i++) {
    float a =  (float)i / (float)iterations;
    CGContextSetRGBFillColor(context, 1.0f, 0.85f, 0.35f + a,0.4);
    a*=2;
    CGContextMoveToPoint( context, 0.0 + a,  0.6);
    CGContextAddLineToPoint( context, -0.2 + a, -0.3);
    CGContextAddLineToPoint( context, 0.2 + a , -0.3);
    CGContextClosePath(context);
    CGContextFillPath( context );
  }
}
```

In both cases, the CPU has 100% utilization when using Quartz, whereas with OpenGL a few commands are passed to a command buffer for the GPU and then the

CPU is effectively idle, waiting for those commands to finish. Both cases also feature low-powered CPUs by modern standards.

In addition to benefitting special-purpose hardware, GPUs can also take advantage of the massive parallelism available in graphics workloads and the huge numbers of transistors available on current technology chip dies to exploit that parallelism. CPUs have similar transistor budgets, but simply do not have nearly the same parallelism available in their workloads.

So whereas CPU designers have to resort to ever more elaborate schemes in order to squeeze ever smaller performance gains out of their largely serial instruction streams, additional hardware resources thrown at GPU workloads tend to translate almost linearly to increases in performance. This is the main reason that GPU performance is not just much higher than CPU performance (for applicable workloads), but the performance improvement curve is also much steeper, meaning that the gap widens with every year.

## From Quartz Extreme to Core Animation

Exploiting the performance potential of modern GPUs for system-wide graphics rendering rather than just for OpenGL-based games has been a driving force in the evolution of Mac OS X and iOS graphics APIs, starting with pure Quartz CPU-based rendering and slowly adding accelerated components such as Quartz Extreme, Quartz GL, and most recently Core Animation.

The most obvious way of leveraging GPUs for Quartz drawing is to map the Quartz primitives to GPU commands. The problem with this approach is that the graphics hardware implements OpenGL-compatible primitives, and those OpenGL primitives do not match the Quartz primitives. OpenGL does not have filled paths; it has triangle or quadrilateral polygon meshes, no curves. Instead of stroked paths, there are polylines. While mapping these primitives is possible, for example, tessellation for converting filled paths to polygons, that translation is expensive. In addition, OpenGL has a loosely defined rendering model, meaning that hardware has significant leeway in interpreting commands in a way that is efficient. This looseness is in conflict with Quartz's strictly defined imaging model and Apple's requirements in terms of graphics fidelity.

However, there is one primitive that translates readily: raster images. And there is a (hidden) subsystem that deals entirely in raster images: the Window Manager, which multiplexes the single physical screen between windows owned by a different process so that every process can draw into its own windows without having to worry about what other processes are doing.

Via the Window Manager, every graphics API on Mac OS X, whether immediate or retained, in fact becomes a retained API with the window bitmaps the retained state, with all the advantages of a retained-mode API: Windows can be moved around and the consequences of content becoming visible can be handled entirely within the Window Manager. Unlike many earlier windowing systems, and unlike the view hierarchy in AppKit or UIKit, there is no need to involve client code to repaint any revealed sections, and therefore window manipulation is always smooth, even if a process is nonresponsive.

Quartz Extreme, introduced with Mac OS X 10.2, took advantage of this architecture to add at least some level of hardware-accelerated graphics to the system. Every window in the system was turned into an OpenGL rectangle and the window's contents (provided by Quartz or another graphics API) into an OpenGL texture that is mapped onto that rectangle. Each window's contents are drawn with whatever API is deemed appropriate, and the bitmap window contents are then composed together using OpenGL and the graphics hardware.

This change not only takes advantage of the hardware support in the graphics card for better performance, for many operations it also removes the load from the CPU almost completely: in order to move a window, the Window Server just has to change the coordinates of the rectangle, and in order to bring a window to front or back it just adjusts the rectangle's z-value.

Core Animation brings this basic architecture from the WindowServer to the client programs. Instead of drawing into a shared backing store, each `CALayer` maintains its own raster image, and these images are then composed together by a separate process (the *render server* on iOS) with hardware support. In essence, each `CALayer` acts like a window under Quartz Extreme, and changes to the layer's location, transparency or rotation, and so on, can again be handled by adjusting the geometry of the OpenGL primitive it is mapped to, off-loading the actual bitmap compositing to the graphics hardware.

Figure 14.6 shows the development from the first, non-hardware-accelerated window server via Quartz Extreme to Core Animation. As you can see, the increase in hardware acceleration corresponds with an increase in raster backing buffers in this graphics architecture. In the extreme case of graphical assets, there is no software rendering at all apart from decoding those assets; the entire rest of the pipeline is hardware accelerated. The cost is memory, the resolution-dependent nature of those assets, and the decoding time of image assets, which can also be significant.

Just like the separate WindowServer process makes window manipulation smooth, this architecture makes animations run smoothly regardless of the client. Once all the layers have been set up, the animations run independently of the calling program, in a separate process and with hardware support.

This is a highly non-obvious approach to performance optimization because its basis is the most expensive primitive, the raster image. Raster images take significant amounts of memory and prodigious amounts of memory bandwidth as those images are composited into the final result. All other things being equal, the Core Animation architecture would make things significantly slower, but all other things are not equal because these operations can easily benefit from the graphics hardware.

In addition, we get gains in simplicity and corresponding predictability, making it possible to hand off the operations to a separate process, which just sends small instruction streams to the graphics hardware.

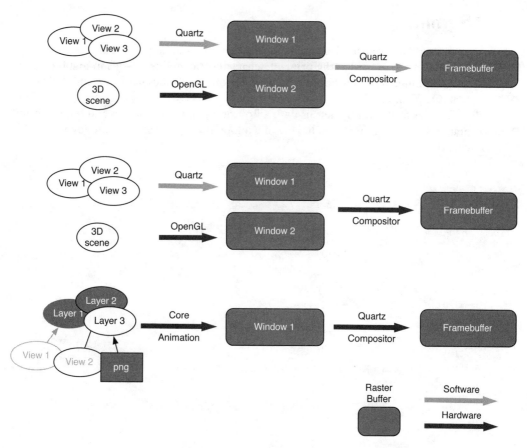

**Figure 14.6** Window Server (top), Window Server extended with Quartz Extreme (middle), Core Animation (bottom)

Drastically reducing the work the CPU has to do to composite the different layers then creates the headroom to animate these compositions. The fact that the animations are orchestrated by a separate process and executed on the highly capable GPU hardware means the system can guarantee much greater degrees of smoothness and performance than if the client programs were involved.

The performance guarantees in turn allow animations to become a central part of the user experience. Apart from making the user experience much more "solid" and realistic, the animations are also extremely useful in order to improve perceived responsiveness.

If the system starts an animation immediately it will feel responsive to the user, even if it doesn't actually have the final answer yet. The time taken by the animation can potentially be used to come up with that final answer, as long as we can come up with a good enough proxy for the animation target.

# Summary

In this section, we briefly examined the psychophysical basis for application responsiveness, looked at the principle characteristics and trade-offs in graphics programming, and then traced the co-evolution of graphics hardware and APIs in Mac OS X and later iOS.

This co-evolution has left us with a host of different approaches and trade-offs for graphics programming, which we will explore in more detail in the following chapters.

# 15

# Graphics and UI: Measurement and Tools

Just as with other areas of performance, optimizing graphics is usually pointless without knowing what is slow, and most importantly, knowing whether what you just did helped or hurt performance.

Measuring graphics performance and responsiveness is in many ways more difficult than other forms of performance measurement. Typically, the action is happening deep inside opaque system libraries, separate processes you don't necessarily have access to and even separate pieces of hardware that may or may not be introspectable.

What's more, when it comes to graphics performance, you really start to care about the timing of individual events, down to the level of tens of milliseconds. In previous chapters, we cheated a bit by measuring a large number of individual events and then dividing to get the "timing" for the individual event. This is not entirely correct; what we got was the *average* timing.

As we saw in Chapter 14, averages are only marginally useful in graphics timing: Having all frames of a second of animation delivered in less than 16.6 ms is not at all the same as having 50 frames delivered in 1 ms and the remaining 10 frames take 90 ms each. Even though the second version is slightly faster on average, it will look unacceptably jerky, whereas the slightly slower first variant is perfectly smooth.

Fortunately, there are mitigating factors: The system and the tools have a much better idea of what you are trying to do, and therefore can give you much better insight into whether you are accomplishing this goal effectively. As an example, if you are overdrawing a pixel with the same value, this effective no-op can be flagged.

This chapter will look at some of those specialized instruments and the specific aspects of the graphics pipeline they are designed to report on, as well as show how to use these tools with the more general tools and techniques we have seen earlier.

# CPU Profiling with Instruments

In the previous chapter, we briefly examined the performance difference between CPU-based drawing using Quartz and hardware-based drawing using OpenGL. Figure 15.1 shows the Instruments time profile of the Quartz example.

The top 11 entries of the profile contain the user code, but as you can see, the total time spent there is only 3.3%. The last user-code entry is a block defined inside the -[GLBenchView drawOn:inRect:] method and called from -[MPWAbstractContext ingsave:]. The entire 96.7% remainder of the total running time is within the Quartz function CGContextDrawPath(). While it may be interesting that around 50% of that is spent in CGSColorMaskSover ARGB8888() or rather, its apparently SSE-enabled worker function CGSColor MaskSoverARGB8888_sse(), that doesn't really help you much.

The fact that you are spending a lot of time drawing paths may be useful information, but it doesn't really tell you why that is the case. Are your paths too complex, are you doing redundant drawing, or is what you are trying to do simply too complex for the system to handle? The latter shouldn't really be the case, because even Quartz can at least theoretically fill every pixel on screen at animation frame rates.

When using hardware acceleration, the problem is even worse, because now the CPU is actually mostly idle and waiting for the GPU. Figure 15.2 shows the benchmark program profiled for the same amount of time, but this time using the OpenGL code path that uses the CPU to draw.

| Running Time ▼ | | Self | | Symbol Name |
|---|---|---|---|---|
| 2176.0ms | 100.0% | 0.0 | | ▼-[NSView displayIfNeeded]  AppKit |
| 2176.0ms | 100.0% | 0.0 | | ▼-[NSView _displayRectIgnoringOpacity:isVisibleRect:rectIsVisibleRectForView:]  AppKit |
| 2176.0ms | 100.0% | 0.0 | | ▼-[NSThemeFrame _recursiveDisplayRectIfNeededIgnoringOpacity:isVisibleRect:rectIsVisibleRectForView:topView: |
| 2176.0ms | 100.0% | 0.0 | | ▼-[NSView _recursiveDisplayRectIfNeededIgnoringOpacity:isVisibleRect:rectIsVisibleRectForView:topView:]  App |
| 2176.0ms | 100.0% | 0.0 | | ▼-[NSView _recursiveDisplayAllDirtyWithLockFocus:visRect:]  AppKit |
| 2170.0ms | 99.7% | 0.0 | | ▼-[NSView _recursiveDisplayAllDirtyWithLockFocus:visRect:]  AppKit |
| 2170.0ms | 99.7% | 0.0 | | ▼-[NSView _drawRect:clip:]  AppKit |
| 2170.0ms | 99.7% | 0.0 | | ▼-[GLBenchView drawRect:]  GLBench |
| 2169.0ms | 99.6% | 0.0 | | ▼-[GLBenchView drawOn:inRect:]  GLBench |
| 2168.0ms | 99.6% | 0.0 | | ▼-[MPWAbstractCGContext ingsave:]  EGOS_Cocoa |
| 2165.0ms | 99.4% | 1.0 | | ▼__29-[GLBenchView drawOn:inRect:]_block_invoke  GLBench |
| 2105.0ms | 96.7% | 4.0 | | ▼CGContextDrawPath  CoreGraphics |
| 2098.0ms | 96.4% | 0.0 | | ▼ripc_DrawPath  libRIP.A.dylib |
| 2072.0ms | 95.2% | 0.0 | | ▼ripc_Render  libRIP.A.dylib |
| 1093.0ms | 50.2% | 2.0 | | ▼RIPLayerBltShape  libRIP.A.dylib |
| 1074.0ms | 49.3% | 3.0 | | ▼argb32_mark  CoreGraphics |
| 1071.0ms | 49.2% | 0.0 | | ▼CGSColorMaskSoverARGB8888  CoreGraphics |
| 1071.0ms | 49.2% | 1071.0 | | CGSColorMaskSoverARGB8888_sse  CoreGraphics |
| 7.0ms | 0.3% | 0.0 | | ▼ripd_Lock  libRIP.A.dylib |
| 7.0ms | 0.3% | 1.0 | | ▼CGSDeviceLock  CoreGraphics |
| 6.0ms | 0.2% | 1.0 | | ▼_CGSLockWindow  CoreGraphics |
| 1.0ms | 0.0% | 1.0 | | CGSDisplaySynchronizeSeed  CoreGraphics |
| 1.0ms | 0.0% | 0.0 | | ▼<Unknown Address> |

**Figure 15.1**   GLBench CPU profile, Quartz

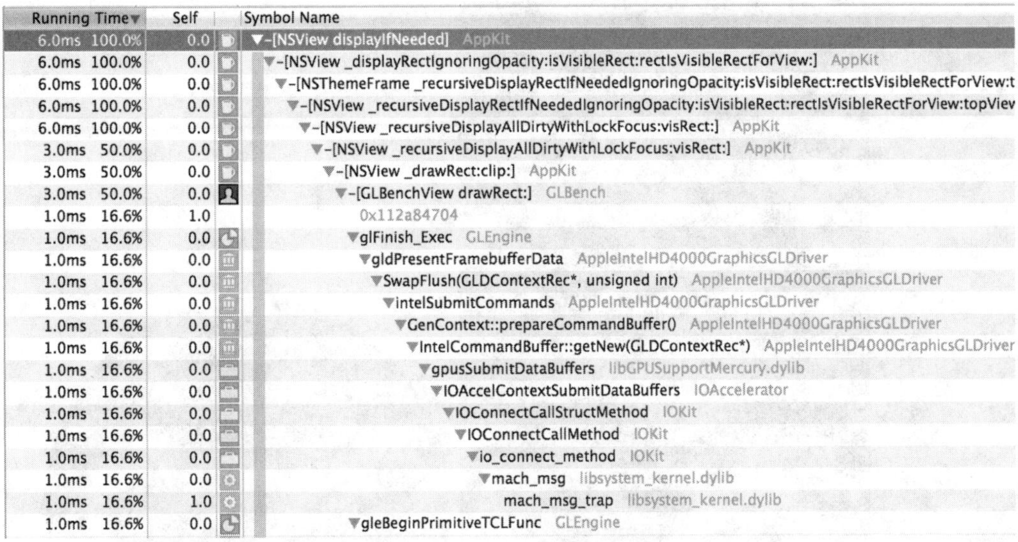

| Running Time ▼ | | Self | Symbol Name |
|---|---|---|---|
| 6.0ms | 100.0% | 0.0 | ▼-[NSView displayIfNeeded] AppKit |
| 6.0ms | 100.0% | 0.0 | ▼-[NSView _displayRectIgnoringOpacity:isVisibleRect:rectIsVisibleRectForView:] AppKit |
| 6.0ms | 100.0% | 0.0 | ▼-[NSThemeFrame _recursiveDisplayRectIfNeededIgnoringOpacity:isVisibleRect:rectIsVisibleRectForView:t |
| 6.0ms | 100.0% | 0.0 | ▼-[NSView _recursiveDisplayRectIfNeededIgnoringOpacity:isVisibleRect:rectIsVisibleRectForView:topViev |
| 6.0ms | 100.0% | 0.0 | ▼-[NSView _recursiveDisplayAllDirtyWithLockFocus:visRect:] AppKit |
| 3.0ms | 50.0% | 0.0 | ▼-[NSView _recursiveDisplayAllDirtyWithLockFocus:visRect:] AppKit |
| 3.0ms | 50.0% | 0.0 | ▼-[NSView _drawRect:clip:] AppKit |
| 3.0ms | 50.0% | 0.0 | ▼-[GLBenchView drawRect:] GLBench |
| 1.0ms | 16.6% | 1.0 | 0x112a84704 |
| 1.0ms | 16.6% | 0.0 | ▼glFinish_Exec GLEngine |
| 1.0ms | 16.6% | 0.0 | ▼gldPresentFramebufferData AppleIntelHD4000GraphicsGLDriver |
| 1.0ms | 16.6% | 0.0 | ▼SwapFlush(GLDContextRec*, unsigned int) AppleIntelHD4000GraphicsGLDriver |
| 1.0ms | 16.6% | 0.0 | ▼intelSubmitCommands AppleIntelHD4000GraphicsGLDriver |
| 1.0ms | 16.6% | 0.0 | ▼GenContext::prepareCommandBuffer() AppleIntelHD4000GraphicsGLDriver |
| 1.0ms | 16.6% | 0.0 | ▼IntelCommandBuffer::getNew(GLDContextRec*) AppleIntelHD4000GraphicsGLDriver |
| 1.0ms | 16.6% | 0.0 | ▼gpusSubmitDataBuffers libGPUSupportMercury.dylib |
| 1.0ms | 16.6% | 0.0 | ▼IOAccelContextSubmitDataBuffers IOAccelerator |
| 1.0ms | 16.6% | 0.0 | ▼IOConnectCallStructMethod IOKit |
| 1.0ms | 16.6% | 0.0 | ▼IOConnectCallMethod IOKit |
| 1.0ms | 16.6% | 0.0 | ▼io_connect_method IOKit |
| 1.0ms | 16.6% | 0.0 | ▼mach_msg libsystem_kernel.dylib |
| 1.0ms | 16.6% | 1.0 | mach_msg_trap libsystem_kernel.dylib |
| 1.0ms | 16.6% | 0.0 | ▼gleBeginPrimitiveTCLFunc GLEngine |

**Figure 15.2**    GLBench CPU profile, OpenGL

Whereas the Quartz example used 2,176 ms of CPU total, this time the CPU usage is 6 ms, and the actual place where drawing is done is using only 16% of that CPU time.

When you are using hardware assist, CPU profiles will not tell you where the bottleneck of your application is.

# Quartz Debug

For Mac OS X, a specialized tool for debugging graphics performance problems is the aptly named tool *Quartz Debug*. Figure 15.3 shows its main options window and the framerate meter. Quartz Debug enables global debugging parameters in Mac OS X's graphics stack, so it won't affect just your program, but all running programs, including Quartz Debug itself, so it is best to quit or at least hide all other applications except the one under test.

The option I personally find most useful is *Flash identical screen updates*, pretty much in the middle of the options window. With this option enabled, Quartz flashes a red rectangle around areas of the screen that were updated with identical content, meaning that the drawing was completely redundant and should be eliminated. There really isn't any good reason to draw identical content.

Next up is the *Flash screen updates* setting, which is similar to the previous option except that it flashes a yellow rectangle on all updates, not just redundant ones. This option allows you to identify drawing that, while different, may not have to be refreshed quite as often as it is. Enabling this option can produce a lot of clutter.

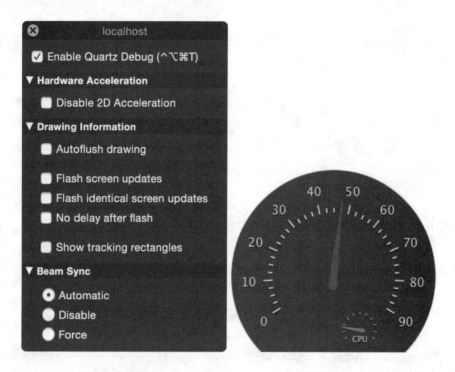

**Figure 15.3**    Quartz Debug options and framerate meter

The *Autoflush drawing* option disables the coalescing that usually happens, so every drawing operation gets flushed to the screen (and potentially flashed using the previous two options) individually. This produces even more clutter, but the more fine-grained rectangles may give you a better idea of what exactly was changed/drawn.

Finally, it should be noted that with Quartz Debug running, your application won't perform as usual; all the extra drawing of rectangles imposes a significant overhead, and usually there is an additional small delay so you can actually see the rectangles that are being flashed. Try dragging a window with one of the flash options enabled! Not only do you get lots and lots of flashing, the drag will be very sluggish. Disabling the delay gets the performance closer to normal, but at the cost of the flashes becoming even more difficult to identify.

# Core Animation Instrument

iOS has somewhat more sophisticated measurement tools available, probably because the graphics architecture is even more complicated, the hardware still overall significantly less powerful, and the requirements more stringent. In short, you really need those tools!

Probably the primary tool is the Core Animation instrument that's part of Instruments, rather than a stand-alone tool like Quartz Debug. This integration with Instruments can be extremely helpful because you can combine multiple instruments to correlate problems with possible root causes.

Figure 15.4 shows a problem we saw with animation performance while developing Wunderlist 3.

The trace is for an iPhone 5S; the dip in animation performance was far more noticeable on a 4S. By focusing on the area with the dip in animation performance and then switching to the CPU instrument, we were able to figure out what was happening—one of our routines was performing a computation that was repeatedly calling `valueForKeyPath:` to compute some counts. As you may recall from Chapter 3, using keyed accessing is orders of magnitude slower than direct access or a message send.

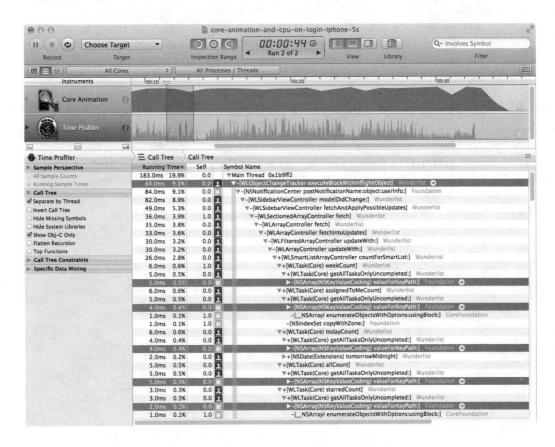

**Figure 15.4**    Core Animation and CPU instruments working together

The simple solution was to make the routine that did the counting faster by switching away from `valueForKeyPath:` to using a loop and normal message sends. Had that not been possible, other options for dealing with this would have been to delay that computation until later, perform it on a background thread rather than the main thread, or compute it incrementally.

## When the CPU Is Not the Problem

In the previous example, we were fortunate that the problem actually did turn out to be the CPU, identifiable with the profiling tools we are familiar with from Chapter 2. But what if that's not the case? The Core Animation instrument for iOS has a set of options similar to the Quartz Debug tool we just had a look at, except that the options are more extensive and tailored to the special iPhone/iPad environments.

As explained in Chapter 14, iOS standardizes on the most bulky and arguably least efficient representation for graphics: the full bitmap image. This is offset by being able to leverage the GPU universally, but it means that seemingly small inefficiencies in data access get magnified hugely due to the sheer bulk of the data being moved. The Core Animation global options shown in Figure 15.5 focus on these small inefficiencies with potentially large effects, showing the results visually on the screen similar to the Quartz Debug coloring options.

Specifically, the following options are supported.

- **Color Blended Layers**—Alpha blending the source with the target means that we need to read from the target as well as the source. Not blending eliminates one read. This flag colors blended layers red and non-blended layers green.

- **Color Hits Green and Misses Red**—This refers to a cache used by the system to support the *shouldRasterize* flag. Usually Core Animation

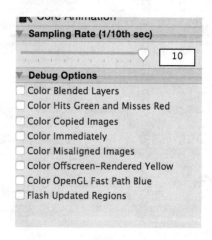

**Figure 15.5**    Core Animation instrument global options

copies/blends the entire layer tree on an update. The *shouldRasterize* flag on a layer tells Core Animation to instead cache the rasterized representation of the sublayers of the layer that the flag is set on.

It does *not* keep the rasterized bitmap of all the layers with this flag set, however, but instead has a global cache where a limited number of bitmaps are kept for a limited amount of time.

- **Color Copied Images**—This flag shows whether a specific image was able to be used directly by the GPU or had to be copied/converted by the CPU first (it colorizes the latter case).
- **Color Misaligned Image**—This is another flag for fine-tuning memory access patterns. When images are aligned on word boundaries, all memory access is done at least a full word at a time. When images are not aligned, multiple source words need to be read in order to produce each word of output, and the GPU has to shift and mask the source bits.

  Depending on how smart the GPU is, the extra memory accesses either occur for every target word or just at the edges of the image. Either way, it is better to avoid misaligned images, and this setting will show you the images that were misaligned.
- **Flash Updated Regions**—This flag works the same as the similarly named Quartz Debug feature: When an area on the screen is changed, the area flashes in a distinctive color. I haven't yet found a feature on iOS analogous to the Quartz Debug "flash identical regions" feature that is so useful for finding redundant drawing.
- **Color OpenGL Fast Path Blue**—This shows regions of the screen that avoid the main compositor and instead are directly rendered using OpenGL.
- **Color Offscreen Rendered Yellow**—This flag shows regions that were first rendered offscreen and only then copied to the screen. The extra copy is obviously a potential performance problem.

Note that like Quartz Debug, these options globally affect rendering on the affected device, they don't just affect the application run with Instruments.

To illustrate some of these options, let's look at the thumbnail view of a PostScript/PDF viewer for the iPad. Figure 15.6 shows the thumbnail view as it looks normally, without any colorization enabled. Scrolling performance was a bit laggy, so I used some of the options here to find out what was wrong.

Figure 15.7 shows the thumbnail view with the *Color Blended Layers* option selected. Every single thumbnail is colored red in Instruments (shown as dark gray in the printed book), meaning that blending was used. As we don't really want the background to show through, blending shouldn't be needed.

The first idea was that the UIImageView was not set to be opaque and that there was a shadow, which usually requires blending. However, setting the view to opaque

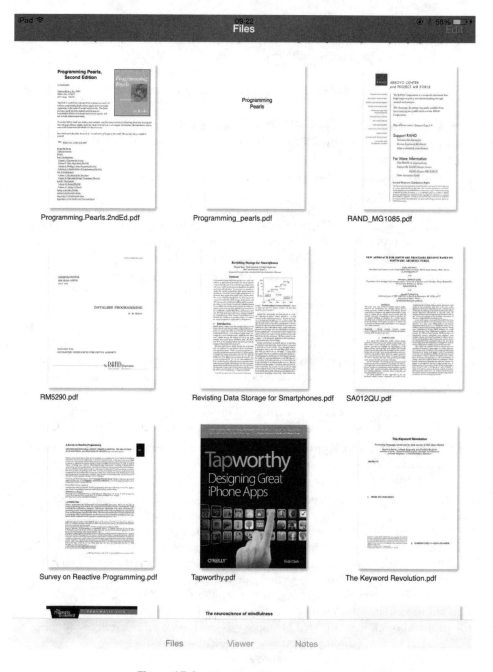

**Figure 15.6** The view without any coloring

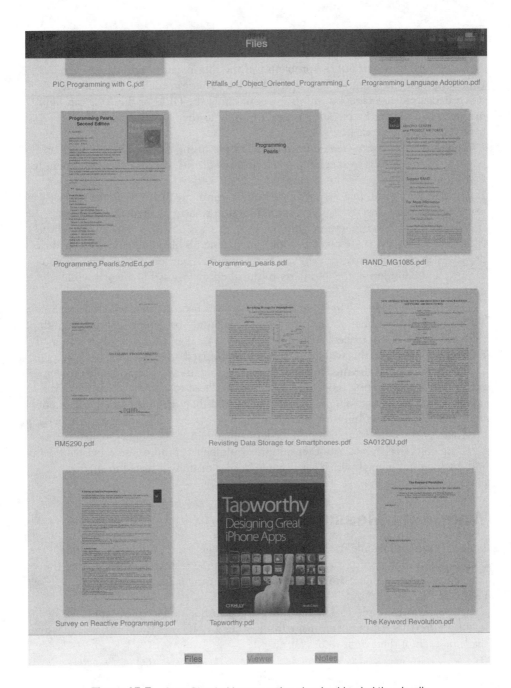

**Figure 15.7**   Color Blended Layers option showing blended thumbnails

and removing the shadow did not make a difference; all the thumbnails were still colored red due to using blending.

In the end, it turned out the problem was the thumbnail images themselves contained an alpha channel. This alpha channel was not needed because all the pixels had full/opaque coverage, but this is not something the GPU or the APIs can figure out, so it had to run the blending operation, only to then always completely overwrite the target pixel.

The thumbnails were created from the PDF files using a Core Graphics bitmap context, so the fix was to specify `kCGImageAlphaNoneSkipLast` as argument to `CGBitmapContextCreate()`, instead of `kCGImageAlphaPremultiplied Last`. Specifying `kCGImageAlphaNone`, the seemingly obvious choice for not wanting an alpha layer, did not work; the function returns an error at runtime.

Figure 15.8 shows the result of the fix: everything is now green in Instruments (shown as light gray in the printed book), indicating no blending, and with shadows drawn. Alas, the performance gain was fairly minimal, but sometimes that's all you can get, and considering the also fairly minimal effort, it was still a worthwhile optimization.

Finally, I also looked at the misaligned image (see Figure 15.9), which does show a few misaligned thumbnail images. As the images should be centered and the width of the image can't be controlled, there is no easy way to align the currently misaligned images, so potentially this will need to stay unoptimized.

If it turns out that the misaligned accesses are a significant performance problem, the thumbnail-generating procedure could be modified to round the widths of the image up to the nearest "alignment-safe" value and then draw the actual document thumbnail centered within the larger thumbnail. However, this would require making the edges of the image transparent in order to maintain visual fidelity, which incurs blending costs (see above). Another option would be to compromise on visual fidelity and draw the thumbnail with a small white border or draw it scaled to slightly different dimensions.

## What Am I Measuring?

We were trying to decide whether to use static image assets or draw using code. One consideration, though not the only one by far, was the relative performance of the different techniques. The sample task was drawing the gradient shown in Figure 15.10.

The code in Example 15.1 draws this gradient using either CoreGraphics or by loading a prerendered gradient image from either a PNG or a JPEG file, and measures the time each of these approaches take.

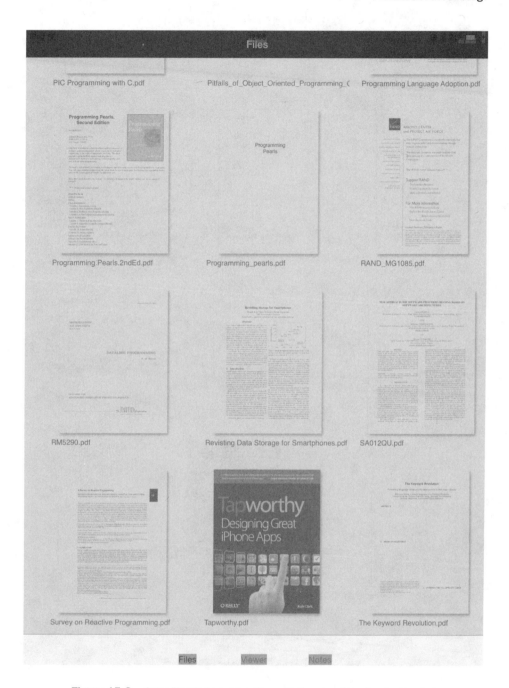

**Figure 15.8** Color Blended Layers option with thumbnails no longer blended

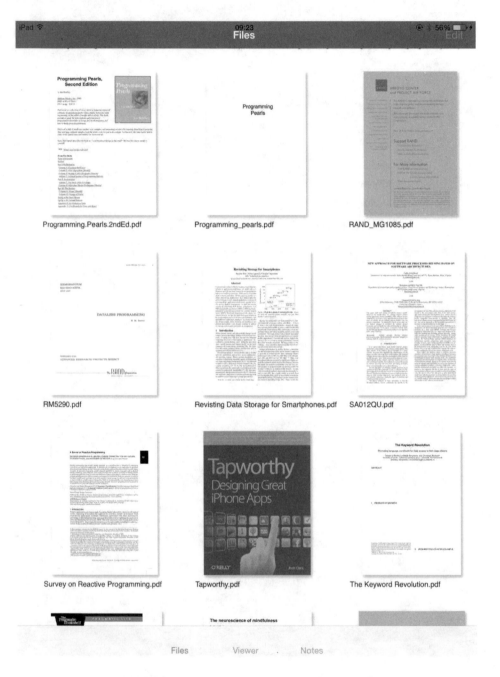

**Figure 15.9**    Core Animation instrument, color misaligned

**Figure 15.10**    The gradient to draw

### Example 15.1    Trying to time image loading vs. image creation

```
-(void)timeImageDrawingAndLoading
{
  CGFloat drawnTime, PNGTime, JPGTime;

  CFTimeInterval startTime, endTime;

  startTime = CACurrentMediaTime();
  self.drawnImageView.image = [self drawnImage];
  endTime = CACurrentMediaTime();
  drawnTime += 1000*(endTime - startTime);

  startTime = CACurrentMediaTime();
  self.PNGImageView.image = [UIImage imageNamed:@"Image.png"];
  endTime = CACurrentMediaTime();
  PNGTime += 1000*(endTime - startTime);
  SEL flusher = NSSelectorFromString(@"_flushSharedImageCache");
  [[UIImage class] performSelector:flusher];

  startTime = CACurrentMediaTime();
  self.JPGImageView.image = [UIImage imageNamed:@"Image.jpg"];
  endTime = CACurrentMediaTime();
  JPGTime += 1000*(endTime - startTime);

  [[UIImage class] performSelector:flusher];

  NSLog(@"Drawing %f, PNG %f, JPG %f", drawnTime, PNGTime, JPGTime);
}
```

The times measured were: Drawing 11.1 ms, PNG 3.89 ms, JPG 0.51 ms, so it's a clear case for prerendering everything and storing as JPG, right? We can also superficially explain the figures: as we saw in Chapter 14, Core Animation is bitmap based, so drawing is an extra step, whereas images are loaded and stored more or less directly as the layer's backing storage.

Not so fast!

It turns out that those timings come from measuring on the simulator (the numbers are suspiciously low). Also, what's up with JPG being 8 times faster than PNG? It's all a bit weird.

First, I fired up my trusty Instruments to get a rough idea of what was going on, and there was no image decoding going on in method `-timeImageDrawing AndLoading`. Instead, I saw a bit of PNG decoding going on later, during actual drawing of these views. I did not see any JPEG decoding; it was too quick. This confirms what we know about image loading and decoding on iOS: It is extremely lazy, only loading/decoding images when it is absolutely necessary, such as when drawing.

Some books claim that decoding is also forced by assigning the `image` property of an `UIImageView` or the `image` property of a `CALayer`, but I have not actually seen this in practice.

Running the code on an actual device (an iPhone 5s) yielded the following numbers: Drawing 3.26 ms, PNG 67.2 ms, JPG 49.1 ms. This time, the roles are reversed, with drawing being more than 20 times faster than PNG decoding and 15 times faster than JPG decoding. However, the result is also puzzling—since iOS isn't actually decoding the images here (which another Instrument run confirms), what is it doing?

If you look closely using Instruments, it turns out that the times for JPG and PNG "decoding" in this case are one-time initialization costs of the respective decoders. So "loading" a second copy of the image is many times faster: Drawing 3.50 ms, PNG 2.54 ms, JPG 1.91 ms. But of course those still aren't the times for actually decoding the image; the image times are just reading some metadata for the image from disk and preparing it for future decoding.

In order to force decoding separately from drawing the image in a view (where it is difficult to disentangle), we need to "draw" the image in a bitmap context, and using this we get the following times: Drawing 3.41 ms, PNG 7.19 ms, JPG 8.39 ms. That is the closest we got to the true time, though it is still not quite correct because we had to combine decoding and drawing. Apple claims that this is essentially the same thing as a pure decode, but we can't be 100% certain of it.

Another anomaly was that although we could now clearly identify the PNG decode times in a CPU sample, there was no trace of the JPEG decoding. Running the CPU Profile Instrument with the "Record Waiting Threads" option shows that the JPEG decoding is sitting in `mach_msg_trap()`, that is, waiting for another process that also doesn't show any CPU activity. The answer, of course, is that iPhones have a hardware JPEG decoder, use of which doesn't show up as CPU activity.

This hardware decoder is very fast for large images, but for small images the overhead is sufficiently high that even the fairly slow zlib/flate decompressor used for PNG is faster overall, and specialized software JPEG libraries like TurboJPEG can be several times faster.

## Summary

I hope this chapter demonstrated just how intricate measuring graphics performance can be. Apart from the complexities due to the number of subsystems involved, latencies of individual operations actually matter. We can't just average lots of operations and get a meaningful result.

However, there is also some hope—for example, the Mark 1 eyeball is a very good detection mechanism, particularly when coupled with a good electronic stopwatch (one with large mechanical buttons, not an iPhone). We actually used manual measurements as a crucial part of performance evaluation at Apple and successfully diagnosed problems down to one tenth of a second.

In the next chapter, we will take a look at what to do when we find a problem.

# 16

# Graphics and UI: Pitfalls and Techniques

Fast graphics programming is, in effect, an entire industry unto itself with many books worth of techniques and much more lore passed around online, so we can't possibly cover it exhaustively nor even do it justice. For example, we will be taking at best a cursory glance at OpenGL. What we can do is look at techniques that work for non-game end-user applications using the regular graphics stack.

## Pitfalls

For responsiveness, one of the biggest pitfalls is to perform long or unpredictable operations on the main thread. This includes all I/O, because as we saw in the previous sections, even the smallest I/O operation can potentially take a long time. On the other hand, just putting operations in the background without actually making the I/O responsive is even worse, and this is something I've also seen quite a bit of: there is no spinning cursor and all the UI seems operational, but nothing happens. In this case, being on the main thread is preferable as it at least triggers the system-busy cursor, giving the user an indication of what is going on.

For graphics, one of the biggest and most visible blunders is also one of the most pervasive techniques for delivering graphics: having all your assets prerendered and delivered as bitmaps. The likely most extreme example of this technique was the way magazine apps were created using certain Adobe publishing tools for delivery on the iPad, with every page of the magazine prerendered as a full-page bitmap, once for portrait and once for landscape. With I/O being the slowest part of the modern computer experience, both over the (cellular) wireless and from disk, even if solid state, this was not exactly a stellar user experience. And when Retina displays came out, everything looked even more fuzzy instead of getting better.

With the advent of high-resolution retina displays, anything that is artwork, so digitally generated, should probably be available as vector artwork, if it isn't drawn directly as code. Bitmaps are just much larger and don't scale, so they have to be supplied at every resolution, but the idea of "pixel perfect" artwork just won't die.

No more.

The iPhone 6 Plus has a 1,920×1,080 panel, but rendering actually takes place at 3 times the resolution, so 2,208×1,242 pixels. These two resolutions don't match, and so the pixels are downsampled by a factor of 1.15× to the display resolution. Whether that is accomplished by downsampling pixel art (which happens automagically with Quartz and the proper device transform set) or as a separate step that downsamples the entire rendered framebuffer doesn't matter (much). Either way, there are no more "pixel perfect" prerendered designs. And what's more, it doesn't matter—at 400-dpi screen resolution, nobody cares about, or can even identify, individual pixels and users love the screen of the 6 Plus.

If you absolutely have to use bitmapped artwork, there are different optimization techniques that can reduce file sizes and loading times dramatically, even over the "optimized" PNG files that Xcode produces. We will look at these in more detail in Chapter 17.

In terms of basic drawing, the biggest problems tend to be things like overdrawing (drawing the same pixels multiple times) and redrawing parts of the screen that haven't changed. Fortunately, the tools discussed in Chapter 15 will help you diagnose and resolve those issues, so use the tools!

# Techniques

Getting good graphics performance generally means starting with the screen and the pixels that need to be displayed and working backward, rather than beginning with the changes to your model and pushing those out to the screen.

On one hand, this means respecting the *dirty rectangle(s)* provided to you by AppKit and UIKit when you do draw, and on the other hand it means setting up those rectangles when notifying the UI layer of changes. The "Too Much Communication Slows Down Installation" section of this chapter contains a larger example showing the obstacles we had to overcome in one particular project in order to exploit these effects, and how drawing performance improved from unacceptably slow to almost immeasurably fast as a result.

Large complex paths used to be a huge problem in Quartz, due to the fact that self-intersections need to be computed for antialiasing to work properly and the geometric algorithm used was quadratic in the number of segments (checking each segment for intersections against every other). The underlying algorithms have improved a lot, so this isn't a huge problem anymore, but path length is still something to consider, with the sweet spot being medium-length paths.

Instead of repeatedly drawing shapes, use the Quartz pattern facilities. The same goes for gradients: Use what is built in. The `CGLayer` facility doesn't really help much in terms of drawing performance any longer; the great `CGImage` rewrite basic image drawing is as fast as can be, whereas image drawing has been problematic ever since the NeXTStep days. However, `CGLayer` is still an advantage when generating PDFs, as it will preserve vector information for repeated elements. So `CGLayer` is a good thing if you plan to have print or PDF output and have repeated elements.

Considering the potential performance advantages of OpenGL seen in Chapter 15 and the obvious performance of modern games rendering incredibly complex scenes at high frame rates, accelerating drawing using OpenGL appears to be an absolute no-brainer. Conceptually this is true, but actually implementing such acceleration has turned out to be anything but (a no-brainer). Apple made several attempts at incorporating OpenGL acceleration into Quartz at the OS level, and to my knowledge all of these were all cancelled. The additional transaction costs tended to eat up any gains in those parts of the graphics drawing that could be accelerated. A particular problem is the very immediate, call/return nature of the Quartz APIs, which maps reasonably well onto the OpenGL API but not so well onto the actual hardware interface (see the OpenGL/Metal discussion in the "Metal" section in Chapter 14).

Another is that the graphics primitives are different: Quartz uses filled and stroked bezier paths, which have to be expensively tesselated to turn them into the shaded triangles used by the graphics hardware and exposed by the APIs. If shapes are reused, that translation cost would be easier to amortize over many uses, but the APIs don't really provide for that.

# Too Much Communication Slows Down Installation

One investigation that had an unexpected result was looking into the mysterious slowdown of an installer in a new Mac OS X version. The installer was installing several thousand small files and previously had performed as expected. With the new version, the installer had slowed down several-fold, almost an order of magnitude. I/O rates were much slower than the disk subsystem could support and CPU usage was negligible, so there did not seem to be an actual bottleneck to explain the drop in performance.

## The Display Throttle

After much head-scratching and tool usage, the culprit was found to be the status updates the installer was providing. It was displaying the name of every single file it installed, and in order to make sure the user had a chance to see every single one of those filenames, it was flushing its drawing to screen after every name. This eagerness to keep the user abreast of its progress fell afoul of a throttling mechanism inside the Mac OS X graphics subsystem that limits graphic updates to roughly the screen refresh rate, nowadays set somewhat arbitrarily at 60 Hz. Trying to flush the screen more often will simply block your program, as illustrated by Example 16.1.

**Example 16.1    Running at 60 Hz**

```
import Cocoa

class AppController: NSObject, NSApplicationDelegate {
  var mainWindow: NSWindow?

  func applicationDidFinishLaunching(n: NSNotification) {
    let window = NSWindow(contentRect: NSMakeRect(0, 0, 320, 200),
                          styleMask: NSTitledWindowMask,
                          backing: NSBackingStoreType.Buffered,
                          defer: false)
    window.orderFrontRegardless()
    self.mainWindow = window

    NSApp.activateIgnoringOtherApps(true)
    dispatch_async(dispatch_get_main_queue()) {
      for i in 1...60 {
        self.drawSomething(i)
      }
      NSApp.terminate(true)
    }
  }
  func drawSomething( i:Int ) {
    let window=self.mainWindow!
    window.contentView?.lockFocus()
    NSColor.redColor().set()
    NSBezierPath.fillRect( NSMakeRect( 10,10,200,120 ))
    let labels=String(i)
    let label:NSString=labels
    NSColor.blackColor().set()
    label.drawAtPoint( CGPoint(x:20,y:20),   withAttributes:nil)
    window.contentView?.unlockFocus()
    window.flushWindow()
  }
}

NSApplication.sharedApplication()

let controller = AppController()
NSApp.delegate = controller

NSApp.run()
```

Running this program with 600 iterations of the display loop on my 8-core Mac
Pro takes almost exactly 10.0 s, same as on my MacBook Pro, with the CPU at over
90% idle on both systems.

Note that Quartz is smart enough to figure whether there has been any drawing at all, so just calling `flushWindow()` in a tight loop will return almost immediately because it doesn't actually attempt to do a flush in that case. You need to actually draw something, though it doesn't actually have to be different.

## Working with the Display Throttle

While there are ways of working around the display throttle, games using OpenGL can get much higher refresh rates, and it is probably better to actually take its fundamental lesson to heart: Status updates can happen much more frequently than the user cares to know about them. For example, I measured an `NSURLSession DataTask` via its delegate methods, and it was giving me status updates 273 times a second when downloading via a 6-MBit/s home DSL line.

Not only am I quite confident that users don't care about knowing about their exact download status 273 times a second—I certainly don't—you actually won't be able to read a byte count that gets refreshed that often. For the byte count text, once a second is probably plenty, whereas progress bars might be slightly smoother if updated at a higher rate, for example, around 10 times per second.

I have so far used three techniques to avoid excessive UI refresh rates, two of which actually work. The first technique tends to be very good for essentially continuous progress monitoring, for example, of download or disk progress. It uses a timer running at around 10 Hz that queries the progress and updates the display. Apart from smoothing and limiting progress display, this technique also avoids model → view communication, which is desirable from an architectural point of view. The drawback of the timer technique is that the timers have to be started and stopped independently of the underlying operation.

The second technique, update-request batching, avoids introducing explicit timers, but does not manage to avoid model → view communication. One way of implementing update-request batching is to store the update request and then send a message to deliver the updates at a later point in time, for example, 0.1 s later, a technique we demonstrate in Example 16.4 in the next section.

The third technique I thought would work was being clever with `performSelector:afterDelay:` and canceling previous requests, and in fact I have seen this technique used many times. Alas, it doesn't actually work, at least if there is high enough load for the intervals to be shorter than the delay. In that case, we just keep cancelling the sending of the update message until the updates stop coming.

## Installers and Progress Reporting Today

Considering how egregious this particular problem is, you may think it is rare, obvious, and simply no longer happens. You'd be wrong—in January 2016, it was reported that the node package manager `npm` could be slowed down by 50% to 200% when the progress bar was turned on, and Microsoft's auto-updater still uses around 150% CPU (as measured by `top` on a two-core machine), displaying its progress bars during updates.

In OS X 10.9 and iOS 7, Apple introduced explicit support for reporting progress of long running tasks with the NSProgress class and NSProgressReporting protocol. The basic idea is to have objects report on progress of individual activities and then combine those individual reports to obtain the overall progress. Having implemented a very similar system back in the late 1990s, I can say that this is very well done.

Alas, Apple completely dropped the ball, or maybe just punted, when it came to actually reporting progress. The recommended technique for actually *reporting* progress to the UI is to observe the percentCompleted property of the top-level NSProgress object. That doesn't solve any of the problems we've seen, and it adds the problem that the KVO notification is going to be delivered on the same background thread that changes the progress status.

In fact, Apple admonishes us: "Don't update completedUnitCount in a tight loop," so they are aware of the problem, and they realize they haven't actually solved it.

## Overwhelming an iPhone

A couple of years ago, I was asked to help out with a newspaper app that was managing a number of items in RSS-like feeds, displayed using the ubiquitous UITableView. Every item had UI for indicating the different states it could be in: not yet downloaded at all, some metadata complete, thumbnail received, with or without audio, and so on. In addition, it would indicate incremental progress while downloading audio data because those files could take a significant time to download.

This all worked fine as long as we were working with a single feed of up to 10 items, but once we went into production with 10 or more feeds of 30 or more items each the app started experiencing significant problems. We tried some obvious optimizations, for example, moving long-running operations such as thumbnail generation onto a background thread and refraining from doing unnecessary work such as synchronizing the entire defaults database for every state change of every item, but to no avail.

The symptom was that the UI would freeze, sometime for a significant amount of time, before the app became usable again. This happened especially on first launch of the app, as it had to do an initial fetch/update of all the items in all the feeds. Subsequent launches tended not to have as much of a problem because data was already cached, but there was a bad initial user experience to contend with.

Profiling showed that the time was being spent in UIKit drawing code (text drawing, table layout). The Cell reuse mechanism advocated by Apple was being used and working as expected, with no particular overhead from Cell creation. Not much to do there, right?

Wrong! The problem turned out to be the code in Example 16.2.

**Example 16.2    Model to view notification code**

```
-(void)notifyChanged
{
    [[NSNotificationCenter defaultCenter]
            postNotificationName: @"UserStatusChanged"
            object:nil];
}
```

Although this code may seem OK and matches a lot of the published example code for `NSNotificationCenter`, it actually suffers from two problems. First is the lack of update-throttling discussed in the previous section, the second is that it is too unspecific: it just says that something has changed, not what has changed. Without this important piece of context information, the UI element receiving the notification (in this case, a table view) has no other choice but to update all of its UI. Not only is this quadratic in the number of (visible) elements, it also updates the display for items that aren't even visible and may not be in the current list at all!

The simple way of overcoming this problem is of course to include the current object in the notification, which fortunately `NSNotification` is set up to handle. Example 16.3 shows this improvement.

**Example 16.3    Model to view notification code with context**

```
-(void)notifyChanged
{
    [[NSNotificationCenter defaultCenter]
            postNotificationName: @"UserStatusChanged"
            object:self];
}
```

The receiving code was then able to retrieve the object in question from the notification, figure out whether it was relevant at all (contained in the current table), and then update only that particular row. The code in Example 16.4 combines this context-dependent refresh with the batched refreshing from the previous section. It assumes that the table view is managing a list of "items." A client calls `-refreshItemsFromBackground:`, for example, via a `NSNotification`, which then determine the index for the item and subsequently uses just that index.

**Example 16.4    Code for batched refreshing of table view items**

```
@property (retain)  NSMutableSet  *indexesToRefresh;

-(void)refreshAccumulatedItems
```

```
{
  NSSet *items=nil;
  @synchronized(self) {
    itemIndexes=[self indexesToRefresh];
    [self setIndexesToRefresh:nil];
  }
  [tableview reloadRowsAtIndexPaths:[itemIndexes allObjects]
                    withRowAnimation:UITableViewRowAnimationNone];
}

-(void)triggerRefresh
{
  [self performSelector:@selector(refreshAccumulatedItems)
          withObject:nil afterDelay:0.2];
}

-(void)refreshItemFromBackground:item
{
  NSIndexPath* index=[self indexPathForItem:item];
  if ( index ) {
    @synchronized(self) {
      if ( !indexesToRefresh ) {
        [self setIndexesToRefresh:[NSMutableSet setWithObject:index]];
        [self performSelectorOnMainThread:@selector(triggerRefresh)
                    withObject:nil waitUntilDone:NO];
      } else {
        [indexesToRefresh addObject:index];
      }
    }
  }
}
```

The batching is essentially performed by the code that follows; if we don't have a batched set of results, we create one and schedule the refresh. If, on the other hand, we already have a batch going, then we just add the result to that batch. Picking up is simple—we pick up the batch, clear it, and refresh the table view. Note that you will want to clear the batch if anything happens to invalidate those indexes in the meantime.

## It's Just an Illusion

One of the most important techniques I have learned for dealing with UI performance issues is faking it. If actually doing the thing you're supposed to be doing is too slow, you can often present a facsimile to the user while you catch up and do the remainder of the work. Or you can animate.

Consistently using animation to hide latencies was one of the really brilliant moves that made the original iPhone appear to be so fast and immediate/solid, despite the relatively puny hardware, and allowed it to maintain this lead even as competitors rolled out higher-performance hardware and arguably better accelerated graphics.

For example, opening a PDF file and rendering the first page (or double page) takes some time. However, animating the thumbnail of the file from its thumbnail size to full screen means that the user is occupied while the system is busily preparing the PDF. Since the animation can be handled by the GPU, it also mean that CPU resources aren't taken away from the underlying task.

## Image Scaling and Cropping

In the 1990s, I created various pieces of NeXT software for driving different output devices, from a high-quality alternate driver for the NeXT Color Printer to high-end Color Laser Copiers costing tens of thousands of dollars. One of these programs was eXTRASLIDE (see Figure 16.1), which drove the Polaroid CI-5000S Digital Palette Film Recorder.

From an engineering point of view, the main part of those programs were the actual low-level drivers, which frequently employed the SCSI ports to ship

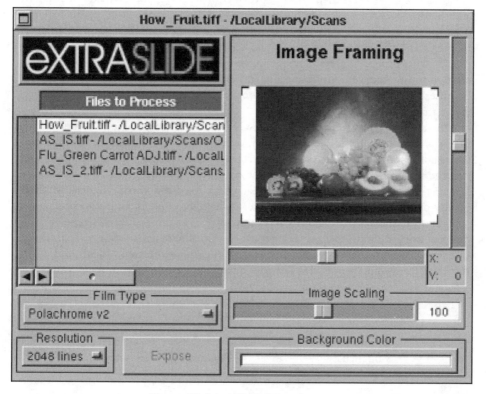

**Figure 16.1**    eXTRASLIDE application

high-resolution bitmaps rendered by Display PostScript to the devices using custom and usually poorly documented protocols.

All of this tended to be performance critical. The Polaroid recorder, for example, had 4,000-line resolution, which made for 48-MB images, and there were some real-time requirements for delivering those images. With 1–GB memories on phones, that doesn't seem a lot, but our highest-end box was a Canon object.station 41 with around 32 MB of DRAM and a 100–MHz 486 processor. Although the clock rate difference suggests a factor 10 to 20 between that CPU and modern ones, benchmarks show more of a factor 100. In short, this is a much, much slower machine than even a middling phone today. We considered it "blazingly fast."

For eXTRASLIDE, we had an additional problem; it needed a little front-end application to position, scale, and crop the source material (shown in Figure 16.1). Not a big deal, except that the hardware we had took a significant amount of time to redraw the source material, meaning live redraw was not possible. Instead, the standard practice was to draw a rectangular outline to aid positioning and then redraw the full image once the outline had been positioned.

This was one time that NSImage was actually extremely helpful. It automatically creates and caches a screen-resolution preview of whatever source material you have and then renders that. This often causes problems because people forget that they are dealing with a wrapper, rather than the image the name suggests (NSBitmapImageRep is the class for an actual bitmap image), but in this case it is exactly what is needed. The preview image used in eXTRASLIDE was always small enough for interactive performance, regardless of the size of the original, especially because, as you can see from the screenshot, we chose to make the actual preview fairly small.

One last problem was that NSImage will only consider the screen cache valid if the resolution matches the screen exactly, otherwise it will recreate the cache from the original representation. Alas, that is exactly what happens during scaling; at each step the resolution no longer matches and a full redraw is triggered. This is the "correct" behavior, as resampling an already resampled thumbnail will lead to drastic quality problems, but of course it also meant that live scaling was not possible.

The trick, shown schematically in Figure 16.2, is to create a new NSImage instance using only the cached representation from the original NSImage. In this case, the NSImage has no choice but to scale the low-resolution bitmap, and therefore live scaling is possible. The low quality of scaling the thumbnail is no

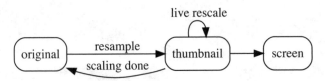

**Figure 16.2**   Live image scaling in eXTRASLIDE

problem because while the image is moving, the human eye can't discern much detail anyway. Once the live scale is done (button released), we switch back to the original NSImage, which will then recache a new screen bitmap.

The lesson I learned is that when it comes to interactive programs, you are allowed to cheat, as long as you don't get caught. In this example, we can scale the low-resolution bitmap as long as we're scaling. While not quite as good as scaling the source, the difference is not very noticeable as long the image is in motion, and of course it is much more realistic than moving a rectangle around, so customers absolutely *loved* this feature.

## Thumbnail Drawing

While working on the award-winning Livescribe Desktop software, the subject of image, particularly thumbnail drawing, came up again, and again cheating without getting caught turned out to be the right answer. The Livescribe Smartpen uses an infrared camera to precisely capture its position as you write on paper with an aperiodic dot pattern. The desktop application displayed and organized those captured pages of writing and/or drawing.

For each notebook, the overview mode was supposed to show thumbnails of the captured vector strokes superimposed on the background of the paper used, which for obvious reasons was not captured by the pen. Two issues were that those backgrounds were high-resolution PNG images that were quite slow to render, and the file format that contained the pen strokes had significant initialization overhead for reading.

## How Definitely Not to Draw Thumbnails

The first approach for drawing the thumbnail, shown in Figure 16.3, ran with the word "thumbnail." A thumbnail is typically a small image generated from a larger graphic or document. Our Windows client took that very literally and created thumbnail images for every page that it saved to disk.

Our Mac team thought they would do the same thing, just better, because OS X supports high-quality PDFs and Apple had just introduced the CGImageSource CreateThumbnailAtIndex() function specifically for loading thumbnails from disk. What could possibly go wrong?

Well, everything went wrong with the approach taken: Because PDF is a resolution-independent format, every PDF "thumbnail" contained the full-resolution

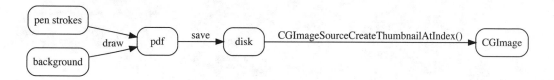

**Figure 16.3**   How not to draw thumbnails

PNG, drawing it to the PDF required the PNG to be decompressed and then recompressed for the PDF generation. Those PDFs "thumbnails" were also very slow to render, as they contained much more detail than one would ever need. The inherent slowness of the process was countered by spawning a new thread for every PDF to generate.

Trying this out just once required a hard reboot of the machine as 200 threads hogged the CPU and the memory consumption caused continuous heavy swapping.

## How to Not Really Draw Thumbnails

While writing PDFs to disk and then rendering those was obviously a classic *Bad Idea*™, we were still wedded to the idea that a thumbnail is a specific image, though we were now willing to entertain the idea that a bitmap image might be sufficient at low resolution. Apple's *ImageKit* (also new) and specifically the `IKImageBrowser View` seemed to provide the answer: a fast (OpenGL accelerated!), ready-made view for images. Perfect, right?

The API is simple enough, all we had to do was provide a data source that would return individual images of just about any format imaginable.

Alas, the result was still far from ideal, as the screenshots in Figure 16.4 illustrate: While everything was super fast once all the thumbnails were generated, initial load was quite slow and visually quite jarring as the individual thumbnails rendered one by one. What's even worse is that during the delay that was caused by the overhead of opening the file, we couldn't draw anything.

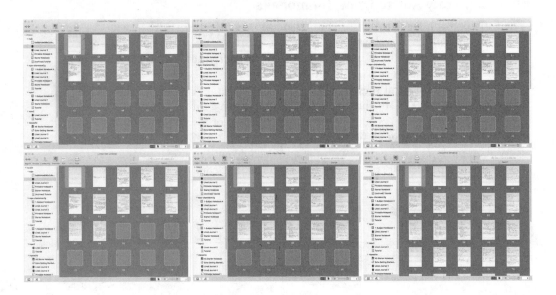

**Figure 16.4**    Atomic thumbnail drawing

This got us no love from Amazon customer reviews:

> If you have hundreds of pages of notes, it is odd that the software needs to reload the thumbnails every single time you load up the software. If you wait a long enough time, as long as the software is open, the thumbnails will be in memory. But this takes too long! If you close the program, and re-open the desktop software, guess what? You have to start over in waiting for the thumbnails to reappear. I don't know if this is also true in the windows version, but it happens in the Mac.

The problem was fundamentally still the same as before: we didn't actually have the thumbnail images the `IKImageBrowserView` wanted to display for us. Instead we had a single large, shared, and slow-to-render background image and vector data obtained from a separate source, and we had to combine the two to give the `IKImageBrowserView` what it wanted, which was fundamentally a slow process.

## How to Draw Non-Thumbnails

Fortunately, that very structure that was causing us problems also turned out to contain the seeds of the solution. Instead of delivering each page thumbnail as an atomic unit and actual image, we could use plain old Quartz/AppKit drawing to draw all the pieces to the screen individually in the `-drawRect:` method of our `ThumbView` class.

Just like with eXTRASLIDE image scaling, `NSImage` was helpful for caching an optimized, screen-resolution-sized version of the background PNG. We only needed to do this once per notebook and could then draw that single background `NSImage` for every thumbnail. This made the drawing of the background effectively instantaneous.

However, we still had the problem that getting the stroke data out of the file format was taking a bit of time. Here again, the solution was to cheat: instead of waiting until all stroke data was available, we drew all the thumbnails immediately after having rendered the background so there was *something* to draw and to look at, even if it wasn't the final image.

The result is illustrated in Figure 16.5. First all the backgrounds are drawn while at the same time the stroke data is retrieved. In the next step, all the stroke data appears essentially simultaneously.

The on-screen effect was dramatic: Thumbnails seemed to appear immediately and always be live, touchable objects. The reason is that the thumbnails appear immediately and then change slightly, rather than appearing one by one fully formed. This was the solution that shipped and provided users with "immediate" responsiveness, at which point it feels like you are manipulating the on-screen items directly rather than giving commands to which the computer responds.

This technique is similar to the launch images (or launch files) that Apple requires iOS apps to have in order appear fast and responsive "because it appears instantly and is quickly replaced by the first screen of your app."

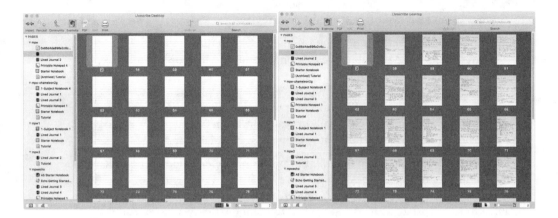

**Figure 16.5**   Decomposed thumbnail drawing

The crucial insight for achieving this was to stop viewing the thumbnail as an indivisible unit, and instead use the structure of our thumbnails (background + strokes) to our advantage: first, factor out the slow drawing of the background so that is only done once instead of once for each page, then realize we could display those backgrounds while waiting for the strokes to decode. The differences in the flows are illustrated in Figure 16.6.

What we didn't actually need were faster graphics routines or OpenGL. In fact, the method that did use OpenGL internally (`IKImageBrowserView`) was significantly slower for our purposes than the ostensibly much slower method we used, which just used plain old Quartz and AppKit drawing. As is often the case, the structural advantages far outweighed the API costs.

## Line Drawing on iPhone

Another aspect of the Livescribe software discussed in the "It's Just an Illusion" section in this chapter is a feature called *Paper Replay*: The pen can record audio along with pen strokes, and when such an audio session is played, the strokes are animated in sync with the sound. More specifically, so-called *future ink* that hadn't been written yet at the time currently playing in the recording was colored gray and turned green as the play-head passed. The effect was that you could see the written text (or graphic) appear essentially as it had been written in the first place.

On the Mac client, this wasn't ever a problem. We had straightforward Quartz code to draw strokes and called that in our `PageView`'s `drawRect:` method. For paper-replay we just added a `time-from` and a `time-to` parameter (all the individual strokes were time-stamped) and drew the strokes twice: once after setting the stroke color to gray and with `time-to` set to the current time in the recording, and once again after setting the stroke color to green and now with `time-from` set to the current time in the recording.

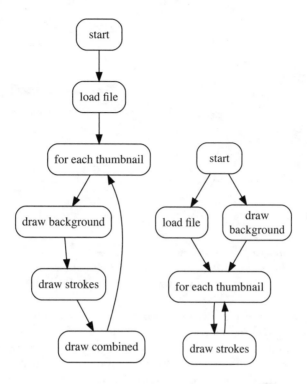

**Figure 16.6**    Atomic vs. decomposed thumbnail drawing flow

When we ported this code over to iPhone, we made sure to use CoreAnimation, which was the recommended high-speed API and we were, after all, animating. More specifically, we used a `CATiledLayer` because we had to support zoom, and `CATiledLayer` even supports internal multithreading, so things should be faster still. Except they weren't: on complex graphics, Instruments showed us barely hitting 3 to 4 frames per second with the CPU pegged at 100%. Since we were pushing the redraws from the animation, redraw commands would also pile up, making the app completely unresponsive. The Paper Replay feature was effectively unusable, especially for more complex pages.

What had we done wrong? It's not that we hadn't cared about performance; in fact, our primary technology choices were driven primarily by performance concerns. We had even investigated speeding up line-drawing performance variations due to stroke length and had derived a near optimal segmentation of our strokes, but that only made a 10% to 20% difference; the impact on our problem was negligible. We started looking at OpenGL, but the problem nagged at me because it didn't seem like the problem should be this hard.

Of course, the problem really wasn't that hard, we had just been blinded by the shiny technology instead of actually thinking about the problem. Figure 16.7 shows

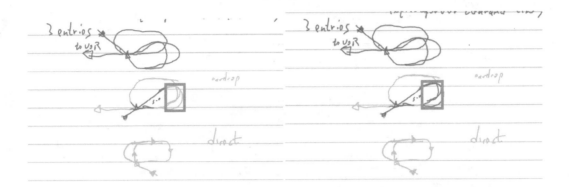

**Figure 16.7**    Two frames of Paper Replay animation with the changed rectangle

two frames of a paper-replay session with some notes for an instrument flying course—specifically, different ways of entering a hold. The region that actually needs to be redrawn to get from the first snapshot to the second snapshot is indicated by the rectangle.

A pen is a physical object moved by a hand; it can only move so far in a given amount of time. In 1/60th of a second, the time for one frame of smooth animation, it can't move very far at all. So only a very small region of the screen can possibly change between frames, and only that small region needs to actually be redrawn.

Our focus on CoreAnimation had prevented us from seeing this because CoreAnimation only allows the entire backing bitmap of a layer to be replaced at once. Both AppKit and UIKit's view mechanism, on the other hand, allow drawing arbitrary small rectangular subregions (or unions of rectangular subregions) using the `drawRect:` methods and invalidating rectangular sections of a view using `setNeedsDisplayInRect:`. On iOS these rectangles are drawn *into* the layer bitmap.

Once we realized that UIKit, not CoreAnimation, was the answer, adapting the code was an easy task. We added a `PageView`, moved the drawing code there, added some utilities for obtaining changed rectangles from sets of time codes, and then only invalidated the rectangular regions for a specific frame. The effect was dramatic: Where before we had barely reached 3 to 4 frames per second by pegging the CPU, we were now effortlessly pegged at 60 frames per second, with CPU usage only rarely exceeding the 2% to 3% range, largely independent of the overall complexity of the page. Even better, the UI animation was now achieved by pulling from the UI, rather than being pushed from the audio, so there was no chance of getting permanently overwhelmed or out of sync.

# Summary

In this chapter, we looked at graphics performance and overall responsiveness. Although low-level drawing performance is more easily measurable and a frequent topic for developer discussions, I find that architectural patterns and domain-specific optimizations usually have a far larger impact. In fact, architectural restrictions of ostensibly faster low-level techniques that prevent high-level optimizations often have a far larger impact than the benefits of the low-level optimizations. One particularly significant point is model-to-view communication, which has become much more relevant in our network-connected devices because the model can change rapidly without user input. We will look at a more comprehensive solution to this problem in the next chapter.

# 17

# Graphics and UI: Examples

This chapter will look at two concrete examples of tuning larger applications in their totality: a highly image-centric weather app and the Wunderlist 3 task manager.

## Beautiful Weather App

A couple of years ago, I was approached by a young Berlin start-up that had hitherto worked primarily on puzzle apps and had been very successful with that. Their goal was to build the most beautiful weather app on the planet, and now that they were almost done making it beautiful (see Figure 17.1) they hit some snags actually getting it shippable.

The app was so image heavy that it would routinely crash with out of memory errors. In addition, there were performance problems. I've already discussed some of the lessons learned in earlier chapters, but one of the most remarkable is still the rather nasty interaction between memory warnings and threading: If you run your memory consumer on the main thread, your process will be blocked from receiving and acting on memory warnings and will likely get killed, even if you could in principle do something about them. On the other hand, if your memory consumer runs on a background thread, it is likely that it will continue to consume memory even as the main thread is trying to do something about the memory warning, also leading to the process getting killed.

The solution was to have the background thread occasionally "check in" with the main thread by sending a message to the main thread and waiting for the result, especially before large allocations. The result would be to give the main thread a chance to react to any memory warnings and to stall the background thread if such processing was taking place.

### An Update

The main task described in this chapter, however, is the work done for an update of the application. By this time, iOS device screen sizes and resolutions had multiplied, and a mix of old and new devices meant that there was a vast gulf in capabilities

**Figure 17.1**    Beautiful Weather app

between the most and least powerful devices. Of course the design team wanted even more animations, more realistic graphics, and an added parallax effect.

At the time I got involved, starting the app could take several minutes, and a single high-resolution version of the image assets alone took 491 MB all by itself, and those assets weren't complete. Adding optimized assets for each device and the missing graphics would have easily propelled the app to more than 1 GB, but the goal was staying under the 100-MB limit Apple imposes for over-the-air purchases and updates.

So the task at hand was to reduce the size of the assets by more than a factor of five, add support for all current iOS devices without multiplying those assets, and at the same time dramatically reduce loading times. I have to admit it seemed impossible at the time.

## Fun with PNG

The original version of the app used PNG images, despite the somewhat photo-realistic nature of the images. I was somewhat skeptical of that choice at the time, but it was really too late to do anything about it so close to the release, and the team certainly seemed to know what they were doing with regard to images.

Furthermore, although the images *looked* quasi-photo-realistic, they were in fact synthetic, and PNG is generally considered more suitable for synthetic images than JPEG. The PNGs were highly optimized, using lossy compression to 8-bit/256-color palette images and even reducing the color palette further than 8 bit, sacrificing color resolution for spatial resolution.

Sacrificing color resolution is a good idea in principle because human vision has much higher resolution for brightness changes than for color changes, but the effort was probably skewed by the method used: The images were examined in an interactive tool at several times the original size, and parameters adjusted until a minimum size was achieved that still "looked OK." The problem with this approach is that, due to the fact that images are displayed magnified, spatial defects are emphasized over color defects. The solution would be to also "magnify" color resolution, but I am not aware of a way of doing this.

The way the prototype app attempted to avoid having multiple versions of the assets for each device was also problematic—it saved a version optimized for the particular device in question (in essence, it downsampled to the appropriate resolution). In order to not impact the existing rendering code, this subsampling and saving was done before the normal loading code (see Figure 17.2), resulting in a horrific first launch experience: The app would just sit for several minutes with a loading screen and spinner, unable to interact, and the device would get hot.

In addition, iOS's PNG writing code does not feature the optimization mechanisms of external tools, so the images saved were 32-bit RGBA, significantly larger than the originals despite being lower resolution.

## Brainstorming

To me, it seemed obvious that the use of PNG format "as-is" would have to be at least reconsidered. My first ideas revolved around a pyramidal encoding scheme either similar to or directly using wavelet encodings such as JPEG 2000. The beauty of a pyramid encoding scheme is that the image is compressed by extracting lower and lower resolution versions of an image and storing only the differences between those versions. This means that the act of decompression automatically extracts lower-resolution versions, and therefore multiple resolutions can be provided with just one image file.

Alas, JPEG 2000 support on both iOS and Mac OS X is quite slow, so JPEG 2000 itself was not an option. There is also quite a bit of evidence that this lack of performance is not for lack of trying, but rather inherent to the format and the technique. So this approach seemed quite daunting, even though our needs would have allowed for a simpler implementation with fewer levels in the pyramid, and possibly using other compression mechanisms for encoding those base images.

We also looked at alternative to the *flate* compression method used in PNG. Flate compression is a very good general-purpose lossless compressor, but our requirements aren't general purpose, they are very specific. For example, we only compress images, and we care much less about compression speed than decompression speed (flate is intentionally pretty symmetric). One alternative we looked at was LZ4, which boasts decompression speeds at least 10 times faster than flate with only slightly worse compression ratios.

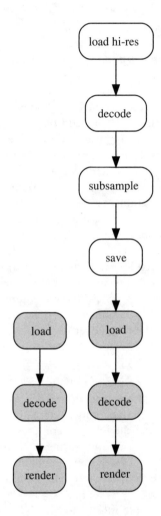

**Figure 17.2**    Original loading flow and subsampling/saving pre-pended

In addition, there were even more exotic options such as the precompressed PVRTC texture format directly supported by the Apple's mobile graphics chipset. This data format needs no decoding by the CPU; it can be fed directly to the GPU, for best possible performance. On the other hand, both compression and quality are at best mediocre. I also experimented with using actual MPEG movies, which also have a hardware decoder, but there can only be one of these at a time on iOS and it is difficult to compose with other objects in the scene.

## Data Points to JPEG

In the end, there were a lot of options on the table, and it wasn't clear at all what the right choice might be. We needed data, so I started running experiments, starting with the common JPEG and PNG image formats.

Not surprisingly, the JPEG format files came out ahead in size, with the 491 MB of assets compressing down to 87 MB at very conservative 0.7 quality setting with no visible loss in quality. A bit more surprising was that despite Apple's recommendation of Xcode-"optimized" PNGs as the default format, JPEG compressed files decoded much more quickly, at least on the Mac on which I was running the tests.

The more we looked at JPEG decoding, the more the good news flooded in—using the TurboJPEG library improved speeds by another 20% to 200%. What's more, the `CGImageSourceCreateThumbnailAtIndex()` that turned out to be completely useless for our needs in the "How Definitely Not to Draw Thumbnails" section of Chapter 16 actually did the fast extract of lower-resolution images we were hoping to get out of JPEG 2000!

## A Measuring Hiccup

Of course, I had made the cardinal mistake of not actually running these tests on the device, and when we actually did run the tests on devices there was a huge downer: The performance was much worse, especially relative to PNG, which now turned out to be faster after all! The relative performance difference didn't make sense to me because the CPUs are sufficiently alike that even if one is slower, relative performance differences between the two codecs shouldn't be as large as we were measuring. The plot thickened when I compiled a version the Independent JPEG Group's `libjpeg` software, the official reference implementation for JPEG, and got better results than the Apple libraries.

The answer lies in the fact that Apple actually has JPEG decoder hardware on the iPhone system on a chip (SOC). This decoder hardware can actually be slower than software, but always uses much less power, so Apple prefers it even when it is slower. There is also some constant overhead involved in talking to the hardware, which sits behind a Mach IPC interface.

Fortunately, it turned out that these overheads are fixed and I was measuring fairly small images. Figures 17.3 through 17.5 show a more representative set of measurements with images of different sizes and at different subsampling settings.

For larger images, the fixed overheads are amortized over more data being decoded, and Apple JPEG easily beats the alternatives, with TurboJPEG coming in a good second and PNG just unacceptably slow. Furthermore, PNG actually gets substantially slower when subsampling, whereas the JPEG decoders are really able to get generous speedups by doing only partial decoding.

In the end, while the relative performance degradation of small images is significant, the absolute slowdown is not that much because the images are small. Just

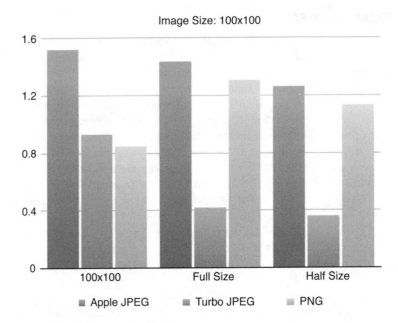

**Figure 17.3**   Time to load small image with downsampling (ms)

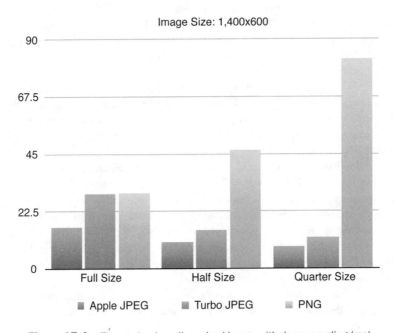

**Figure 17.4**   Time to load medium-sized image with downsampling (ms)

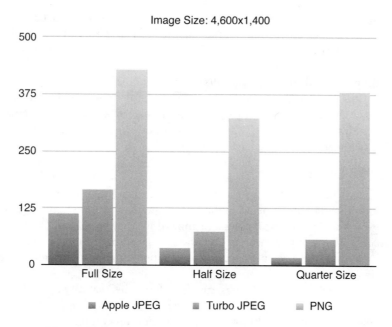

**Figure 17.5**    Time to load large image with downsampling (ms)

one medium-sized JPEG "pays" for the cost of almost a hundred small images, and if there is a really large image there just is no contest. Additionally, the hardware slowdown was model specific, with the device I had been testing being one of the slowest.

So things were actually much better than our first device tests had suggested, and if all else failed we could fall back on the `libjpeg` code or get TurboJPEG to work. So it looked like we didn't need the frankly slightly scary rocket-science ideas we had thought up after all; JPEG was going to give us all we need.

## JPNG and JPJP

There was one final hurdle: many of our assets were composited together to form the final scenes, and so used a lot of transparency, but JPEG doesn't support transparency. Again, we were fortunate that someone else had been here before and solved that particular problem: Nick Lockwood came up with the JPNG file format, which combines a JPEG and a PNG into a single file, with the JPEG providing the color information and the PNG the alpha mask.

At first, using a PNG for the alpha channel seems a little oxymoronic. Yes, PNG supports alpha, but we are not encoding an image with alpha, we are encoding just a simple grayscale image that *acts* like an alpha channel for a different image. On the other hand, alpha channels are usually much more blocky than images, and so even flate compression should work quite well. Despite this, there really isn't a good reason *for* having the alpha channel being a PNG, and for us it was a serious limitation because it would mean that one fourth of the data would have to be downsampled from highest resolution after all.

Instead, we decided to update the JPNG format so that it would also use a (grayscale) JPEG image for the alpha channel. In addition, we modified the library's APIs to allow specification of an image resolution/size, as well as the implementation to use `CGImageSourceCreateThumbnailAtIndex()` in order for the extraction of lower-resolution images to work.[1]

## A Beautiful Launch

In the end, we pulled off the impossible task we set ourselves at the start. The app stayed within the 100-MB limit, it supported all the new devices, and the designers were happy with all the new graphics and animations they could add. And the users? They *love* it, with the app garnering 4.5+ star ratings on both the U.S. and the German App Stores, and frequent reports of the app being the right pick-me-up in the morning.

One final benefit of our JPEG subsetting mechanism is that on very old and slow devices, we can very quickly load a significantly reduced-resolution image (one fourth or even one eighth resolution) so the user sees something resembling the final scene while the high-resolution artwork is loading.

There is still more we could do. We never integrated software JPEG decoding, so all decoding has to funnel through the hardware decoder. This is obvious from the CPU profiles, which show CPU utilization substantially below 100%. Even if the hardware is generally faster, adding two software decoders seems like it could at least double decoding throughput, especially if we manage to sort the images so that larger images are preferentially decoded by hardware and smaller images preferentially decoded by software. We could also add a few images in PVRTC format that work well with that compression, and maybe decode a few of the animation sequences from MPEG movies. The idea is to utilize as many of the available hardware resources as possible, as long as they don't start stepping on each other.

But that is for later.

# Wunderlist 3

In late 2013, I was asked to help out the 6Wunderkinder team with the launch of Wunderlist 3, particularly the architecture of what we collectively, and still unironically, call the Objective-C clients: Mac and iOS. I was so impressed with the team and the product that I joined.

---

1. The code is at https://github.com/mpw/JPNG/.

A year and a half later, Microsoft was so impressed with the team and the product
we had built in the meantime that they bought the company, meaning your loyal
Apple scribe is now in the employ of the evil empire of Redmond. And loving it!

## Wunderlist 2

Version 2 of Wunderlist was in many ways a wonderful product, and users generally
loved it, but performance and stability were not its strong suits. After I downloaded
and launched it for the first time, it crashed almost immediately and consistently for a
couple of times before finally stabilizing.

The Mac and iOS clients used CoreData for their data model as well as for
connecting UI components. As we saw in Chapter 12, CoreData is OK for small
amounts of data and simple use-cases with lax performance requirements. High
performance with medium to large data sets is at best challenging, and the team
found they had to create ever more elaborate and fragile workarounds to keep
CoreData from blocking the main thread with I/O.

## Overall Architecture

The overall architecture of the Wunderlist 3 Objective-C clients is shown in
Figure 17.6. There is really not that much special about this architecture. It has an
in-memory model, which is initialized from a persistent (disk) store at start-up. The
memory model is kept in sync with the UI (bi-directionally) and with the back end
(also bi-directionally). We also keep the disk store in sync with the memory model,
but there is no need to go in the other direction because the disk store is private to
the application.

However, it is exactly this simplicity that makes excellent performance possible:
The boundaries between the different subsystems are clearly delineated and the
division of responsibility is obvious. For example, neither the model objects nor the

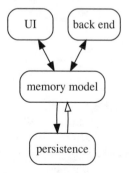

**Figure 17.6**   Overall Wunderlist architecture

in-memory store know anything whatsoever about storage or network I/O, therefore it is not possible to have surprising interactions. At most, they know how to turn themselves into dictionaries, which outside code can then serialize to some eternal data format.

Another way of expressing the same architecture, this time in code, is Example 17.1. The $|=$ and $=|=$ operators (like the solid arrows in Figure 17.6) denote *dataflow constraints*, which act very much like spreadsheet formulae and can be regarded as permanent assignments, so just like a normal assignment except that the system maintains the relationship.

**Example 17.1   Wunderlist client architecture expressed as dataflow constraints**

```
memory-model := persistence.
persistence  |= memory-model.
ui           =|= memory-model.
backend      =|= memory-model.
```

## URIs and In-Process REST

The underlying architectural model for the memory-model and the persistence store is *In-Process REST*, an adaptation of the REST architectural style for use within an application. All the entities are referred to via identifier objects that take on the role of URIs; in Wunderlist these are instances of the `WLObjectReference` class that encode an *entity type*, a *container id*, and *object id*. A container id is the id of an enclosing object, for example, the list id of the list that a task belongs to. Not all objects have an explicit container; for example, lists or the logged-in user are located directly under root. Example 17.2 shows a couple of example `WLObjectReferences` represented as string URIs.

**Example 17.2   Internal URIs**

```
task://container/2/id/3
list://id/2/
task://container/2/
task://id/3
```

URIs are structured. For example, the first URI in Example 17.2 refers to the task with the object id 3 within the list with id 2. The second URI is the list object with id 2. The third URI is the array of all tasks in the list with id 2. The last URI refers to just the task with id 3, without giving a list id. In our current implementation, that requires searching for that task in all lists.

Storage is organized as a series of objects that act like little Web servers, except that they don't use the HTTP protocol to communicate, but rather the ordinary Objective-C message protocol shown in Example 17.3. As you can see, the message roughly correspond to the GET, PUT, and DELETE verbs, with the only wrinkle being that we generally talk about arrays of objects, rather than single objects at a time.

**Example 17.3    Storage protocol**

```
@protocol WLStorage <NSObject>

- (NSArray*)objectsForReference:(WLObjectReference*)ref;
- (void)removeObjectsForReference:(WLObjectReference*)ref;
- (void)setObjects:(NSArray*)new forReference:(WLObjectReference*)ref;

@end
```

This same protocol is used by the in-memory store, the disk store, and the objects representing the REST back end, so stores are largely interchangeable. For testing, we can substitute a second in-memory store for the disk store or the back end or both, speeding up testing significantly. The fact that the protocol is so simple also means that it is composable. For example, we have filters that add computed entities to the store hierarchy that can be accessed in the same way, or multiple persistent stores that optimize storage for specific entities.

We can compute with `WLObjectReferences` independently from their referenced objects. For example, we can determine the disk path and the back-end URL. As we saw in Example 17.2, we can also determine the group an object is in just by chopping off the last pieces of the URI.

## An Eventually Consistent Asynchronous Data Store

Considering the previous experience with CoreData, keeping the data store simple and fast was one of the biggest priorities in the initial design. I think we succeeded: our CTO likes to shock people at conferences by telling them we store our data as individual JSON files on disk. This has worked remarkably well—as you may recall from Chapter 12, the JSON format is one of the fastest to encode and decode using Foundation methods, and it also happens to be our wire format for talking to the back end, so keeping those formats the same has proved to be fantastic for debugging.

This simple mechanism has proved to be surprisingly fast. Our other clients use databases or sophisticated serialization formats, yet the Objective-C clients are consistently fastest, especially when dealing with our stress-test accounts that have more lists and tasks than a sane—no, than even an insane user would ever have. This is despite the fact that there are many things obviously *wrong* with this format. For example, we write way too many small files. However, whenever I thought I had found a problem that warranted finally changing to something more sophisticated (otherwise known as less brain-dead), the problem turned out to be caused by a simple bug that was solvable with an easy fix.

The simplicity of the data store is helped by the fact that our back end consists of a loose federation of microservices that at best offer eventual consistency between different entities. This means that our consistency requirements are no more than the canonical store, so keeping the individual files consistent by passing YES to the NSData method `writeToFile:atomically:` is quite sufficient.

All writes to disk are asynchronous from the main thread; however, they are executed synchronously in a loop from a single background thread responsible for the disk. The main thread just sends the URIs of objects it wishes to save to the background writer thread via a queue. When the background writer thread gets to the a particular URI in the queue, it fetches the current up-to-date entry from the memory store and serializes that to disk.

Since the disk writer always saves the most current version, multiple write requests can be coalesced by simply discarding duplicate write request URIs from the queue. This helps minimize the load on the disk subsystem.


## RESTOperation Queues

In the previous section, I mentioned that write requests to the file writer are sent via a queue. This queue is a `WLRESTOperationQueue`, instances of which we use throughout the system to connect asynchronously acting entities. They are, so to speak, the secret sauce for keeping Wunderlist responsive while at the same time interacting with the network and managing persistence.

As the name suggests, a `WLRESTOperationQueue` consists of a Queue of REST operations, each of which consists of an `WLObjectReference` coupled with a REST verb (GET, PUT, DELETE) that tells the target what it should with the reference. What that operation means depends on the specific target. For the disk store, receiving a PUT means that the objects specified by the URI should be saved to disk; for the Web interface it means to send an HTTP PUT to the back end.

Each queue can be added to from any thread and maintains its own worker thread to service the entries. It can optionally deliver results to a specified target thread that's different from the service thread; for example, the main thread. Compared to GCD, having a single worker thread per queue drastically reduces the number of threads with their corresponding resource consumption.

`WLRESTOperationQueue` objects support coalescing by automatically rejecting duplicate entries. Getting this right crucially depends on the entries in the queue only being references. It took us quite some time to figure this out, with the `WLRESTOperationQueue` in its present form only appearing after about a year of development.

All the variants we tried with actual object pointers led to undesirable results (here with the example application of writing to disk).

- Writing mutable objects to the queue and mutating them after they've been written has the object potentially being modified as it is being saved. That's a bad idea, and the solutions would involve incredible amounts of locking while probably still allowing conflicting mutations.

- Placing copies in the queue would potentially mean the same object being written one time for every modification made. This would lead to massive performance degradation during high-load situations, just the time when you need performance to remain good.

- Purging the most recent addition (the way we do with the URIs) would mean that only the first update gets written; later updates get lost until the object is modified again.

- Purging the oldest addition can easily lead to situations where an object that keeps getting modified is never written to disk.

With our URI queues, high-load situations simply mean that more changes are accumulated together, with the disk subsystem maintaining its highest possible throughput. So far, we've had very few situations where disk writing wasn't able to keep up, and they were all due to minor bugs that were easily fixed.

## A Smooth and Responsive UI

For the UI (Figure 17.7), we used effectively a classic MVC approach, which is expressed as the `ui =|= model` line of the Wunderlist architecture. In classic MVC,

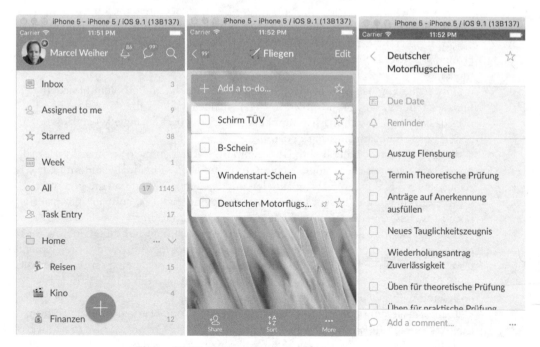

**Figure 17.7**   Principal Wunderlist UI elements

the UI pulls data from the model when it is ready and the data is needed, compared to Apple's take on MVC that features controllers pushing data to the UI from the model.

Leaving the UI in charge to update itself when it is ready has always been a fundamental tenet of MVC that is largely ignored by current ViewController programming practice, but it becomes even more crucial when coordinating animations with asynchronous operations adding more data while those animations are running. Trying to coordinate this in a push model becomes almost impossible and has led to complex solutions such as FRP and React, but good old MVC always had the answer: just notify the UI (without pushing data) and let *it* decide when to update itself.

In our case, UI elements are parametrized with the URIs of the objects they are supposed to represent. They can then obtain the most up-to-date version of those objects from the memory store by sending the `objectsForReference:` message with that URI.

That same URI is also used in update notifications. We use the basic Cocoa `NSNotificationCenter` approach and parametrize it with the URI in question. The UI element can then compare the URI to the one it is responsible for to figure out whether it needs to update itself.

As we saw earlier, URIs can be related to one another, so for example if a task with the URI `task://container/2/id/3` is modified, a list view showing the list `task://container/2` can also update itself.

We use the `WLRESTOperationQueue` objects to decouple the UI thread from model changes that can happen on any thread. When the model changes a particular object, it posts the URI of the object to a queue that is set up to deliver "model did change" `NSNotifications` to the default `NSNotificationCenter` on the UI thread.

The coalescing behavior of those queues neatly resolve the problem of keeping update latencies as low as possible for single changes while at the same time not overloading the UI with massive numbers of back-to-back changes when those occur, but also not missing any updates.

For the UI, we actually had to add one more feature: auto-coalescing. In normal operations, we want every single element to be updated individually and immediately. As load increases, however, this makes less and less sense. When you are getting hundreds of new list tasks sent to your device, having each one animate into place is not just useless, it becomes downright annoying and confusing.

The way auto-coalescing works is by monitoring the depth of the queue. As the queue gets fuller, the coalescing level is increased, removing more and more elements from the back of the URIs entered into the queue. With coalescing set to its default, a URI like `task://container/2/id/3` is entered into the queue as is, and coalescing will only affect changes to that specific task.

If auto-coalescing bumps the coalescing level to 1, one element is removed from the back of the URI, leaving only the container: `task://container/2`. This has two effects: on one hand, the entire list will now be refreshed in the UI, instead of just the specific task. On the other hand, coalescing will now also merge all updates to individual items in that list, so instead of having multiple updates to items in the list, we get one update to the entire list.

Finally, if updates still outpace the ability of the UI to keep up, coalescing level 2 chops everything off the end of the URI, leaving just a general "UI needs to updated" and merging all UI update requests into one at the rate the UI can refresh itself.

With this mechanism in place, we've never again had to worry about the UI not being able to keep up with changes or becoming unresponsive during heavy updates. Except when we introduced bugs.

### Wunderlist in Short

The architectural elements presented here are obviously not the full Wunderlist 3 performance story. We also had our tremendous back-end team giving us fast HTTP and WebSocket interfaces, and the team did low-level and detailed performance investigations and tweaks as necessary. The architectural elements, however, ensured that these investigations tended to be rare and straightforward, the tweaks small and simple, rather than fighting performance all the time.

I also don't want to imply that this is the only way to achieve performance, or that it is impossible to achieve good performance using any of the technologies that we avoided. I do think that applying these techniques and the underlying principles makes it not just possible, but straightforward to achieve amazing performance given the tools at our disposal, and awesome performance is a crucial ingredient for apps to get to 5 million monthly active users, as well as rave reviews and regular 4.5- to 5-star ratings in the app stores.

# Summary

In this chapter, we looked at two examples of "putting it all together" to make great, high-performance apps. The Beautiful Weather app was the more extreme case, pushing the boundaries on a very specific performance aspect (loading and displaying large image sets) and achieving something that seemed utterly impossible, in the end with room to spare. It required careful analysis of hardware and software capabilities, tweaks to the requirements, a bit of thinking outside the box...and defining a new custom image file format that's a version of another custom image format.

Wunderlist is a more typical example of a modern mobile application with a mix of data storage, real-time network access, and fluid UI updates. It puts together lessons learned from earlier chapters—for example, working mostly in-memory and eschewing database engines, whether relational or not, for simpler and faster storage mechanisms. It generalizes the update mechanism from Chapter 16 for throttling UI updates into an architectural element now used to coordinate and simplify all the parts of the app: network layer, data storage, memory model, and UI.

Both examples showed what is possible with today's pocket supercomputers, and neither, in the end, required pushing the hardware to its limits in order to achieve extraordinary performance.

# Index

# REGISTER YOUR PRODUCT at informit.com/register
## Access Additional Benefits and SAVE 35% on Your Next Purchase

- Download available product updates.

- Access bonus material when applicable.

- Receive exclusive offers on new editions and related products.
  (Just check the box to hear from us when setting up your account.)

- Get a coupon for 35% for your next purchase, valid for 30 days. Your code will
  be available in your InformIT cart. (You will also find it in the Manage Codes
  section of your account page.)

Registration benefits vary by product. Benefits will be listed on your account page
under Registered Products.

---

InformIT.com—The Trusted Technology Learning Source
InformIT is the online home of information technology brands at Pearson, the world's foremost
education company. At InformIT.com you can
- Shop our books, eBooks, software, and video training.
- Take advantage of our special offers and promotions (informit.com/promotions).
- Sign up for special offers and content newsletters (informit.com/newsletters).
- Read free articles and blogs by information technology experts.
- Access thousands of free chapters and video lessons.

Connect with InformIT—Visit informit.com/community
Learn about InformIT community events and programs.

## informIT.com
the trusted technology learning source

Addison-Wesley • Cisco Press • IBM Press • Microsoft Press • Pearson IT Certification • Prentice Hall • Que • Sams • VMware Press

ALWAYS LEARNING                                                                                    PEARSON